A MUSICOLOGY
OF PERFORMANCE

A Musicology of Performance

Theory and Method
Based on Bach's Solos for Violin

Dorottya Fabian

http://www.openbookpublishers.com

© Dorottya Fabian

Version 1.1. Minor edits made, October 2015.

Version 1.2. Minor edits made, June 2016

This work is licensed under a Creative Commons Attribution 4.0 International license (CC BY 4.0). This license allows you to share, copy, distribute and transmit the work; to adapt the work and to make commercial use of the work providing attribution is made to the author (but not in any way that suggests that they endorse you or your use of the work). Attribution should include the following information:

Dorottya Fabian, *A Musicology of Performance: Theory and Method Based on Bach's Solos for Violin*. Cambridge, UK: Open Book Publishers, 2015. http://dx.doi.org/ 10.11647/OBP.0064

Please see the list of images and audio examples for attribution relating to individual resources. Whenever a license is not specified, these resources have been released under the same license as the book. Every effort has been made to identify and contact copyright holders and any omission or error will be corrected upon notification to the publisher.

In order to access detailed and updated information on the license, please visit https://www.openbookpublishers.com/isbn/9781783741526#copyright

Further details about CC BY licenses are available at http://creativecommons.org/licenses/by/4.0/

All external links were active on 31/06/2016 unless otherwise stated and have been archived via the Internet Archive Wayback Machine at https://archive.org/web

The Australian Academy of the Humanities has generously contributed to the publication of this volume.

Digital material and resources associated with this volume are available at https://www.openbookpublishers.com/isbn/9781783741526#resources

ISBN Paperback: 978-1-78374-152-6
ISBN Hardback: 978-1-78374-153-3
ISBN Digital (PDF): 978-1-78374-154-0
ISBN Digital ebook (epub): 978-1-78374-155-7
ISBN Digital ebook (mobi): 978-1-78374-156-4
DOI: 10.11647/OBP.0064

Cover image: Juan Gris, 'Violin' (1913), http://commons.wikimedia.org/wiki/File:Juan_Gris_-_Violin.jpg

All paper used by Open Book Publishers is SFI (Sustainable Forestry Initiative) and PEFC (Programme for the Endorsement of Forest Certification Schemes) Certified.

Printed in the United Kingdom and United States by Lightning Source for Open Book Publishers

In memory of my father, Otto Somorjay.
Your appreciation of performing musicians and your love
of listening to music have been life-long inspirations.
Thank you!

Contents

Acknowledgments	i
1. Dancing to Architecture?	1
1.1 The Problems of Researching and Writing about Music Performance	3
Problems with Historical Investigations of Music Performance	7
Is HIP a Modern Invention/Aesthetic or Does it Have Historical Grounding?	12
Data versus Narrative–Letting Go of Dancing or Returning to the Dance Floor?	13
1.2 Summary: Recordings, Aims and Method	17
2. Theoretical Matters	25
2.1 Cultural Theories	28
HIP and Modernism	28
Modernism versus Postmodernism	31
HIP as a Mirror of Cultural Change	35
Aesthetics and Value Judgment: Beauty and the Sublime	39
2.2 Analytical Theories	42
Music Performance Studies	42
Empirical and Psychological Studies of Performance	48
2.3 Music Performance and Complex Systems	51
Gilles Deleuze and Difference in Music Performance	52
Music Performance as Complex Dynamical System	56
2.4 Performance Studies, Oral Culture and Academia	61
Research Roles: Performing Music or Analysing Performance?	62
Oral Cultures and the Aurality of Music Performance	65
Keeping Music Performance in the Aural Domain	69
Academia Once More	71
2.5 Conclusion	73

3. Violinists, Violin Schools and Emerging Trends ... 75
   3.1 Violinists ... 76
   3.2 Violin Schools ... 87
   3.3 The Influence of HIP on MSP ... 95
   3.4 Diversity within Trends and Global Styles ... 106
   3.5 Overall Findings and Individual Cases ... 116
      Trends in Particular Movements ... 118
      The Importance of Ornamentation ... 120
   3.6 Conclusion ... 122

4. Analyses of Performance Features ... 127
   4.1 Tempo Choices ... 130
   4.2 Vibrato ... 137
   4.3 Ornamentation ... 146
      Problems of Aesthetics and Notation Practices ... 146
      The Role of Delivery ... 149
      The Performance of Embellishments ... 153
      Diversity—Once More ... 166
      Ornamenting or Improvising? ... 169
      Summary ... 170
   4.4 Rhythm ... 172
      Dotted Rhythms ... 173
      Rhythmic Alteration ... 181
      Rhythm and Musical Character ... 183
   4.5 Bowing, Articulation and Phrasing ... 184
      Bowing and Timbre ... 184
      Multiple Stops ... 190
      Phrasing and Dynamics ... 193
   4.6 Conclusions ... 197

5. Affect and Individual Difference: Towards a Holistic Account of Performance ... 201
   5.1 Differences within the MSP and within the HIP Styles ... 202
      The Loure ... 202
         MSP Interpretations ... 203
         HIP Interpretations ... 206
      The Gavotte en Rondeau ... 207
         HIP: Wallfisch and Huggett ... 208
         MSP: Lev and Girngolts ... 210
      Menuet I-II ... 211

5.2	Multiple Recordings of Violinists	217
	Gidon Kremer	218
	Rachel Barton Pine	221
	Christian Tetzlaff	223
	Sigiswald Kuijken	229
	Viktoria Mullova	230
5.3	The Holistic Analysis of Interpretations	233
	"Subjective" Aural Analysis: The D minor Giga	234
	"Objective" Measures:	238
	The A minor Grave and G minor Adagio	
	Perception of Affect	241
5.4	Idiosyncratic Versions and Listeners' Reactions	247
	Thomas Zehetmair	247
	Monica Huggett	251
	The E Major Preludio	254
5.5	Conclusions	268

6. Conclusions and an Epilogue: The Complexity Model of Music Performance, Deleuze and Brain Laterality — 273
   6.1 Summary — 286
   6.2 Where to from Here? — Epilogue — 287
        The Brain and its Two Worlds — 288

List of Audio Examples — 297
List of Tables — 303
List of Figures — 305
Discography — 307
References — 313
Index — 333

Acknowledgments

The publication of the book was assisted by subventions from the Australian Academy of Humanities and the School of the Arts and Media of UNSW Australia.

This project has also been supported by an Australian Research Council Discovery Grant (DP0879616) and a UNSW Australia Faculty of Arts and Social Sciences Special Studies program in 2010, during which I took up a visiting fellowship at Clare Hall, Cambridge University which proved an ideal environment for focused work. In 2014 I received some tutoring and marking relief from the School of the Arts and Media at UNSW that contributed significantly to my ability to bring this project to a close.

I would like to thank my research assistants Bridget Kruithof, Elizabeth Cooney, Hae-Na Lee and Amanda Harris for help with data collection and some measurements; Daniel Bangert, Jennifer Butler, Daniel Leech-Wilkinson, Eitan Ornoy, Sean Pryor, Dario Sarlo, and Emery Schubert for insightful and corrective comments on earlier drafts; Kumaran Arul for encouragement and Ellen Hooper for stimulating discussions about performance research and Deleuze; two anonymous reviewers for their valuable comments and suggestions; Rachel Barton-Pine for her generosity in providing me with recordings of her concerts; and Alessandra Tosi and Bianca Gualandi of the superb editorial team at Open Book Publishers who helped make the multi-media presentation possible. I thank Corin Throsby for preparing the index.

Although I prepared a rough draft in 2011, due to other work commitments I could not return to it until 2014, so this book has had a long gestation and underwent substantial rethinking and re-writing. Sections, mostly on ornamentation and the interaction between period and mainstream playing styles have been presented at various academic gatherings. I wish to note my gratitude to Jane Davidson (University of Western Australia, Perth), Gary McPherson (Music, Mind and Wellbeing, University of Melbourne, Australia), Clive Brown and David Milsom (Leeds University), Ingrid Pearson (Royal College of Music, London), Jane Ginsborg (Royal Northern College of Music Manchester) for the invitations. Thanks are also due to the organizers of conferences in Aveiro (Portugal) and at the Orfeus Institute (Ghent), for the opportunity to present, and to the audiences for valuable questions and comments. An article on ornamentation in recent recordings of J. S. Bach's Solos for Violin was published in *Min-ad*, the Israeli Musicological Society's peer-reviewed journal. I thank them for kindly allowing me to re-use some of that material in chapter four of this book.

I would also like to record the generosity of John Butt, Janice Stockigt, Samantha Owens, and Neal Peres da Costa who wrote supporting letters to the Australian Academy of Humanities when I applied to them for a publications subvention. Thank you!

I am grateful to Katalin Komlós for noting some additional misprints and notation errors in one of the score examples and thank Open Book Publishers, especially Bianca Gualandi, for their prompt action in correcting them for edition 1.2 (June 2016).

1. Dancing to Architecture?

> Framing all the great music out there only drags down its immediacy. [...] Writing about music is like dancing about architecture—it's a really stupid thing to want to do.
>
> Elvis Costello (b. 1954), singer-songwriter[1]

Starting this book with such a quote is not just a flippant rhetorical device. It flags my very strongly felt unease regarding the subject matter of the undertaking and my research in general. It is not that I agree with music theorist Heinrich Schenker (1868-1935), who famously began his thesis *The Art of Performance* by stating that "a composition does not require a performance in order to exist. [...] The reading of the score is sufficient,"[2] thus similarly negating the importance of his topic. No, I believe all perception of music is performative whether it is reading a score, hearing with one's inner ears, imagining, playing and singing, or listening to someone else performing. I even contend that when we say "music," when Elvis Costello speaks of "great music," we think of performances, sounds that "live" in our bodies, in our memories. We do not think of inscriptions on pages (scores) even if we are speaking of western art music with its long tradition of notated, authored compositions. And this is exactly why it is so difficult—if not stupid—to talk or write about it. When we do, we are trying to express in words that is in effect, a subjective, physical-affective experience. So a better question might be, "Why is it that we cannot readily recover for our ordinary speech what is so tantalizingly offered

---

1 Cited from *Quote Investigator: Exploring the Origins of Quotations* ("Writing about Music is like Dancing about Architecture"), available at http://www.quoteinvestigator.com
2 Heinrich Schenker, *The Art of Performance*, ed. by Heribert Esser, trans. by Irene Schreier Scott (New York: Oxford University Press, 2000), p. 3.

© Dorottya Fabian, CC BY   http://dx.doi.org/10.11647/OBP.0064.01

by practice?"³ If this question seems sensible then we have identified the reason why we need a musicology of *performance*.

Musicology—a discipline invented in nineteenth-century Austria and Germany along the analogies of philology, historical and literary studies—has traditionally been concerned with the written text of music. To a great extent it still is. However, over the past few decades there has been an exponential growth in scholarship that focuses on music performance. The contention of this book is that we need a better theoretical framework for such studies; a framework that enables engagement with this richly complex phenomenon so that "talking about music" may be regarded less like "dancing to architecture," less of "a stupid thing to want to do."

The theoretical framework and analytical approaches I propose in this book are for studying musical performance. They do not shift the thinking about music to the different paradigm advocated by Nicholas Cook: music *as* performance.⁴ I am interested in a musicology that might assist us to deconstruct the complex that music performance entails: the act and its perception, the aesthetic and the technical, the cultural and the historical, the personal and the common. Therefore I propose a model that engages not only with the various elements and aspects but, importantly, with the interactions of these. I argue that music performance shows overwhelming similarities to the characteristics of complex dynamical systems. We may gain a better understanding of its layers and the functioning of its contributing elements if we approach it with an adequately complex method. I will demonstrate this by studying forty recordings of Johann Sebastian Bach's *Six Sonatas and Partitas for Solo Violin* (BWV1001-BWV1006, dated 1720) made during the past thirty years or so. In this introductory chapter I will first outline the problems we face when studying classical music performance as well as some of the specific questions and debates that relate to playing music composed almost 300 years ago. In the second part of the chapter I will introduce my material and outline how I proceed in the rest of the book.

---

3   Bruno Latour, *Pandora's Hope: Essays on the Reality of Science Studies* (Cambridge, MA: Harvard University Press, 1999), p. 266.
4   Nicholas Cook, 'Between Process and Product: Music and/as Performance,' *Music Theory Online*, 7/2 (April 2001), 1-12, http://www.mtosmt.org/issues/mto.01.7.2/mto.01.7.2.cook.html

1.1. Problems in Researching and Writing about Music Performance

Music perception is multi-modal, whence it lays the crux of our problem. The role of visual, spatial and kinaesthetic inputs and sensations has been repeatedly demonstrated. What we hear depends on the context, on what we see, on our disposition and health, and our prior experiences and knowledge; on our mental and muscle memory, and the function of mirror neurons, not to mention "species-saving" mechanisms of evolutionary significance.[5] Edmund Husserl (1859-1938) considered perception an extraordinarily creative mental act while Maurice Merleau-Ponty (1908-1961) called for a more "holistic theory incorporating embodiment and action."[6] The music theorists David Lewin argued that "musical perception was a type of skill, built over time, which can manifest in an infinite number of creative responses."[7] He claimed that it was erroneous and leading to false dichotomies to "suppose that we are discussing *one* phenomenon at one location of phenomenological space-time when in fact we are discussing *many* phenomena at many distinct such locations."[8]

It is indeed difficult to accept the view that our perceptual experiences may be understood on cognitive terms alone. However, it is equally difficult to be convinced by models that discount the role of cognitive processes and endeavour to explain everything in neurological or evolutionary terms. As Merleau-Ponty noted, "the distinction between subject and object is blurred in my body [...]."[9] Or, as Günther Stern [Anders] (1929-1930) opined, "When listening to music we are *out* of the world and *in* music."[10]

---

5   Anthony Gritten, 'The Subject (of) Listening,' *Journal of the British Society for Phenomenology*, 45/3 (2015), 203-219; Ian Cross and Iain Morley, 'The Evolution of Music: Theories, Definitions and the Nature of the Evidence,' *Communicative Musicality: Exploring the Basis of Human Companionship*, ed. by Stephen Malloch and Colwyn Trevarthen (Oxford: Oxford University Press, 2009), pp. 61-81.
6   Brian Kane, 'Excavating Lewin's "Phenomenology,"' *Music Theory Spectrum*, 33 (2011), 27-36.
7   Kane, 'Excavating,' p. 27.
8   Here and elsewhere italics in original unless otherwise stated. David Lewin, 'Music Theory, Phenomenology, and Modes of Perception,' *Music Perception*, 3/4 (Summer 1986), 327-392 (p. 357).
9   Maurice Merleau-Ponty, *Phenomenology of Perception* (London: Routledge and Kegan Paul, 1962 [1945]), p. 167 cited in Kane, 'Excavating,' p. 33.
10 Günther Stern [Anders], 'Philosophische Untersuchungen zu musikalischen Situationen,'

This sounds rather romantic, does it not?—even though it goes beyond the romantic notion of music communicating the inexpressible. Anders' formulation, as I see it, implies that listening to music is inwardly in direction. It is internalized (unlike sight that canvasses the outside world); it has no objective subject, and in this regard John Lennon's quip might ring quite true as it evokes another very internalized and personal experience: "Listen, writing about music is like talking about fucking. Who wants to talk about it? But you know, maybe some people do want to talk about it."[11]

The "talking about" music performance has long been the domain of music critics on the one hand, and music psychologist on the other hand, both with characteristics that duly raises the question of "why bother." The former deals in metaphorical description and tends to reflect normative thinking. Given the space limits of most magazines and dailies, reviews tend to be very short, having no room for detailed observation or definition of subjective terms. More recently they often include phrases to the effect, "you really need to hear the disk, it is not possible to describe it properly." The latter, that is music psychology, is driven by empiricism and laboratory testing. As such it is limited to what it can measure and test. Although recent developments in technology make their investigations increasingly sophisticated and influenced by neuro-science, the tendency to look for universals through what is measurable yields results of moderate interest to musicians and lovers of music. These studies are not really concerned with either the phenomenological experience or the aesthetic-affective impact of technical and stylistic differences. And when they do, the results do not necessarily provide particularly penetrating new insights. Instead, they simply confirm what practicing musicians have known for long through practice.[12] For example, they have rightly noted the importance of visual cues in music performance and drew attention to it when most investigations focused on audio-only formats—both in terms of performer-to performer communication and, more importantly, perhaps, for listeners' enjoyment and aesthetic judgement.[13] By now, however, psychological research into

---

typescript, Österreichisches Literaturarchiv der Österreichischen Nationalbibliothek, Vienna. Nachlass Günther Anders. ÖLA 237/04, p. 6 cited in Veit Erlmann, *Reason and Resonance: A History of Aurality* (New York: Zone Books, 2010), p. 312.

11 From an Interview with Playboy magazine in 1980. Cited in http://www.quoteinvestigator.com ['Writing about music is like dancing to architecture'].

12 The reasons for the musician's frustration with these studies is discussed, for instance, in J. Murphy McCaleb's recent book *Embodied Knowledge in Ensemble Performance* (Farnham: Ashgate, 2014).

13 One of the first researcher of the visual aspect (body movements, appearance, etc.) of music performance was Jane W. Davidson, see, for instance, her 'What Type of

the multi-modal perception of music performance seems to be focusing on *anything but* the aural sensation and perception, as witnessed at a highly successful conference on the topic held at the University of Sheffield in March 2015. Yet musical gestures—aurally perceived gestures as well as gestures made visible to the mind through aural stimulus—are crucial in the affective communication between performer and listener, between "the music" and the perceiver.

I mention gesture because it is a "hot topic" nowadays. Three edited books have been published on music and gesture in the past ten years and they provide important propositions that would benefit from systematic psychological, cognitive or neurological investigations.[14] Several of the contributing writers address the multi-modal and experiential perception of music. Rolf Godøy, for instance notes that "music perception is embodied in the sense that it is closely linked with bodily experience" and it "is multi-modal in the sense that we perceive music with the help of both visual/kinematic images and effort/dynamics sensations, in addition to the 'pure' sound."[15] Tapping into the mentioned debate between the Husserlian emphasis on "cognitive processes" and the Merleau-Pontian emphasis on the embodied sensation, that "thought and sensation as such occur only against a background of perceptual activity that we always already understand in bodily terms,"[16] Godøy states that *"ecological knowledge* in listening, [means] knowledge acquired through massive experience of sound-sources in general and musical performances in particular." He adds: "[…] the main point is […] not so much the kinematics (the gesture trajectory shapes that we see) as it is the dynamics of movement (the sensation of effort that we feel through our embodied capacity for mental simulation of the action of others)."[17]

Information is Conveyed in the Body Movements of Solo Musician Performers?,' *Journal of Human Movement Studies*, 6 (1994), 279-301.

14 *Music and Gesture* and *New Perspectives on Music and Gesture*, ed. by Anthony Gritten and Elaine King (Farnham: Ashgate, 2006 and 2011). See also *Musical Gestures: Sound, Movement, and Meaning*, ed. by Rolf Inge Godøy and Marc Lehman (New York and London: Routledge, 2010).

15 Rolf Inge Godøy, 'Gestural Affordances of Musical Sound,' In *Musical Gestures: Sound, Movement, and Meaning*, ed. by Rolf Inge Godøy and Marc Lehman (New York and London: Routledge, 2010), pp. 103-125 (p. 106).

16 Taylor Carman, 'The Body in Husserl and Merleau-Ponty,' *Philosophical Topics*, 27/2 (1999), 205-226 (p. 206), cited in Kane, 'Excavating,' p. 33.

17 Godøy, 'Gestural Affordances,' p. 118, referring to Vittorio Gallese and Thomas Metzinger, 'Motor ontology: The Representational Reality of Goals, Actions and selves,' *Philosophical Psychology*, 16/3 (2003), 365-338.

In a similar vein, Lawrence Zbikowski proposes the possibility of "no correlation between the gesture and the sound that produced it" and argues that "gesture [and music] give access to a dynamics, imagistic mode of thought that is inaccessible to language."[18] As such it may function like a metaphor by reflecting "a conceptual mapping" of knowledge in one domain to the experience in another domain. The multi-modal perception of music and the subjectivity of meaning are underlined by such assertions, and highlight the difficulties commentators on music performance face. Yet our fascination is such that we do not give up easily. The dance to architecture goes on.

Focusing on actual rather than metaphorical gestures but similarly building on James Gibson's ecological theory of hearing and listening,[19] Luke Windsor argues: "Gestures are actions that musicians make, and the supreme virtue of music in this respect is that it can make audible gestures that are near invisible."[20] I propose that deciphering these gestures that are made audible by music is a key to a better understanding of aural modes of communication, of our capacity for "imagistic thought" that are visible only to our minds but triggered by sound. We want to talk about music because we are fascinated by our experience and want to understand why and how these strongly felt reactions come about.

A comprehensive approach to the study of music performance is therefore important. It paves the road towards such insights. How, in what manner does sound specify the actions of performers and how do these aural cues give meaning to the musical experience? My analyses will aim to answer these questions step by step. First looking at the separate performance elements and then contemplating their contribution to the overall effect. Given our multi-modal, cognitive as well as embodied and affective perception of music, analysis must attempt to consider cues not in isolation but in their complex, non-linear and dynamic interactions with each-other as well as with both the performer's and the listener's historical-cultural disposition. This complexity hints at the biggest

---

18 Lawrence M. Zbikowski, 'Musical Gesture and Musical Grammar: A Cognitive Approach,' in *New Perspectives on Music and Gesture*, ed. by Anthony Gritten and Elaine King (Farnham: Ashgate, 2011), pp. 83-98 (pp. 84, 97).

19 James Gibson, *The Senses Considered as Perceptual Systems* (London: Unwin Bros, 1966); idem, *The Ecological Approach to Visual Perception* (New Jersey: Lawrence Erlbaum, 1979).

20 Windsor, Luke W., 'Gesture in Music-making: Action, Information and Perception,' in *New Perspectives on Music and Gesture*, ed. by Anthony Gritten and Elaine King (Farnham: Ashgate, 2011), pp. 45-66 (p. 63).

problem experimental investigations of music performance face: for such an understanding "we must imagine a hearing that involves no lapse of attention and a perfect operation of all the faculties—sensation, memory, understanding, imagination, and so on. In an actual, empirical hearing it is difficult to imagine such perfection."[21] In contrast, in an analytical, contemplative framework that relies on rich, empirically derived data and a transdisciplinary approach the chances seem better to achieve this goal. It is this kind of musicology of performance that I propose.

Problems with Historical Investigations of Music Performance

It is not only the multi-modal nature of our engagement with music that causes problems in investigations of musical performance. There are also the historical, cultural and aesthetic dimensions to be accounted for. How and why does a performance evolve? How and why do styles of interpretation change? How do performers interact with the past and the present; how do they influence each-other? Are stylistic practices developing through communities sharing aesthetic sensibilities, geographical location, cultural or educational history? What is the current scene of performing the music of Bach like compared to earlier times? Are there trends and if so, who are the trend setters? The availability of more than one hundred years of recordings makes such investigations possible. In fact the study of sound recordings as evidence of changing performing styles has been a growing field of musicological investigation since the mid-1990s.

The explosion of digital reissues of old recordings at the end of the twentieth century suddenly put the history of music performance on centre stage as hundreds of items from early catalogues have had again become easily accessible. These provided fascinating and undeniable evidence for considerable changes in the interpretations of canonical compositions within the European concert tradition. Normative thinking regarding how Beethoven, or Bach, or any other composer's music "should go" was challenged, eventually leading to Nicholas Cook's call for a re-evaluation of the framing of musicological investigations to be not music as text (scores, compositions), but music as performance. Or how I prefer to think about it: music as sound.

---

21 Christopher Hasty, 'The Image of Thought and Ideas of Music,' in *Sounding the Virtual: Gilles Deleuze and the Theory and Philosophy of Music* (Farnham: Ashgate, 2010), pp. 1-22 (p. 5).

Anything that develops so rapidly brings with it the danger of "running ahead of itself." Understandably, historians have focused on the earlier recordings and on the playing of musicians of bygone eras. Many of them (e.g. Jascha Heifetz, Fritz Kreisler, Beniamino Gigli, Tito Gobbi, Adelina Patti, Pablo Casals, Ignacy Jan Paderewsky, Alfred Cortot, the Lehner Quartet, Willam Mengelberg, Bruno Walter, to name a few) are legendary and becoming familiar with their artistry is not only informative regarding earlier styles of playing or singing but also satisfies curiosity. But a narrative of the history of twentieth-century performance styles that is based primarily on studying earlier musicians while relying on impressionistic information regarding more recent or living artists, leads to false conclusions. In this book I aim to supplement this near singular focus of detailed research on early recordings and pre-war artists by similarly engaged, systematic work on current musicians. This is important to do for an accurate picture to emerge and to prevent potentially unwarranted conclusions regarding a "golden age" (that is, pre-1930s) from taking hold.[22]

A lack of sufficient balance in scholarly attention may also foster premature notions about the roles various stakeholders and cultural-historical-social forces play in the development of performing styles and interpretative approaches. I will explore these at length in the next chapter. So here I only introduce some of the key issues that are problematic and need further investigation.

A commonly expressed view is that the recording industry has fostered a de-personalisation of musical expression through its demand for technical perfection and repeatability, that performances have become much less individual than they used to be during the proverbial "golden age" prior to and at the beginning of sound recordings.[23] Theorists of music performance in the second half of the twentieth century also seem to be of

---

22 The only study I am aware of that focuses on the performance characteristics of a more recent musician is Kevin Bazzana's brilliant book, *Glenn Gould: The Performer in the Work* (New York: Oxford University Press, 1997). There are also biographies and autobiographies of Yehudi Menuhin, Nikolaus Harnoncourt, and Isaac Stern, among others.

23 For instance Timothy Day, *A Century of Recorded Music* (New Heaven and London: Yale University Press, 2000); Robert Philip, *Performing Music in the Age of Recording* (New Heaven and London: Yale University Press, 2004); Eric Wen, 'The Twentieth Century,' in *The Cambridge Companion to the Violin*, ed. by Robin Stowell (Cambridge: Cambridge University Press, 1992), pp. 79-91. This view is also evidenced in several authors' contributions to *The Cambridge Companion to Recorded Music*, ed. by Nicholas Cook et al. (Cambridge: Cambridge University Press, 2009).

the opinion that performances today are less communicative because they are less detailed.[24]

The individual liberties observed in early recordings, including piano rolls, are of course stunning for a modern listener. Performances have an air of spontaneity because they do not seem to strive for uniformity of tone or phrasing, steadiness of tempo, or ensemble and (in case of pianists) hands co-ordination, and because they freely arrest the musical movement to highlight a melodic pitch, or glide and "scoop" to notes of affective significance. Importantly, the flexibilities heard in these recordings are of a "fluid" nature; they sound very engaged because they seemingly follow unhinged the texture and assumed dramatic impetus of the music. However, closer study reveals that these performance characteristics were quite common during the turn of the nineteenth and twentieth centuries; they represent the general trend, the convention.[25] They seem individual and idiosyncratic to us only because our current conventions are very different. Systematic and comprehensive analyses are important—whether dealing with old or recent performances—if we wish to avoid the problems of premature generalizations and misrepresentation of historical-cultural developments. Performances are constantly changing and evolving. The impressions about conventions in the 1980s and 1990s reported in narratives of the recorded history of performing western classical music may not hold water when considering more recent performances, or specific repertoires.

Nevertheless, broad and unsystematic listening to classical music seems to confirm, at a basic level, that performance has been "tidied up."[26] There is ample evidence of current players' dazzling technical proficiency, and this precision of intonation and ensemble, steadiness of

---

24 Richard Taruskin, 'How Things Stand Now?' Keynote address delivered at the *Performa 11* conference, Aveiro Portugal, on 19 May 2011. Daniel Leech-Wilkinson, 'Recordings and Histories of Performance Style,' in *The Cambridge Companion to Recorded Music*, pp. 246-262.

25 Several authors have presented ample evidence for this claim. See for instance, Neal Peres Da Costa, *Off the Record: Performing Practices in Romantic Piano Playing* (New York: Oxford University Press, 2012); David Milsom, *Theory and Practice in Late Nineteenth-Century Violin Performance: An Examination of Style in Performance, 1850-1900* (Aldershot: Ashgate, 2003); Dorottya Fabian, 'Is Diversity in Performance Truly in Decline? The Evidence of Sound Recordings,' *Context*, 31 (2006), 165-180; idem, 'Commercial Sound Recordings and Trends in Expressive Music Performance: Why Should Experimental Researchers Pay Attention?,' in *Expressiveness in Music Performance: Empirical Approaches Across Styles and Cultures*, ed. by Dorottya Fabian, Renee Timmers, and Emery Schubert (Oxford: Oxford University Press, 2014), pp. 58-79.

26 Philip, *Performing Music*, p. 232.

tempo, accuracy of rhythm, bow and vibrato control, dexterity, virtuosity and so on have become minimum standards. The often less polished and more wayward playing on early recordings, on the other hand, may make such performances sound more personal and musically engaged because of their seeming vulnerability and the *ad hoc*, "in the moment" solutions musicians are able to pull off.[27] But what are the assumed characteristics of the modern style?

Since in this book I study performances of Bach's Solos for violin, it seems appropriate to report how the "modern" style is described in literature specific to violin playing. Eric Wen refers to a "codification of violin technique," namely a focus on the left hand and "overemphasis on vibrato at the expense of shadings in the bow." This, Wen claims, "led to an increase in digital facility [and] set a standard in sound production which lacked variety."[28] Jaap Schröder explains the situation by highlighting that the modern legato stroke, which is based on the whole bow being under a certain pressure, "tend[s] to produce a straight and uninteresting tone that must be made more attractive through vibrato."[29] Mark Katz agrees but also posits a direct link between the increased prominence of vibrato and the advent of sound recording. In his view, during the 1910s-1920s vibrato may have been considered an aid in adding personality in the absence of visual contact and also helped project the tone into the recording equipment—while also hiding imprecision in intonation.[30] In short, a more homogeneous tone has developed aided by standardized and continuous vibrato and seamlessly even up-and-down bow strokes. The aesthetic preference for unity and smoothness has also fostered fingering that enables the use of single strings for the entire length of phrases. As each

---

27 How spontaneous these interpretations are is, of course, questionable. In fact comparisons of multiple recordings by the same artists from the early period tend to show important similarities in terms of expressive gestures suggesting deliberate and controlled choice rather than momentary artistic impulse. Apart from the analytical investigations already cited, a recent doctoral thesis also provides corroborating evidence: Dario Sarlo, 'Investigating Performer Uniqueness: The Case of Jascha Heifetz' (PhD Thesis, Goldsmith College, University of London, 2010).

28 Wen, 'The Twentieth Century,' 89.

29 Jaap Schröder, *Bach's Solo Violin Works: A Performer's Guide* (London: Yale University Press, 2007), p. 29.

30 Mark Katz, *Capturing Sound: How Technology has Changed Music* (Berkley and Los Angeles: University of California Press, 2004). This is not the place to discuss vibrato at length. Katz and others provide a detailed discussion that is much more complex than the citation here may imply. See also Daniel Leech-Wilkinson, *The Changing Sound of Music: Approaches to Studying Recorded Musical Performance* (London: CHARM, 2009), especially chapter five, http://www.charm.rhul.ac.uk/studies/chapters/intro.html

string of the violin has a slightly different timbre and because one cannot use vibrato on open strings, violinists have tended to shift hand position to avoid open strings and create a unified tone by remaining on the same string for a given melodic passage. Later I will explain the differences between this way of playing and what historical sources tell us about early eighteenth-century practice. However, it remains to be seen if currently recording violinists subscribe to this modern aesthetic when performing J. S. Bach's Solos.

As I have already mentioned earlier, in spite of these observations, their general arguments regarding the current state of affairs are not necessarily entirely accurate. Although the grand narrative of increasingly less "interesting," more homogeneous performance practice dominates public and scholarly opinion, these are based on broad impressions, not systematic examinations. Yet by now several data-rich studies exist that demand a more refined account of how performance styles are developing and what characteristics are typical today (cf. fn. 25). On the one hand, they point to the fact that trends and fashions existed in earlier times also, while on the other hand, they reveal considerable variety among recent versions of given repertoires, thus throwing the theory of growing homogeneity into doubt.[31] Furthermore, it is recognized that every generation expresses nostalgia towards a "golden age" which invariably seems to refer to the period during which that generation gained its formative musical experiences.[32] Whether idealizing the performances of certain teachers and older artists or gradually canonizing particular aspects of their playing or musical approach, when a performance style becomes a convention it also becomes normative, fostering a level of uniformity: one orthodoxy gradually

---

31 Bruno Repp, 'Patterns of Expressive Timing in Performances of a Beethoven Minuet by Nineteen Famous Pianists,' *Journal of the Acoustical Society of America*, 88 (1990), 622-641; idem, 'Diversity and Commonality in Music Performance: An Analysis of Timing Microstructure in Schumann's "Träumerei,"' *Journal of the Acoustical Society of America*, 92 (1992), 2546-2568; Richard Turner, 'Style and Tradition in String Quartet Performance: A Study of 32 Recordings of Beethoven's Op. 131 Quartet' (PhD Thesis, University of Sheffield, 2004); Dorottya Fabian and Emery Schubert, 'Musical Character and the Performance and Perception of Dotting, Articulation and Tempo in Recordings of Variation 7 of J.S. Bach's *Goldberg Variations* (BWV 988),' *Musicae Scientiae*, 12/2 (2008), 177-203; Eitan Ornoy, 'Recording Analysis of J. S. Bach's G minor Adagio for Solo Violin (Excerpt): A Case Study,' *Journal of Music and Meaning*, 6 (2008), available at http://www.musicandmeaning.net/issues/showArticle.php?artID=6.2

32 Kenneth Hamilton, *After the Golden Age: Romantic Pianism and Modern Performance* (Oxford and New York: Oxford University Press, 2009).

replaces another.[33] The problems with currently available historical studies of music performance are becoming increasingly transparent.

Is HIP a Modern Invention/Aesthetic or Does it Have Historical Grounding?

Another problem, perhaps more pertinent for the case study in this book, is the reception and critical theory of what we call historically informed performance, or HIP. Without wanting to pre-empt the discussion of this complex area in chapter two I should explain here some of the stakes involved.

At the beginning of sound recordings the most often performed repertoire was from the nineteenth century and many works from periods prior to Mozart were hardly known at all. The revival of early music became an important preoccupation of musicians throughout the twentieth century but in particular during the post WWII decades of the 1950s to the 1980s. The history and aesthetics of the "early music" or "authenticity movement," as it was originally called, have been mapped from a range of viewpoints. Harry Haskell wrote primarily about its history; I investigated its stylistic development; Richard Taruskin and John Butt theorized its ideologies and cultural connections; while Bruce Haynes focused on articulating stylistic and aesthetic differences among various twentieth-century approaches to repertoire, to name but only a few larger studies.[34]

During the course of the movement not only forgotten repertoire but also old instruments and past performance conventions have been revived. Or so people specializing in HIP claim. They assert that by studying period instrumental treatises, by playing on historical instruments or copies thereof and by implementing ornamentation, articulation, bowing, tonguing and fingering techniques recommended in historical sources, they are able to recreate performing conventions that were typical at the time of composition. Critics of the movement argue, on the other hand,

---

33 Taruskin, 'How Things Stand Now?'
34 Harry Haskell, *The Early Music Revival: A History* (London: Hudson, 1988); Dorottya Fabian, *Bach Performance Practice, 1945-1975: A Comprehensive Review of Sound Recordings and Literature* (Aldershot: Ashgate, 2003); Richard Taruskin, *Text and Act: Essays on Music and Performance* (New York: Oxford University Press, 1995); John Butt, *Playing with History: The Historical Approach to Musical Performance* (Cambridge: Cambridge University Press, 2002); Bruce Haynes, *The End of Early Music* (New York: Oxford University Press, 2007).

that HIP is not much else than a selective cherry-picking of elements our modern sensibilities like; their sum total has little historical credence, in fact they are essentially similar to the mainstream performance (MSP) style.

Although currently less discussed, the extent to which HIP is an invented, modern aesthetic tradition is still a matter for debate. As I will show in the next chapter, and throughout the book, a systematic and comprehensive analysis of recordings and repertoire does not support a generalized view of HIP. The analogies between the styles of MSP and HIP are not water tight when it comes to performances of Bach's Solos for violin. "It depends" – as a lawyer would say and as I will show in chapters three to five. More importantly, performers have moved on, and believing that what might have been true of the 1970s and 1980s still holds today is naive. One constantly has to re-evaluate findings about "current practice," because practice never stands still. When the theoretical framework and analytical approaches proposed in this book are implemented a more nuanced picture develops that allows for the complexities to shine through and a fairer account of what performers do to be formulated.

Data versus Narrative–Letting Go of Dancing or Returning to the Dance Floor?

Having outlined problems encountered in various approaches to investigating music performance it is time to address the dilemma the "systematic and comprehensive" analyst faces: How to "talk" (write) about recordings meaningfully and interestingly? When interpretations are played one after the other, the differences between them seem all too obvious. Yet, when enlisting scientific apparatus to account for these differences, the resulting descriptive words, numerical tables and graphs often seem opaque and thus hopelessly inadequate; really, like overkill. As Taruskin put it, "data can't solve aesthetic issues. To think it can is utopian, and all utopian thinking ends up being authoritarian."[35] I might retort that without data all we have is opinion. But what knowledge do we gain? How much and what kind of detail do we need? On what grounds and through what kinds of expression can we verbalise sensed aural and temporal experiences? What do we learn that we did not know already, even if only intuitively or perceptually? This, of course, may be asked of many academic

---

35 Taruskin, 'How Things Stand Now?'

endeavours, especially in the arts. In this book I argue that we need much more detailed empirical data before an evidence-based narrative of the historical-cultural evolution of performance styles can be written because the devil is indeed in the detail. We need not only more data but we need to approach our subject, music performance, differently because it is like a complex system and complex systems are not "constituted merely by the sum of [their] components but also by the intricate *relationships* between these components. In 'cutting up' a system, the analytical method destroys what it seeks to understand."[36]

I argue that individual performances are so varied and unique that making generalizations on the basis of a select few samples is simply not adequate from a scholarly point of view. It is impossible to know whether an observed element is typical until we have widespread evidence for it. Furthermore, personal traits cannot be distinguished from conventions until a representative sample has been thoroughly investigated. As José Bowen noted, "It is altogether too easy to mistake a performance characteristic for a unique interpretive feature when it is, in fact, a general style trait of an unfamiliar style."[37] For instance, a-synchrony between parts (e.g. melody versus accompaniment) could be regarded as a unique feature of, say, Paderewsky's playing, until one realises that most pianists trained during the nineteenth century performed that way. The seemingly idiosyncratic style turns out to be a historical convention.

Groups of performers belonging to the same generation or "school" of performing practice and playing within broadly similar stylistic conventions nevertheless exhibit personal characteristics otherwise they would not likely become soloists with established careers. To account for these individual artistic signatures one has to study differences in degree, not just in kind. The problem is that once such evidence is carefully amassed and examined with a fine-toothed comb, the richness and variety of observations are staggering. The resulting picture tends to be so complex that drawing neat conclusions appears to be farcical, if not outright untenable, for anybody intimately familiar with the data. The modernist scientific project of categorizing, of putting products in the either/or baskets quickly fails. It is all too clear that for any particular finding there

---

36 Paul Cilliers, *Complexity and Postmodernism: Understanding Complex Systems* (London: Routledge, 1998).
37 José A. Bowen, 'Performance Practice versus Performance Analysis: Why Should Performers Study Performance?,' *Performance Practice Review*, 9/1 (1996), 16-35 (p. 20).

could be several counter examples. Take for instance Richard Tognetti's recording of Bach's *Six Sonatas and Partitas for Solo Violin*. If one listens to the B minor Partita's Sarabande movement, one may come to the conclusion that Tognetti adds ornaments and embellishments where appropriate, at least in slow movements. However, the only other movements in which a few additional embellishments are heard are the E Major Gavotte and the Andante of the A minor Sonata.

To preview some of the results of my analyses of tempo in chapter four, here is a more general example of how varied some findings can be. In conversations people often claim that HIP performers play faster than MSP instrumentalists. However, my systematic study of Bach recordings reveals three important characteristics that correct this generalization. Firstly, it is not so much the tempo that is faster in HIP versions of slow movements, but the *perception* of the tempo. The overall duration is frequently similar but because of the different approach to articulation and rhythm, the HIP versions tend to move along at an apparently brisker pace. Secondly, HIP players tend to play slow movements faster while MSP players often have a more virtuosic speed in fast movements, especially in finales. The exceptions among HIP violinists include Rachel Podger, whose tempos are usually fast all round, and Monica Huggett, whose tempos are among the slowest regardless of movement type. Thirdly, and as a consequence of the second observation, HIP performers tend to use less extreme tempos than MSP performers (i.e. the differences between the speeds of fast and slow movements is less pronounced). It is clear then, that generalizing on the basis of select examples (e.g. an impression gained from listening to fast or slow movements) can lead to incorrect claims. But of course preparation of comprehensive data is time consuming and the results are likely to be valid only for the particular repertoire examined. Moving along at a snail pace is not conducive for an academic career and many people rather read provocative assertions written in an engaging and persuasive style then hair-splittingly detailed accounts with no neat or debatable conclusions, however accurate they might be. After all, most of us prefer to dance (especially when it comes to music) than to labour in a lab.

Finally, we circle back to the issue of subjectivity of perception and the problems with quantification. Aural analysis is often more instructive in identifying nuanced but clearly audible individual differences that may "disappear" once measured data are averaged, percentages calculated and other means of numerical-statistical or graphic representations are enlisted to show "scientifically" potential trends and regularities. Surely, one has to decide if the aim is to find generalizable trends or to account for individual differences. Yet in either case quantification or visualization are essential because without them the aurally based observations may be tainted by the researcher-listener's own biases, musical attention and memory. To recall Hasty cited earlier, in empirical investigations of listening it is difficult to maintain the "perfect operation of all the participating faculties—attention, sensation, memory, understanding, imagination, and so on." What one can hope for is to constantly move back and forth (or in and out) of all these faculties and engage with them one by one while also paying attention to their interactions and combined effect. My proposed approach entails exactly such a conduct and my analytical comments throughout chapters three to five are peppered with cross references looking forward and back across the various observations made according to a particular "faculty" and questioning or confirming previous or later conclusions.

Overall the aim of my analyses is to emphasize the importance of individual differences and to advocate for a more nuanced, more circumspect picture of "general trends"; to be less lofty and more honest about "how things are." I posit that for a while—until we have accumulated significant quantities of systematically gathered, specific information—the main goal of historical studies of performance and sound recordings needs to be the provision rather than the explication of data. And the data must be generated by a combination of quantitative and qualitative-descriptive analyses and be supported by ample Audio examples.[38] If we are serious about putting the performer centre stage and claiming for her or him a pivotal role in the identity and reception of western classical compositions (or "pieces," to make their identity more fluid than the words "work" or "composition" may imply),[39] we must undertake the painstaking data gathering and analytical tasks that were typically applied to written texts / scores until the

---

38 Anthony J. Onwuegbuzie and Nancy L. Leech, 'On Becoming a Pragmatic Researcher: The Importance of Combining Quantitative and Qualitative Research Methodologies,' *International Journal of Social Research Methodology*, 8/5 (2005), 375-387.

39 Several authors have argued for this recently. For instance José A. Bowen, 'Finding the Music in Musicology: Performance History and Musical Works,' in *Rethinking Music*, ed. by Nicholas Cook and Mark Everist (Oxford and New York: Oxford University Press, 1999), pp. 424-451; Cook, 'Between Process and Product'; Daniel Leech-Wilkinson, 'Compositions, Scores, Performances, Meanings,' *Music Theory Online*, 18/1 (2012), 1-17, http://www.mtosmt.org/issues/mto.12.18.1/mto.12.18.1.leech-wilkinson.php

1980s. We need to deconstruct and name the specifics constituting players' artistry, because style history is the history of choices performers make. If we wish to understand how these choices fit with or reflect broader cultural movements we first need to know their exact nature as far as it is possible to know, and how they vary from one generation to the next.

1.2. Summary: Recordings, Aims and Methods

Being a historical musicologist, this book is primarily a historical-analytical investigation of music performance. Given the diverse approaches noted throughout the introduction and problems encountered in all of them, my contention is that we need a different approach and a different theoretical framework. I propose to consider music performance as a complex dynamical system and to use comprehensive analytical methods that are commensurate with the object of study. My aim is to model such an approach through the case study of Bach recordings and meanwhile demonstrate the complex, non-linear and dynamic nature of music performance.

As I have noted, there seems to be a lack of systematic work on contemporary styles of music performance; the depth and detail of discussion rarely going beyond that of a record review.[40] Therefore I intend to start correcting the balance by putting the contemporary performer in the spotlight. Because the earliest recordings featured singers and violinists, much has been written about legendary violinists of the early twentieth century.[41] It seems appropriate then to also focus on violinists, but (mostly)

---

40 Post 1950s recordings of Bach's Cello Suite No. 6 are analysed in the context of postmodernism, individual difference and interaction between historically informed and mainstream performance styles in Alistair Sung and Dorottya Fabian, 'Variety in Performance: A Comparative Analysis of Recorded Performances of Bach's Sixth Suite for Solo Cello from 1961 to 1998,' *Empirical Musicology Review*, 6 (2011), 20-42, http://hdl.handle.net/1811/49760

41 For instance, Milsom, *Theory and Practice*; Mark Katz, 'Beethoven in the Age of Mechanical Reproduction: The Violin Concerto on Record,' *Beethoven Forum*, 10 (2003), 38-54; idem, 'Portamento and the Phonograph Effect,' *Journal of Musicological Research*, 25 (2006), 211-232; Heejung Lee, 'Violin Portamento: An Analysis of its Use by Master Violinists in Selected Nineteenth-Century Concerti' (Doctor of Education Thesis, Columbia University, 2006); Dario Sarlo, *The Performance Style of Jascha Heifetz* (Farnham: Ashgate, forthcoming); Leech-Wilkinson, *Changing Sound*; Ornoy, 'Recording Analysis'; Dorottya Fabian and Eitan Ornoy, 'Identity in Violin Playing on Records: Interpretation Profiles in Recordings of Solo Bach by Early Twentieth-Century Violinists,' *Performance Practice Review*, 14 (2009), 1-40.

living ones. As for repertoire, J. S. Bach's *Six Sonatas and Partitas for Solo Violin* (BWV1001-BWV1006) are ideal because of their long and varied performance history that enables engagement with HIP / MSP debate.[42] Importantly, they are unaccompanied pieces, making the examination of performance choices less complicated.

The forty recordings selected for study were all made between 1980 and 2010 except for Sergiu Luca's. His was issued in 1977 and is included here because it was the first to use a baroque bow and to attempt a historically informed interpretation of the Solos.[43] I do not at all claim that my selection is fully inclusive of all recordings made during the designated period of 1980 to 2010, but I certainly believe they form a substantial collection and a representative cross section of such recordings (Table 1.1).[44] I also believe that recordings can be studied as if they were performances because the listener experiences them as such, regardless of how they might have come about.

In a study like this, it is not enough to note the date of a recording and its release on the market. It is also important to be aware of the age of the performers. It has been shown that performers develop their personal style early on and then tend to stick with it by and large throughout their careers.[45] The majority of violinists studied here were born in or after 1945, except for Oscar Shumsky (b.1917), Ruggiero Ricci (b.1918), Jaap Schröder (b.1925), Gérard Poulet (b.1938), Rudolf Gähler (b.1941), Sergiu Luca (b.1943), Ugo Ughi (b.1944) and Sigiswald Kuijken (b.1944). The younger players, born since 1970, are represented by Lara St John (b.1971), Isabelle Faust (b. 1973), Rachel Barton Pine (b.1974), James Ehnes (b.1976), Hilary Hahn (b.1979), Ilya Gringolts (b.1982), Julia Fischer (b. 1983), Sergey Khachatryan (b.1985) and Alina Ibragimova (b.1985). Table 1.1 and the Discography provide the complete list and full details.

---

42 Dorottya Fabian, 'Towards a Performance History of Bach's Sonatas and Partitas for Solo Violin: Preliminary Investigations,' in *Essays in Honor of László Somfai*, ed. by László Vikárius and Vera Lampert (Lanham, MD: Scarecrow Press, 2005), pp. 87-108.

43 Another exception might be Oscar Shumsky's. My recording is dated 1983 but I have come across a NIMBUS re-issue (NI2557, 2010) which states that the recording was made by Amreco Inc. in 1979. By the same token, Paul Zukovsky's disk issued by Musical Observations in 2005 is not included because it is a remixed and remastered copy of his Vanguard recording from 1971-1972 (VSD 71194/6).

44 Bernard Sherman, 'The Bach Violin Glut of the 2000s and its Strange Gender Gaps,' lists twenty-six complete set recordings of the Bach Solos just from the period between 2000 and 2010. Out of these there are eleven (two HIP and nine MSP) that I have not heard, available at http://bsherman.net/BachViolinGlutofthe2000s.htm

45 Daniel Leech-Wilkinson, 'Recordings and Histories'; Fabian and Ornoy, 'Identity in Violin Playing'; Sung and Fabian, 'Variety in Performance.' Throughout my research into various repertoires and performers I find this to be true in the majority of cases.

Table 1.1. Studied Recordings Listed by Chronology of Violinists' Year of Birth

Name	Year of birth	Recording / CD Release Date
Shumsky, Oscar	1917	1979 / 1983
Ricci, Ruggiero	1918	1992 (Concerts from 1988, 1991)
Schröder, Jaap HIP	1925	1985
Poulet, Gerard	1938	1996
Gähler, Rudolf	1941	1997
Luca, Sergiu HIP	1943	1977
Kuijken, Sigiswald HIP	1944	1981 / 1983
Kuijken, Sigiswald HIP	1944	2001
Perlman, Itzhak	1945	1986
Edinger, Christiane	1945	1991
Van Dael, Lucy HIP	1946	1996
Kremer, Gidon	1947	1980
Kremer, Gidon	1947	2005
Holloway, John HIP	1948	2004 / 2006
Szenthelyi, Miklós	1951	2001
Wallfisch, Elizabeth HIP	1952	1997
Huggett, Monica HIP	1953	1995
Poppen, Christoph	1956	2000
Mintz, Shlomo	1957	1984
Mullova, Victoria	1959	1987
Mullova, Victoria	1959	1992-3 / 2006
Mullova, Victoria	1959	2009
Buswell, James	1950s/1960s?	1989 / 1995
Lev, Lara	1950s/1960s?	2001
Beznosiuk, Pavlo HIP	1960	2007 / 2011
Brooks, Brian HIP	1960s?	2001
Zehetmair, Thomas	1961	1983
Tognetti, Richard	1965	2005
Tetzlaff, Christian	1966	1994
Tetzlaff, Christian	1966	2005
Matthews, Ingrid HIP	1966	1997 / 2001
Schmid, Benjamin	1968	2000
Podger, Rachel HIP	1968	1998
St John, Lara	1971	2007
Faust, Isabelle	1973	2010
Barton Pine, Rachel	1974	1999 (Radio Broadcast)
Barton Pine, Rachel	1974	2004
Barton Pine, Rachel	1974	2007 (Festival Concert, private recording)
Ehnes, James	1976	1999
Hahn, Hillary	1979	1997
Gringolts, Ilya	1982	2001
Fischer, Julia	1983	2005
Khachatryan, Sergey	1984	2010
Ibragimova, Alina	1985	2008

In this selection approximately twenty-five[46] recordings represent non-specialist or "mainstream" violinists, with multiple recordings by Gidon Kremer, Viktoria Mullova, Christian Tetzlaff and Rachel Barton Pine. There are eleven violinists representing the historically informed performance movement, with two recordings by Sigiswald Kuijken. Initially (and in this summary) I categorized violinists who play on modern violins and perform the broad gamut of the violin repertoire as representing "mainstream performance" (MSP), while those playing with eighteenth-century violins and bows (whether originals, copies, or reconstructions) *and* specializing in performing largely pre-1800 repertoire are regarded as "period" (HIP) violinists. However, it has been pointed out that the distinction between HIP and MSP is increasingly difficult to make as time passes. For instance, Colin Lawson and Robin Stowell noted the application of "period principles […] to mainstream situations" whereas in 2006 Eitan Ornoy demonstrated "clear similarities" between the styles of playing.[47] This trend began when Nikolaus Harnoncourt and other HIP specialists started conducting large symphonic orchestras in the early 1980s, demonstrating that the HIP style was transferable to modern instruments. However, as noted in the previous section, there are also commentators who believe HIP was never really different from MSP. This book explores where things are now in this regard and one of its main findings is the revision of this initial categorization.

As a practical note, it needs to be said, that throughout the book I generally refer to Bach's *Sei Solo a Violino senza Basso accompagnato* as the Solos and I abbreviate the identification of movements by stating the key of the sonata or partita of which they are a part, followed by the movement title. This ignores the fact that certain movements are in a different key from the work's main tonality (e.g. the Andante of the A minor Sonata is actually in C Major) but should cause no confusion as to the identity of the excerpt. The spelling of the movement titles follows Bach's own indication in the autograph manuscript.

To foreshadow some elements of this analysis, it can be noted that many of the younger players in the sample claim to have been influenced by HIP

---

46 The number is approximate because not all of the studied recordings are complete sets of all Six Solos (see Discography) and only a selection of them will be commented on in detail.

47 Colin Lawson and Robin Stowell, *Historical Performance: An Introduction* (Cambridge: Cambridge University Press, 1999), p. 160; Eitan Ornoy, 'Between Theory and Practice: Comparative Study of Early Music Performances,' *Early Music*, 34/2 (2006), 233-247 (p. 243).

ideology (e.g. Zehetmair, Tetzlaff) and quite a few of them undertook periods of specialist training (e.g. Ibragimova) or regularly play with period ensembles (e.g. Barton Pine). According to the liner notes for their respective recordings, three MSP violinists use a baroque bow and / or gut strings: Rachel Barton Pine, Richard Tognetti, and Viktoria Mullova in 2008. On the other hand, Rudolf Gähler plays with the so-called curved-bow, also referred to as "Bach-bow" or "Vega-bow." Although the arguments for using such a bow bespeak of a search for period practices, the playing style enabled by such bows is closer to the aesthetic principles upheld by the MSP tradition. The historical existence of such a bow has been discredited by researchers since the 1960s.[48]

This book is not the place to discuss at length what constitutes the performance characteristics of MSP or HIP *in principle*; there is plenty of literature on that as mentioned earlier. I will refer to them in detail later on, particularly in chapters two and four, as they relate to performance features I analyse. Here it should suffice to recall that, as we have seen in earlier comments on twentieth-century violin playing, in MSP the aesthetic ideal is essentially a purity and evenness of tone (achieved through vibrato and seamless bowing) in service of power and projection of the melody. Inflections are kept to the minimum to foster long-spun phrasing shaped through graded dynamics. In contrast, HIP takes its cue from the bass line and meter of a piece and inflects melodic-rhythmic-harmonic groups accordingly. The use of shorter, uneven bow strokes, bouncing rhythm and locally nuanced articulation of smaller musical units are among the main characteristics of such interpretations. These and other differences will of course be explored and expanded upon since they are key matters to consider when teasing out the qualitative differences between performances. Identifying them and explaining their characteristics and interactions provide the basis for a more textured description of performances and a more nuanced "categorization" of violinists.

Importantly, although versions on period instruments are contrasted with mainstream ones, my goal is *not* to assess historical verisimilitude or whether an interpretation reflects Bach's possible intentions. The futility of such exercises has been well argued by others many times over, as discussed in the next chapter. The aim is neither a search for the ultimate "authentic," "definitive," or "normative" performance nor the matching

---

48 Fabian, 'Towards a Performance History,' p. 22, n. 26. For its disappointingly strange sound effect see also Sergiu Luca, 'Going for Baroque,' *Music Journal*, 32/8 (1974), 16-34.

of interpretations to particular editions, analytical observations, or performance suggestions, even though certain specific differences between HIP literature and execution are noted.[49] My goal is, rather, to conduct a thorough examination of these recordings as a model for analysing performances as complex dynamic systems. Such an approach is likely to unveil the actual level of uniformity versus individuality in playing Bach's Solos at the turn of the twentieth and twenty-first centuries and thus contribute to a more circumspect narrative of baroque performance styles on record. Throughout I aim to problematize methods to show their limitations and how misleading the results of any one approach might be when used in isolation. Yet when used cumulatively, the various analytical approaches unpack the complex, dynamic network of interactions at play and allow us to see what performers do to achieve particular effects and how differences in execution lead to different readings of the music. At this point the "talking about music" ceases to be "like dancing to architecture"; it starts tapping into the holistic experience.

The different interactions and transformations such an approach unveils can be elucidated by reference to Deleuzian terminology and thinking. I will introduce these in chapter two as part of my argument for tackling music performance as a complex dynamical system. Once I modelled such an approach through chapters four and five but also chapter three, I return to this crucial matter in the final chapter to make the parallels more explicit.

To achieve my goals, both descriptive and quantitative methods need to be employed based on repeated close listening (aural analyses) and software assisted measurements of audio signals. When working with variants of a musical "text" the human brain is often more effective than current computer programs in discerning and sorting individual resemblances or nuances. The use of software is more advantageous in identifying basic or categorical differences and trends across the larger body of data. Moreover, since music performance is ephemeral—"evanescence is its essence" even if recorded—what is available to the listener-analyst is "only what is present

---

49 Such issues are discussed in Joel Lester, *Bach's Works for Solo Violin: Style, Structure, Performance* (New York: Oxford University Press, 1999); Carl Schachter, 'The *Gavotte en Rondeaux* from J.S. Bach's Partita in E Major for Unaccompanied Violin,' *Israel Studies in Musicology*, 4 (1987), 7-26; Richard Efrati, *Treatise on the Execution and Interpretation of the Sonatas and Partitas for Solo Violin and the Suites for Cello by Johann Sebastian Bach* (Zürich: Atlantis Verlag, 1979); David Ledbetter, *Unaccompanied Bach: Performing the Solo Works* (New Haven and London: Yale University Press, 2009); Frederick Neumann, 'Some Performance Problems in Bach's Unaccompanied Violin and Cello Works,' in *Eighteenth-Century Music in Theory and Practice: Essays in Honour of Alfred Mann*, ed. by Mary Parker (Stuyvesant, NY: Pendragon Press, 1994), pp. 19-48; Robin Stowell, *The Early Violin and Viola: A Practical Guide* (Cambridge: Cambridge University Press, 2001).

in the moment, what is remembered of the past, and expectations for the future."[50] The data a computer might provide may have very little ecological validity. Contemplating the subjectively experienced sound is therefore essential, both globally as a whole and also in its details through close listening. While I focus more on the measurable in chapter four, in chapter five I aim to engage with the holistic and affective experience. However, both chapters are cross-referenced to highlight discrepancies between points of view and underscore the importance of the comprehensive, non-linear approach.

Violin technique is examined as far as vibrato is concerned while bowing is discussed in relation to articulation and phrasing as well as multiple stops and timbre. Expressive timing (rhythmic flexibility) is studied in detail as this contributes significantly to the performance style and plays a decisive role in aesthetic perception and in generating homogeneity or diversity among performances.[51] Nevertheless, rhythmic flexibility and phrasing remain somewhat resistant to quantification and categorization. The discussion of them is therefore necessarily limited to a few detailed, striking examples and generalizations. Other elements, such as tempo choices, ornamenting, the shaping of dotted rhythms, the performance of multiple stops, and the extent of reliance on pulse and / or harmony to project musical character and structure lend themselves better to tabulation, transcription or various other forms of visualization. Together, I hope, they provide ample complementary evidence in support of my main points and arguments.

I would like to stress my conviction that, at the time of writing, the methods of studying musical performance have important limitations. Treading the fine line between "impartial" measurements and "subjective" description raises many problems throughout that I do not claim to be able

---

50   Dan Ben-Amos, *Do We Need Ideal Types (in Folklore)? An Address to Lauri Hinko* (Turku, Finland: Nordic Institute of Folklore, 1992), pp. 65-66; cited in Anne Dhu McLucas, *The Musical Ear: Oral Tradition in the USA* (Farnham: Ashgate, 2010), p. 44.

51   Gerhard Widmer, 'Machine Discoveries: A Few Simple, Robust Local Expression Principles,' *Journal of New Music Research*, 31/1 (2002), 37-50; Eric Clarke, 'Empirical Methods in the Study of Performance,' in *Empirical Musicology: Aims, Methods, Prospects*, ed. by Eric Clarke and Nicholas Cook (Oxford and New York: Oxford University Press, 2004), pp. 77-102; Neil Todd, 'A Model of Expressive Timing in Tonal Music,' *Music Perception*, 3 (1985), 33-57; idem, 'Towards a Cognitive Theory of Expression: The Performance and Perception of Rubato,' *Contemporary Music Review*, 4 (1989), 405-416; idem, 'The Dynamics of Dynamics: A Model of Musical Expression,' *Journal of the Acoustical Society of America*, 91/6 (1992), 3540-3550; Luke Windsor and Eric Clarke, 'Expressive Timing and Dynamics in Real and Artificial Music Performance: Using an Algorithm as an Analytical Tool,' *Music Perception*, 15/4 (1997), 127-152.

to solve. But in my account I attempt to retain that semi-conscious moment of perception before I as a critic become "modern"; when I "still possess [a] pristine and unspoiled exoticism" and a sense of wonder about my subject; the moment before one tries to "desecrate" what one believes to be the phenomenon under investigation.[52] I am interested as much in the sonic means that violinists use as the expressive effect that the sound creates. I want to avoid the obvious danger in attempting to use science to account for human experience: the danger that what is quantifiable may become equated with the phenomenon one originally set out to study. More often than not I am frustrated by the recognition that the "objectively" measurable in a performance does not seem to fully explain my impression of it and that words fail to grasp the internalized perception.

In the Epilogue of chapter six I contemplate the implications and significance of the crucial difference between holistic-affective perception and abstract analytical dissecting with reference to Ian McGilchrist's proposition put forward in his 2009 book on brain laterality, *The Master and his Emissary*.[53] The discrepancy between "scientific" data and "sensed experience" underlines the importance of multi-modal approaches; of cross-checking acoustically measured and subjectively perceived data and if in doubt, giving priority to the listening experience. Music performance is a complex aural system rooted in oral cultures, as discussed in chapters two and six. This book is an attempt to explain aspects of it and map interactions in the rather opposite domains of text (language) and sight (the visual) even though I also provide numerous Audio examples, and advocate for the "and / as well as" view instead of the "either / or" dichotomy.

In the next chapter I explore some of these theoretical-aesthetic and methodological concerns in much more detail and present my argument for an approach that embraces the complexity of music performance. Such an approach highlights the interactions among a performance's varied and layered elements, allowing for a more balanced view that accounts for differences in degree, not just in kind. In the subsequent, central chapters I discuss the recordings that provide the empirical data, the case study, for my argument: first a more general overview (chapter three), then considerably detailed analyses (chapters four and five). At the end of the book (chapter six) I return to cultural issues and propose an alternative view of "how things [may] stand now," at the beginning of the twenty-first century.

---

52 Latour, *Pandora's Hope*, p. 276.
53 Iain McGilchrist, *The Master and his Emissary: The Divided Brain and the Making of the Western World* (London: Yale University Press, 2009).

2. Theoretical Matters

Music performance is a rich, multi-dimensional phenomenon that has fascinated philosophers, historians, analysts, psychologists, cognitive and neuro-scientists as well as anthropologists and cultural theorists. People have studied it from various angles and disciplines arriving at important partial insights. In this chapter I review (necessarily very selectively) some of the key developments in this broad field leading to my proposition that music performance is too complex to be understood by any one approach. We need multi-modal and transdisciplinary, comprehensive accounts that are data-driven yet embrace the phenomenological and cultural if we wish to lessen the problem of verbalizing an embodied aural experience. Ultimately I argue that music performance is a complex dynamical system; as such it requires a robust and dynamic investigative approach. Gilles Deleuze's theory of difference and consistency may just provide the necessary theoretical framework and toolbox of terms.

The last twenty years or so has seen an exponential growth in academic studies of musical performance. Previously this area of humanistic musicology was largely limited to investigating historical performing practices of the seventeenth and eighteenth centuries or earlier periods of western literate culture. At the same time, it was maintained that modern-day performances of later repertoires represented an unbroken tradition. Renowned composers and performers of the nineteenth century would hand down their understanding of stylistic requirements to their pupils in conservatoires or private studios, who in turn passed this tradition on to the next generation, in a continuous flow. Subsequent generations constantly interpreted the opinions and insights of past masters—composers, performers and teachers—while holding them to be gospel. The availability of increased quantities of written evidence from the 1800s onwards, including more detailed notated instructions in scores, as well as letters, memoirs, press reports and concert reviews, together with the relatively small, insular, hierarchical and authoritative nature of the world of classical music ("this is how Beethoven goes because the maestro says so, and he knows because he was the student of the student of the student of Czerny who was a student of Beethoven") created the impression of an ongoing, living tradition. The master–apprentice model and prestige of educational institutions ensured that change was slow and seemingly imperceptible. Thus emerged what the musicological literature tends to call "mainstream performance" (MSP) style. This is the style that most experimental music psychologists have been studying since the early 1980s, though systematic investigations began in earnest with Seashore and his group at the University of Iowa in the 1930s.[1] However, recent musicological interest in sound recordings has started to provide important counter-evidence that questions the existence of such an unbroken tradition and supports studies that map a different history.[2]

Meanwhile, generations of twentieth-century musicians and music historians dedicated to the rediscovery of historical performing practices of music composed prior to 1800 (roughly speaking) followed a very different path during the last 70-100 years. Instead of learning their craft from master teachers, they turned to written sources and surviving old instruments. From sporadic, individual endeavours at the end of the nineteenth century and during the first half of the twentieth century (e.g. Edward Dannreuter,

---

[1] Carl Seashore, 'Approaches to the Science of Music and Speech,' *University of Iowa Studies: Series of Aims & Progress of Research*, 41 (1933), 15. This is not the place to chart the history of psychological studies of music performance. For an exhaustive review of the field see Alf Gabrielsson, 'The Performance of Music,' in *The Psychology of Music* ed. by Diana Deutsch, 2nd edn (San Diego: Academic Press, 1999), pp. 501-602 and idem, 'Music Performance Research at the Millennium,' *Psychology of Music*, 31 (2003), 221-272. It is worth noting, however, that an interest in studying systematically what performers do arose already in the last quarter of the nineteenth century, both in musicology (e.g. Matisse Lussy, *Musical Expression: Accents, Nuances, and Tempo in Vocal and Instrumental Music*, trans. by M. E. von Glehn (London: Novello, 1874)) and psychology (e.g. Benjamin Ives Gilman, 'Report on an Experimental Test of Musical Expressiveness,' *The American Journal of Psychology*, 4/4 (1892), 558-576).

[2] For instance, José A. Bowen, 'Tempo, Duration and Flexibility: Techniques in the Analysis of Performance,' *Journal of Musicological Research*, 16/2 (1996), 111-156; Robert Philip, *Performing Music in the Age of Recording* (New Haven: Yale University Press, 2003); Turner, 'Style and Tradition in String Quartet Performance: A Study of 32 Recordings of Beethoven's Op. 131 Quartet' (PhD Thesis, University of Sheffield, 2004); Kenneth Hamilton, *After the Golden Age: Romantic Pianism and Modern Performance* (New York: Oxford University Press, 2008); Daniel Leech-Wilkinson, *The Changing Sound of Music: Approaches to Studying Recorded Musical Performance* (London: CHARM, 2009).

Wanda Landowska, Carl Dolmetsch, Ralph Kirkpatrick) the early music movement, as it was first labelled, gradually grew in popularity during the 1950s and 1960s and, by the late 1970s and early 1980s, had developed into the immensely popular authenticity or period instrument movement. There are many readily available accounts of this development.[3] What concerns me here is what has happened since; however, to explain my views properly, I have to take a detour.

As I showed in my earlier book on the performance history of Bach's works in the twentieth century, this phase of the early music or authenticity movement had developed rather differently in Europe than in England. Contrasting customs, economic circumstances, cultural practices and musical personalities led to different musical results. During the 1970s and early 1980s the recorded performances of leading Continental musicians and ensembles (e.g. Leonhardt, Harnoncourt, Concentus Musicus Wien) had a very different sound and style of playing compared to their UK-based colleagues (e.g. Hogwood, Academy of Ancient Music). This difference was largely ignored by the most important English language criticisms and evaluations of the movement that appeared between 1982 and 1988 and thereafter.[4] Ever since Taruskin's immensely influential

---

3   The most detailed (in English) are Harry Haskell, *The Early Music Revival: A History* (London: Hudson, 1988); Dorottya Fabian, *Bach Performance Practice, 1945-1975: A Comprehensive Review of Sound Recordings and Literature* (Aldershot: Ashgate, 2003), and Bruce Haynes, *The End of Early Music: A Period Performer's History of Music for the Twenty-first Century* (New York: Oxford University Press, 2007). A more philosophical-cultural take can be found in John Butt, *Playing with History: The Historical Approach to Musical Performance* (Cambridge: Cambridge University Press 2002). There are also many journal articles, book chapters and foreign language publications, most of them reviewed in Fabian, *Bach Performance Practice*. The volume of interviews conducted and edited by Bernard Sherman is also invaluable: *Inside Early Music* (Oxford and New York: Oxford University Press, 1997). Richard Taruskin's many essays and short papers on the topic are collected in the volume *Text and Act: Essays on Musical Performance* (New York: Oxford University Press, 1995). The essays collected in *Authenticity and Early Music*, ed. by Nicholas Kenyon (Oxford: Oxford University Press, 1988) provide an excellent snapshot of opinions regarding the movement up to the 1980s, seen primarily from the United Kingdom. A recent book by Nick Wilson, *The Art of Re-enchantment: Making Early Music in the Modern Age* (New York: Oxford University Press, 2013) charts the "business" of early music in the UK.

4   Richard Taruskin, 'On Letting the Music Speak for Itself: Some Reflection on Musicology and Performance,' *Journal of Musicology*, 1/3 (1982), 101-117 and idem, 'The Pastness of the Present and the Presence of the Past,' in *Authenticity and Early Music*, ed. by Nicholas Kenyon (Oxford: Oxford University Press, 1988), pp. 137-207, both reprinted in idem, *Text and Act*; see also Daniel Leech-Wilkinson, 'What We are Doing with Early Music is Genuinely Authentic to such Small Degree that the Word Loses Most of its Intended Meaning,' *Early Music*, 22/1 (1984), 13-25.

essay, *The Pastness of the Present and the Presence of the Past* (1988) that crowned this growing criticism, historical musicologists have looked at the twentieth-century trajectory of music performing styles in a different light and the movement itself gained a new name: historically informed performance (HIP). However, as I will outline below and throughout this book, the differences between performers and groups specializing in HIP have often continued to be ignored. This enabled generalizations that parroted Taruskin's claim that HIP is a modern invention fitting modernist aesthetics to become entrenched in spite of several important refinements of his articulation being voiced in subsequent publications. As this issue is a crucial inspiration for my endeavour to show the importance of detailed and systematic data gathering, analysis and reporting, I will start my discussion of music performance literature with this key debate.

2.1. Cultural Theories

HIP and Modernism

Focusing primarily on British musicians, Taruskin pointed out essential similarities between mainstream and historically informed performing styles and linked both to modernist ideals. He showed that the tendency for rigid tempos, technical accuracy and literal reading of scores was common in both styles of playing and reflected general cultural trends that aimed to eschew the personal, the passionate, the subjective in favour of a distanced stance that paraded as objective, technocratic and scientifically based. An approach that subdues the performer's role into a neutral, impersonal vehicle or narrowly functioning mediator-transmitter that simply allows the music to "speak for itself" is not, he argued, historically accurate at all, but reflective of our own age and preferences: music-making that aims for clarity, precision and economy of language is modernist. The sleek technical proficiency and clockwork-like style of playing may be compared to the smooth lines and functional design of modernist architecture à la Le Corbusier and show closer links to Stravinsky's and Toscanini's aesthetics than to the documented sensibilities of any composer-performer of the seventeenth or eighteenth centuries.

What Taruskin did not mention in his 1988 essay, apart from a short discussion towards the end, was the fact that not all musicians active in HIP at the time played like that, especially not on the Continent. There a different style was gradually emerging that allowed a greater role for the old instruments to guide technique and more time for experimentation, and to put into practice what historical treatises and instrumental tutors seemed to be recommending. As I have shown in my previous book, initially musicians of Leonhardt's and Harnoncourt's circles presented no exception to the modernist approach. They too went through the phase of the depersonalized, no-expression style of playing, but much earlier.[5] Leonhardt reflected on this "new objectivity" period, when he said "Oh well, the *neue Sachlickeit* period [...] We had to strip down our playing to bare essentials in order to find and bring up something different, something new that may be closer to how it was back then centuries ago."[6] However, by the later 1960s-early 1970s they had had their debates about the utopian nature of historical authenticity—a discussion that happened in the English-speaking world only well into the 1980s—and had created a radically different style of playing, rich in novel means of expression.[7]

This new style has since been described and codified by various musicologists and developed into what is currently regarded as the historically informed way of performing music from the seventeenth and eighteenth centuries. It is important to remember, however, that not before it was available in sound did performer-researchers manage to really grasp its essence and find a way to write about it meaningfully.[8] It

---

5   Fabian, *Bach Performance Practice* (esp. chapters one and two).
6   Personal communication, Amsterdam, July 1996.
7   *Alte Musik in unserer Zeit—Referate und Diskussionen der Kasseler Tagung 1967*, ed. by Walter Wiora (Kassel: Bärenreiter, 1968); 'Podiumdiskussion 1978: Zur Situation der Aufführungspraxis Bachscher Werke,' in *Bachforschung und Bachinterpretation heute: Wissenschaftler und Praktiker im Dialog*, ed. by Reinhold Brinkmann (Kassel: Bärenreiter, 1981), pp. 185-204. For similar debates in English see Taruskin, *Text and Act* and *Authenticity and Early Music*, ed. by Kenyon. In terms of the radically different style of playing key Bach-interpretations that date from this period include Leonhardt's second *Goldberg Variations* recording in 1965; the *Mass in B minor* (1968) and *St Matthew Passion* recordings by Harnoncourt's Concentus Musicus Wien, and a recording of the *Brandenburg Concertos* by an ensemble of soloists comprising Leonhardt, the Kuijken brothers and other Dutch and Belgian players in 1976 (see Discography for detail).
8   Key texts capturing the stylistic characteristics of HIP in baroque music include, in chronological order: Anthony Newman, *Bach and the Baroque: A Performing Guide to Baroque Music with Special Emphasis on the Music of J.S. Bach* (New York: Pendragon Press, 1985); George Houle, *Meter in Music, 1600-1800: Performance, Perception and Notation* (Bloomington: Indiana University Press, 1986); John Butt, *Bach Interpretation: Articulation Marks in Primary Sources* (Cambridge: Cambridge University Press, 1990); idem, *Bach: B minor Mass* (Cambridge: Cambridge University Press, 1991); Frederick Neumann, *Performance Practices of the Seventeenth- and Eighteenth Centuries* (New York: Schirmer, 1993); Colin Lawson and Robin Stowell, *Historical Performance of Music: An Introduction* (Cambridge: Cambridge University Press, 1999); Fabian, *Bach Performance*

is also essential to stress that what we currently regard HIP is likely to be quite different from what performances actually sounded like during the eighteenth century. Historical accuracy is not really the issue here. We will never know for sure. What matters is the existence during the second half of the twentieth century of two distinct styles of playing baroque music; one identified as MSP, the other as HIP. I shall explain the differences, as I see them, throughout this book.

Contrary to the style critiqued by Taruskin, this version of HIP is orientated towards creating musical gestures; to make the music "speak" as a good orator would using the conventions and classical art of rhetoric. This approach and aesthetics foster rhythmic flexibility and localized rubato, dynamic inflections, free ornamentation and other expressive liberties. Although a radically different sound is thus created, this is of course no evidence for it being similar to how music-making originally sounded in the baroque period. Without surviving sound objects, aurally perceivable artefacts, it remains impossible to know. Taruskin's argument that the HIP style is reflective of our own time still stands. But is it really *just* a twentieth-century invention, reflective of modernist aesthetic? Does it not have any historical grounding? Should we not need a fresh look at what is happening now instead of mindlessly continuing to repeat Taruskin's finding about practices typical of the 1970s and 1980s in certain commercially successful circles?

Surely I am not the first to ask such questions. Music performance studies have grown enormously during the past two decades and several publications corroborated Taruskin's basic claims while refining the argument. In relation to historically informed contemporary baroque performance, the most important contribution is John Butt's monograph, *Playing with History* (2002) and the most often cited "defence" is the late Bruce Haynes' *The End of Early Music* (2007). Butt's discussion places a premium on linking the HIP movement to broader post World War II cultural developments; Haynes is more concerned with detailing stylistic differences and defending the ideology and historical validity of the HIP approach.

Practice; Haynes, *The End of Early Music*. Earlier publications focused on making the content of treatises available in modern editions or translations and in collated readers. See for instance, Arnold Dolmetsch, *The Interpretation of the Music of the Seventeenth and Eighteenth Centuries* (London: Novello, 1949 [1915]), Robert Donington, *The Interpretation of Early Music* (London: Faber, 1989 [1963]), Frederick Neumann, *Ornamentation in Baroque and Post-Baroque Music* (Princeton: Princeton University Press, 1978).

As I stated earlier, I am not at all interested in the debate about whether any performance of the Six Solos is more historically accurate than any other. The lack of sonic evidence from Bach's time and circle makes this a moot point. Rather, I wish to provide an account of developments in baroque performance practice since the 1980s and explore how Taruskin's and Butt's positions may be applied or expanded. Therefore I will first investigate further the potential links between contemporary performance practice and broader cultural and aesthetic trends.

Modernism versus Postmodernism

In performance studies terms like modernism and postmodernism are often used rather loosely or only implied by way of reference to qualities and modes of thinking associated with broadly held modern or postmodern viewpoints and aesthetics. In a simple formulation the modernist stance pursues absolutes, believing in the possibility of an objective (scientific) knowledge of a dispassionately observed world. It tends to put a premium on abstraction; it tends to be logocentric, authoritarian, and hierarchical. Modernist art tends to be austere or ascetic to the degree of being unpleasant or incomprehensible. Its promotion of the cult of genius and originality goes hand in hand with denigrating conventional attitudes: the "philistines" and products that cater to such tastes.[9] The postmodern stance rejects this and values relativism and pluralism instead. Postmodernism is linked to post-structuralism and deconstruction, which are "often presented in anti-scientific terminology that stresses the proliferation of meaning, the breaking down of existing hierarchies, the shortcomings of logic, and the failures of analytical approaches."[10] It emphasizes the importance of culture and its products, holding entertainment and the decorative in the same elevated esteem that the modernists would prefer to reserve for "High Art."

However, what modernism is or is not is a complicated matter and has been argued and reviewed by many, much better qualified to do so than I. It is common to posit that modernism stems from the emergence of self-consciousness made explicit by Descartes's famous *"cogito ergo sum"* and the Enlightenment's attempts at empiricist rationalism (or indeed from the radically changed sensibility that emerged with the Renaissance, Humanism

---

9 Fredric Jameson, *A Singular Modernity* (London and New York: Verso, 2012 [2002]), p. 1.
10 Paul Cilliers, *Complexity and Postmodernism: Understanding Complex Systems* (London: Routledge, 1998), p. 22.

and Copernicus' discovery). Others link its beginning to Baudelaire's mid-nineteenth century definition of *modernité* as the new aesthetic. Modernism's various strands mean that it also entails aspects of romanticism and the cult of the individual.[11] Complications regarding definitions and periodization show clearly in literary studies, for instance. They seem to form two camps: those who see modernism as late romanticism, and those who see it as anti-romanticism. Both are probably right; a situation that reflects modernism's fraught relation with its past.

In music studies, modernism is more closely related to compositional style; the break-down of tonality, the rejection of melody, the cultivation of mathematically derived material, and the eschewing of the emotional, the expressive. In relation to music performance, and perhaps mirroring debates in literature, Butt distinguishes between romantic-modernism and classical-modernism, the latter aligning more closely with what Taruskin describes as typical of modernist performance style.[12] The romantic-modernist (Taruskin calls them "vitalists"[13]) tends to read the musical score with the modernist aesthetic of seriousness and reverence granted to deserving artefacts representing "High Art"—for instance slow tempi, monumental sound, intensely felt and expressed melody lines in performances of Bach's Passions as on recordings conducted by Karl Richter, or Wilhelm Furtwängler's Fifth *Brandenburg Concerto* recording much discussed by Taruskin,[14] or, to remain closer to repertoire under examination here, Itzhak Perlman or Oscar Shumsky's recordings of the Violin Solos. The classical-modernist approach is dispassionate, matter-of-fact, clear, precise, sleek and smooth; "modern" in the most general and commonly understood sense of the word—for instance Shlomo Mintz's

---

11 Jameson in *A Singular Modernity* draws important distinctions between modern, modernity and modernism. He also reviews several discussions of modernism, including Heidegger's. Most show a tendency to periodization and Jameson explores how this influences different takes on what modernism may entail. See also Gabriel Josipovici, *What ever Happened to Modernism?* (New Haven: Yale University Press, 2010). Baudelaire's definition of modernity reads: "By 'modernity' I mean the ephemeral, the fugitive, the contingent, the half of art whose other half is the eternal and the immutable." Charles Baudelaire, 'The Painter of Modern Life,' in *The Painter of Modern Life and Other Essays*, ed. and trans. by Jonathan Mayne (London: Phaidon Press, 2012 [1995]), pp. 1-41 (p. 12). For a counter or parallel history of aspects of modernism, see Veit Erlmann, *Reason and Resonance: A History of Modern Aurality* (New York: Zone Books, 2010).
12 Butt, *Playing with History*.
13 E.g., Taruskin, *Text and Act*, p. 131.
14 Taruskin, 'Pastness of the Present.'

version of the Solos, or the "sportive" *Brandenburg Concerto* recordings of the Boyd Neal Orchestra, the Busch Chamber Orchestra or those conducted by Karl Münchinger as well as most of Taruskin's examples.

Similarly, commentators' discussion of what is or is not postmodern varies greatly. There are authors who regard postmodernism to be essentially a continuation of modernism, "except that confidence in [...] reason has been abandoned."[15] Fredric Jameson identifies "a moment of late modernism" and posits that for "the late modernists themselves, what is often called postmodernism or postmodernity will simply document yet a further internal break and the production of yet another, even later, still essentially modernist moment."[16]

To me this resonates well with the view that at times Taruskin labels as modernist certain attitudes manifest in some HIP recordings that may also be regarded as postmodernist. In his richly textured argument, Taruskin highlights the aiming for novelty and variety evident in many HIP projects and interprets this as a sign of modernist aesthetic. In discussing Christopher Hogwood and the Academy of Ancient Music's 1985 recording of Bach's *Brandenburg Concertos*, he criticises their decision to replace the famous sixty-five-bar harpsichord cadenza at the end of the first movement of the fifth concerto with a mere nineteen-bar solo found in secondary eighteenth-century sources. Taruskin recalls the archmodernist Stravinsky's "strictures [...] about the 'seduction of variety'" and notes the commercial ploy of the recording being "billed [...] as the *Urfassung*, the original version of the set, bringing with it a promise of hitherto unprecedented 'authenticity.'" He argues that "the elevation of what amounts to a rejected draft to the status of a viable alternative—and even a preferable one—because it is earlier [...] and less demanding on the listeners" amounts to "immoderate irony"; non-reverence for the canon and devaluing "both the work and the critical sensibility that impelled its revision" by Bach. Taruskin concludes, "By being rendered so much less impressive [...] Hogwood's Bach is rendered correspondingly more modern."[17] Maybe so, but perhaps the diversification, the commercial orientation, the de-canonization, the simplification, the "frivolization" if you will, could also be signs of postmodernism.

---

15 Latour, *Pandora's Hope: Essays on the Reality of Science Studies* (Cambridge, MA: Harvard University Press, 1999), p. 308.
16 Jameson, *A Singular Modernity*, pp. 150-151.
17 Taruskin, 'The Pastness of the Present' (in *Text and Act*), pp. 138-139.

Taruskin's explanation of this potential paradox is provided on the next page, where he writes:

> The same critics who can be counted upon predictably to tout the latterday representatives of High Modernism of music—Carter, Xenakis, Boulez—and also who stand ready zealously to defend them against the vulgarian incursions of various so-called postmodernist trends, are the very ones most intransigently committed [...] to the use of "original instruments" and the rest of "historical" paraphernalia. For we have become prevaricators and no longer call novelty by its right name.[18]

One reason for the paradoxical situation may be that postmodernism also thrives on novelty, increasingly so. In a fully commercialized and commoditized art world, novelty is essential although can be retro in style.[19]

Whether postmodernity is regarded a continuation of or a break with modernity, most authors define the terms in relation to each other. Jean-François Lyotard, in the classic text on the subject, explains that "scientific knowledge" and the modernist quest for it, "legitimates itself with reference to a metadiscourse [...] making an explicit appeal to some grand narrative." He posits that postmodernism can therefore be defined as "incredulity toward metanarratives" even though "[t]his incredulity is undoubtedly a product of progress in the sciences"[20]—another reason perhaps for seeing postmodernism as simply another stage in modernism. Jameson describes postmodernism by listing those features of modernism that it rejects, including authoritarianism and "the non-pleasurable demands made on the audience or public." He also notes the "refusal of concepts of self-consciousness, reflexivity, irony or self-reference in the postmodern aesthetic and also in postmodern values."[21]

How might such "incredulity toward [historical] metanarratives" manifest in music performance and its research? In terms of current performing styles of Bach's music one might look for signs of an acceptance that it is impossible to accurately recreate bygone historical styles or

---

18 Taruskin, 'The Pastness of the Present' (*Text and Act*), p. 140.
19 See also Fredric Jameson, 'Postmodernism and Consumer Society,' in *The Cultural Turn: Selected Writings on the Postmodern, 1983-1998* (London: Verso, 2009 [1998]), pp. 1-20 and Jameson, *A Singular Modernity*, pp. 5, 152.
20 Jean-François Lyotard, *The Postmodern Condition*, trans. by Geoff Bennington and Brian Massumi (Minneapolis: University of Minnesota Press, 1984), pp. xxiii-xxiv.
21 Jameson, *A Singular Modernity*, pp. 1, 93. Some of this seems to be contradicted by Latour, who writes about postmodernity's "overemphasis on reflexivity" (*Pandora's Hope*, p. 22). Perhaps what Jameson means here is that reflexivity is so typical of postmodernism that it has ceased to be a mere concept; it has become the way of being.

to gauge long-dead composers' intentions. A rejection of the authority of sources—manifest in increasing tempo and rhythmic flexibility, ornamentation, improvisation and transcriptions / arrangements—may also be indicative of "incredulity toward the metanarrative" of canonical composers, "fetishized" versions of scores and "etalon" performances. The postmodern tendency to discard attitudes that made "non-pleasurable demands" on audiences is also demonstrable in current performances of baroque music. It is evidenced in the revival of more sensuous sounds, less rigid tempi, less geometric meter, more modulated tone and varied use of vibrato, and more general freedom and flexibility to bring expressive qualities to the fore. In short, postmodern aesthetics—defined as "incredulity toward scientific knowledge" and "elevation of the decorative"—is seen in the increasing number of recordings that dare to "interpret" rather than just "dispassionately transmit" pieces; that show violinists being more personally invested in the performance, experimenting and *playing with* the music.

HIP as a Mirror of Cultural Change

Comparing performance aesthetics to modernist or postmodernist thinking seems fruitful up to a certain point. There are obvious similarities between the two: the modernist-scientific search for absolute truths and the concern for the composer's intention; the establishing of correct scores (Urtext), execution, instruments, ensemble size and constitution; the searching for performance rules; the revering of great masters and their texts / scores; the pursuit of technical mastery, machine-like reliability and evenness, and so on. On the other hand, parallels can also be drawn between the postmodern focus on the "obsolescence of the metanarrative apparatus"[22] or the "overwhelming failure of the rationalist project"[23] and recent crossover and arrangement projects such as Uri Caine's jazz versions of Bach, Beethoven and Mahler, The Bad Plus arrangement of Stravinsky's *The Rite of Spring* or the liberal approach to Bach's or Vivaldi's pieces (among others) by the British ensemble, Red Priest, to name but a few. Musicians' publicly stated opinions convey a decidedly loosened verbal rhetoric regarding the possibility of ever knowing the composer's precise intentions and the subjectivity of these intentions. Artists and researchers alike have started

---

22 Lyotard, *The Postmodern Condition*, p. xxiv.
23 Latour, *Pandora's Hope*, p. 22.

to emphasize the role of the perceiver (whether performer, listener, or reader), and the inadequacy of musical notation to convey how the music may sound.[24]

There are more covert analogies as well. Jameson notes that "classical modernism was an oppositional art; it emerged [...] as scandalous and offensive [...] subversive within the established order."[25] This could also be said of the early music movement of the 1950s to 1970s. Back then it represented an alternative performance tradition, often belittled and ridiculed by the academic and musical mainstream,[26] which became more and more standardized and aggrandized by commodification through the recording industry and the promotion of stars.[27] Jameson suggests dating the emergence of postmodernism to the early 1960s, when "the position of high modernism and its dominant aesthetics [became] established in the academy and [were] henceforth felt to be academic by a whole new generation of poets, painters and musicians."[28] In terms of music history this was the time when modernist composers, from the safety of university posts and state subsidies, shrugged at the lack of audience support, and when a positivistic outlook gave impetus to philological and analytical studies and the rise in prestige of musicology and music theory.[29] With a delay of a decade or two (i.e. by the end of 1980s or later) the once radical art of HIP had also become established in pockets of Western Europe (e.g.

---

24 Here I mention only two sources that are among the earliest where this shift in mentality is registered: Michelle Dulak, 'The Quiet Metamorphosis of "Early Music,"' *Repercussions*, 2/2 (1993), 31-61 and *Inside Early Music*, ed. by Sherman. I will cite the views of violinists under study in chapters three and five.

25 Jameson, 'Postmodernism and Consumer Society,' p. 18.

26 Comments like "they can't play the piano so play the fortepiano" or "s/he can't play Liszt/Paganini so s/he plays early music" were common, and Harnoncourt's appointment in 1973 as Professor of Early Music at the Salzburg Mozarteum was not without controversy. See Monica Mertl, *Vom Denken des Herzens. Alice und Nikolaus Harnoncourt — Eine Biographie* (Salzburg and Wien: Rezidenz Verlag, 1999).

27 For a cultural study of record sleeve covers see Nicholas Cook, 'The Domestic *Gesamtkunstwerk*, or Record Sleeves and Reception,' in *Composition, Performance, Reception: Studies in the Creative Process in Music*, ed. by Wyndham Thomas (Aldershot: Ashgate, 1998), pp. 105-117.

28 Jameson, 'Postmodernism and Consumer Society,' p. 19.

29 Joseph Kerman, *Musicology* (London: Fontana Press, 1985). See also Milton Babbitt, 'The Composer as Specialist' (reprinted in *The Collected Essays of Milton Babbitt*, ed. by Stephen Peles et al. (Princeton: Princeton University Press, 2003), pp. 48-54), a paper originally published in *High Fidelity* (February 1958) as 'Who cares if you listen.' According to Babbitt, this title was chosen by the Editor without his approval (Milton Babbitt, 'A Life of Learning,' *Charles Homer Haskins Lecture for 1991*. ACLS Occasional Paper, 17 (New York: American Council of Learned Societies, 1991), p. 18.

The Netherlands) and in British and North American higher education institutions. So much so that it was common in the 1980s to jokingly refer to the "Early Music Police," an umbrella term for purists who would insist on the use of period instruments and would sanction certain solutions and practices while vehemently condemning others as inauthentic.

The long-standing debate regarding the performance of dotted rhythms is a good example to illustrate the point. Two of the key contributors to twentieth-century scholarship on seventeenth- and eighteenth-century performance practice, Robert Donington and Frederick Neumann, were at loggerheads for decades about the "correct" delivery of dotted rhythms. Many others, such as David Fuller, Graham Pont, Matthew Dirst and Stephen Hefling, have joined in, generating innumerable articles, books and responses to each other examining and interpreting the same sources.[30] A more recent example is the debate regarding the size of Bach's ensembles, especially the vocal forces in his Passions, Cantatas and the *Mass in B minor*.[31] The modernist appeal to scientific truth and confidence in reason are clearly in evidence in these writings, making it is easy to agree with Taruskin and regard HIP as just another manifestation of musical modernism. However, noting the "immense weight of seventy or eighty years of classical modernism," Jameson explains an aspect of the postmodern condition that also clearly resonates with the HIP project:

> [I]n a world in which stylistic innovation is no longer possible, all that is left is to imitate dead styles, to speak through the masks and with the voices of the styles in the imaginary museum.[32]

So is HIP modern or postmodern? Does it matter? One way to reconcile the seeming contradictions is to examine the stylistic aspects of performance more closely. The differences may point to problems with dates: There is a discrepancy between the emergence of the broader manifestations of both

---

30 Tellingly, Matthew Dirst's paper is entitled, 'Bach's French Overtures and the Politics of Overdotting,' *Early Music*, 25/1 (1997), 35-44. The sources are too numerous to list here. I have reviewed this literature in my previous book (Fabian, *Bach Performance Practice*) and also in a series of follow up studies in which I adopted a completely different, perceptual approach. These experiments demonstrated the existence of an auditory illusion whereby tempo and articulation mask the perception of dotting, leading us to hear the performance as if over-dotted and thus proving the debate misplaced. For a summary see Dorottya Fabian and Emery Schubert, 'A New Perspective on the Performance of Dotted Rhythms,' *Early Music*, 38/4 (2010), 585-588.
31 For an interim summary see Andrew Parrott, *The Essential Bach Choir* (Woodbridge: The Boydell Press, 2000).
32 Jameson, 'Postmodernism and Consumer Society,' p. 7.

modernism and postmodernism in general and the appearance of these attributes in performances of western art music. As far as twentieth-century music performance history is concerned, a change of style is more evident around the 1930s and then again since the late 1980s, rather than around the 1890s and the 1960s. The performances from the period between ca. 1930 and 1985 are what Taruskin originally labelled "modernist," using the term "authentistic" for those that identified with the HIP movement. But is Taruskin's verdict still valid? What has happened since 1988? What is the current style of playing? The next three chapters will explore these questions in great depth by examining the chosen violinists' views and affiliations as well as analysing the performance features that characterise their respective interpretative styles.

For now we can note that already in the 1990s Michelle Dulak wrote about a mellowing of rhetoric regarding the possibility of recovering past practices or indeed the composer's intentions.[33] John Butt agreed while also aiming to explain the cultural roots of this new relativism:

> As soon as it becomes acceptable to dislike what Bach might have done it is easier to allow [choices]. [...] [H]istorical evidence can be treated critically, and one can acknowledge that there is no absolute distinction between the choice of personal insight—or opinion—and historical accuracy. [...] If postmodernism means a more liberated attitude toward historical evidence, a less guilty (and more conscious) inclination to follow one's own intuitions, then there are certainly more postmodern performers around than there were ten years ago.[34]

It is my intention to show how or to what extent pluralism and relativism conquered Bach performance practice at the turn of twentieth and twenty-first centuries; whether parallels can be found between performance styles and broader cultural trends. Butt has already paved the way. In this book I focus on subsequent decades to investigate further how performance practice issues have developed since Taruskin's critique and Butt's revisionist reading. It must be kept in mind, though, that this book only deals with recorded performances and only of Bach's Six Solos for Violin. How valid my findings might be for other repertoires or what one may hear on concert platforms across the world is a task for another day!

---

33   Dulak, 'The Quiet Metamorphosis.'
34   John Butt, 'Bach Recordings since 1980: A Mirror of Historical Performance,' in *Bach Perspectives* 4, ed. by David Schulenberg (Lincoln and London: University of Nebraska Press, 1999), pp. 181-198 (pp. 191, 194).

Aesthetics and Value Judgment: Beauty and the Sublime

Trying to apply cultural theory to music performance, although potentially illuminating, also has limitations. It is worth looking for alternative explanations as well. Additionally, ideologically I tend to find myself agreeing with those who are frustrated by the relativism of postmodernism, "its overemphasis on reflexivity, its maddening efforts to write texts that do not carry any risk of presence."[35] Yet I much prefer performances that are unique, personally engaged, flexible, inventive and "interventionist" even to a degree when the interpretation considerably de-familiarizes or "recomposes" the piece. Music performance always carries risk and should not be impersonal. But is it not the modernist style that is criticised for lacking a presence, the performer's personal conviction and "authenticity"?[36] What about stylistic requirements? If prescriptive performance analysis necessarily leads to normative and thus authoritarian and absolutist-modernist expectations as Taruskin posits, then how are we to decide the quality of a performance?[37]

Jameson touches on this problem when he reviews the philosophy of aesthetics and its distinction between the sublime and the beautiful. He notes that "[m]odernism aspires to the Sublime as to its very essence, which we may call trans-aesthetic, insofar as it lays claims to the Absolute, that is, it believes that in order to be art at all, art must be something beyond art."[38] This is very much the standpoint of many mainstream musicians, who emphasize the timelessness of Bach's music and reject the importance of historical practices when performing his works in the twenty-first century. Adorno's oft quoted critique of the 1920s organ movement and bourgeoning music festivals that "reduce" Bach to Telemann is a famous quip stemming from such a modernist aesthetic.[39] Itzhak Perlman's contempt for HIP approaches to Bach's violin works, or indeed for using period instruments, is another.[40]

---

35 Latour, *Pandora's Hope*, p. 22.
36 Taruskin, *Text and Act*.
37 Richard Taruskin, 'How Things Stand Now?' Keynote address delivered at the *Performa 11* conference, Aveiro, Portugal, on 19 May 2011.
38 Fredric Jameson, '"End of Art" or "End of History"?,' in *The Cultural Turn*, pp. 73-92 (p.83).
39 "The Philistines' [...] sole desire is to neutralize art since they lack the capacity to comprehend it [...] They say Bach, mean Telemann and are secretly in agreement with the regression of musical consciousness which even without them remains a constant threat under the pressures of the culture industry." Theodor W. Adorno, 'Bach defended against its devotees,' in *Prisms*, trans. by Shierry and Samuel Weber (Cambridge, MA: MIT Press, 1981), pp. 133-146 (pp. 137, 145).
40 See, for instance the interview with Perlman on the *The Art of Violin* DVD (written and

40 A Musicology of Performance

Taruskin also discusses the difference between beauty and sublimity.[41] In his view, the confusion started with Eduard Hanslick (1825-1904), who considered beauty "the legitimate domain of art," the attribute that appeals to our intellect and invites contemplation.[42] In contrast, as Taruskin shows, during the eighteenth-century, writers associated not the beautiful but the sublime with "boldness and grandeur," with "the Pathetic, or the power of raising the passions to a violent and even enthusiastic degree."[43] Taruskin quotes Edmund Burke, who decreed: "Sublime objects are vast in their dimensions, beautiful ones comparatively small; beauty should be smooth and polished; the great is rugged and negligent [...] beauty should be light and delicate; the great ought to be solid and even massive."[44] Taruskin then explains how, in the nineteenth century, the sublime encroached "upon the domain of the beautiful—of the 'great' upon the pleasant" to an extent that was "profoundly repugnant to the early generation of modernists" who wanted "art [...] to be full clarity, high noon of the intellect."[45] Herein lies the source of Hanslick's conflation of beauty and the sublime and the elevation of beauty to the centre of aesthetic contemplation. The smooth and polished, impeccably precise playing and the evenly vibrated, homogenous tone of contemporary mainstream musicians are the enactment of such a conception of beauty and art. In modernist performance there is no room for ruggedness or negligence. Rough sounds, risk taking, boldness are attributes one hears in recent recordings of select HIP and cross-over musicians; these, as I will show, blur the divide between the modern and the postmodern yet again.

This imperceptible yet confusing swap between the sublime and the beautiful underlies the difficulty in distinguishing between the modern

---

  directed by Bruno Monsaingeon). Warner Music Vision NVC Arts, 2001, 8573-85801-2.
41 Taruskin, 'Pastness of the Present,' *Text and Act*, pp. 132-133.
42 Taruskin, *Text and Act*, p. 132 referring to Eduard Hanslick, *The Beautiful in Music*, originally published as *Vom Musikalisch-Schönen* (Leipzig: R. Weigel, 1854). One commonly available English translation by Geoffrey Payzant is based on the 8th edition (1891), *On the Musically Beautiful* (Indianapolis: Hackett Publishing, 1986).
43 Taruskin (*Text and Act*, p. 132) quoting Longinus in William Smith's eighteenth-century translation as cited in *Music and Aesthetics in the Eighteenth and Early Nineteenth Centuries*, ed. by Peter le Huray and James Day (Cambridge: Cambridge University Press, 1981), p. 4.
44 *A Philosophical Enquiry into the Origin of Our Ideas of the Sublime and the Beautiful* (1757), in Le Huray and Day, eds., *Music and Aesthetics*, pp. 70-71 as cited in Taruskin, *Text and Act*, p. 132.
45 Taruskin, *Text and Act*, p. 133, citing José Ortega y Gasset, *The Dehumanization of Art and Other Essays on Art, Culture and Literature*, trans. by Helene Weyl (Princeton: Princeton University Press, 1968), p. 27.

and the postmodern in music performance. According to Jameson it was not until the 1960s that we came to the "end of the Sublime, the dissolution of art's vocation to reach the absolute."[46] Thus began a celebration of the *decorative* and the return to seeking beauty; art as pleasure for the senses, which, incidentally, was very much the view of music's function during Charles Burney's (1726-1814) time.[47] The new-found expressivity and playfulness of HIP that have been evolving on the Continent since the late 1960s and have become much more widespread since the late 1990s reflect this postmodern (as well as late eighteenth-century) sensibility: the geometrical, literal, smooth, modernist playing started to give way to a more engaged, flexible, interventionist, and reflexive interpretative style. What seems unique about this development is that while baroque music performance is apparently becoming more "decorative" (note the added embellishments, greater rhythmic freedom, etc.), it is also reclaiming boldness and depth through varied bowing and articulation, stronger pulse and a broader spectrum of dynamics, among others. While giving up on dogmas and rules, it is again becoming capable of "raising the passions," to be daring and expressive; in letting go of absolutes, it is finding a way to resurrect the sublime.

It may be fruitful, then, to reverse the question of our investigation. That is, rather than trying to fit music performance into broad cultural trends, it could be instructive to examine instead if what is happening in music performance may provide cultural theorists with new ways of evaluating the status quo. Nowadays the performance of classical music is a small, peripheral phenomenon in global culture. Yet, through its technical discipline and concern with past repertoires and their aesthetic ideals, it upholds certain seemingly conservative values while managing to readjust and renew; to generate affect and move listeners. It is neither modern nor

---

46 Jameson, 'End of Art,' p. 84.
47 See for instance "[...] I expected to have my ears gratified with every musical luxury and refinement which Italy could afford." Charles Burney, *The Present State of Music in France and Italy* (London, 1771), p. 291 (cited in *Strunk's Source Readings in Music History: The Late Eighteenth Century*, ed. by Leo Treitler and Wye Jamison Allanbrook, rev. edn (New York: Norton, 1998), p. 255. In his *A General History of Music* (1776), Burney famously wrote: "music is an innocent luxury, unnecessary indeed, to our existence, but a great improvement and gratification of the sense of hearing" (New York: Dover Books, 1957), vol. 1, p. 21. Burney was of course writing in and of the classical period not the heyday of North-German Protestant seriousness often associated with Johann Sebastian Bach's compositions. However, Bach wrote the Violin Solos in Cöthen, while employed as Capellmeister of Prinz Leopold's Italianate court so it is fair to assume that entertainment and "luxury" as well as virtuosity were not far from his mind.

postmodern, neither absolutist nor relativist, neither scientific nor reflexive, but a never-ending search to get closer to the essence of pieces according to what this means to successive generations of performers and audiences.

2.2. Analytical Theories

The field of music performance studies (as opposed to historical performance practice studies) has generated its own theories. Here I am thinking of analytical and empirical models developed by music theorists, cognitive scientists and performers. The richest literature comes from music psychology and as such is of limited importance here because its questions relate more to psychological processes rather than stylistic considerations. Therefore my consideration of them will be necessarily selective. The main aim of this section is to provide an overview; to introduce different approaches and to discuss a select few recent theoretical propositions starting with musicological work and continuing with experimental and empirical contributions from the cognitive sciences.

Music Performance Studies

In the English-speaking world the study of music performance had originated in music analysis. As Nicholas Cook, among others, has pointed out the significant side-effect of this has been that the "flow of signification [in performance analyses] is from analysis to performance, from text to act" in both analytically and historically informed performance theory.[48] Yet changes in performance style tend to precede their theoretical formulation. If Cook's perception is correct, and reading the literature it seems apt, the situation betrays a lack of true dialogue between leading performers and academic music studies. Or rather, it indicates a one-way flow of innovation and an opposite flow of normative thinking that needs to be highlighted to correct the record.

---

48 Nicholas Cook, 'Bridging the Unbridgeable? Empirical Musicology and Interdisciplinary Performance Studies,' in *Taking it to the Bridge: Music as Performance*, ed. by Nicholas Cook and Richard Pettengill (Ann Arbor: Michigan University Press, 2013), pp. 70-85 (p. 71). It is also important to note a difference between "Performance Studies," that "is located at the intersection of theatre and anthropology" and situates what is referred to as MAP (Music as Performance) and the Study of Music Performance, with what I am concerned here. MAP tends to write on popular music from a cultural studies perspective. See Todd J. Coulter, 'Editorial: Music as Performance—The State of the Field,' *Contemporary Theatre Review*, 21/3 (2011), 259-260 (p. 259).

My earlier comparative review of the development of HIP theory and HIP practice clearly showed performers leading the way and academically argued analysis and style description lagging behind. Key formulations of the essential characteristics of what is called the HIP style started to appear some two decades *after* the first recordings in which such characteristics can be heard (see fn. 8 above for references).[49] While the performance style of Leonhardt and his circle or the Concentus Music Wien attained, by the late 1960s, a markedly different sound through its altered approach to articulation and musical meter, published performance practice research continued to be preoccupied with tabulating and debating the "correct" delivery of ornaments and dotted rhythms or, perhaps more usefully, with making sources available.[50] Once the new style of playing had become wide-spread and its practice analysed and explained (primarily during the 1980s), the theory of performance practice (again) quickly became normative and prescriptive rather than descriptive, reinforcing the text to act flow of signification in academic writing while performers have again moved on, mostly unnoticed. This tendency of researchers limits insights into what actually happens in music performance at any particular time and is one of the reasons, I contend, why Taruskin's verdict regarding HIP being modernist and "authentistic" prevails.

The reality is that in the wake of Taruskin's criticism during the 1980s, HIP and *performance practice* research appear to be moving away from the "purist" standpoint. Nowadays many performers play on both period and modern instruments, and specialist groups and soloists emphasize the significance of their own sensibilities and readings of scores rather than

---

49 In an interview, answering a question about a possible "Netherlands HIP school," Gustav Leonhardt emphasized the importance of playing over theorizing: "We never thought about developing much. We never talked about any issues. We didn't make a point of anything ever. We played, and each one studied the pieces. We played—we had no theories. Perhaps in secret; but no, I never had theories. I was investigating all the time, but from a tradition to a wealth of general concepts. And maybe it [our style] is all wrong; I don't know, it could be." Gustav Leonhardt, '"One Should not Make a Rule": Gustav Leonhardt on Baroque Keyboard Playing,' in *Inside Early Music: Conversations with Performers*, ed. by Bernard D. Sherman (New York: Oxford University Press, 1997), pp. 193-206 (p. 203). The quote is also a testimony to the aural and practical nature of music performance; something I shall return to later in this chapter.

50 The "abstract" nature of musicological theory is indicated by such publications as *The Art of Ornamentation and Embellishment in the Renaissance and Baroque*, ed. by Denis Stevens (New York: Vanguard Records BGS 70697/8, 1967); a two-LP album with extended liner notes where the musicological explanation is illustrated by the most mundane, literal and uninspired examples of added trills and mordents in movements played in a completely MSP style.

the importance of knowing the "rules" and abiding by the fine print of historical sources. This more relaxed and relativist attitude is less typical of *analytical* and *empirical* music *performance studies*. Explicitly or implicitly these seem to hold on to the primacy of the notated text and to the view that the quality of a performance is dependent on how well it reflects or brings out compositional structure.[51] Although such publications also seem to have had their apex around the turn of the 1980s and 1990s, the importance of structural signification has proven to be a notion even harder to let go of than the belief in the utopian ideal that the performer's duty is to recreate exact historical practices and realise the dead composer's ultimate intentions as represented by critical (Urtext) editions.

One example of these criteria continuing to make their mark is the work of pianist-researcher Julian Hellaby.[52] He proposes a "framework" for analyzing performance: a "tower" based on nine "informants" grouped into four "levels"—all neatly fitting the broader principles of being historically and stylistically-analytically accurate, aware of the composition's structural, genre-specific and affective content, and thus well disposed towards fulfilling the composer's intentions (Figure 2.1). At the bottom of the tower Hellaby lists historical era and the score, followed by genre and topic (i.e. musical type associated with a particular function) one level up, then topical mode (i.e. performance qualifiers that appeal to imagination or emotion) and characterizers (i.e. distinctive musical features such as rhythmic, melodic or harmonic devices). Finally, on top of the tower, are tempo, duration and sonic manipulators.

---

51 For instance, expressiveness in music performance is often analyzed (and theorized) in relation to the music's structure (from a long possible list, see for instance, Wallace Berry, *Musical Structure and Performance* (New Haven: Yale University Press, 1989); Eric Clarke, 'Structure and Expression,' in *Musical Structure and Cognition*, ed. by Peter Howell, Ian Cross, and Robert West (London: Academic Press, 1985), pp. 209-236; idem, 'Expression in Performance: Generativity, Perception and Semiosis,' in *The Practice of Performance*, ed. by John Rink (Cambridge: Cambridge University Press, 1995), pp. 21-54; Caroline Palmer, 'Mapping Musical Thought to Musical Performance,' *Journal of Experimental Psychology*, 15 (1989), 331-346. See also the public lecture held on 27 May 2013 at Zentrum für systematische Musikwissenschaft (Karl-Franzens Universität Graz, Australia) entitled: *How Does Music Expression Depend on Structure?* available at https://systematische-musikwissenschaft.uni-graz.at/en/neuigkeiten/detail/article/vortrag-erica-bisesi/

52 Julian Hellaby, *Reading Musical Interpretation—Case Studies in Solo Piano Performance* (Farnham: Ashgate, 2009).

Figure 2.1. Hellaby's *Interpretative tower*.[53]

level four	Tempo	Duration manipulator	Sonic moderator
level three	Topical mode	Characterizer	
level two	Genre	Topic	
level one	Era (style)	Authorship (score)	

executive ↑↓ ideal

Although he states that the model represents an essentially interactive hierarchy, Hellaby implies that the top level is the most significant in terms of explaining variability between performances when he asserts: "level four [includes] those informants that engage most directly with a performer's acoustic formations."[54] The sample analyses (Bach Toccata in D, BWV 912, among other works, each performed by four different pianists) are primarily descriptive, briefly commenting on the nine informants. The results are then summarized in a grid within the tower. Hellaby indicates the relative importance of both the nine informants and the four levels of an analyzed recording by varying the thickness of arrows that highlight the relationships. He thus provides a testable model that seems quite powerful in summarizing basic differences among performances. At the same time, its breadth and ability to show differences in detail (i.e. differences of degree rather than of kind) seems limited. Furthermore, while it aims to provide an objective account of a performance, it remains not just descriptive in its evaluation of the nine informants but also prescriptive regarding what a performer should consider when embarking on an interpretation of a composition. In other words, the model is an example of the "page to stage"[55] approach to performance analysis.

This aesthetic seems a natural or logical standpoint in a literate culture where the functions of composing and performing have been separated. Yet the identity of a composed piece is not a simple matter, prompting several

---

53 Adapted from Hellaby's Figure 2.2. Hellaby, *Reading Musical Interpretation*, p. 47.
54 Hellaby, *Reading Musical Interpretation*, p. 48.
55 Nicholas Cook's expression borrowed from Susan Melrose, *A Semiotics of the Dramatic Text* (London: Macmillan, 1994), p. 215. See Nicholas Cook, 'Between Process and Product: Music and/as Performance,' *Music Theory Online*, 7/2 (April 2001), 22, http://www.mtosmt.org/issues/mto.01.7.2/mto.01.7.2.cook.html

philosophers to argue about it.[56] Adorno maintained, for instance, that "while neither the score nor the performance is in fact the actual 'work,' the score is closer than the performance, suggesting the need to examine the score when evaluating performances."[57] Exploring Adorno's views, Paddison states:

> While at the level of work as score multiple and contradictory readings may coexist as infinite potential performances, at the level of the work in performance, as 'sounding object,' no particular realization of the piece can fully meet the contradictory demands of the work as score.[58]

These contradictory demands of the score speak differently to diverse generations, leading to a variety of performance styles and interpretative approaches.[59] When lamenting the "Urtext mentality" of modernist performers, we should keep in mind that earlier generations were often as well-versed in composition as in performance, and they often played more than one instrument (consider the violinist-pianists Fritz Kreisler, Jascha Heifetz and George Enesco, the last named being also noted for his original compositions, not just transcriptions or period pieces published under pseudonyms as in the case of Kreisler or Nathan Milstein and others).[60] The renewed interest in improvisation since the turn of the twenty-first century may take performers back to composing as well. Some performers (e.g. Rachel Barton Pine among violinists) are already

---

56 Most influentially by Lydia Goehr, among others: *The Imaginary Museum of Musical Works*, rev. edn (Oxford: Clarendon Press, 2007). See also Stan Godlovitch, *Musical Performance: A Philosophical Study* (London: Routledge, 1998) or Stephen Davies, *Musical Works and Performances: A Philosophical Exploration* (New York: Oxford University Press, 2001).

57 Cited in Dario Sarlo, 'Investigating Performer Uniqueness: The Case of Jascha Heifetz' (PhD Thesis, Goldsmith College, University of London, 2010), p. 21.

58 Max Paddison, *Adorno's Aesthetics of Music* (Cambridge: Cambridge University Press, 1993), p. 197, cited in Sarlo, 'Investigating Performer Uniqueness,' pp. 20-21, fn. 17.

59 A forcefully presented challenge to the equation of scores with "the" composition and a plea to pay more attention to the role performers play in creating meaning and musical communication have recently been put forth by Daniel Leech-Wilkinson ('Compositions, Scores, Performances, Meanings,' *Music Theory Online*, 18/1 (2012), 1-17). In his concluding paragraph (5.4) Leech-Wilkinson states: "In view of this it would be wise to try to get out of the habit of ascribing much of what we hear in scores either to the composer or to the inherent nature of a work. The agency is in fact the listener's or the analyst's in response to the performer's responding to the notation determined by editors making their own sense of whatever was left by the composer or the nearest surviving sources."

60 George Enescu (1881-1955), the Romanian composer, violinist, pianist and conductor eventually settled in Paris after WWII where he was known as Enesco and in the English-speaking world this version of his name is more commonly used.

playing their own cadenzas and preparing transcriptions to expand their instrument's repertoire.[61] Once they feel confident in their command of speaking the musical language of particular eras or composers, performers can take scores as scripts rather than as literal texts. In any case, the fine line between fulfilling the composer's assumed intentions and maintaining the performer's prerogative of breathing life into the "work" by creating a "sound object" of it will always have to be negotiated anew, historically as well as culturally. Hellaby's "tower" is a possible framework for analysing this negotiation.

Rink, writing earlier than Hellaby, proposed a framework for the study of music performance that illuminates the "process of refraction," which may lead to performances "reflecting personal conviction and individual choice, at the same time demonstrating historical and analytical awareness and a given 'programming' (both physical and psychological)."[62] The constituent parts of this "process of refraction" are similar to Hellaby's "informants," namely "genre, performing history, notational idiosyncrasies, compositional style, structure as 'shape' and physicality." In Rink's model these inform the "performer's artistic prerogatives," which then produce the performance conception.

The similarity of Rink's and Hellaby's lists of elements with which a performer should be concerned in developing an interpretation underline the currently accepted boundaries within which musicians of the western classical tradition work. In Rink's conception, though, there is no preordained hierarchy among the constituents impacting on the performer's decisions. Presumably each artist's personal disposition and training dictates the process. As such, this framework seems more open-ended and less prescriptive than Hellaby's; more accommodating of cultural and historical norms of any given era or performer. It is not a testable model, but it provides the analyst of performances with more room to actually study what performers do without channelling the investigation into an assessment of the "sound object" against predetermined hierarchical criteria. Hierarchical conceptions may easily lead to normative thinking

---

61 *The Rachel Barton Pine Collection: Original Compositions, Arrangements, Cadenzas and Editions for Violin* (New York: Carl Fischer, 2009). See also her recording of violin concertos by Brahms and Joachim (Cedille CDR 90000 068, 2002) and the Witches' Sabbath movement from Berlioz' *Symphony Fantastique* ('Instrument of the Devil,' Cedille CDR 90000 041, 1998).

62 John Rink, 'The State of Play in Performance Studies,' in *The Music Practitioner*, ed. by Jane Davidson (Aldershot: Ashgate, 2004), pp. 37-51 (p. 48).

and as such are not far removed from the modernist-absolutist standpoint. Framing performance and its analysis as a "process of refraction" allows for greater plurality, subjectivity and reflexivity. This can be useful if one seeks a diagnosis rather than an evaluation of the state of performance.

Empirical and Psychological Studies of Performance

Perhaps not surprisingly, investigations of music performance by the scientific community reflect even clearer preferences for the modernist approach. This is not necessarily for ideological-philosophical reasons but, as Richard Parncutt argues, because there is not enough time in a researcher's life to keep up with all the musicological literature and knowledge to develop a deeper understanding of performance history and conventions.[63] Also, music psychologists and cognitive scientists tend to look for "general mechanisms" rather than "individual manifestations."[64] For instance, when studying expressiveness in musical performance, they tend to focus on the relationship between the normative (notated) compositional structure and deviations from it in performance. Using scientific, empirical and experimental methods, they measure how performers mark musical units like cadence points or phrase boundaries and study listeners' perceptual thresholds and aesthetic judgments.[65] Once scientists have observed and mapped regularities they develop models for musical performance. In these rule-based systems preferences masquerading as normative "consensus" are programmed in, and even though the authors of algorithms keep fine-tuning the rule parameters, the systems remain reflective of stylistic characteristics common in a particular era (among currently available programs these largely mirror the mainstream aesthetic ideals of the 1950s to 1980s period).[66] Such systems remain paradigmatic of the modernist

---

63 Richard Parncutt, 'Introduction: "Interdisciplinary Musicology,"' *Musicae Scientiae*, 10/1 (Special Issue 2005-2006), 7-11.
64 Clarke, 'Expression in Performance,' p. 52.
65 For instance, Bruno Repp, 'A Constraint on the Expressive Timing of a Melodic Gesture: Evidence from Performance and Aesthetic Judgment,' *Music Perception*, 10/2 (1992), 221-241; idem, 'Diversity and Commonality in Music Performance: An Analysis of Timing Microstructure in Schumann's "Träumerei,"' *Journal of the Acoustical Society of America*, 92/5 (1992), 2546-2568.
66 One such system is the KHT rules for musical performance (*Director Musices*) developed by Anders Friberg at the Royal Institute of Technology in Stockholm. For a description of its current state see Anders Friberg and Erica Bisesi, 'Using Computational Models of Music Performance to Model Stylistic Variations,' in *Expressiveness in Music Performance: Empirical Approaches across Styles and Cultures*, ed. by Dorottya Fabian, Renee Timmers, and Emery Schubert (Oxford: Oxford University Press, 2014), pp. 240-259.

approach, working with abstract forms of meaning (representation) and central control.

But music performance changes constantly, even if this is difficult to detect within shorter periods of time. Musicians, especially competition judges and teachers, often assert their conviction regarding what they believe to be artistic norms—for instance how Beethoven or Mozart "should" sound. Yet music performance changes because taste changes. Instead of taste, Leonhardt speaks of imagination. He explains:

> I think that the changes made in the last fifty years are based on the fact that the imagination has changed. [...] the crucial element behind the wish of some players not to play Bach on the piano was that they wanted to get rid of that dripping Romanticism they did not like. [...] In the last fifty years, we have gradually begun to see that Baroque music is, if anything, *more* expressive than Romantic music, but in details rather than in large lines. With that, a technique developed, but not by itself; it's only that the wish has changed, that our imagination of the music has changed completely.[67]

This ever renewing thinking and musical imagination is one reason why I propose—more fully in the next section—that music performance should be considered a "self-organising process in which meaning is generated through a dynamic process." In other words, it is *not* the result of "the passive reflection of an autonomous agent" who authoritatively decides how the performance should go.[68] Expressiveness is a feature of performance that can establish an artist's personal authenticity; it is a performer's way of interacting with and responding interpretatively to musical stimuli according to her or his cultural-educational background and musical persona.[69] What may be a convincing gesture in one performance may sound alien in another; what one generation finds appealing and "true," may be rejected by another as uninformed or false. This can be demonstrated by studying listeners' reactions to old recordings or subsequent published reviews of earlier performances re-issued first as long playing record and then as compact disk. It is also evidenced in diverse generations' emphatic assertion that they are "serving the composer's intention" while playing completely differently from each-other.

The constraints a performer brings to what may be heard as appropriate expression has been confirmed scientifically as well. Through a set of

---

67 Leonhardt, 'One Should not Make a Rule,' p. 197.
68 Cilliers, *Complexity and Postmodernism*, p. 116.
69 Hellaby, *Reading Musical Interpretation*, p. 15.

experiments Renee Timmers showed that "choices at the beginning of a phrase provide constraints and expectations for the rest of the phrase [...] if ornaments are chosen to be performed long, this may set the trend for future ornaments."[70] The musical context, the quality of the measured gesture and the historically-culturally defined aesthetic expectations are crucial and provide the basis of the infinite variety and creativity manifest in music performance. The various mathematical models developed so far tend to neglect these more intuitive interactions between a performer and a piece of music.[71] Although some computer controlled piano performances sound very successful (because they come close to current aesthetic criteria), they lack dynamism: the potential for creativity and renewal.

Nicholas Cook also advocates a more complex approach that embraces ethnographic-cultural as well as empirical-experimental methods. He takes his cue from Philip Auslander, starting with the premise that "to be a musician [...] is to perform an identity in a social realm." This approach, Cook claims, "involves not a predefined meaning reproduced in performance but rather a meaning that emerges from performance."[72] It assures the foregrounding of the performer and his or her "relationships to audiences."[73] Referring to Robert Philip's work, Cook too notes the abyss between the quantifiable and the qualitative, how "empirical analysis can leave behind essential aspects of the phenomenon" it studies.[74] For instance, Philip claims that although an accelerando can be measured, to a listener it "can seem impulsive, or uncontrolled, it can seem to be aiming precisely at a target, or to be dangerously wild. It can seem spontaneous or calculated."[75] In other words, the *meaning* of the accelerando is not deciphered by acoustic-physical measurements; the same measured value

---

70 Renee Timmers, 'On the Contextual Appropriateness of Expression,' *Music Perception*, 20/3 (Spring 2003), 225-240 (p. 225).
71 For instance Neil Todd, 'A Model of Expressive Timing in Tonal Music,' *Music Perception*, 3 (1985), 33-58. Idem, 'The Dynamics of Dynamics: A Model of Musical Expression,' *Journal of the Acoustical Society of America*, 91 (1992), 3540-3550. More recent refinements of earlier work allow for stylistic and other nuances to be taken into account. See for instance, Gerhard Widmer, 'Machine Discoveries: A Few Simple, Robust Local Expression Principles,' *Journal of New Music Research*, 31/1 (2002), 37-50; or Friberg and Bisesi, 'Using computational models.'
72 Cook, 'Bridging the Unbridgeable?,' p. 72.
73 Philip Auslander, 'Musical Personae,' *The Drama Review*, 50/1 (2006), 100-119 (p. 117), cited in Cook, 'Bridging the unbridgeable?,' p. 73.
74 Cook, 'Bridging the Unbridgeable?,' p. 76.
75 Robert Philip, 'Studying Recordings: The Evolution of a Discipline,' Keynote paper at the CHARM/RMA conference *Musicology and Recordings* (Egham, Surrey), September 2007,' available at http://www.open.ac.uk/Arts/music/RMAkeynote.pdf, p. 9.

may be perceived to create varied and even contrasting affects, it may move the listener in diverse ways while different listeners may also hear the same performance differently.[76] Similarly, performers regularly note how they adjust their playing according to the venue or the instrument at hand (and various other "externals").[77] The solution Cook proposes is to adopt a broadly ethnographic approach, with the performer and analyst taking part in a participant-observational dialogue or the analyst ensuring that empirical data is contextualized adequately through detailed engagement with cultural, biographical, historical and other available sources.[78] Cook concludes by asserting

> Performance […] is an indefinitely multi-layered and complex phenomenon, the multiple aspects of which demand multiple analytical perspectives. […] [T]he approach of interdisciplinary performance studies helps to clarify what performances mean, while more empirical approaches help to clarify how performances mean what they mean.[79]

2.3. Music Performance and Complex Systems

Given the considerable achievements of the various approaches reviewed so far, it seems useful to try to develop an understanding that may assist in moving away from the "either / or" divide both in terms of cultural theory (modernist versus postmodernist) and also in terms of approach

---

76 That perceived performance characteristics can differ greatly was observed experimentally by a study of dotted rhythms. Identical dotting ratios contributed to five different clusters of musical character (bright, lyrical, calm, vehement, and angry). It was shown that certain kinds of interactions between articulation, tempo and dotting determined the perceived character and not any specific, measured value of performed tempo, articulation or dotting ratio on its own. Dorottya Fabian and Emery Schubert, 'Musical Character and the Performance and Perception of Dotting, Articulation and Tempo in Recordings of Variation 7 of J. S. Bach's *Goldberg Variations* (BWV 988),' *Musicae Scientiae*, 12/2 (2008), 177-203.

77 To again cite Leonhardt ('One Should not Make a Rule,' p. 198), "[…] one should not make a rule […] you use [a certain] means in order to achieve [say] a dynamic effect. Now, on one instrument in one hall you do it a little, and in another you do it a lot, in order to achieve the same effect." A systematic analysis of interviews conducted with several contemporary baroque violinists and cellists also highlighted the relative, context-dependent, and thus difficult to quantify nature of expressive gestures. See Daniel Bangert, 'Doing Without Thinking? Processes of Decision-making in Period Instrument Performance' (PhD Thesis, The University of New South Wales, 2012).

78 Georgia Volioti also argues for an ethnographic approach in her 'Playing with Tradition: Weighing up Similarity and the Buoyancy of the Game,' *Musicae Scientiae*, 14/2 (2010). Special Issue (CHARM II), 85-111.

79 Cook, 'Bridging the Unbridgeable?,' pp. 83-84.

(empirical or analytical, ethnographic or experimental). Both the study of music performance and its object (i.e. performance) are multi-faceted. Acknowledging that music performance is a complex phenomenon, indeed a complex *system*, fosters the "and / as well as" outlook; the possibility of multiple characteristics and groupings. An understanding of complex systems can be developed by finding the simplest aspects and building on those; or by working with the complexity. Cook has argued we need both and I agree. However, the former approach has been privileged long enough and therefore I would like to shift the attention, without becoming dogmatic, to the latter. As Cilliers states:

> Instead of looking for a simple discourse that can unify all forms of knowledge, we have to cope with a multiplicity of discourses, many different language games—all of which are determined locally, not legitimated externally.[80]

Such a standpoint may prove productive for a study of the current landscape of Bach performance practice: the differences between MSP and HIP, but especially the varied strands within these broad categories readily lend themselves to explication once it is accepted that "[d]ifferent institutions and different contexts produce different narratives which are not reducible to each other."[81] But before I discuss similarities between music performance and complex dynamical systems I want to turn to philosophy, the more traditional seat of theoretical thinking about music. My contention is that Gilles Deleuze's theory of difference and consistency can be usefully harnessed as it fosters non-hierarchical thinking and the non-linear inter-relationship of individual constructs and elements or "intensities."[82]

Gilles Deleuze and Difference in Music Performance

In performing arts, thinking categorically and scientifically can easily lead to stifling rules and the formation of one dominant type of thought: "This is how Beethoven goes because Czerny says so." Aiming to pin

---

80 Cilliers, *Complexity and Postmodernism*, p. 114, building on Jean-François Lyotard, *The Postmodern Condition* (Minneapolis: University of Minnesota Press, 1984).
81 Cilliers, *Complexity and Postmodernism*, p. 114.
82 These are developed in Gilles Deleuze, *Difference and Repetition*, trans. by Paul Patton (New York: Columbia University Press, 1994) and Gilles Deleuze and Felix Guattari, *A Thousand Plateaus: Capitalism and Schizophrenia*, trans. by Brian Massumi (London: Bloomsbury Academic, 2013 [1987]).

down what the composer might have wanted leads to "territorialization"; normative, recurring patterns of thinking and a limitation of possibilities. The emphasis on Urtext scores leads to "Urtext"—and "Maestro"— mentality, an authoritative hierarchy that discourages experimentation and to be different. Instead it promotes "obedience" and repetition, resulting in homogeneity of performing style. Hierarchical conception of difference reduces performance styles to static, binary opposites and (negative) categories. For instance, a performance is considered to be either HIP or not; it is evaluated against a specific category such as HIP or MSP, a context within which one or the other tends to be regarded inferior to the alternative.

As Sally Macarthur notes while discussing the binary between male and female composers, "In its pluralism and chaos, Deleuzian philosophy enables the construction of a web of interrelations for [performance styles] which opens [them] out to multiple possibilities."[83] Instead of "subordinating difference to instances of the Same, the Similar, the Analogous and the Opposed," Deleuze argues for "the state of free, oceanic differences, of nomadic distributions and crowned anarchy."[84] He claims that "to ground is to determine. [...] Grounding is the operation of the logos, or of sufficient reason."[85] And later reiterates "that to ground is to determine the indeterminate."[86] On the other hand

> Systems in which different relates to different through difference itself are systems of simulacra. Such systems are intensive; they rest ultimately upon the nature of intensive quantities, which precisely communicate through their differences. [...] Systems of simulacra affirm divergence and decentring: the only unity, the only convergence of all the series, is an informal chaos in which they are all included. No series enjoys privilege over others, none possesses the identity of a model, none the resemblance of a copy. None is either opposed or analogous to another. Each is constituted by differences, and communicates with the others through differences of differences. Crowned anarchies are substituted for the hierarchies of representation; nomadic distributions for the sedentary distributions of representation.[87]

---

83 Sally Macarthur, *Towards a Twenty-first Century of Feminist Politics of Music* (Farnham: Ashgate, 2010), p. 5. I have substituted "women's music" for "performance styles."
84 Deleuze, *Difference and Repetition*, p. 265.
85 Ibid., p. 272.
86 Ibid., p. 275.
87 Ibid., pp. 277-278.

As Deleuze considers such systems "sites for the actualisation of Ideas," in other words active, individuating "multiplicities constituted of differential elements, differential relations between those elements, and singularities corresponding to those relations,"[88] they are open and dynamic systems with ever expanding potential for something new and different. In these systems

> Repetition is no longer a repetition of successive elements or external parts, but of totalities which coexist on different levels or degrees. Difference is no longer drawn *from* an elementary repetition but is *between* the levels or degrees of a repetition which is total and totalizing every time; it is displaced and disguised from one level to another, each level including its own singularities or privileged points.[89]

Individual performances of western art music, with its history, traditions, conventions, and ever renewed imagination, easily fit this description: when we compare recordings (or live performances) of a particular composition we are not dealing with "repetition of successive elements" but with "totalities which coexist on different levels or degrees." And the differences between them are as Deleuze describes in the above quote.

Because Deleuze considers the "highest object of art […] to bring into play simultaneously all these repetitions, with their differences in kind and rhythm, their respective displacements and disguises, their divergences and decentrings," he critiques the pursuit of universally agreed-upon suppositions. In his view these create an impasse; they deny the potential to renew, to create difference:

> The more our daily life appears standardized, stereotyped and subject to an accelerated reproduction of object consumption, the more art must be injected into it in order to extract from it that little difference which plays simultaneously between other levels of repetition […]"[90]

If this is (one) role of art, including western classical music performance, then it is questionable what we gain by categorizing its various specimens. Description and interrogation of music performance as "systems of simulacra," as examples of "multiplicities" and "difference" might be more meaningful. The analytical chapters demonstrate the rich diversity and interaction of performance features that come to light when we are

---

88 Ibid., p. 278.
89 Ibid., p. 287.
90 Ibid., p. 293.

willing to forget about neat categories or wanting to explain, to "ground [...] the indeterminate." Chapter three shows that hardly any of the selected recordings fits perfectly the opposing "One" of MSP or HIP. It is much more appropriate to think of a continuum along a vector or even a three-dimensional space of performance style where each performance hovers over several instances of "multiplicities." These findings are further explored and illuminated in chapters four and five until enough evidence is amassed to demonstrate the analogies between complex dynamical systems and music performance. The pointing out of these parallels is assisted by occasionally referring to certain terms borrowed from Deleuze and Guattari.

For Deleuze's philosophy of difference provides not just a broad aesthetic and analytical framework but also a toolbox of concepts. I hasten to say that my analysis is *not* going to use Deleuzian terminology directly. I am not conducting a Deleuzian analysis. But throughout chapters four to six I am signposting the parallels between Deleuze and Guattari's concepts and my more mundanely formulated analyses of the recorded performances to highlight their persuasive support for the argument of this book. Therefore it is important to introduce them here while noting that since these terms are used only as potential analogies they are always placed in double quotation marks.

In his opus magnum co-authored with Felix Guattari, Deleuze distinguishes three "lines" in relation to *strata* (i.e. "phenomena of thickening; accumulations, coagulations, sedimentations, foldings"), *assemblages* ("produced in the strata by extracting a *territory* from the milieus") and *rhizome* (a heterogeneous, non-linear chaotic system / multiplicity): The "molar lines" segment and categorize, they are subordinated to the "One"; they form a circular and binary system. The "molecular lines" are rhyzomic, they break and twist and pass *"between* things, *between* points." They organize in a non-hierarchical fashion and are no longer subordinated to the "One" but are "multiplicities of becoming, or transformational multiplicities." Finally there are the "lines of flight or rapture."[91] This is where transformation or metamorphosis occurs. They do not segment but completely break out of one form of construction (the "territorialized" and "repetitive" normative) and move towards an emerging other. Deleuze and

---

91 Deleuze and Guattari, *A Thousand Plateaus*, pp. 584-597. At the beginning of the book (p. 5) they explain the "rhizome" thus: "Subtract the unique from the multiplicity to be constituted [...] A system of this kind could be called the rhizome."

Guattari emphasize the lack of symmetry which enables "the masses and flows" to constantly escape and invent new connections.[92]

I would argue that we can think of performance features as functioning like these three types of lines. "Molar lines" would constitute elements that define and categorize performance style. They "territorialize" and make a performance belong to a type (the "One"); for instance a clear example of seamless portato bowing denoting the MSP style. "Molecular lines" would be features that interact with other features and blur categories. They "deterritorialize," in Deleuzian language, and create difference. They contribute to the transformation of style such as when articulation and bowing emulate period performance practice without using a period bow. The "lines of flight" might be those elements of a performance that create radical departures from the usual; for instance through extreme tempo or novel ornamentation and other variations. To analyse the complex interplay between these "lines" is a major aim of this book and Deleuze and Guattari's conceptualization of difference and how it may be constituted in non-linear dynamical systems ("assemblages" and "multiplicities") provides fitting theoretical underpinnings.

Music Performance as Complex Dynamical System

As I have indicated already several times, I propose that it is time for researchers to investigate music performance in its complexity because it is a phenomenon that displays the characteristics of complex dynamical systems. These need to be approached with an appropriately complex method. The aim, therefore, is to provide a theoretical framework and a model for such a comprehensive and multimodal approach. The ensuing chapters demonstrate the necessity of dealing with music performance in its complexity if the goal is to understand the phenomenon and its experience. Studying merely its constituent parts is not just inadequate for a proper insight but often leads to misconstrued information. To introduce my position, a review of what I consider important about complex dynamical systems is in order. How these characteristics manifest in music

---

92 Ibid., p. 588.

performance is argued more fully in chapter six, once sufficient evidence has been established through chapters three, four and five.

As is well known, music and its performance is a cultural product with a rich history. Paul Cilliers asserts that complex cultural phenomena are "never symmetrical" because the "*history* of the system is vitally important for the way in which meaning is generated."[93] Self-organizing complex systems make self-adjustments "to improve [their] own performance."[94] Music performance is no exception. As I have shown and will detail further in subsequent chapters, post-1980s HIP had embraced valid criticisms and altered its verbal rhetoric and, more gradually, its interpretative practices to "improve" and renew. The history of performing styles is never circular or symmetrical. The study of sound recordings shows, when older styles of expressive mannerisms seem to resurface at a later time, these tend to be ever so slightly or fundamentally different from their previous incarnations. It is quite unlikely that we would ever recreate the sound as it was originally produced, whether we have aural evidence or only verbal descriptions of a particular performing convention.

The current scene of HIP in nineteenth- and early twentieth-century repertoire is a case in point. The majority of such performances adapt precious little of the original conventions evidenced on early recordings and piano rolls. One fledgling exception, the work of Neal Peres Da Costa and the Ironwood Ensemble, shows preliminary attempts at re-instating nineteenth-century piano, string and ensemble practices.[95] I say preliminary, because the extent to which they use particular characteristics (such as dislocation of hands, arpeggiating chords, portamento, asynchrony of parts, non-unified bowing, tempo irregularities, etc.) is far more modest than what one hears on early sound recordings. Eventually they may go further with some or all of these performance techniques but whether they will ever sound like a carbon copy of artists recording at the beginning of the twentieth century is highly doubtful and not particularly desirable.

---

93 Cilliers, *Complexity and Postmodernism*, p. 117.
94 Ibid.
95 For a taste see: http://www.youtube.com/playlist?list=PL78D10D0EE7FB7345. See also the work of violinist David Milsom and recent performances of MSP pianists Murray Perahia, Stephen Hough, Steven Osborne, Evgeny Kissin and Yulianna Avdeeva showing signs of documented nineteenth-century concert practices such as "preluding" before and between pieces.

Rachel Barton Pine, among others, has noted that the clear and rich sound achieved through current recording technology makes her look for a style of portamento (sliding between notes) and bowing that she feels is more suitable than a direct imitation of what one hears on old recordings.[96] Barton Pine seems to refer here to a pre-conscious affect, a sensation of intensity. Listening to her playing and comparing it to the recordings of Maud Powell—in homage of whom Barton Pine's recording was issued—I think I know what she means, but I am unable to objectively show the difference. My measuring tools (software that can be used to visualize and analyze audio signals) are not sophisticated enough to help quantify the differences in kind and degree. Lacking empirical evidence, we are left with our aural impression. This confirms a difference in the frequency of introducing portamento and a tendency to mostly use it in upward motion while Powell and others used it in both directions, often more frequently downward. The fascinating revelation, however, is not this. Rather, the techniques by which expressive gestures like portamento are delivered, but at least the resultant sound, are utterly different. I would venture to propose that the modern expressive portamento is fingered and bowed much more lightly while those heard in old recordings are more intense. When late nineteenth-century violinists introduce portamento for expressive purposes they play them with more weighted bow-strokes and greater definition. Performance does not circle back, it is "not symmetrical"; it moves more like a spiral because each generation reinterprets and further develops what it learns from the past. We simply may not have the right vocabulary to adequately describe what we hear nor the technology to study it empirically.

Music performance is a complex system not just because it is a culturally constructed yet individual artistic practice that is temporal and ephemeral, resisting verbal discourse, but also because the act of performance involves a multitude of elements from the technical to the aesthetic, and from the physical and measurable to the embodied, implied and subjectively perceived. All of these are inter-dependent, forming a complex web of non-linear interactions. The non-linear and asymmetrical nature of complex systems means that

---

96 Personal interview conducted in Chicago, April 2008. The remark was made in relation to her CD tribute to Barton Pine's famous nineteenth-century compatriot, violinist Maud Powell (American Virtuosa, Cedille 9000 097). Maud Powell's playing can be heard, for instance, on NAXOS HISTORICAL 8.110961.

"the same piece of information has different effects on different individuals, and small causes can have large effects."[97] The infinite variability of music performance and its diverse effect on listeners are well established facts, lending further support to viewing it as a complex system. As such it is best grasped, at least metaphorically, by models that "can dynamically adjust themselves in order to select that which is to be inhibited and which is to be enhanced."[98] Music performance is robust and flexible, constantly changing and adjusting to cultural norms and expectations as well as to individual artistic personalities and technical abilities.

Interdisciplinary approaches and collaborations are therefore important because complex systems are more than the sum of their parts; the "intricate relationship" among these parts is equally, if not more, significant. By cutting up the system, by focusing on one or the other of its aspects, the "analytical method destroys what it seeks to understand."[99] Complexity is misrepresented by simplistic explanation but "an analysis of [its] characteristics […] can be attempted in order to develop a general description that is not constrained by a specific, *a priori* definition."[100] Distortions are inevitable since only certain aspects of a performance can be analysed at a time.

Frustratingly, even attempts at describing the holistic effect leads to dissecting because of the linearity of words and sentences: we can only speak of one thing at a time while our mind can decode-perceive the full aural image at once (surely not in all its detail at a conscious level but in its essence, something that can prove very elusive otherwise). I will try to overcome this linearity by frequent cross-referencing to earlier and later discussions of the same excerpts. Ultimately, we simply need to accept that our inquiries lead along a road of discoveries and increasing knowledge rather than towards absolute truth (or how the performance "ought to go"). If investigators of music performance adopt such an attitude they will make less lofty claims and act as researchers of the "nonmodern" era as opposed to assertive modernist scientists or postmodernist debunkers.[101] An approach that focuses on the complex of what we hear and experience

---

97 Cilliers, *Complexity and Postmodernism*, p. 120.
98 Ibid., p. 119.
99 Ibid., p. 2.
100 Ibid., p. 2.
101 "Nonmodern" is a term used by Latour (*Pandora's Hope*) to distinguish current research practice that is neither modern nor postmodern.

when we listen to a particular recording; an approach that acknowledges and interrogates the dynamical, non-linear interactions at play promises to enrich our knowledge and understanding of music performance in a way that science and its reductionist, positivist paradigm cannot.

But what are these potential non-linear, dynamical interactions? According to Cilliers, the characteristics of complex systems include:

1. A large number of elements are necessary but not sufficient [...] the elements have to interact and their interaction must be dynamic. A complex system changes with time. The interactions do not have to be *physical*; they can also be thought of as the transference of *information*.
2. The interaction is fairly rich, i.e. any element in the system influences, and is influenced by, quite a few other ones.
3. The interactions themselves have a number of important characteristics. Firstly, the interactions are non-linear [...] [which means] that small causes can have large results and vice versa. This is a precondition for complexity.
4. There are loops in the interactions. The effect of any activity can feed back onto itself, sometimes directly, sometimes after a number of intervening stages.
5. Complex systems are usually open systems, i.e. they interact with their environment.
6. Complex systems operate under conditions far from equilibrium [or stability]. There has to be a constant flow of energy [...] to ensure survival.
7. Complex systems have history. Not only do they evolve through time, but their past is co-responsible for their present behaviour.
8. The interactions often take the form of clusters of elements which co-operate with each-other and also compete with other clusters. An element in the system may belong to more than one clustering. Clusters should not be interpreted in a special sense, or seen as fixed, hermetically sealed entities. They can grow or shrink, be subdivided or absorbed, flourish or decay.[102]

Looking at this list, I see many parallels with music performance. As we all know, music performance has many elements and they interact with each other in many ways. We do not just hear pitch but also its timbre and therefore the same pitch or note can have different character and

---

102 Cilliers, *Complexity and Postmodernism*, pp. 3-4, 7. The compilation and numbering is entirely mine.

affect; phrasing and articulation interact with tempo and intensity to create diverse meanings while articulation and tempo impact on the perception of rhythm and pulse, just to name the most obvious interactions. These may also form "loops," and differences in nuances can have significant impact ("small causes having large results"). My analyses in the subsequent chapters show the history of performing Bach's music in recent times; how the past is "co-responsible for present behaviour"; how this evolving style interacts with the players' personality and musical biography as well as their cultural environment, and how all this is fed by the dynamism of ever new generations of musicians wanting to make their mark, providing a "constant flow of energy" and change. The discussion of similarities and differences between current MSP and HIP highlights the "clusters of elements which co-operate with each other and also compete with other clusters." They also show how certain features may belong to several clusters. This in turn explains why their *relative* importance (as well as interaction with other elements) in a particular context determines their function; how strongly, at any given moment, the feature contributes to the style of the performance and its overall effect. There are no absolute indicators, only "multiplicities" with different proportions of "molar" and "molecular" lines "territorializing" and "deterritorializing" various "assemblages."

Whether we see the relevance of Deleuze's thinking or take heed from Cilliers' assertion—that clusters are not "hermetically sealed entities" but "can grow or shrink, be subdivided or absorbed, flourish or decay"—we are surely facing a complex dynamical system in the phenomenon of music performance. The exploration of these parallels between music performance and complex systems infuses all of the subsequent chapters of the book. I return to engage with them specifically in the last one.

2.4. Performance Studies, Oral Cultures and Academia

There are two more issues I wish to touch upon before turning to the chosen repertoire. These are, firstly, the respective roles of "practice-based musician-researchers" and musicologists, and secondly, the differences between aural / oral and literate cultures.[103] Although the notions of

---

103 It was Ingrid Pearson's conference paper that first drew my attention to this second issue: Ingrid E. Pearson, 'Practice and Theory; Orality and Literacy: Performance in the 21st Century,' paper delivered at *Performa 11* conference, Aveiro, Portugal, 19-21 May

modernism and postmodernism could be adequate to explain certain observations, looking at them from these additional angles adds further depth and nuance to the study of music performance.

Research Roles: Performing Music or Analysing Performance?

During the last few years there has been an increased emphasis, especially in the UK, but also in Australia, on "practice-based" or "practice-led" (practice-informed) research and a questioning of the adequacy of performance research conducted by musicologists "to get to the heart of what underlies performed music."[104] The proliferation of self-reflections and musical self-analyses (at times referred to as auto-ethnography) is clearly noticeable, causing some concern in science-based circles of academia. I sense a growing tension between two camps, a tension that, to me, seems to be perpetuated and exacerbated primarily by simplistic, "one-size-fits all" funding models. The situation is not unique to music performance research. Speaking of academia more broadly Latour states:

> One camp deems the sciences accurate only when they have been purged of any contamination by subjectivity, politics, or passion; the other camp, spread out much more widely, deems humanity, morality, subjectivity, or rights worthwhile only when they have been protected from any contact with science, technology, and objectivity.[105]

He argues for synthesis and mutual respect, adding:

> We are [...] so accustomed to taking for granted the abyss between the wisdom of the practice and the lessons of theory, that we seem to have entirely forgotten that this most cherished analytical clarity was reached at the price of an incredibly costly invention: one *physical world* "out there" versus *many mental worlds* "in there."[106]

I could not agree more, as everything else so far in this book hopefully demonstrates. Surely, the study of phenomenology, dialogue, collaboration,

---

   2011.
[104] This is manifest, for instance in the bourgeoning symposia around performance studies organized by conservatories, the proliferation of doctoral programs in artistic practice and the projects undertaken by the AHRC Research Centre for Musical Performance as Creative Practice (CMPCP) at Cambridge University. The citation is from the abstract of the closing Roundtable discussion at the 17 June 2011 study day for research students entitled *Performing Musicology* and held at City University London (organized jointly with Guildhall Research Work and supported by the Royal Musical Association).
[105] Latour, *Pandora's Hope*, p. 18.
[106] Ibid., p. 284.

and genuine communication are in the interest of all who wish to gain a better understanding of artistic processes. But none of this should mean changing or abandoning roles and giving up on rigorous standards. Musicological performance studies as I perceive them are not primarily for the benefit of performers but for the listening public and those interested in culture and history. Practicing musicians' main contribution to society is to create high-quality performances and my task as a music performance researcher is to account for how and what they achieve and offer to listeners. These are two entirely separate activities, with different goals and means, in the contrasting domains of aurality and textuality. Both are valuable in their own right and dependent on the other to gain greater insight. If musicologists are not asked to perform why are performers required to write?

I am not denying that performers should be well-informed about and reflect on what they do, or that they may even wish to communicate their thoughts in the form of published research. These can offer different and important perspectives and I am always curious to read them. I simply would like to reaffirm the right of performers to "just" perform, to communicate their knowledge aurally, through performance. By the same token, I wish to affirm the validity of "traditional" musicological investigations of performers and performance that deal with the product of performance, the "sound object." Or, whether in collaboration or not, with the process that helped it come to life.

I find it contentious to do away with the subject-object dichotomy and agree with Latour that we need to *overcome* it instead because "the object that sits before the subject and the subject that faces the object are *polemical* entities, not innocent metaphysical inhabitants of the world."[107] The self-reflective practitioner may not be the most reliable source for exploring certain processes and mechanisms. Psychologists speak of demand characteristics and attribution as essential problems that may arise in such contexts. Patrik Juslin asserts that "because many of the processes and mechanisms are 'implicit' in nature and could occur in parallel, researchers cannot rely merely on phenomenological report or introspection to explain musical emotion. (The music experience is the thing that needs explaining, rather than being that explanation). Most of what goes on in the causal process might, in fact, not be consciously available."[108] Juslin refers to Paul

---

107 Ibid., p. 294.
108 Patrik N Juslin, 'From Everyday Emotions to Aesthetic Emotions: Towards a Unified Theory of Musical Emotions,' *Physics of Life Reviews*, 10 (2013), 235-266 (p. 259).

64 A Musicology of Performance

Silvia who also "notes that 'perceived causality and true causality diverge,' since 'processes irrelevant to causality influence the attribution that people make': 'people tend to attribute causality to salient stimuli, even when salient is unrelated to the effect.'"[109] From a more philosophical, humanistic and subjectively felt viewpoint we may ask: "Who has ever mastered an action? Show me a novelist, a painter, an architect, a cook, who has not, like God, been surprised, overcome, ravished by what she was—what *they* were—no longer doing."[110]

The problem as I see it is that the performer is not necessarily better placed than the musicologist to verbalize the characteristics of a sound object or the processes that generated it. As introduced in chapter one, the typical inadequacy of words (including metaphors) for the particulars of bodily, somatic, kinaesthetic, aural and psychological experience (or action) is the biggest obstacle in researching music, especially performance. A good example comes from a recent DVD where the eminently articulate and inquisitive Pieter Wispelwey is struggling to explain the difference between the sounds of his two different baroque cellos. First he states that "at 392 the sound is even more relaxed" but also "rustic and raw" adding that "it's all a matter of colour."[111] Later he comes back to this issue and again notes the difference in tuning but then simply keeps repeating "it's very different" while shaking his head and eventually just plays a passage on both instruments ending with raised open arms and shoulders and a huge smiling question mark on his face, as if saying with delight "don't you hear? It's all very different—wonderful / amazing, no?"[112] I am not sure the audible difference is so noticeable, or entirely stemming from the instrument (or the tuning) rather than the way he plays the passage on each cello. It is possible though, that he plays differently because the different instruments "prompt" him or react differently. What this episode makes blatantly clear, however, is the phenomenon that what is in the mind (arms, fingers, ears, whole body) of a performer may not always be audible for the outside listener. Still, I wonder with Latour "Why is it that we cannot

---

109 Paul J. Silvia, *Exploring the Psychology of Interest* (New York: Oxford University Press, 2006), cited in Juslin, 'From Everyday Emotions,' p. 259.
110 Latour, *Pandora's Hope*, p. 283.
111 2:37-3.36 on the DVD documentary—in discussion with Lawrence Dreyfus and John Butt—accompanying Pieter Wispelwey's third compact disk recording of Bach's Six Suites for Cello released in 2012 (Evil Penguin Records Classics EPRC 0012).
112 Idem, 4:22-5:08.

readily recover for our ordinary speech what is so tantalizingly offered by practice?"[113] and suggest we look for the answer in contrasting oral and literate cultures.

Oral Cultures and the Aurality of Music Performance

Others have also drawn attention to the importance of aurality in music making.[114] But in relation to the study of western art music performance this issue has largely been neglected. Instead, there has been an increase in "how to" books, tutors, and manuals (just like in the empiricist eighteenth century!) that provide written accounts of how to play the piano, the violin, the flute, the guitar; how to have a healthy singing technique; how to interpret particular repertoire, how to compose hit songs; how to be creative; how to practice, how to memorize, and so on. Almost every "famous" teacher since Carl Czerny (1791-1858) and Rodolphe Kreutzer (1766-1831) has put pen to paper to disseminate their knowledge—accrued from learning mostly by ear from other famous musicians—to eager students and interested amateurs around the globe.

This emphasis on the written word is at odds with our multi-modal but primarily aurally perceived appreciation of music. As neuroscience has shown, "Musical activity involves nearly every region of the brain that we know about, and nearly every neural subsystem."[115] If so, we are limiting our potential to understand our interaction with music if we over-emphasize the analytical, the abstract, the written or notated; what we can verbalize. It leads us to look for what we can measure and make us think we explained what is not (yet) measurable. Such an approach fosters categorization, ossification, homogenization and normative thinking. Oral cultures thrive on variation, on "thinking forward,"[116] on experiential and communal learning, communicating and being in the world.

Music performance parallels oral cultures in that it is based primarily on experience—kinaesthetic, aural and emotional memory—that is honed and kept alive through repetition and daily practice. Although music notation

---

113 Latour, *Pandora's Hope*, p. 266.
114 One recent contribution is Anne Dhu McLucas, *The Musical Ear: Oral Tradition in the USA* (Farnham: Ashgate, 2010).
115 Daniel Levitin, *This is your Brain on Music: Understanding a Human Obsession* (London: Atlantic Books, 2008), pp. 85-86.
116 Albert B. Lord, *The Singer of Tales*, 2nd edn (Cambridge, MA: Harvard University Press, 2000 [1960]), p. 128; cited in McLucas, *The Musical Ear*, p. 121.

has become increasingly sophisticated over time and western classical musicians rely on score reading, much of the musician's training and active professional life takes place in the aural realm. Surely teachers often use metaphors and imagery, occasionally specific musical terms, but most often they demonstrate, playing their instruments or singing / humming.[117] Anyone who has observed rehearsals of experienced musicians knows how little they speak and how well they seem to communicate through sound and gestures in shaping their interpretation. This is also confirmed in experimental music psychologists' research.[118] If there is any discussion at a rehearsal, it is often combined with brief demonstrations on the instrument, as if to confirm proper understanding. Knowledge is "conceptualized" *in sound* and movement rather than words. As Mine Doğantan-Dack states, "music making requires mentally hearing and imagining the notation *as music*."[119] Because of this and because western music notation is limited in capturing phrasing, articulation, rhythm, intensity / volume (dynamics) and tempo while being silent on timbre, the cognitive processes of the performer's musical world resemble those typically found in oral cultures and this is what we need to tap into and investigate.

The perception of sound is limited to a few seconds—similar to the time-limitations of short-term memory—and experienced as "the now." According to cognitive science,

> Echoic memory is an auditory sensory memory that persists for several seconds, after which it is lost unless attended to. [...] Echoic memory enables us to relate what we are hearing at this very moment to what we

---

[117] Interview studies with musicians confirm this as they frequently report the musicians singing / humming and demonstrating on their instrument as they respond to questions or reflect on problems raised. See for instance Daniel Leech-Wilkinson and Helen Prior, 'Heuristics of Expressive Performance,' in *Expressiveness in Music Performance*, pp. 34-57. According to a 2003 study, less experienced student musicians do not necessarily like such teaching, however common it is in the "master-apprentice" setting. See, Erik Lindström, Patrik Juslin, Roberto Bresin, and Aaron Williamon, '"Expressivity Comes from within Your Soul": A Questionnaire Study of Music Students' Perspectives on Expressivity,' *Research Studies in Music Education*, 20/1 (2003), 23-47. It should be noted that this study only focused on learning to play expressively while I am discussing performance in general, inclusive of technical and expressive-interpretative matters (as much as the two are separable).

[118] Peter Keller, 'Ensemble Performance: Interpersonal Alignment of Musical Expression,' in *Expressiveness in Music Performance*, pp. 260-282.

[119] Mine Doğantan-Dack, 'Philosophical Reflections on Expressive Music Performance,' in *Expressiveness in Music Performance*, pp. 3-21 (p. 10).

have just heard. It permits us to maintain a temporal window wide enough to recognize a dynamic sound or parse a phrase.[120]

Importantly, "this sensory memory is image-like [...], in that it exists independent of and prior to language and it is often difficult to capture in words."[121]

In contrast, reading texts engages sight and sight isolates, dissects. As Walter Ong has argued in his foundational text on orality, "A typical visual ideal is clarity and distinctness, a taking apart." Listening to sound is the opposite. "The auditory ideal [...] is harmony, a putting together."[122]

> Whereas sight situates the observer outside what he views, at a distance, sound pours into the hearer. [...] Vision comes to a human being from one direction at a time: to look at a room or a landscape, I must move my eyes around from one part to another. When I hear, however, I gather sound simultaneously from every direction at once: I am at the centre of my auditory world, which envelops me, establishing me at a kind of core of sensation and existence.[123]

Noting that the concepts of interior and exterior are "existentially grounded concepts, based on experience of one's own body," Ong also explains that

> Interiority and harmony are characteristics of human consciousness. The consciousness of each human person is totally interiorized, known to the person from the inside and inaccessible to any other person directly from the inside. [...] What is "I" to me is only "you" to you. And this "I" incorporates experience into itself by "getting it all together." Knowledge is ultimately not a fractioning but a unifying phenomenon, a striving for harmony. [...] In

---

120 Jamshed J. Bharucha, 'Neural Nets, Temporal Composites, and Tonality,' in *The Psychology of Music*, 2nd edn, ed. by Diana Deutsch (San Diego: Academia Press, 1999), pp. 413-440 (p. 422).
121 McLucas, *The Musical Ear*, p. 39.
122 Walter J. Ong, *Orality and Literacy: The Technologizing of the Word* (London: Routledge, 1988), p. 71.
123 Ong, *Orality and Literacy*, p. 71. Although it is true that we do not only see with our focal point but also with our peripheral vision, Ong's argument highlights an important and useful distinction. It is possible, of course, to focus attention to a particular sound or a particular attribute of a sound and to filter out other sounds, including background noise, but unless it is segmented out and "frozen in time," it is considerably harder to do than to focus on, say, a detail of a landscape. I should note, that I am not advocating an "either-or" division between vision and hearing. I am using Ong to explain certain essential differences arising from these senses to argue for a more balanced appreciation and approach to perception and the study of music performance.

> a primary oral culture [...] the phenomenology of sound enters deeply into human beings' feel for existence.[124]

As musicians tend to spend long hours playing music from an early age, we can think of them as living in a "primary oral culture." In such worlds words or musical notes are not thought of as something "laid out before their eyes [...] ready to be explored," dissected, analysed, understood; they are experienced and acted, although they can also be mentally represented.[125] Pianist-musicologist Mine Doğantan-Dack has recently formulated something similar in relation to classical music performance:

> The experiential reality for the performer is such that the visual symbols in a score are always already perceived as "music," together with various expressive details that are understood *immediately* as constitutive of the music and are not *inferred* from the score. [...] Consequently, the visual, objectively identifiable and fixed entity that researchers regard as the musical score, and the audible, subjectively construed phenomenon that defines the score for performers are not ontologically the same phenomenon.[126]

At the end of the book I shall return to the problem that an over-emphasis on seeing, on analytical and abstract thinking may pause. There I shall propose reasons why we should try harder to find ways of interrogating how and why we hear and react to music performance the way we do in a more holistic manner. Here I would just like to note the accumulating literature promoting the "revaluation" and "rehabilitation" of our aural sense.[127]

Exploring Jean-Luc Nancy's phenomenology of listening, Anthony Gritten refers to research on music's role in human evolution and concludes that "there is a strong case for claiming that the ear is the primary sense organ of the human body."[128] He comes to this conclusion by arguing that

---

124 Ong, *Orality and Literacy*, pp. 71-72.
125 Ibid., p. 72. It is outside the scope of my discussion here, but these points could be further developed in contemplating the importance of music in all cultures and from the dawn of human existence right to the present day.
126 Mine Doğantan-Dack, 'Philosophical Reflections,' p. 10.
127 In *Reason and Resonance* Erlmann points out that his evidence "does not bear out the tenet that modernity is, at root, a period dominated by vision, images, and distanced observations." As I will explain in chapter six I essentially agree with his cautioning against "modernity's either-or logic" (p. 341). At the same time, I believe an emphasis on aurality is due to correct the balance and counteract the prevalence in modern epistemology to promote "such a distanced stance as the sine qua non of reason" (ibid).
128 Anthony Gritten, 'The Subject (of) Listening,' *Journal of the British Society for Phenomenology*, 45/3 (2015), 203-219 (p. 217). Gritten refers to a wide variety of sources on listening and seeing while engaging with Jean-Luc Nancy, *Listening*, trans. by Charlotte Mandell (New York: Fordham University Press, 2007). His main source of

the extraordinarily deep-seated and often unthinking bias towards visual modes of cognition, action and judgement is a necessary detour in human development that finds its real significance within the narrow context of the rise of Enlightenment Modernity in the techno-scientific developed world. [...] we should acknowledge that we have been listening for longer, and that we have been listening quicker for that matter (the human brain processes audio data faster than visual data). Given that listening is central to many ways of being in the world otherwise than, and often older than, the dominant Western model of communicative consensus [...] it behoves us to rethink the function of listening, and by extension musicking.[129]

How can we do that, in our current academic climate where even visual artists, let alone musicians employed by tertiary institutions are required to write as much as to produce creative work? When we are fixated on the written, we miss an opportunity to study our ability of sensing and communicating aurally. Yet this is what musicians do best.

Keeping Music Performance in the Aural Domain

Although my focus is on performing western art music, there is no need to underline that most other musical traditions do not use notation but pass on everything purely aurally. There is considerable emphasis on learning by ear even among pedagogues of western classical music as well, especially during the foundational years. According to Ong, people who have no recourse to writing and have to rely on their memory for everything tend to think much more functionally and eschew abstraction. For instance, if they are asked to define an object, they do not provide "a sharp-focused description of visual appearance [...] but a definition in terms of its operations"—in our case, a demonstration of a musical phrase or gesture, rather than a scientific explication.[130] Oral cultures do not

> deal in such items as [...] abstract categorization, formally logical reasoning processes, definitions, or even comprehensive descriptions, or articulate

---

information regarding the role of music in evolution is the chapter by Ian Cross and Iain Morley, 'The Evolution of Music: Theories, Definitions and the Nature of the Evidence,' *Communicative Musicality: Exploring the Basis of Human Companionship*, ed. by Stephen Malloch and Colwyn Trevarthen (Oxford: Oxford University Press, 2009), pp. 61-81.
129 Gritten, 'The Subject (of) Listening,' 217.
130 Ong, *Orality and Literacy*, p. 54. Telling examples of how differently pre-literate people think are provided by James Flynn (with reference to the work of neuropsychologist Alexander Luria, 1902-1977) in a February 2013 TED lecture available at http://www.ted.com/talks/james_flynn_why_our_iq_levels_are_higher_than_our_grandparents.html

self-analysis, all of which derive not simply from thought itself but from text-formed thought.[131]

Although modern musicians of the western art tradition have recourse to sound recordings as well as music notation and thus are able to take a snapshot of sound or the score for close inspection, their learning or polishing performance still largely parallels oral cultures in its ways of enabling recall of solutions. Just as in oral cultures, musicians learn to *express the full existential context* of performing particular pieces through repetitions and the adoption of conventions.

Back in the seventeenth and eighteenth centuries there was no sound recording technology and notation was much more skeletal. Oral traditions were even more alive partly because fewer people were (fully) literate. Also, musicians came from families of musicians stretching several generations. They learnt composition and ornamentation primarily by imitation and daily practice as well as absorption of a formulaic "vocabulary." Unlike their modern-day colleagues, they only played in their local, contemporary style and were not required to "speak in dialect,"[132] let alone the different "languages" of music composed over a period of more than 400 years. For them, just like for the bards of ancient times and oral cultures, thinking of a single text, of one fixed version was still quite an anathema. Notation was severely limited in conveying information essential for an ideal performance so they interpreted them at will, adding and changing according to their fancy even if relying on local customs. They performed a living, vernacular tradition that was malleable and fluid typical of the artistic output of oral cultures. They also tended to play their own music and so had control over the contributing elements. They worked with patterns and "templates," and the learning of articulation and figuration were embedded in their instrumental training. What we find in modern institutionalized musical learning is a process, at least partly, of "training [the professional musicians] *out of* that flexible mode of thinking."[133]

An overemphasis on text, on being "true to the score," on playing exactly as the score prescribes, goes against the long tradition of living in the aural realm, especially since scores are so hopelessly inadequate in

---

131 Ong, *Orality and Literacy*, p. 55.
132 For instance, the average English or German small-town musician of the seventeenth- and early eighteenth centuries was unlikely to be well-versed in playing the French way.
133 McLucas, *The Musical Ear*, p. 123.

conveying what a musician is required to do when performing a piece (and equally inadequate to transcribe what performers have actually done).[134] Similarly, in my view, an overemphasis on self-reflective research, on insisting that musicians verbally articulate and publish academic papers about what they are doing simply reinforces the primacy of literacy and delegates an unwarranted superiority to verbal discourse. It is a sign of a dominant left-hemisphere, according to Ian McGilchrist.[135] The question to which I will return in the Epilogue of this book is whether an over-reliance on what the left hemisphere does best (such as analysis, categorization and abstraction) is ever going to be adequate to investigate processes (like music performance and listening) that are deeply multi-modal and heavily implicating the involvement of the right-hemisphere.

Academia Once More

As I indicated at the start of this section, people lament the complacency of analysts taking the upper hand in performance analysis (the text to act flow of signification), or the unequal balance of power between academics and performers or between musicology and performance.[136] Yet funding principles of tertiary institutions perpetuate the situation by insisting that performers should write and publish "original research"; verbal discourses rather than (or as well as, in somewhat better scenarios) create exciting and illuminating performances (whether informed by research or not). I find it

---

[134] It is probably not a coincidence that the "work" concept and canonic thinking started to develop in earnest from about Beethoven's time (see Goehr, *Imaginary Museum*). Once print music became accessible and affordable the aural cultures of close musical communities broke up and "internationalization" became inevitable. In view of this, one may argue that the elevation of the score to its status of representing "the work" could, in fact, be regarded as an utopian attempt to keep this aural culture alive, no matter how contradictory this may seem to the logical mind.

[135] Ian McGilchrist, *The Master and his Emissary: The Divided Brain and the Making of the Western World* (London: Yale University Press, 2009). See more on his ideas in chapter six (Epilogue).

[136] There is a growing list of musicological writing where such statements are routinely offered. Rink and Cook were among the first to explore the dichotomy and the consequences of the hierarchy more generally, while Taruskin critiqued it from the point of view of historical performance practice: John Rink, 'In Respect of Performance: The View from Musicology,' *Psychology of Music*, 31/3 (2003), 303-323; Cook, 'Between Process and Product'; Taruskin, *Text and Act*, p. 13. Where analysis is at a decade later is discussed in, for instance, Nicholas Cook, 'Introduction: Refocusing Theory,' *Music Theory Online*, 18 (2012), http://mtosmt.org/issues/mto.12.18.1/mto.12.18.1.cook.pdf. The artificial impact of funding and employment structures tends to go unmentioned, however.

a demeaning situation that stifles creativity when musicians are required to demonstrate "original research" in their performance or recording of a repertoire piece. It is not just difficult but near impossible to do so when performing a Beethoven or Brahms sonata or Bach's Solos for Violin, for that matter, or any other oft performed music. Yet the performance may be stunning and worth a hundred "original" research papers about them!

In oral cultures the "integrity of the past [is] subordinate to the integrity of the present. […] Oral traditions reflect a society's present cultural values rather than idle curiosity about the past."[137] The musical mainstream's claim to a living tradition reaching back to Beethoven reflects a mind-frame focusing on the integrity of the present. Even the development of HIP is a testimony to the residual power of this aural mode of existence: When the written sources were first recovered and studied musicians could only interpret them according to their modern experiential boundaries of aural and operational memory. That is why the use of old instruments proved so crucial yet it took so long to let go of playing them with modern technique.[138] The older generation of HIP practitioners sometimes note that the younger players are not familiar enough with the sources but try to "cut corners" by quickly learning the essential "tricks" from their teachers and then use them liberally and routinely.[139] This might be a lamentable attitude, but it also shows that music performance is primarily an aural practice that thrives on imitation and variation rather than abstraction and analysis. Musicians are like "skilled oral narrators [who] deliberately vary their traditional narratives because part of their skill is their ability to adjust to new audiences and new situations or simply to be coquettish," to entertain.[140] We should let them play and rejoice in the sensual pleasures they offer. We should let "the phenomenology of sound enter deeply into [our] feel for existence" because listening to music brings us closer to our own inner world, to our "interiorized consciousness" more than a thousand academic words.[141] When we listen to music we are not "out there" contemplating an object but "in the music," living it in the now.[142]

---

137 Ong, *Orality and Literacy*, p. 48.
138 Fabian, *Bach Performance Practice*.
139 See interviews with Leonhardt and Bylsma, for instance 'Dirigieren ist der leichteste Beruf,' *Concerto*, 2/1 (1984), 61-64.
140 Ong, *Orality and Literacy*, p. 48.
141 Ibid., p. 72.
142 Compare to the quote from Günther Anders cited in chapter one: "When listening to music we are *out* of the world and *in* music." Günther Stern [Anders], 'Philosophische Untersuchungen zu musikalischen Situationen,' typescript, Österreichisches Literaturarchiv der Österreichischen Nationalbibliothek, Vienna. Nachlass Günther

As a final point in my argument regarding practice-led / practice-informed research, I cite Latour again to reiterate "that action is slightly overtaken by what it acts upon, that it drifts through translation; that an experiment is an event which offers slightly more than its inputs; that chains of mediations are not the same thing as an effortless passage from cause to effect."[143] The "experiment" Latour refers to in this quote can easily be exchanged for "music performance" or its analysis. There are innumerable examples when performers' verbal discourse does not match their performing practice. It may be that the intention was not executed (or not perceptibly executed) for a variety of reasons, or the verbal pronouncement might have been just empty rhetoric. The fact of the matter is that performers practice, research and reflect but then the performance takes over, and the musician's preparation "drifts through translation."[144] The musicologist in turn tries to make sense of this translated act but while looking for adequate words and methods a new "chain of mediations" arises and the perceived or analytically derived cause and effect may not match entirely the performer's understanding and mental construct of her own act. And this is all well and good, for the musicologist is primarily a listener and as such writes for other listeners. The performer on the other hand may best communicate to other performers and listeners her knowledge about performance and the work she is performing through the act itself, within the experiential aural domain.

2.5. Conclusion

At the end of this meandering tour of theoretical and methodological approaches to music performance we seem to be well positioned to launch into our designated material, the forty-odd selected recordings of Bach's Violin Solos made since Sergiu Luca's ground-breaking first with period apparatus from 1977. The development of and current views on HIP and MSP have been mapped from multiple angles—cultural, historical,

---

Anders. ÖLA 237/04, p. 6 cited in Veit Erlmann, *Reason and Resonance: A History of Aurality* (New York: Zone Books, 2010), p. 312.
143 Latour, *Pandora's Hope*, p. 298.
144 This process is documented in a longitudinal study that examined musical decision making in preparation for commercial recording. See Daniel Bangert, Dorottya Fabian, Emery Schubert, and Daniel Yeadon, 'Performing Solo Bach: A Case Study of Musical Decision Making,' *Musicae Scientiae*, 18/1 (2014), 35-52. Other studies have also documented this phenomenon, e.g. Roger Chaffin, Gabriela Imreh, and Mary E. Crawford, *Practicing Perfection: Memory and Piano Performance* (Mahwah, NJ: Lawrence Erlbaum, 2002).

analytical—and the proposition to consider the recordings as manifestations of multiple, non-linear, looping interactions in a complex dynamical system that is music performance has been put forth. Through the review of analytical, empirical and experimental research into music performance we realized the need for a more comprehensive approach that would offer an adequately complex and more nuanced account of this multifaceted human activity. My position that both objective and subjective, aural and written (as well as visual) representations and discussions are absolutely essential for a balanced and fair evaluation of what is happening in music performance has also been made clear.

In the following chapters I endeavour to showcase a method that engages with music performance in its complexity. I examine the selected recordings of Bach's solo violin music against this theoretical backdrop and explore the potentials and limits of an academic approach to the study of music performance. Some might readily object that recordings are not performances but I believe they are.[145] Those disputing it generally cite the unnatural environment of the recording studio, the inhibiting effect of the microphone and, above all, the editing processes involved. But in my experience the differences between Arturo Toscanini and Herbert von Karajan or Sviatoslav Richter and Alfred Brendel are fairly clear. According to empirical data I collected in 2006, most recordings are released when all parties are satisfied with it and the majority of soloists would agree that their recordings reflect their ideal performance of the work at the time of recording.[146] Most importantly, recordings are experienced by listeners as performances, in my experience they may even sound different each time one listens to them, and so I make no apologies for studying them as such.

---

[145] For my main reasons see Dorottya Fabian, 'Classical Sound Recordings and Live Performances: Artistic and Analytical Perspectives,' in *Recorded Music: Philosophical and Critical Reflections*, ed. by Mine Doğantan-Dack (London: Middlesex University Press, 2008), pp. 232-260.

[146] Most of these points and findings have now been corroborated by several contributors to *The Cambridge Companion to Recorded Music*, ed. by Nicholas Cook, Eric Clarke, Daniel Leech-Wilkinson, and John Rink (Cambridge: Cambridge University Press, 2009), for instance chapters one-three. See also Susan Tomes, *Beyond the Notes: Journeys with Chamber Music* (Woodbridge: The Boydell Press, 2004).

3. Violinists, Violin Schools and Emerging Trends

To introduce and contextualize the recordings analysed in chapters four to five and to account for cultural, personal and educational influences this chapter starts off by surveying the violinists whose Bach performance is in the focus of attention. Almost all discussions of violinists and their playing visit the issue of violin teachers and schools.[1] As noted by some of these studies, the usefulness of such accounts is doubtful even regarding earlier violinists, but given the greater mobility and internationalization of musical training since the second half of the twentieth century, sorting out influences and delimiting stylistic boundaries are of interest in the present study only to the extent to which these inform the discussion of homogeneity versus plurality of styles or the possible blending of HIP and MSP. While Milsom largely deals with earlier artists, Ornoy provides a "genealogy" of teachers and schools of most of the violinists considered here.[2] Biographical information on most of them is also readily available on the internet and various encyclopaedias. Therefore I provide only a very basic overview, focusing on those violinists who will be mentioned more frequently and on information regarding their Bach-playing. I cite potentially decisive influences and events as well as some violinists' opinions on certain issues

---

1 For instance, David Milsom, *Theory and Practice in Late Nineteenth-Century Violin Performance: An Examination of Style in Performance, 1850-1900* (Aldershot: Ashgate, 2003); Eitan Ornoy, 'Recording Analysis of J. S. Bach's G minor Adagio for Solo Violin (Excerpt): A Case Study,' *JMM: Journal of Music and Meaning*, 6 (Spring 2008); Walter Kolneder, *Amadeus Book of the Violin*, trans. by Reinhard G. Pauly (Pompton Plains, NJ: Amadeus Press, 1998); Dorottya Fabian and Eitan Ornoy, 'Identity in Violin Playing on Records: Interpretation Profiles in Recordings of Solo Bach by Early Twentieth-Century Violinists,' *Performance Practice Review*, 14 (2009), 1-40.

2 Ornoy, 'Recording Analysis,' Table 2, section 2.1.3.

in the "Influence of HIP on MSP" section, in so far as they seem relevant to the main focus: the musical interpretation of Bach's Solos for Violin.

3.1. Violinists

The recordings under study showcase roughly four generations of violinists (cf. Table 1.1). The smallest cohort is the oldest, born during the first three decades of the twentieth century: Oscar Shumsky (1917-2000), Ruggiero Ricci (1918-2012), Jaap Schröder (b.1925), and Gérard Poulet (b.1938). Out of these, the Philadelphia-born **Oscar Shumsky** studied with the famed Leopold Auer and, after his death, with Efrem Zimbalist, but as a child prodigy he was also in close contact with Fritz Kreisler. Later he became a teacher at various US conservatories, including the Curtis Institute of Music (Philadelphia) and also the Juilliard School of Music (New York) from 1953. His Bach recording is interesting because of his reputation among fellow violinists and also because of his association with Glenn Gould through the Stratford Festival in Ontario during the early 1960s. There he played with Gould and the cellist Leonard Rose in all Bach programs as well as other repertoire.[3]

Ruggiero Ricci, like Yehudi Menuhin, was from the West Coast of the United States and, just like him, first studied with Louis Persinger,[4] and then went to study in Europe. He chose to go to Berlin, though, to study with Georg Kulenkampff, rather than George Enescu in Paris, as Menuhin did. Thus he was exposed to the German tradition best represented by Adolf Busch. As with most violinists, Ricci studied with others as well, including Paul Stassevich and Michel Piastro. His distinguished career as virtuoso and promoter of nineteenth-century violin repertoire spanned over seventy-five years. He gave master classes all over the world (including at the Mozarteum in Salzburg) and also taught at Indiana University and the Juilliard, among others. His Bach-playing is represented here by concert recordings from 1988 and 1991 of the A minor Sonata and D minor Partita only, both displaying his celebrated sweet tone and romantically inclined expression.

---

3 Kevin Bazzana, *Wondrous Strange: The Life and Art of Glenn Gould* (Toronto: McClelland and Stewart, 2003), pp. 210-211.

4 Persinger (1887-1966) was trained in Leipzig but also studied with Ysaÿe and Thibaud. He eventually succeeded Auer (in 1930) as professor of violin at Juilliard. Apart from Menuhin and Ricci he also taught Isaac Stern and, more importantly for this study, Almita Vamos, Rachel Barton Pine's teacher.

The Frenchman **Gérard Poulet** studied at the Paris Conservatoire with André Asselin. After winning the Paganini International Competition in 1956 he continued his studies with a series of renowned violinists of the mid-twentieth century, most of whom were also famed for their Bach interpretations: Zino Francescatti, Yehudi Menuhin, Nathan Milstein and Henryk Szeryng. Poulet's recording of the complete set from 1996 is interesting as it has many movements that are lightly bowed and clearly articulated while elsewhere his playing exhibits the hallmarks of MSP.

Jaap Schröder stands out in this oldest group of violinists for being closely associated with the early music movement. He studied at the Amsterdam Conservatory between 1943 and 1947 with Jos de Clerck and with Jean Pasquier at the Ecole Jacques Thibaud in Paris. He joined Gustav Leonhardt, Anner Bylsma and Frans Brüggen around 1960, establishing the Quadro Amsterdam to explore historical performance practices of eighteenth-century music. He became a well-known teacher[5] and chamber musician (e.g. Concerto Amsterdam, Quartetto Esterhazy) of the baroque and classical violin, as well as an orchestral leader (e.g. Academy of Ancient Music). Schröder has lectured widely on historical playing conventions and also published on performing the Bach Solos.[6] His interpretation will often be referred to as it offers an interesting case. Although he was the oldest violinist among HIP specialists who made a recording of the Solos, he did so quite late in his career (1985) and considerably later than the earliest such versions (1977, 1981). His performance thus provides insights into generational boundaries and developments in period violin technique.

The pool of the youngest players, hardly in their late twenties as the first decade of the twenty-first century came to its close, is similarly small: Ilya Gringolts (b.1982), Julia Fischer (b.1983), Sergey Khachatryan (b.1985), and Alina Ibragimova (b.1985). The four of them have diverse paths but some shared backgrounds as well.

Ilya Gringolts went from St Petersburg and the tutelage of Tatiana Liberova and Jeanna Metallidi to the Juilliard and studied with Dorothy DeLay and Itzhak Perlman but then returned to Europe. Currently he resides in Switzerland and is professor of violin at the Basel Hochschule für

---

5   Amsterdam Conservatory from 1963; Basel Schola Cantorum from 1973; and also as guest at Yale University and the Helsinki Sibelius Academy, for instance.

6   Jaap Schröder, *Bach's Solo Violin Works: A Performer's Guide* (London: Yale University Press, 2007); idem, 'Jaap Schröder Discusses Bach's works for Unaccompanied Violin,' *Journal of the Violin Society of America*, 3/3 (Summer 1977), 7-32.

Musik. In an interview with Inge Kjemtrup in 2011 Gringolts claims that he had been "at a crossroads musically, where I was questioning everything" while he was studying with Perlman. "I was not happy with my playing in many respects," he says.

> I was looking around, trying to absorb a lot of influences and trying to make sense of them. I don't know if any teacher would have helped at that point. He was there for me, but he didn't really know how to handle me at that time[…].[7]

In this same interview Gringolts states that his Bach Solos recording was a "real transition, meaning that I just started moving in one direction and I was still moving as I was recording. But later I did really explore period performance and Baroque playing." The "transitory" stage of his approach to Bach at the time of making the recording under study here will be evidenced and commented upon on multiple occasions. His onward move towards HIP can be witnessed in his collaboration with Masaaki Suzuki, performing the Bach accompanied sonatas.[8]

Julia Fischer mostly remained in her native Germany, her main teacher being Helge Thelen. Her 2005 recording was well received by reviewers who praised the recording's "immaculate finish" and Fischer's "ability to trace a smooth, even line" while desiring "more in the way of expressive flexibility."[9] As we will see, her approach on this disk to interpreting Bach is much closer to the traditional MSP style and, like Sergey Khachatryan's from 2010, somewhat fades into grey eminence in comparison with many others issued around the same time. As the reviewer in *Gramophone* noted, Fischer's performances "are in general lightly pressured, leisurely and at times rather austere […] a sort of half-way house between period-style asceticism and a more emotive style associated with the various twentieth-century schools."[10]

---

7   'Ilya Gringolts: The Man, the Myth, the Musician on the Move,' Interview by Inge Kjemptrup, posted in February 2011, available at http://www.allthingsstrings.com/layout/set/print/News/Interviews-Profiles/Ilya-Gringolts-The-Man-the-Myth-the-Musician-on-the-Move [last accessed October 2015].

8   Available at http://www.youtube.com/watch?v=fY-rbsei_rY. Apparently they played the entire set at the Verbier Festival in 2010. I thank Daniel Bangert for both these references.

9   Rob Cowan, 'Bach: Violin Sonatas and Partitas, BWV1001-BWV1006, Julia Fischer *vn*, Pentatone PTC 5186072 (150 minutes DDD),' *Gramophone*, 89/993 (June 2005), 72.

10 Ibid. I am not sure what "period-style asceticism" might be but if it refers to literalism then the recordings should be labelled classical-modernist. It is not at all in what is regarded HIP style and such slippage can contribute to considerable misrepresentation.

Khachatryan is Armenian but has been living in Germany since 1993, when he was eight, and in 2000 became the youngest ever winner of the Jan Sibelius competition. In relation to his debut compact disk with EMI the reviewer in *Gramophone* noted already in 2003, that his Bach performance "is impressive [...] for its polish and fine rhythmic control but Kachatryan does have something to learn about playing eighteenth-century music—in particular to use the slurs to add light and shade to the phrasing, rather than ironing out the difference between slurred and separate notes."[11] The advice was apparently not taken on board, for the disk of the Six Solos recorded seven years later shows very similar ironed-out traits.

Of this youngest generation only **Alina Ibragimova**'s set exhibits the influence of HIP. She was born in Russia and studied with Valentina Korolkova in Moscow before moving to London and joining the Menuhin School under the tutelage of Natasha Boyarskaya. Later she completed her training at the Guildhall and the Royal College of Music (under Gordan Nikolitch). She also studied with Christian Tetzlaff, which is noteworthy given all the observations I will make about his two recordings throughout the book but especially in chapter five. Ibragimova's interest in HIP is most unequivocally demonstrated by her founding of Chiaroscuro, a period-instrument string quartet that focuses on performing the classical repertoire.

In between the oldest and youngest performers represented by the recordings, there are two further generations: those born in the 1940s to early 1960s and those born between the mid-1960s and the end of the 1970s. Discussion will inevitably centre on those players who are either better known or contributed interpretations of particular note. From the first group these include Sergiu Luca (1943-2010), Sigiswald Kuijken (b.1944), Gidon Kremer (b.1947), Elizabeth Wallfisch (b.1952), Monica Huggett (b.1953), Viktoria Mullova (b.1959) and to a lesser extent Itzhak Perlman (b.1945), Lara Lev (birth year not known) and James Buswell (not known). From the younger group Thomas Zehetmair (b.1961), Richard Tognetti (b.1965), Christian Tetzlaff (b. 1966), Rachel Podger (b.1968), Lara St John (b.1971), Isabelle Faust (b.1973), Rachel Barton Pine (b.1974), James Ehnes (b.1976) and Hilary Hahn (b.1979) will be repeatedly mentioned.

---

11 Duncan Druce, 'Sergey Khachatryan—An Engaging and Persuasively Virtuosic Debut from a Young Violinist to note EMI Debut 575684-2 (71 minutes DDD),' *Gramophone*, 80/962 (January 2003), 56.

Originally from Rumania, **Sergiu Luca** lived in Israel from 1950 and later studied with Max Rostal in Europe before emigrating to the United States of America, where he studied with Galamian at the Curtis Institute and won the Leventritt Award before turning to period instruments and becoming a pioneer of HIP. His recordings of Mozart's sonatas with Malcolm Bilson are no less revolutionary than his solo Bach; each being the first of its kind by far.[12] The Belgian **Sigiswald Kuijken**, on the other hand, remained close to home, joining the innovative Flemish-Dutch branch of the early music movement during the 1960s-1970s. He eventually became a seminal figure not just as one of the first professors of baroque violin and consequently the teacher of many later players, but also as founding conductor of La Petite Bande (1971) and as a chamber musician in several projects involving Gustav Leonhardt, among others.

Monica Huggett first studied at the Royal Academy of Music (London) with Manoug Parikian and Kato Havas and later became one of the first students of Kuijken at the Royal Conservatory in The Hague. She was a close associate of Ton Koopman, with whom she established the Amsterdam Baroque Orchestra and whose influence she frequently acknowledges. Apart from her solo career she is also well known as a professor of baroque violin (in Bremen and, since 2008, also at Juilliard) and as a concertmaster and conductor of period orchestras. Huggett has frequently mentioned in interviews her youthful desire to be a rock musician and her reluctance to conform.[13] Her recording from 1995 is infused by this strong sense of individuality through and through. Hence it is worth noting further what she tells us about her life and inspirations.

As a kid, Hugget's brother introduced her to jazz giants Charlie Parker and John Coltrane while later she became a fan of the Beatles, Jimi Hendrix and the Beach Boys. Most importantly, "[f]rom an early age I didn't like the way that I had to play if I was playing with a big Steinway. It wasn't my idea of what a violin should sound like and I always felt that the instrument

---

12 Wolfgang Amadeus Mozart, *Sonatas for Fortepiano and Violin* (3 vols), Malcolm Bilson, Sergiu Luca. Nonesuch Digital 9 79112 (New York: Electra/Asylum/Nonesuch, 1985). Luca's untimely death in December 2010 cut short his plan to record the Beethoven sonatas, which I for one was awaiting with great expectations and curiosity.

13 Lindsay Kemp, 'Going Solo—Monica Huggett on Playing Solo Bach,' *Gramophone*, 75/897 (January 1998), 16; Naomi Sadler, 'Unpredictable Passions—Monica Huggett [Profile],' *The Strad*, 110/1310 (June 1999), 595. Shulamit Kleinerman, 'A Mix of Images: Women in Baroque Music,' *Early Music America*, 10/4 (Winter 2004), 28-34 (pp. 31-32); Laurence Vittes, 'From Rock to Bach—Monica Huggett,' *Strings*, 21/6 (January 2007), 53-57.

had more possibilities in terms of tone quality and nuance."[14] She felt immediately happier when a friend "said my style would suit a gut fiddle, and she lent me one. "Oh yes," I thought, "this is really nice.""[15] Huggett also notes how much she admired "Henryk Szeryng's amazing set of Bach (Sony MP2K 46721) for its "mind-bogglingly [technical] perfect[ion]"[16] but how, at the time of recording the set, she rather took inspiration from jazz-rock guitarist John McLaughlin's album *My Goals Beyond*. Apparently the "first recording she heard of authentic instruments" was Rameau's *Pièces de Clavecin en Concert* performed by Gustav Leonhardt with Sigiswald and Wieland Kuijken (Teldec 9031-77618-2).[17] Characteristically Huggett is not afraid to admit listening to and imitating others' performances and recordings.

> I believe that imitation is the sincerest form of flattery, and I'm not afraid to imitate something that really works. Some musicians have got a thing about not ever sounding like other artists, but that doesn't worry me at all. If I think somebody else did something really well, I'll happily copy it. But funnily enough, I generally find that the end result doesn't sound like any of them.[18]

Perhaps most tellingly, Huggett sees

> Bach as this big North German with huge hands who could stretch a tenth and play all the parts in between, a great big chap who was difficult, passionate, overwhelming and larger-than-life. His music should be full-blooded; you shouldn't be feeling 'I mustn't do this, it's too much,' but really go for it![19]

Huggett's performance of the set certainly "goes for it." She often takes slow tempos paying attention to every little detail but also joyously plays around with certain dance movements, like the E Major Gavotte en Rondeau, adding a showy cadenza. Elsewhere she deepens the music's sad or melancholy character through soulful embellishments (e.g. D minor Sarabanda) or rapturous tempo and rhythmic flexibilities. Her unique style will be the focus of attention in the final part of chapter five.

The similarly flamboyant **Elizabeth Wallfisch** (only one year senior to Huggett) was born in Australia but also trained in the Royal Academy of

---

14 Kemp, 'Going Solo,' p. 16.
15 Vittes, 'From Rock to Bach,' p. 54.
16 Sadler, 'Unpredictable Passions,' p. 595.
17 Ibid.
18 Kemp, 'Going Solo,' p. 16.
19 Ibid.

Music under Frederick Grinke. Currently residing in England, she became a specialist HIP violinist during the early 1970s, and is renowned for founding the Locatelli Trio and for her appearances with the Australian Brandenburg Orchestra, the Hanover Band and many other European period-instrument orchestras. She also teaches baroque violin at the Royal Conservatory in The Hague and the Royal Academy of Music in London. She recorded the set just a few years after Huggett did and her reading is almost the polar opposite of Huggett's; much faster, more virtuosic, strongly accented and displaying an entirely different timbre.

Although approximate contemporaries of the above named players, the artistic trajectories of Perlman, Kremer, Mullova, Lev and Buswell are quite different. **Itzhak Perlman** was thirteen years old when he was "talent-hunted" from Israel by Ed Sullivan for his touring show, "Cavalcade of Stars," which eventually led to studies with Ivan Galamian and Dorothy DeLay at Juilliard. He was barely eighteen when he won the Leventritt Award in 1964, an achievement that launched his solo career. For many years he has taught at Brooklyn College and at the Perlman Program, a summer school on Long Island established by his wife. In 1998 he started co-teaching with DeLay at Juilliard, eventually succeeding her.

Gidon Kremer was David Oistrakh's prized student before he emigrated to the West, a fully formed virtuoso soloist, in the late 1970s. He followed his own path, playing the staple repertoire of classical and romantic concertos, commissioning and promoting new works, collaborating with diverse conductors (from Herbert von Karajan to Nikolaus Harnoncourt) and chamber orchestras, and eventually forming his own ensemble, Kremerata Baltica, in 1996. He is known for his musical integrity, wide ranging repertoire and promotion of new music.

Lara Lev and **Viktoria Mullova** could have followed a similar path, both having been trained in Soviet Conservatoires: Lev studied with Yuri Yankelevich and Vladimir Spivakov in Moscow, while Mullova's teacher was Leonid Kogan. Lev played in orchestras before taking a teaching post in Helsinki during the 1990s and then joining the Chamber Music Faculty of Juilliard in 2008. In contrast, Mullova focused on solo performance: she won the Sibelius competition in 1980 and the Gold Medal at the Tchaikovsky Competition in 1982, before defecting to the West in 1983. She became an internationally known soloist and over time completely overhauled her playing of baroque music as evidenced by her three recordings under study here, the B minor Partita from 1987, the three Partitas from 1992-1993 and the complete set from 2007-2008.[20]

James Buswell, currently professor of violin at the New England Conservatory (Boston, Massachusetts), initially trained at Juilliard with Ivan Galamian and then worked at both the Lincoln Centre in New York and the Music School of Indiana University. His interest in Bach's Solos led to a documentary for the PBS Network and a recording on the Centaur label. He is highly respected for his dedication to new music and performances of the chamber repertoire. His recording of the Solos is of special interest because he was one of the last teachers of the Canadian Lara St John, whose interpretation will often be mentioned.

Among the younger group of mid-career violinists Rachel Podger (b.1968) and Ingrid Matthews (b.1966) are baroque specialists while Thomas Zehetmair (b.1961), Richard Tognetti (b.1965), Christian Tetzlaff (b.1966), Benjamin Schmid (b.1968), Lara St John (b.1971), Isabelle Faust (b.1973) and Rachel Barton Pine (b.1974) are not, even though some of them may opt for a baroque bow and gut strings, or speak of being influenced by the tenets of HIP, as I will detail later.

In terms of his age, the Austrian **Thomas Zehetmair** could belong to the previous, older group. However, his radical performing style makes it more natural to regard him as belonging to this third generation of violinists. Among non-specialists he was one of the first to "cross-over" and learn from Nikolaus Harnoncourt's classes while at the Salzburg Mozarteum, eventually making a recording with the conductor (Mozart Haffner Serenade, Teldec 1986). Nowadays Zehetmair works mostly as a conductor but earlier in his career as violinist he undertook master classes with Nathan Milstein and Max Rostal.

Benjamin Schmid, also an Austrian, is renowned for playing jazz as well as classical music. He tends to mention the influence of Yehudi Menuhin and Stéphane Grappelli, and studied in Salzburg, Vienna and at the Curtis Institute. His recording exhibits an interesting, at times rather idiosyncratic, combination of MSP and HIP features.

The Germans Tetzlaff and Faust both have international reputations and both play the gamut of the standard violin repertoire. **Christian Tetzlaff** first studied with Uwe-Martin Haiberg (Lübeck Hochschule für

---

20 The details of all these recordings are provided in the Discography.

Musik) and then with Walter Levin at the University of Cincinnati. He is a regular soloist with many orchestras and has an extensive discography covering works from Bach to Bartók and beyond. The younger **Isabelle Faust** is one of the more original players on the current scene. She studied with Denes Zsigmondy and Christoph Poppen, whom she often cites as inspirational. Having established her first string quartet at the age of 11, she continues to be an active chamber musician. In 2004 she was appointed professor of violin at the Berlin University of the Arts. Faust is well-known for her interest in exploring different musical idioms and new repertoires, including contemporary music. She has also collaborated with performers who specialise in baroque and classical music and for her recording of three of the Bach Solos she worked closely with fortepianist-harpsichordist Andreas Staier. The second disk of her Bach Solos (containing the G minor and A minor Sonatas and the B minor Partita) came out only in 2012; too late for me to include it in the current discussion. Suffice to say perhaps, that she tends to choose rather fast tempos in all movements on this second disk that gives the interpretation a rather hurried and somewhat routine feel in spite of the original added embellishments in the A minor Andante and B minor Sarabande movements. The tone could also be warmer although this may reflect recording technology more than her playing. Overall, I find Faust's first disk containing the D minor and E Major Partitas and the C Major Sonata much more revelatory and convincing. All my comments regarding her interpretation refer to that disk from 2009 unless specifically indicated otherwise.

One of the first teachers of the Australian **Richard Tognetti** was William Primrose (1904-1982), the famed viola player, once a pupil of Eugène Ysaÿe. Perhaps more influential were Tognetti's teachers at the Sydney Conservatorium High School (Alice Waten) and at the Bern Conservatoire (Igor Ozim). Since his return to Australia in 1989 Tognetti has been the leader and artistic director of the Australian Chamber Orchestra, an ensemble that plays a wide variety of repertoire (often especially transcribed by Tognetti or crossing boundaries with world music and other styles) on modern instruments. He has made several recordings as a soloist too, including Bach's complete works for violin (Solos, Accompanied Sonatas and Concertos). For his recording of the Bach Solos, Tognetti chose lower tuning, gut E and A strings and a classical period bow. Reviewing it for *Gramophone*, Duncan Druce noted his varied bow strokes, limited use of vibrato and "persuasive ornamentation." He described Tognetti's interpretation as conveying

> remarkable freedom and imaginative range, stemming from what is clearly a deep understanding of eighteenth-century performance style. The set, in fact, offers a closer comparison with the best period instrument versions than with a modern player such as Julia Fischer who, by the side of Tognetti, sounds smooth and bland, for all her sensitivity and stylistic awareness. […] His view of the music is so well founded that he is able to communicate with an air of complete spontaneity.[21]

In 1992, Chicago-based **Rachel Barton Pine** became the youngest American to win the gold medal at the Leipzig International Johann Sebastian Bach competition. A virtuoso musician, she performs her own cadenzas; prepares transcriptions and arrangements of all sorts of music; promotes the music of little known composers and black musicians; and plays with heavy metal bands (e.g. Earthen Grave) and early music groups (e.g. Trio Settecento). When performing baroque music, she opts for a period bow and gut strings. She issued one commercial disk containing the G minor Sonata and D minor Partita but she kindly made available to me two of her live concert recordings of the complete set: a series of radio broadcast concerts from 1999 and a marathon single day event (afternoon and evening) in 2007.

Barton Pine's close Canadian contemporary **Lara St John** started learning the violin with Richard Lawrence in her home town, London Ontario, and later studied with Linda Cerone in Cleveland and Gérard Jarry in Paris. She received her degree from the Curtis Institute (studying with Felix Galimir and Arnold Steinhardt) and continued at the Moscow Conservatoire. This was followed by further studies at the Guildhall in London (under David Takeno), the Mannes College in New York (again with Felix Galimir) and finally the New England Conservatoire in Boston with James Buswell. Her Bach Solo album was described by one critic as "wild, idiosyncratic, and gripping."[22] Her interpretation of the G minor Adagio and A minor Grave are improvisatory in character and the fugues are light and fast; there are also a few idiosyncratic moments in other movements that I will discuss in chapter four. St John plays with a modern bow but uses little vibrato

---

21 Duncan Druce, 'Reviews: Bach 3 Sonatas and 3 Partitas BWV1001-BWV1006, Richard Tognetti *vn*, ABC Classics CD ABC 4768051 (145 minutes: DDD),' *Gramophone*, 84/1010 (October 2006), 80.

22 *Los Angeles Times*, 9 December 2007. Available at http://www.larastjohn.com/ancalagon#

when playing Bach; her repertoire is wide-ranging but remains primarily within the concert tradition. In that she is less like Barton Pine and closer to Ehnes and Hahn, who represent the most traditional mainstream within this group of violinists.

James Ehnes studied at the Juilliard with Sally Thomas, graduating in 1997. He is one of the most prolific recording violinists of the past decade, covering mostly nineteenth- and twentieth-century works. According to his website (http://www.jamesehnes.com), *The Guardian* described his playing as "effusively lyrical [...] hair raising virtuosity." His 1999 recording of the Solos has all the hallmarks of MSP at the end of the twentieth century, but his more recent recording of the accompanied sonatas (with harpsichordist Luc Beauséjour) indicates that he too has started to adopt characteristics of the HIP style.

In contrast, **Hilary Hahn** remains true to her upbringing and initial aesthetic ideals. She studied with Klara Berkovich (who taught in the Leningrad School for the Musically Gifted for twenty-five years previously) from the age of five and with Jascha Brodsky for six years at the Curtis Institute. In a 2003 interview Hahn stated that although she "keeps abreast" with her own generation, she feels closer to "an older period, the artists of the same generation of my teacher and musical grand-father, Jascha Brodsky."[23] This is indeed quite clear when listening to her recording of three of the Solos (1999) and also a much more recent disk of Bach arias with violin obligato (2010).[24]

Out of the two HIP specialists in this generation of violinists **Rachel Podger** will feature more than Ingrid Matthews, partly because her disk came out earlier (1998 versus 2001) and also because it contains more variations from the score.[25] Both of them have many recordings to their credit but Matthews seems to appear more frequently as leader of ensembles whereas Podger is primarily a soloist and guest director who also teaches at several institutions (including the Guildhall, the Royal Academy of Music, the Royal Welsh College and the Royal Danish Academy of Music). Her

---

23 Michael Quinn, 'Bach to the Future' [Hilary Hahn Interview], *Gramophone*, 81/973 (Awards/Special Issue 2003), 30-31.
24 Bach—Violin and Voice, CD. Hilary Hahn (violin), Mattias Goerne and Christine Schäfer (voice), Munich Chamber Orchestra, Alexander Liebreich (conductor), Deutsche Grammophon 477 8092.
25 Nevertheless one critic considered the latter his "favourite complete set of these works on either period or modern instruments" and praised Matthews' version as a "superb recording" and "top recommendation" (Joseph Magil, 'Bach: Solo Violin Sonatas and Partitas' [Ingrid Matthews], American Record Guide, 63/4 (Jul/Aug 2000), 83-84.

teachers at the Guildhall were David Takeno, Micaela Comberti and Pauline Scott. The American **Ingrid Matthews** studied at Indiana University with Josef Gingold and Stanley Ritchie. She won the Erwin Bodky International Early Music Competition in 1989 and served as leader of the Seattle Baroque Orchestra between 1994 and 2012, which she co-founded with harpsichordist Byron Schenkman. Apart from baroque music she has also made recordings of contemporary works.

3.2. Violin Schools

Having surveyed some of the main violinists in my sample, a few words about so-called violin schools are also in order. Traditionally discussions of violin playing distinguished a German and a Franco-Belgian school of playing, the latter subsuming aspects of the Italian style. Nineteenth- and early twentieth-century representatives of the former were Joseph Joachim and his disciples, while the French school was embodied by Henri Vieuxtemps and Eugène Ysaÿe. The German school was regarded as analytical and sober and was epitomized by the "Berlin circle" and Carl Flesch's famous studio in the first half of the twentieth century. The French school on the other hand was considered flamboyant and virtuosic, cultivating warmth of sound. Around the turn of the twentieth century a Russian school came to the fore headed by Leopold Auer at the St Petersburg Conservatoire. From his classes came such violinists as Jascha Heifetz, Misha Elman, Efrem Zimbalist, and also Nathan Milstein.[26] Auer (1845-1930) himself studied mainly with Joachim, but stated that it was Jacob Dont in Vienna who "gave me the foundation of my violin technique."[27] Auer chose teaching rather than playing at the age of only twenty-three when he was appointed to the St Petersburg Conservatory; and later famously refused to premiere Tchaikovsky's Violin Concerto, leaving the honour to Adolph Brodsky (1851-1929).[28] He remained in his post for nearly 50 years, until the

---

26 Apart from Auer's studio in St Petersburg, Piotr Stoliarsky's classes in Odessa (of which Milstein was a "graduate") also contributed significantly to the notion of a Russian School, especially since his star pupil, David Oistrakh, remained in the Soviet Union and continued the tradition locally, developing it into a national "industry" while nurturing many competition-winning virtuosos.

27 Auer's memoir cited in Boris Schwarz, *Great Masters of the Violin: From Corelli and Vivaldi to Stern, Zukerman and Perlman* (New York: A Touchstone Book, 1983), p. 414.

28 Auer did perform publicly throughout his life, including concerts at Carnegie Hall in his 70s, but his fame rested on his reputation as a pedagogue.

Bolshevik revolution in 1917 forced him to move to the United States. There he continued to teach for another twelve or so years, privately and at the Juilliard School as well as at the Curtis Institute.

According to Nathan Milstein, Auer hardly ever demonstrated during a lesson and neglected to teach technique: he encouraged his students to use their head, not their hands.[29] This may be one reason why all his famous students sound so different. Milstein also claims that the students "almost never played Bach in Auer's class. Bach was not at all popular in Russia then. […] Auer wasn't interested in listening to Bach. He didn't know what to say, and he said practically nothing."[30]

Apparently Auer was "deliberately vague as to how to grip the bow" relying instead on "the physical structure of the student's arm."[31] Yet the so-called Russian bow hold is often linked to Auer because Carl Flesch observed it in the playing of Heifetz and Elman, two of Auer's best known pupils. This bow hold places the index finger lower and more over the bow while the Franco-Belgian grip has the index finger positioned so that the bow touches it around the middle joint.[32] In an article about his career, Schröder is cited explaining that it was the French tradition of bowing that attracted him to study with Pasquier.

> I observed how their bows not only sang, but also talked and danced. The extreme flexibility of their fingers on the bow shaped the sound with refined articulation. Their bow strokes could abruptly change speed and intensity at any part of the bow; slow languid movements were suddenly followed by biting spiccato produced by the finger joints of the bow hand. Their tone palette was full of surprises, from whispering sounds to an open and bright

---

29   Nathan Milstein and Solomon Volkov, *From Russia to the West: The Musical Memoirs and Reminiscences of Nathan Milstein* (New York: Limelight Editions, 1990), p. 22. This opinion contrasts that of Carl Flesch, who believed "that for Auer violin playing came first, while musical considerations were of subordinate significance. Technique and tone were his main concerns; rhythm, agogics and dynamics took second place. The typical Auer pupil values sensuous sonority and an attractive smoothness of tone much more highly than the differences between strong and weak beats and the shaping of musical ideas as such." Carl Flesch, *The Memoirs of Carl Flesch*, trans. by Hans Keller (Bois de Boulogne: Centenary Edition, 1973), p. 254.

30   Milstein, *From Russia to the West*, p. 23. Milstein's impression may be correct, but Auer does discuss the Bach Solos (especially the Ciaccona) in his book on violin repertoire. See Leopold Auer, *Violin Master Works and their Interpretation* (New York: Carl Fischer, 2012), pp. 21-29.

31   Schwarz, *Great Masters*, p. 419.

32   See, for instance, Robin Stowell, 'Technique and Performing Practice,' in *The Cambridge Companion to the Violin*, ed. by Robin Stowell (Cambridge: Cambridge University Press, 1992), pp. 122-142 (p. 134).

tone that has always been a hallmark of French string playing. I noticed that Jean's wrist and elbow were not high, that his index finger was clearly steering the bow and had absolute control over the tone production.[33]

According to Schwarz, photographs show Auer holding the bow with the Franco-Belgian grip (so named by Flesch as well). He also claims that, if anybody, perhaps Wieniawski held the bow the way that came to be known as the Russian grip. He may have introduced it to Russia when teaching at St Petersburg during the nineteenth century.[34] Later in his teaching career Flesch advocated the Russian grip; although it makes bowing less flexible, he still regarded it to be superior to the Franco-Belgian and old German grips because it produces a bigger tone.[35] The rather uniform bowing typical of much violin playing on record from the second half of the twentieth century may be a result of this grip gaining ground through Flesch's pupils and their pupils. However, bow hold may not be the main reason. According to pictures in Galamian's method book, he seems to be teaching the Franco-Belgian grip.[36] Perlman also describes his grip as Franco-Belgian.[37] Furthermore, some players say they use both types of bow hold. Aaron Rosand, for instance, uses the Franco-Belgian grip for "Mozart, Bach, and pyrotechnical works."[38] Looseness of wrist, bow pressure and speed all contribute to tone and variation in tone.[39] Without close study of visual documentation one can only speculate the constituents contributing to the impression of a more uniform style of bowing during the 1950s to

---

33 Kjell-Ake Harmen, 'French Master' [Profile: Jaap Schröder], *The Strad*, 113/1349 (September 2002), 954-957 (p. 954).
34 Schwarz, *Great Masters*, p. 336.
35 Carl Flesch, *The Art of Violin Playing: I. Technique in General*, trans. by Frederick H. Martens (New York: Carl Fischer, 2000), p. 51.
36 Ivan Galamian, *Principles of Violin Playing and Teaching*, 3rd edn, with postscript by Elizabeth A. H. Green (Englewood-Cliff: Prentice Hall, 1985 [1962]), pp. 45-53.
37 [Itzhak Perlman], 'Itzhak on Bow Grip,' available at http://www.youtube.com/watch?v=6r0WW-KN6VM
38 [Aaron Rosand], 'Aaron Rosand on How to Produce a Beautiful Tone,' available at http://www.thestrad.com/latest/blogs/aaron-rosand-on-how-to-produce-a-beautiful-tone. I am indebted to Daniel Bangert for this and the previous references. He also cautioned about attributing too much to a potential preference for the Russian bow hold during the second half of the twentieth century.
39 According to Eales, Paul Rolland's original thesis, *Basic Principles of Violin Playing* (American String Teacher's Association, 1959), provides "superlative descriptions" regarding the "physical factors of tone-quality" including "proximity to fingerboard, bow speed, bow hair, bow distribution, vibrato, bow weight and finger articulation, as well as instruments and accessories." Adrian Eales, 'The Fundamentals of Violin Playing and Teaching,' in *The Cambridge Companion to the Violin*, ed. by Robin Stowell (Cambridge, Cambridge University Press, 1992), pp. 92-121 (p. 104).

1980s period compared to the beginning of the century and since its last decade. The aesthetic ideal regarding a big, even sound may have been the most important driving force behind it.

Many Russian-Jewish violinists escaped to the United States of America at the end of the First World War and thereafter thus making the US the new home of the "Russian school," whatever that might actually be. Among them was Jascha Brodsky (1907-1997), who became professor at the Curtis Institute, a music academy of equal prestige to the Juilliard School, thus influencing innumerable players (e.g. Hilary Hahn, as noted earlier). It is important to note, however, that Brodsky studied not only with his father but also with Lucien Capet and Eugène Ysaÿe, two key figures of the "Franco-Belgian School," before moving to Philadelphia in 1930 (on advice from Mischa Elman) to study further with Efrem Zimbalist at the "newly founded Curtis Institute of Music."[40] So perhaps rather than a special technique or grip, the main attribute of the Russian school may well be its fairly stern pedagogical approach, a method that was typical of Auer as well as Flesch and many less famous teachers coming from Eastern Europe. This is related in numerous first-hand accounts and reminiscences, including Perlman's:

> With my first teacher, who was of Russian background, I would play something and she would say, "That's wrong. You do this and you do that." It was more like you'll play and I'll give you instructions, and Galamian was in a sense the same way.[41]

So the "American school," dominated by Juilliard and Curtis, essentially became a continuation of the Russian school established by Auer. The two most famous and influential teachers associated with these institutions were Ivan Galamian (1903-1981) and Dorothy DeLay (1917-2002). According to Perlman, who studied at the Juilliard School with both of them for about seven years, "they had different approaches to teaching, but similar systems technically speaking, especially with the bow and the way it works. The goals of the two were basically similar — certainly technically they were."[42] Both DeLay and Galamian placed special emphasis on tone production

---

40 Allan Kozinn, 'Jascha Brodsky, 90, Violinist at Curtis Institute' [Obituary], *The New York Times* [Arts], 6 March 1997. Available at http://www.nytimes.com/1997/03/06/arts/jascha-brodsky-90-violinist-at-curtis-institute.html
41 Cited in Barbara Lourie Sand, *Teaching Genius: Dorothy DeLay and the Making of a Musician* (New Jersey: Amadeus, 2000), p. 58.
42 A 1995 interview cited in Sand, *Teaching Genius*, p. 188.

and projection. According to Arnold Steinhardt, a pupil of Galamian, his students "were given two basic principles which he delivered with a heavy Russian accent: one was 'More bow' and the other was 'Play so that the last person in the last row of the hall can hear you.'"[43] Other pupils also emphasized this aspect of Galamian's teaching: "He stressed warmth and good sound," noted David Nadien, while James Buswell stated: "Galamian had a revolutionary technique for the bow arm [...] the ability to project the violin sound at a time when halls are getting bigger [...] has become ever more critical." DeLay agreed that Galamian's "students had good sound. Big healthy sounds."[44] DeLay seemed to have shared this principle with Galamian as her training routine focused a lot on developing sound, including vibrato. Cornelius Duffalo remembered how when he first came to her, he was directed to develop "a clean sound, a nice, clean, beautiful sound. Then we worked on vibrato." Peter Oundijan also noted that DeLay gave him "terrific vibrato exercises," while he "never heard [Galamian] teach vibrato." According to Duffalo, DeLay expected her students to "work on every note so that every note has a beautiful beginning, a beautiful middle, and connects beautifully into the next note."[45]

Where they differed was their pedagogy. The Armenian Galamian was educated in pre-revolutionary Moscow at the Philharmonic School by former Auer student, Konstantin Mostras, followed by a brief period with Lucien Capet in Paris between 1922 and 1924. Although he performed for a while, his focus had soon become teaching, first at the Russian Conservatory in Paris and from 1937 in New York. He eventually joined the faculties of both the Juilliard School (1946) and the Curtis Institute (1944) where he remained until his death in 1981. According to Sand, he "instructed and *intimidated* two entire generations of violinists" during his near forty years of tenure, and "his influence on performance style continues undiminished."[46] Sources agree that his teaching style was "old school authoritarian," focusing on technical work and leaving nothing to chance. He believed that anybody could become a fine violinist if only they practised ("suffered through exercise") and therefore "the first goal must

---

43 Sand, *Teaching Genius*, p. 50. Both of these principles had lasting impact on overall performing styles contributing to a kind of homogeneity in interpretations that stems first and foremost from the aim to project a big, even sound (see also Mullova's and Gringolts' comments cited later in this chapter).
44 Ibid., pp. 50-51, 53.
45 Ibid., pp. 58, 113-114.
46 Ibid., p. 43, emphasis added.

be perfect control of the instrument."[47] According to Isaac Stern "it was never his forte or basic interest to teach a very large musical style" because he believed that the violinist's musical personality could be developed later, once their technical command had been achieved.[48]

These aesthetic ideals and pedagogical views are important factors contributing to the much lamented homogeneity in classical music performance during the second half of the twentieth century. Leaving nothing to chance, focusing on technique rather than style and expression hinders spontaneity and exploration of what a composition may require to sound unique. Assuming that many other teachers had similar approaches, it becomes questionable whether it was primarily the demand of the recording industry that fostered uniformity and precision and discouraged risk-taking and experimentation in performance. Conservatoires and competition judges might have played a more crucial role.

Although sharing a similar aesthetic and technical outlook, the American DeLay was the complete opposite of Galamian when it came to pedagogy. She was motherly and had a holistic approach to developing not just technique but the musician and the personality as well. Not that she was less methodical or lenient. She provided her charges with practice sheets that mapped out the tasks of a five-hour daily routine.[49] But she was interested in teaching her students how to think and how to become independent musicians. She would constantly probe them with questions like "Well, what do you think of that phrase? What could the composer want with such a passage? Why should it sound like this? Why don't you experiment a little with bowing until you are satisfied with the sound?" She also routinely advised them "to get hold of as many recordings of a work as they can […] to compare the various performance styles."[50] Comparing her approach to Galamian's, DeLay once remarked that having come from a traditional Armenian family where

---

[47] Galamian in Samuel Applebaum, *The Way They Play: Illustrated Discussions with Famous Artists and Teachers*, Book 1 (Neptune, NJ: Paganini Publications, 1983), p. 340.

[48] Stern is cited in Sand, *Teaching Genius*, p. 55. Apart from Sand's book such information transpires from articles in *The Strad* and also *Time Magazine* ('Violinists: Cry Now, Play Later' (06 December, 1968), available at http://content.time.com/time/magazine/article/0,9171,844647,00.html; and in Schwarz, *Great Masters*. Galamian's teaching is also discussed by Pauline Scott, former teacher at the Guildhall, on *The Strad* blog site, posted on 26 February 2013, available at http://www.thestrad.com/cpt-latests/pauline-scott-recalls-ivan-galamians-inspirational-teaching/

[49] Sand, *Teaching Genius*, p. 53.

[50] Ibid., pp. 57-58, 44.

the father's word is law [...] Mr Galamian felt that formalities must be adhered to and that in a situation with a child, he was the authority—that children were there to do as they were told. I just don't feel that way about children, but then I'm an American and I'm a woman, and I have two children of my own.[51]

Her goal was to get inside the pupil, to help them find their own solution. Whether her students ended up being or sounding more individual than those who only studied with Galamian is beyond the scope of my investigations here because very few of them have recorded the Bach Solos. The lesson that bears significance for the present discussion is DeLay's and Galamian's shared principle of aesthetics and technique, which was rooted in a beautifully controlled, even, well-projected, warm sound. Given the reputation of the Juilliard School as "the real seat of stringed instrument power" in terms of "producing solo virtuosos," the influence of this ideal should not be underestimated.[52]

Meanwhile, on the European Continent the pre-war era was dominated by the equally famous Carl Flesch in Berlin and George Enescu in Paris. After the Second World War various renowned music institutions have carried the torch for international "best practice" in violin playing and pedagogy. As the biographies above show, the most important of these have been the Guildhall, the Royal College and Royal Academy of Music; the Salzburg Mozarteum, and the conservatories in Amsterdam and The Hague. The last two institutions were also instrumental in pioneering the institutionalized training of historical performing practices.

The very first school to teach specialization in "early music" was the Schola Cantorum in Basel (established in 1933), where Leonhardt completed his studies in 1950.[53] The Schola developed curricula; provided a forum for workshops, master classes and concerts; and brought together many continental musicians interested in reviving earlier performing practices. It was there that the Los Angeles based Sol Babitz, a much neglected and maligned violinist pioneer of the movement, was given the opportunity to demonstrate his findings regarding articulation and bowing. These masterclasses inspired the post-war generation. He was also invited by

---

51   Ibid., p. 52.
52   Ibid., p. 42.
53   Some of its history is recaptured in Dorottya Fabian, *Bach Performance Practice, 1945-1975: A Comprehensive Review of Sound Recordings and Literature* (Aldershot: Ashgate, 2003), pp. 30-31. See also Hans Oesch, *Die Musikacademie der Stadt Basel* (Basel: Schwabe, 1967).

the Kuijken Quartet to give lecture demonstrations in The Hague.[54] This openness and rapid embracing of the period instrument movement on the Continent meant that during the 1970s and early 1980s Amsterdam and The Hague were the places to go if one wanted to study harpsichord playing or to learn to play the baroque version of a string or wind instrument. From 1973 the Salzburg Mozarteum also offered courses in early music theory taught by Nikolaus Harnoncourt.[55]

Decca saw the commercial success of the continental groups and, apparently, wanted to recreate it in England. Christopher Hogwood recounted in an interview how the company recruited him to create an orchestra that would specialize in performing the music of the eighteenth century on period instruments.[56] Of course there were many scholars and musicians in England, attached to various universities and cathedrals, who had been engaged with the early music movement all along. Yet formal training opportunities were not introduced until the 1980s and many of these institutions' future leaders and first teachers had to gain specialist qualifications in the Netherlands. By now, however, most conservatoires around the world have an early music department. Many offer full degrees specifically in period instruments while others reserve the learning of such instruments for post-graduate training or as an optional or supplementary opportunity. The extent to which HIP has become accepted is demonstrated by the institutional recognition that knowledge of HIP maximises a musician's employment prospects, thus it needs to be an essential part of tertiary or post-tertiary training. When the bastions of tradition like the Juilliard consider it important to introduce such a program at least at the graduate level as happened in 2008, then we can be certain that HIP is here to stay—it is current, it is fashionable, it is the contemporary style of playing baroque music.

As this brief overview shows, HIP is exerting an increasing influence on MSP not just at the individual but also at the institutional level. This may lead to a possible relaxing of dogma on both sides of the divide regarding how a piece of music "should go." Music schools are establishing early

---

54 Babitz published several *Early Music Bulletins* during the 1960s and 1970s and a few peer-reviewed articles which created controversy but in retrospect seem quite insightful. See Fabian, *Bach Performance Practice*, p. 49.
55 Monika Mertl, *Vom Denken des Herzes. Alice and Nikolaus Harnoncourt—Eine Biographie* (Salzburg and Vienna: Residenz Verlag, 1999).
56 Gerhard Persché, 'Authentizität ist nicht Akademismus—ein Gespräch mit Chrtistopher Hogwood,' *Opernwelt*, 25/2 (1984), 58-61.

music departments and many younger players are interested in or feel obliged to gain specialist knowledge, to diversify. I now turn to tracing the qualitative details of this trend.

3.3. The Influence of HIP on MSP

Chronologically speaking, the period under discussion shows an initial decline in the number of recordings made by MSP violinists of the Bach Solos during the 1980s and 1990s with a concurrent increase in those made on period instruments, especially during the 1990s. By the mid-2000s however this is reversed, with several non-specialists releasing complete sets. What is important to note, as mentioned earlier, is the fact that quite a few of them use a baroque bow (and often gut strings as well) or acknowledge in interviews or compact disk liner notes the inspiration gained from discussions and collaborations with period performance practitioners and musicologists (e.g. Barton Pine, Faust, Gringolts, Ibragimova, Mullova, Poppen, Schmid, Szenthelyi, Tetzlaff, Tognetti, Zehetmair). How far each of them goes or in what sense they adopt period performing aesthetics varies considerably and provides a fascinating landscape of performing Bach's Solos at the beginning of the new millennium. I will discuss individual differences in more detail later on.

In general, the influence of HIP manifests most clearly in bowing and articulation, in vibrato use, and in an increase in added ornaments and embellishments during repeats. Recordings of period violinists also show this trend as their playing becomes more locally nuanced, metrically and harmonically articulated and richer in ornamentation.[57] In both the HIP and MSP versions of more recent years one can observe greater flexibility in the timing of notes and shaping of phrases. This is largely due to the stronger articulation of smaller musical units and rhythmic groups. The trend towards a more interventionist (or less literal) approach reflects increased freedom and subjectivity and results in a pluralism that may be linked to the postmodern condition observed by Butt, among others.[58]

---

57 By metric-harmonic articulation I mean a delivery that is governed by the bass line and the pulse of a movement and highlights metric-harmonic units rather than longer melodic phrases as is customary in many nineteenth-century and later compositions.

58 John Butt, *Playing with History: The Historical Approach to Musical Performance* (Cambridge: Cambridge University Press, 2002) and also John Butt, 'Bach Recordings since 1980: A Mirror of Historical Performance,' in *Bach Perspectives* 4, ed. by David Schulenberg (Lincoln and London: University of Nebraska Press, 1999), pp. 181-198.

This development becomes even more apparent when the findings of the examination are ordered according to the age of the violinists rather than the recording date (cf. Table 1.1). The very strong correlation between similarities in performance characteristics and date of birth indicates, first and foremost, that soloists develop their distinctive interpretations early in their career and divert from it only rarely.[59] This, in turn, assists us to see what the dominant interpretative modes are in any given decade or so; the aesthetic "common ground," if you wish, that provides the framework for individual differences.

The much lamented "Urtext mentality" of the post-war era can be observed in recordings of violinists born between approximately 1945 and 1960 (e.g. Perlman, Mintz, Kremer 1980). The few even older players (e.g. Shumsky, Poulet) also displayed a similarly literal approach to the works, supporting the view that a decidedly literalistic (either "reverential / romantic-modernist" or "objective / classical-modernist"), technically highly polished playing of Bach had become an ideal already by the 1930s. As such readings were also detected in the recordings of four of the youngest MSP violinists (Ehnes, Hahn, Khachatryan, and to a lesser degree Fischer), this aesthetic seems to have a strong grip on the musical psyche of modern performers. It is tempting to think that the horrors of the First and then Second World Wars, followed by a series of radical social and cultural changes, induced lasting shifts in sensibilities or in willingness to exhibit the deeply personal.[60] Perhaps less dramatically and unconsciously but in a rather more systematic and inevitable way, essentially musical developments must also have contributed to this new aesthetic. The canonization of the classical repertoire that brought about an increased reverence for composers and their scores had started already in the nineteenth century.[61] Yet it seems to have been accomplished only around

---

Increased flexibility and pluralism is also observed in recent performances of Bach's Suites for Cello. See Alistair Sung and Dorottya Fabian, 'Variety in Performance: A Comparative Analysis of Recorded Performances of Bach's Sixth Suite for Solo Cello from 1961 to 1998,' *Empirical Musicology Review*, 6 (1), 20-42.

59 Observed also by Daniel Leech-Wilkinson in 'Recordings and Histories of Performance Style,' in *The Cambridge Companion to Recorded Music*, ed. by Nicholas Cook et al. (Cambridge: Cambridge University Press, 2009), pp. 246-262. See also Eitan Ornoy, 'In Search of Ideologies and Ruling Conventions among Early Music Performers,' *Min-Ad: Israel Studies in Musicology Online*, 6 (2007-2008), 1-19.

60 This view is put forth most pointedly in Daniel Leech-Wilkinson, *The Changing Sound of Music: Approaches to Studying Recorded Musical Performance* (London: CHARM, 2009) and in Leech-Wilkinson, 'Recordings and Histories of Performance Style.'

61 Reinhard Kopiez, Andreas C. Lehmann, and Janina Klassen, 'Clara Schumann's Collection of Playbills: A Historiometric Analysis of Life-span Development, Mobility, and Repertoire Canonization,' *Poetics*, 37 (2009), 50-73.

the 1950s, partly as a drive in historicism and associated preservation of cultural artefacts in the wake of the devastation of the Second World War. The ensuing decades saw further consolidation of this trend through renewed interest in critical editions and musicological dicta based on textual analysis. The more and more formalized and internationalized training of performing musicians—training that emphasized instrumental technique and projection of tone while de-emphasizing the composing and improvising that used to be part and parcel of many earlier virtuosos' skills (e.g. Kreisler, Busch, Milstein, to name only violinists)—fostered an acceptance of the score's authority and the performer's role as an accurate transmitter of the composer's text.[62] Given the very gradual conquest of this ideology and the longevity of musicians' careers in the twentieth century, it is perhaps not surprising that the professors in some of the most famous institutions (e.g. the Moscow Conservatoire, Royal College of Music, Juilliard and Curtis) still seem to produce musicians whose playing displays this trend that started approximately between the 1920s and 1950s.[63]

On the basis of their Bach recordings Hahn, Ehnes, Khachatryan and to a slightly lesser extent Fischer are representative of such violinists. As noted in the previous sections, Hahn and Ehnes were educated at Juilliard and Curtis where famous violin pedagogues (Ivan Galamian, Jascha Brodsky, Sally Thomas, Dorothy DeLay) of a modern "Russian-American" school ruled. It is indicative of Hahn's style of playing that in a lead article about her that appeared in the *Gramophone* in 2000, Milstein, Heifetz, Kreisler and Grumiaux were named as the violinists who influenced her the most. The link between her tutelage under Brodsky and her approach to Bach is also hinted at:

> He wanted me to bring in Bach every week [...] You can't get away with anything in Bach. You can't focus on the technique and forget about the phrasing, and you can't focus on the phrasing and forget the technique because neither will work. You also have to balance voices. It's a challenge to phrase each voice individually, to play everything the way it should

---

62 As discussed in chapter two, Richard Taruskin was among the first to formulate an explanation for this modernist turn that favours the notated score rather than the performer's creative instincts. (Richard Taruskin, *Text and Act: Essays on Music and Performance* [New York: Oxford University Press, 1995], pp. 90-154). See also Eitan Ornoy, 'In Search of Ideologies.'

63 However, even at Juilliard HIP is now present. An advertisement in the October 2010 issue of *The Strad* promotes a graduate program for Period Instrument Performance with "full tuition guaranteed." The names on the faculty include Monica Huggett, Cynthia Roberts (violin), Phoebe Carrai (cello), Robert Nairn (double bass), Robert Mealy (chamber coaching) and annual residency with Jordi Savall and William Christie.

be played technically and make the multiple voices sound like one piece. It takes a lot of thought and a lot of playing to get to where you can feel comfortable with it.[64]

In a 2003 interview she added

Bach is the composer I've played the most—he's the touchstone that keeps my playing honest [...] As long as he is played with good intentions, some thought and an organised approach he will always grab people's attention. Bach never gets old. Something about him is always identifiable.[65]

Julia Fischer, who started with the Suzuki method under the guidance of Helge Thelen in her native Munich, similarly looks to older generations, in particular Oistrakh and Menuhin, when asked to name her idols. She considers Sophie Mutter to be "the greatest German violinist today" and admires Oistrakh because he was

one of the most honest musicians in the world—a real medium between the composer and the listener. He was never, not in one [musical] phrase, on stage to show off, but only to be a servant to music and the composer.[66]

Regarding performing Bach Fischer states:

Bach has been part of my daily diet for years, and recording the Sonatas and Partitas is something I've long wanted to do. One of the things that I love most about Bach is that you can have absolutely your own view—there's no unbroken performing tradition that you're up against.[67]

This seems to be a view shared by the Armenian Khachatryan, another young violinist playing in a decidedly MSP (according to some reviewers "old school") style. When asked about his view on period performance he responded:

People move with the times. In the Baroque period repertoire was played in the way that was modern at that moment. But in time new techniques and

---

64 Adam Sweeting, 'Hilary Hahn [Cover Story],' *Gramophone*, 78/927 (May 2000), 8-13. Importantly, there are also signs that improvisation may again be an important part of the curriculum of high-end classical performance training. The Guildhall School of Music and Drama in London has started offering courses and masterclasses led by David Dolan with contributions from Robert Levin, among others. See also fn. 50 in chapter four.
65 Quinn, 'Bach to the Future.'
66 Martin Cullingford, 'The Experts' Expert—Violinists,' *Gramophone*, 82/986 (November 2004), 46.
67 Harriet Smith, 'Interview: Julia Fischer,' *Gramophone*, 83/993 (June 2005), 19.

new methods have been developed, and if you continued playing Baroque instruments, you'd kind of stagnate. We should approach the pieces from our knowledge now, rather than staying at that earlier level.[68]

What emerges from these quotes is the impression that these violinists have made a deliberate choice regarding their MSP approach to playing Bach and that the decision has been deeply influenced by spending their formative years in musical environments where traditions of mid-twentieth-century aesthetics—including the notion of "letting the music [composer] speak for itself" and thinking of current instruments and playing modes as being all-round better than their period versions—are upheld strongly. Mullova describes these ideals succinctly when she writes,

> When I was at the Conservatory in Moscow [the rules of playing Bach] were based on a widely-held approach of the time that combined a standardized beautiful sound, broad, uniform articulation, long phrasing, if possible, and continuous and regular vibrato on every single note.[69]

She also explains the main differences between her Bach playing then and now:

> During those years [in the Moscow Conservatoire] my Sonatas and Partitas became stiff, monotonous and even more difficult to perform […] I used to play them with very little articulation, and without the distinction between strong and weak beats that is so naturally linked to bow-strokes. But most of all, I didn't understand the harmonic relationships, which are fundamental to a feeling of freedom and involvement in the musical argument.[70]

In her biography she adds information about the MSP style of bowing typical throughout the second half of the twentieth century:

> I was so proud that I could […] play one note, change the bow up or down on the same note and you couldn't hear the join. That was one of the things I had to technically master very young and I was brilliant at it. But now I don't use this technique when I play Baroque music.[71]

---

68 Anonymous, 'One to Watch: Sergey Khachatryan, Violinist' [For the Record], *Gramophone*, 80/962 (January 2003), 11.
69 Viktoria Mullova, 'Liner Notes; Bach: 6 Solo Sonatas and Partitas,' CD recording on a 1750 G. M. Guadagnini violin with gut strings; baroque bow by W. Barbiero (Onyx 4040, 2009).
70 Mullova, 'Liner Notes,' n.p.
71 Viktoria Mullova, and Eva Maria Chapman, *From Russia to Love: The Life and Times of Viktoria Mullova as told to Eva Maria Chapman* (London: Robson Press, 2012), p. 248.

Whereas Mullova has changed her approach radically since her first solo Bach recording in 1987—due to musical encounters with HIP musicians who lured her back to the repertoire which she had abandoned out of frustration, as recounted in the quoted liner notes—it remains to be seen if Hahn and the others cited above ever will and if so, why.[72]

Apart from playing on modern violins with modern bows, the common characteristics of the recordings of Shumsky, Ricci, Perlman, Kremer (in 1980), Mintz, Ehnes, Hahn, Khachatryan and to a slightly lesser extent Poulet and Fischer are the predominantly literal approach to tempo (besides slowing down to mark the end of phrases), rhythm and dynamics; a tendency to use even, portato strokes; projecting longer melodic lines played on a single string as much as possible; not adding ornaments; and playing with regular accenting and an even, vibrato tone. In short, all the features that Mullova so aptly summarized in her liner notes cited above. Other violinists who seem to belong to this modernist school include Gähler, Ughi, Edinger, and to a lesser extent Buswell, Kremer (in 2005), Schmid, Szenthelyi, Schröder, and Kuijken (especially in 2001). Kremer is different in that his interpretation can be linked to his Russian schooling. For instance it is rather intense, serious and grand, a style that upholds Gringolts' opinion that the Russians "always played everything in a romantic manner. Their [...] Bach has a tendency to sound a bit on the never-ending side—a lot of melodic line, shapeless."[73] In Kremer's second version a reviewer heard a "seeming determination to bypass his instrument in pursuit of musical truths" through the "hard hitting, raw, squeezed-out quality of many notes above the stave and loud broken chords." The critic also noted that "[t]he utterly unprettified G minor [is] brisker and

---

72 According to information in another of Mullova's compact disks, she has been "nurturing" a period approach to baroque repertoire since 2000 while performing and touring throughout the world with the Orchestra of the Age of Enlightenment and Il Giardino Armonico (Viktoria Mullova: Vivaldi [with Il Giardino Armonico], Onyx 4001, p. 14). However, her recordings of the 3 Partitas in 1992-1993 already show a strong transformation of style as will be discussed later. In the case of Hahn and Fischer their subsequent Bach recordings do not show such signs of transformation (see their respective disks of the concertos or Hahn's 2009 "Violin and Voice" [DG 477 8092]); Ehnes' recording of the accompanied sonatas, issued in 2005 shows more change of style (Analekta AN 2 9829 and AN 2 9830), whereas Khachatryan's Solo Bach was released in 2010, just at the end of the period under consideration. See also footnote 88.
73 'Ilya Gringolts in Conversation with Jeremy Nicholas,' Liner Notes to Gringolts' recording of two partitas and one sonata for solo violin (Deutsche Grammophon 474 235-2, 2002), p. 5.

grittier than what one usually hears."⁷⁴ Nevertheless, this later recording also shows signs of more recent approaches to baroque music performance adopted in an idiosyncratic way, as I will show in chapters four and five. Similarly, Buswell and Szenthelyi attempt to invoke HIP articulation and bowing but these are usually evident only in the opening bars or phrase of a movement and not across all movements. Schmid's version seems fairly hybrid, with emotionalized dynamics and tone but the pulse often being strong and the articulation detailed. He uses varied bow strokes.

The surprise names in the above list are Schröder and Kuijken, both of them being associated with period performance practice and both playing with period apparatus. Kuijken's first version (recorded in 1981 and issued on compact disk in 1983) is also the most often chosen HIP-comparative recording in reviews published in the *Gramophone*. Nevertheless the evenness of their tempos (Schröder tends to play rather slowly, too), the fairly limited presence of metrical inflections, rhythmic freedom, and additional ornaments, together with a pervasive vibrato, long-range phrasing through dynamics, and occasionally rather sturdy, heavy bowing make their recordings sound quite similar to some of the more "stylish" MSP (alias "authentistic") rather than to the full-blown HIP versions.⁷⁵

---

74   Jed Distler, 'Review: Bach 3 Sonatas and 3 Partitas, BWV1001-BWV1006, Gidon Kremer vn, ECM New Series 4767291 (131 minutes: DDD),' *Gramophone*, 83/1001 (January 2006), p. 63.

75   The term "authentistic" was coined by Richard Taruskin to describe the "modernist" approach to HIP. See his *Text and Act* (esp. p. 99ff). My description of Schröder's and Kuijken's style on these recordings is less valid for Kuijken's first version than his second, and is particularly true of Schröder's recording of certain movements. See Table 3.2. Official reviews tend to be formulated in too general terms to really back up my claim here but I will provide justification in chapters four and five. Published criticism tends to be levelled at technical proficiency and intonation (e.g. Heather Kurzbauer's 'Reviews CDS: Bach Sonatas and Partitas for Solo Violin BWV1001-BWV1006, Sigiswald Kuijken (violin) Deutsche Harmonia Mundi 05472 775 272,' *The Strad*, 113/1341 (January 2002), 81). But in a review captioned "Kuijken's wonderful simplicity of playing allows these works to speak for themselves," Duncan Druce expresses similar views to mine. He finds Kuijken's two interpretations "very similar" but claims that the "more deliberate speed" of the second version "brings a feeling of laboriousness." He continues by saying, "Kuijken's great virtues as a Bach player are his firm grasp of the music's character, particularly its rhythmic character, and his often intense feeling for the overall shape of each piece. Compared to many baroque players, his performances seem very straightforward. [...] the Correnta [sic] of the First Partita gives a good example of their contrasted styles—Podger, with vividly varied bowings and lots of little hesitations to mark the phrase breaks [...] Kuijken much simpler, yet alive to everything in the music that promotes its spirited, dancing character." See 'Reviews: Bach 3 Sonatas and 3 Partitas, BWV1001-BWV1006, Sigiswald Kuijken *vn*, Deutsche Harmonia Mundi 05472 775 27-2 (135 minutes: DDD),' *Gramophone*, 79/947 (2001), p. 93.

Again, the age of the artists and the time of their formative years may provide the explanation. As stated earlier, Schröder was born in 1925 and has been associated with the early music movement since the 1960s, especially for his performances of classical string quartet music and for promoting little known seventeenth- and eighteenth-century works for violin. He once told Kjell Harman that "changing to the Baroque violin was a gradual transition, and in my case it was never complete"; it is well known that even in the early 2000s he was still playing "both the Baroque and Classical violin and occasionally an instrument set up in accordance with modern requirements, but he never uses different instruments in the same programme."[76] In my view, Schröder's published statements regarding historically informed violin playing are much more illuminating and in line with how other period instrumentalists now perform baroque music than his own renderings.[77] This echoes what Sol Babitz reported about the state of early music performance at The Hague in the mid-1970s: "They teach unequal playing to their students, but they don't do it themselves."[78]

Kuijken, although some twenty years Schröder's junior and thus belonging to the next generation of Flemish and Dutch musicians who spearheaded period instrument performance during the 1970s, plays the pieces in a similar fashion. As I will show later, his interpretations go only a little further than Schröder's in the direction of HIP (for details see also Table 3.2). Kuijken's recordings with *La Petite Bande* display much more clearly the characteristically HIP style of closely articulated and metrically orientated playing than either of his two albums of solo Bach (1981, 2001). Perhaps he acquainted himself with the Solos too early in his violin studies to be able to fully shed ingrained readings and executions. The finding that his later recording is even less HIP-sounding than the first may indicate

---

      In my defence, and to clarify my evaluation, I note that perceptual dispositions must be kept in mind. When I listen to Schröder and Kuijken's recordings together with other HIP versions I find them "conservative," but compared to Shumsky or Perlman, for instance, both Schröder and Kuijken are perceived as quite obviously HIP. In chapter five I will consider in detail the differences between Kuijken's 1981 and 2001 recordings that will further tease out my reasoning.

76 Harmen, 'French Master,' p. 955.

77 Jaap Schröder, 'Jaap Schröder Discusses Bach's Works for Unaccompanied Violin,' *Journal of the Violin Society of America*, 3/3 (Summer 1977), 7-32; Jaap Schröder, *Bach's Solo Violin Works: A Performer's Guide* (London: Yale University Press, 2007).

78 Sol Babitz, *Early Music Laboratory Bulletin*, 12 (1975-1977), n.p. These yearly Bulletins were written and published by Babitz from his home in Los Angeles and circulated to subscribers; see Fabian, *Bach Performance Practice*, pp. 48-49.

that as musicians age, the musical conventions and techniques ingrained during their early training could easily resurface.[79]

Contrary to Sigiswald Kuijken, his close contemporary Sergiu Luca (1943-2010) provided listeners with a radically different style of playing Bach's Solos when he recorded them with a period bow and period violin in 1976. His was the first such recording yet it is rarely mentioned in the sources and was never reviewed in *Gramophone*.[80] Although in the USA it stirred some positive reactions—for instance a reviewer voiced his astonishment at hearing the works in such a new light[81]—by and large later recordings tended to be compared to Kuijken's 1981 version as if that was a yardstick for period practice.[82] In many ways Luca's version was so radical and advanced for its time that only recordings from the mid-1990s started to match it in terms of articulation, bowing, added embellishments, rhythmic flexibility and expressive freedom. His story is somewhat similar to Mullova's conversion as related in her liner notes. They both exemplify the rare case when a musician radically changes his or her approach to a composition. The Galamian-trained Luca, who was also playing Sibelius

---

79 Alternatively, this "turning back" could also indicate the loosening of dogma because such a reverse trend can also be observed in Tetzlaff's two recordings. In spite of added embellishments in certain movements, Tetzlaff's 2005 version sounds much more MSP than the 1994 one, primarily because of slower slow movements, longer phrases, weaker pulse, more vibrato tone, and dynamic climaxes (see Table 3.2 for a difference in the proportion of movements sounding HIP or MSP in the two versions).

80 It remains under the radar in spite of its exceptional qualities. For instance it is not mentioned at all in Elste's otherwise exhaustive study of Bach performing practice since 1750. See Martin Elste, *Meilensteine der Bach-Interpretation 1750-2000: Eine Werkgeschichte im Wandel* (Stuttgart: Metzler; Kassel: Bärenreiter, 2000). The 1990 Penguin Guide does not mention Luca's recording either (Ivan March, Edward Greenfield, Robert Layton, *The Penguin Guide to Compact Discs* (London: Penguin, 1990)). Boris Schwarz, on the other hand, includes Luca in his magisterial book *Great Masters*, pp. 608-609, praising him for "branching out into a field of specialization ignored by most virtuosos" and for his "[remarkable] ability to switch from one piece of equipment to the other."

81 Stoddard Lincoln, 'Bach in Authentic Performance: The Technically Impossible Becomes Merely Difficult (Recording),' *Stereo Review*, 40/4 (April 1978), 86-87.

82 Many reviews in *The Strad* or *Gramophone* and other magazines could be listed. Perhaps Stowell's review of Tetzlaff's first recording could be cited as typical (Robin Stowell, 'Review: CDs—J. S. Bach: Sonatas and Partitas for Solo Violin BWV1001-BWV1006, Christian Tetzlaff,' *Strad*, 106/1261 (May 1995), 541-542) or Druce, who stated "Kuijken's 1981 recording convinced us that this music needs a period instrument" (Duncan Druce, 'Review of Bach 3 Sonatas and 3 Partitas, BWV1001-BWV1006, Sigiswald Kuijken,' *Gramophone*, 79/947 (October 2001), 93. One reason for this oversight could be record label distribution, although Deutsche Harmonia Mundi (Kuijken 1981) does not impress as obviously more prominent on the market than Nonesuch (Luca 1977). Daniel Leech-Wilkinson confirmed in a personal communication that Luca's recording was readily available in London at the time of its release (in LP format).

and other late romantic concertos at the time, found inspiration in recorded performances of Gustav Leonhardt and discussions with Alan Curtis, another important harpsichordist. Together they helped him to discard tradition and allow his baroque bow to guide him in finding possible sonic equivalents of written descriptions found in eighteenth-century treatises.[83]

While the recordings of Schröder and Kuijken still showcase many characteristics of the authentistic-modernist MSP style typical of the mid to late twentieth century, younger players born after about 1965, demonstrate an influence of HIP. An interest in recreating eighteenth-century performing practices had started already at the beginning of the twentieth century with publications by Dolmetsch and Landowska. It gained increased momentum from the mid-1950s and eventually became a radical alternative approach and style by the 1980s. Since then it has gradually lost its controversial status. Rather, as the observations in this book also demonstrate, it is the dominant way baroque music is performed nowadays. Some of the violinists born between 1940 and 1960 in the current sample had become leading figures in propelling the HIP aesthetics to the fore (Kuijken, Luca, Wallfisch, Huggett, Beznosiuk, Holloway). This influence is clearly seen in the more lifted bowing of Lev, Mullova, Zehetmair, Schmid, Tetzlaff, Tognetti, Faust, St John, Barton Pine, Gringolts, and Ibragimova. It is also evidenced in their rhythmic and tempo flexibilities, limited use of vibrato, approach to polyphony, and delivery of multiple stops that tend to be (almost) arpeggiated, rather than played as chords. Some of them also embellish the music freely (e.g. Mullova, Tognetti, Tetzlaff, Faust, Barton Pine, Gringolts).

From a broad perspective I found little difference between the general interpretative vocabulary of these players and their contemporary HIP specialists playing on period instruments (Brooks, Podger, Matthews; see Figure 3.1). Short bow strokes with rapid note decay, rhythmic inflections, strong projection of pulse, closely articulated small motivic cells, over-dotting, arpeggiated multiple stops, bouncing, lively dance movements, and dynamic nuances within a basic, "average" volume can be observed in all of these recordings to a greater or lesser extent. The recently released (2008-2010), entirely HIP-sounding, lavishly ornamented performances of Faust (volume one) and, even more so, the much older Mullova are further testaments to this transformation of interpretative style within

---

83 Sergiu Luca, 'Going for Baroque,' *Music Journal*, 32/8 (1974), 16-34.

pockets of MSP. Closer inspection reveals differences in kind (e.g. vibrato or no-vibrato tone, accent rather than metric stress; short but not inflected bow stroke) as well as in degree (e.g. long-range dynamics even if motivic cells are articulated, legato / longer strokes that are nonetheless inflected and varied). These differences will be discussed in the next section.

Noting the similarities, it is intriguing to ponder why these players show such a strong influence of HIP while others of their generation (Ehnes, Hahn, Edinger, Fischer) do not, as discussed earlier. Zehetmair mentions in an interview the decisive influence of attending Harnoncourt's classes in Salzburg and later performing with the conductor.[84] Tetzlaff, Tognetti and Barton Pine are also on record acknowledging the aural appeal of HIP performances of baroque music and, in the cases of Tognetti and Barton Pine, the benefits of using a period bow.[85] But perhaps it is also noteworthy that none of them studied at the Juilliard or the Curtis Institute, not even the American Barton Pine, who is based in Chicago and studied with Roland and Almita Vamos at the Oberlin Conservatory.[86]

Members of the Juilliard-Curtis Schools, in particular Perlman (himself a pupil of Galamian and DeLay, as mentioned before) are well known for their anti-HIP pronouncements.[87] This has likely impacted on the musical horizon of their students, at least at the beginning of their careers when they recorded the Bach Solos.[88] The musical-aesthetic "baggage" that the Solos seem to have accumulated since their re-introduction to the concert repertoire by Joachim in the nineteenth century is manifest even in the

---

84   Nick Shave, 'Star of the North [Zehetmair],' *The Strad*, 116/1377 (January 2005), 18-22.
85   Lawrence A. Johnson, 'An Interview with Rachel Barton,' *Fanfare*, 21/1 (September-October 1997), 81-84; Robin Stowell, *The Early Violin and Viola* (Cambridge: Cambridge University Press, 2001), p. 6.
86   Rachel Barton Pine, *On-line biography*, available at: http://industry.rachelbartonpine.com/bio_medium.php
87   Edward Greenfield, 'Itzhak Perlman talks to Edward Greenfield,' *Gramophone*, 66/787 (1988), 967; Andrew Farach-Colton, 'Perlman,' *The Strad*, 116/1387 (November 2005), 44-51. Pinchas Zukerman, a violinist not studied here because he did not record the Bach Solos as far as I know, has been perhaps the most outspoken. I heard him talk about this on ABC Classic FM in November 2013. Unfortunately the interview is no longer available online.
88   As noted above, Hahn's recent collaboration with Mattias Goerne and Christine Schäfer on Deutsche Grammophon's *Bach Violin and Voice* disk shows no real change in her style of playing (DG 4778092, 2010). Ehnes, on the other hand, plays in a much lighter and more articulated manner on his set of Bach's *Sonatas for violin and harpsichord*, recorded in 2004-2005 (Analekta, AN 2 2016-7). It is very likely that his chamber partners, Luc Beauséjour (harpsichord) and Benoit Loiselle (cello), influenced his approach. The CD booklet does not mention anything in this regard and I was unable to locate any references to Ehnes's thoughts on performing baroque pieces.

much more contemporary-minded Isabelle Faust's reflection. Her goal being "to get into what the composer wants," she worked closely with harpsichordist-fortepianist Andreas Staier, as mentioned earlier, to learn more about baroque performance practice before making the recording. Nevertheless, she admits to finding the process difficult.

> [Bach is] a unique man in his time and his field [...] and it's hard to digest it all. I want to get as close to Bach as I possibly can, and yet still transform it into something that's my own personal vision. Whether to follow rules or be flexible can be very confusing. Still, it's been a fantastic time trying to stretch, at least a little, my approach to Bach. [...] The truth is, with Bach you're never there.[89]

3.4. Diversity within Trends and Global Styles

Notwithstanding the broad trends summarized so far, an examination of the details show great diversity and at times less clear-cut distinction between HIP and MSP characteristics in a given recording.[90] In certain dance movements (especially the Gavotte en Rondeau of the E Major Partita and the E Major and D minor gigues) almost all violinists adopt a lively, rhythmically orientated performance that projects the pulse and articulates the harmonic-metric units clearly. The final fast movements and the E Major Preludio, on the other hand, tend to sound more MSP because of a uniformly virtuosic approach. Although the violinists may employ some accenting to underscore certain structurally, harmonically or figuratively important notes, overall they deliver these movements as virtuosic show pieces (see chapter five for a detailed discussion). The fugues and slow movements of the Sonatas are different, some tending towards MSP, others towards HIP depending on tempo choice, the over-emphasis or not of fugal subjects, and the way polyphony and multiple stops are handled. In case of the lyrical slow movements, the MSP style is reflected in a predilection for phrasing longer melody lines and building major melodic climaxes. Intensification of vibrato and long-range dynamic arches contribute to the effect.

Various authors have identified how the MSP and HIP styles differ along performance scales such as contrasting approach to phrasing, articulation,

---

89 Lorence Vittes, 'Profile: Violinist Isabelle Faust,' *Strings*, 168 (April 2009), available at http://www.stringsmagazine.com/article/default.aspx?articleid=23900 [last accessed October 2015].
90 The spectrum of approaches and allegiances has also been explored by Ornoy through a large-scale questionnaire study. See Eitan Ornoy, 'Between Theory and Practice: Comparative Study of Early Music Performances,' *Early Music*, 34 (2006), 233-247.

bow strokes, multiple stops, ornamentation, rhythmic flexibility, dotted rhythms, and rubato. I summarized my definition of these issues in Table 3.1.[91] Nevertheless, describing the differences in kind often remains elusive and not just because of the subjective nature of perception. For instance, it is generally agreed that in baroque music it is important to articulate smaller rhythmic-melodic units that reflect the beat hierarchy of the meter as well as the harmony implied by a real or imagined bass line. But the execution remains subject to taste within the broadly established parameters. In his seminal study of Bach interpretation, John Butt quotes Leopold Mozart whose advice leaves many doors open for subjective interpretation:

> One must first know how to make all variants of bowing; one must understand how to introduce weakness and strength in the right place and in the right quantity: one must learn to distinguish between the characteristics of pieces and to execute all passages according to their own particular flavour.[92]

Lawson and Stowell also discuss articulation and accenting at length, highlighting the importance of distinguishing between strong and weak beats ("good" and "bad" notes in Quantz's expression) and linking it to bowing, tonguing and fingering patterns.[93]

The trouble is that such articulation can be achieved in a variety of ways with diverse performance features and techniques interacting in seemingly endless degrees of contribution: a bow stroke can be short and light yet not create inflections in terms of dynamic shade-nuance or rhythmic stress; harmonic-metric groups can be created by dynamic accents (such as little sforzandos or fortepianos) rather than timing or "agogic" stress (that is, slight elongation of certain notes or slight delay before sounding the note). Such playing often results in a regular accentual pattern rather than a constantly shifting, nuanced, "hierarchical" one. By the same token

---

91 Most recently by Bruce Haynes, *The End of Early Music: A Period Performer's History of Music for the Twenty-First Century* (New York: Oxford University Press, 2007) but see also Colin Lawson and Robin Stowell, *Historical Performance Practice: An Introduction* (Cambridge: Cambridge University press, 1999) and Fabian, *Bach Performance Practice*, among others.

92 John Butt, *Bach Interpretation: Articulation Marks in Primary Sources* (Cambridge: Cambridge University Press, 1990), p. 38, citing in German Leopold Mozart, *Versuch einer gründlichen Violinschule* (Augsburg, 1756), pp. 254-255 and providing the above English translation. For the original German text see also p. 259 in the 3rd edition of the same book: Leopold Mozart, *Gründliche Violinschule. Fascimile-Nachdruck der 3. Auflage*, Augsburg, 1789 (Leipzig: VEB Deutscher Verlag für Musik, 1968).

93 Lawson and Stowell, Historical Performance Practice, pp. 55-56. See also Johann Joachim Quantz, *Versuch einer Anweisung die Flöte traversiere zu spielen* (1752), trans. by Edward Reilly, *On Playing the Flute*, 2nd edn (Boston: Northeastern University Press, 1985 [1975]).

relatively longer, more sustained bow strokes can nevertheless sound "lifted" because of tiny swells or decays in the sound produced. Phrases articulated in small metric-harmonic groups can still be legato and project a longer line, yet be heard as completely different to a "continuous legato phrase." This latter is achieved primarily through sustained note-lengths (bowing) and a long-range dynamic arch of gradual crescendo and increasing tension followed by decrescendo and rallentando. Furthermore, the less intense tone (lighter bow pressure, less conspicuous vibrato) and looser flow (slight metrical stresses, more decay between notes, not too slow tempos) seem to contribute to the perception that Poulet's, Buswell's and Fischer's recordings are less strictly MSP in style than those of Shumsky, Perlman, Kremer (1980), Mintz, Hahn, Ehnes, or Khachatryan. But in the case of Khachatryan the major difference may be the use of dynamics that create "emotionalized" phrasing, as his bowing is not that intense or heavy even though he uses long bow strokes, often combined with sustained legato. Moreover, the agogic stresses he introduces highlight the harmony or create rhythmic inflections. There are several Audio examples in chapters four and five that will illustrate these subtle and not-so-subtle differences.

Importantly, different movements bring up different issues and possibilities that indicate performance style. In certain movements it is more the phrasing, in others more the bowing and bow pressure; elsewhere it may be the articulation or accenting that seems to determine the perceived style. To put it more accurately, any of these could be the performance feature through which the style can be best described.

Fast movements (E Major Preludio and the finales of the three sonatas) are often just accented and played rapidly with short, non-legato bows even by period specialists. At times these specialists (e.g. Podger) and certain HIP-inspired violinists (e.g. Tognetti, Mullova) relish in the resonances produced by the open gut strings. This creates a fundamentally different effect to the technical brilliance and virtuoso perpetual motion of the typical MSP style. However, to complicate things further, period specialists (e.g. Wallfisch) may also adopt this virtuosic approach as shown in chapter five.

Slow movements (e.g. the C Major Largo and A minor Andante) tend to be played legato yet articulated by several violinists (e.g. Buswell, St John, Barton Pine)—or phrased into longer units through dynamic and tempo arches even by HIP and HIP-inspired players (e.g. Kuijken, Holloway, Tetzlaff). Apart from the kinds of dynamics used, it is often the tone production—intensity of vibrato and bow pressure—that seems to create

3. *Violinists, Violin Schools and Emerging Trends* 109

the real difference. Broader bow strokes and slower tempos may counteract the impact of articulation, especially if this calls upon accenting rather than a projection of meter or pulse. At the same time longer lines may still be heard as "hierarchical-rhetorical" if the small rhythmic values (such as in the G minor Adagio and A minor Grave) are played with some freedom: Flexibility creates a series of gestures that build up to a longer phrase.

So, even if one manages to define the meaning of descriptive categories (e.g. phrasing, articulation, etc.; see Table 3.1), the degree to which the performance features of a given interpretation fit these definitions remains subjective. The overall perceived effect depends on the dominant elements within the interaction of bowing, accenting, articulation, timing, tempo, dynamics, tone and vibrato.

With this in mind, I attempt to summarize my results. Table 3.1 lists the performance features referred to throughout the analyses and my definitions of them. Table 3.2 summarizes the tendency of selected performers to cross over to HIP or MSP styles in particular movements.[94] Table 3.3 provides a more detailed overview of the extent to which HIP and MSP stylistic features are present across all the movements of the more closely studied recordings.[95] It is important to reiterate, however, that styles are necessarily "fuzzy" categories; they often overlap and my discussion of the details in chapters four and five is essential to justify and unpack my judgement tabulated here. As not even movements of a similar type (e.g. fugues, slow movements, opening adagios, allemandes, gigues etc.) are necessarily delivered in a similar vein, I decided to rate each recording as a whole for each category along a ten point scale (10 = maximum) to indicate the consistency of the examined features across all movements in a given recording. These are cumulative scores calculated from rating individually each of the performance features in every movement of the selected recordings and then averaging the result of each scale to obtain the final cumulative score listed in Table 3.3. This way one can see the degree to which a particular performance feature of a given recording belongs to

---

94 Violinists whose performance represents "clearly" or "obviously" MSP or HIP are not included in Table 3.2, only those whose playing shows both styles to a noteworthy degree.

95 I am indebted to Adrian Yeo in devising Table 3.3, which takes his original idea further and adapts it to my purposes. I am also grateful to Daniel Bangert for additional ideas for improvement and to Dario Sarlo for the recommendation to use gradients. See Adrian Yeo, 'A Study of Performance Practices in recordings of Bach's Violin Sonata BWV1003 from 1930-2000' (BMus (Honours) Thesis, Edith Cowan University, 2010).

110   A Musicology of Performance

the MSP or the HIP category; how prominently each manifests in any of the studied albums. Shading the ratings with progressively darker colours aims to aid the visual grasping of the differences. As the categorization is based entirely on repeated listening, issues of instrumental apparatus (e.g. period bow), tuning, choice of score, and artistic intention (if known) are disregarded in this tabulation.[96]

Table 3.1. Definition of stylistic features as listed in column headings in Table 3.3.

Performance feature		Definition
Phrasing	Melodic (MSP)	Melodically orientated; long-spun; created by long-range graded dynamics (crescendo / decrescendo) and tempo rubato (accelerando-rallentando)
	Motivic units (HIP)	Follows bass line / harmony and metric hierarchy; difference between strong and weak beats; delineates small motives and gestures through timing (agogic stress) and bowing inflections; constant ebb and flow of nuance
Articulation and Accentuation	Even, regular (MSP)	Broad, uniform style; semi-detached or legato; all notes equally important, have equal weight; regular or fairly regular accenting; note groups delineated by accenting
	Grouped, metric (HIP)	Inflected according to meter and harmony; follows metrical structure; varied length of notes; first note (or group of notes) under slur stressed / elongated; dissonances leaned-on; hierarchical accentuation (stress) aided by inflected bow strokes
Bowing	Even, sustained (MSP)	Seamless legato or portato strokes; consistent bow pressure / speed; weighted / sustained bowing; little or no decay between notes; often sounding intense
	Uneven, inflected (HIP)	Light or lifted strokes, often short; decay between notes; difference between up and down-bow; constantly shifting dynamic shades; rapidly swelling or receding sound

---

[96] Ornoy ('In Search of Ideologies') lists these and some additional parameters as essential issues to consider when scaling violinists along the MSP to HIP spectrum. I have noted publicly available information regarding apparatus and general intentions earlier and in the Discography. These tables and figures are indicative of the aurally perceivable outcomes along established performance characteristics typically claimed to define HIP versus MSP.

Multiple stops	Together (MSP)	As efficient but weighted blocks (quasi chords), at times harshly accented or broken in 2+2 or 3+1; intense sound and bow pressure; breaking is not always ascending in direction
	Arpeggio (HIP)	Lightly bowed rapid or slower arpeggiation, mostly from bottom up; light and fast bowing of complete, quasi unbroken blocks (often with reverse "hairpin swell"; quick decay)
Ornamentation (HIP)	Graces	Short trills, slides, appoggiaturas, vibrato added in moderate amounts
	Embellished	Melodic embellishments and copious amounts of grace notes added; alternative figurations inserted / improvised
	Improvisational	Smaller note values played as ornamental gestures; delivery reflects the ornamented nature of the notation
Rubato	Tempo (MSP)	Rubato manifest in tempo speeding-slowing to indicate phrases (usually over 4+ bars); the degree of slowing at internal cadence points is varied
Rhythm	Accented (MSP)	Rhythmic-motivic grouping achieved mostly through (dynamic) accenting
	Inflected (HIP)	Taking time and using the inflections of the bow to highlight metrically strong points and hurry weak moments thus flexing rhythm and local tempo; rubato occurs at bar (or half-bar) level; notes inégales and paired slurring
Vibrato	Pronounced (MSP)	Clearly audible, possibly intense (e.g. fast, wide) and fairly continuous; heavy bow pressure creates intense sound
	Light (HIP)	Used occasionally to colour or decorate notes; narrow and inconspicuous; often entirely avoided
Dynamics	Long-range (MSP)	Builds longer phrases or units through large-scale crescendo-decrescendo.
	Local (HIP)	Constant chiaroscuro effect through bow inflections; short / rapid swells and reverse swells; subtle / rapid variation in dynamic nuances and shades

Table 3.2. Movement by movement tendency of selected violinists' interpretative styles listed in DOB order. "H" stands for HIP, "M" stands for MSP. The selection was based on Table 3.3, to provide further information on a few "clear-cut" recordings and most of those displaying a "mixed" approach. This Table was prepared on the basis of renewed listening some 2 years after preparing data presented in Table 3.3. Styles listed in parentheses indicate that the stylistic features are not strong and that characteristics of the other style (or some idiosyncratic style) are also present.

	Gm Sonata				Am Sonata				CM Sonata				Bm Partita				Dm Partita				EM Partita					
	Adagio	Fuga	Siciliana	Presto	Grave	Fuga	Andante	Allegro	Adagio	Fuga	Largo	Allegro assai	Allemanda	Corrente	Sarabande	Tempo di Borea	Allemanda	Corrente	Sarabanda	Giga	Preludio	Loure	Gavotte en Rondeau	Menuet	Bourée	Gigue
Shumsky	H																									(H)
Schröder	(H)	(H)	(H)	M	(M)		(M)	M		M		M		(H)	(M)	(H)	H	H	H	H	M	H	H	(M)	(H)	(H)
Poulet	(H)	(H)	M	(M)			M	M		M	M	M	(H)	H	(H)	H	M	M	H	(H)	M	M	(H)	H	H	(H)
Kuijken '81	(H)	M	M	M	H		(H)	M		(M)	(H)	M	H	(H)	H	H	(H)	H	H	H	H	M	(H)	H		H
Kuijken '01	H	H	H	(M)	M		M	M	(H)	M		(H)	H	(M)	H	H	(H)	(M)	H	(H)	M	(M)	(H)	H	(M)	(H)
Van Dael							(M)	(M)				(M)														
Kremer '05	(M)	M	(M)	M	M		M	(M/H)	(M/H)	M	H	M	M	M	H	(M)	H	(H)	H	(H)	(H)	(H)	(M)	(H)	H	H
Mintz	(M)					(M)																				
Mullova '93												(M)				(M)	(M)	(M)	(H)		(M)				(M)	
Buswell	(H)	(H)	(H)	M	(H)	(H)	(H)	(M)	M	M	(H)	H	(M)	(H)	(M)	(H)	(H)	(M)	(M)	(M)	M	M	(M)	(H)	M	(H)
Lev				M				M	H	H	(M)	M	(H)	(M)	H	(H)	(M)	(M)	H	(H)	M	M	H	H	(M)	H
Beznosiuk	(H)		(H)	(M)	(H)		(H)	(M)	(H)	(M)		M		(M)	(M)	(M)	(M)	(M)	(H)	(M)	(M)	(M)	(H)	(H)	(M)	H
Zehetmair	(M)			(M)			H	M	(M)	(H)	(M)	H	(H)	(H)	(H)	(H)	(M)	(H)	(H)	H	(M)	(H)	H	(H)	(M)	H
Tognetti	(H)	H	H	H	H		(M)	M	H	H		M	(M)	(H)	(H)	(M)	(H)	(M)	(H)	H	(H)	M	H	H	M	H
Tetzlaff '94	H	(H)	M	(M)	H		(H)	M	(M)	(H)	(M)	H	(H)	(M)	(H)	(M)	(H)	(M)	(H)	(M)	M	M	M	H	M	H
Tetzlaff '05	(H)	(H)	H	(H)	H		(H)	M	H	H	(H)	M	H	H	(M)	(H)	(M)	(H)	M	M	M	M	(M)	H	(H)	M
Schmid	H	(H)	(H)	M	(H)		(H)	M	M	M		H	M	(H)	(M)	(M)	(M)	(H)	M	M	M	M	(M)	H	(H)	(M)
St John	H		H	(M)	(H)		(M)	(M)	(M)	(M)	(M)	(M)	(H)	H	(H)	(H)	H	(H)	M	(M)	(M)	(M)	H	H	H	(M)
Barton Pine '99	H	(H)	(H)	(M)	(M)		M	M	H	H	(H)	(H)	H	(H)	(M)	(H)	H	H	H	H	(M/H)	(H)	H	(H)	M	
Barton Pine '07				H	H		(M)	M	H	H		H	H	(H)	H	(M)	M	H	H	(H)	H	H	H	H	(M)	H
Ehnes	M	M	(H)	M	M		M	M	M	M		M	M	(H)	M	(M)	M	M	M	M	M	M	M	(M)	M	(M)
Gringolts	H	H	H	H	H		H	H	H	H		H	H	(M)	H	H	(H)	(H)	H	H	(H)	(H)	H	H	H	H
Fischer	(M)	M	H	M	M		(M)	M	M	M		H	(M)	(H)	(M)	(M)	(H)	(H)	(H)	(M)	M	M	H	H	M	(H)
Khachatryan	(H/M)		(H)	(M)	(H)		(M)	(M)	(M)	(M)		M	(M)	(M)	(H)	(H)	(M)	M	(M)	(M)	(H)	(M)	(H)	(M)	(M)	(H)
Ibragimova	(H)	H	(H)	(H)	H		H	M	M	(M)	(M)	M	(H)	(M)	(H)	(H)	(M)	(M)	(H)	(H)	H	H	H	H	(H)	(H)

112   *A Musicology of Performance*

3. *Violinists, Violin Schools and Emerging Trends* 113

Figure 3.1. Collated scores expressed as percentages of performance features according to style categories (MSP [dark red] versus HIP [light red]) in 40 recordings made between 1976 and 2010 and listed in order of performers' date of birth.

114   A Musicology of Performance

Table 3.3. Summary of MSP and HIP performance features (as defined in Table 3.1) in 40 selected recordings, expressed as a score out of 10 reflecting data collapsed across all movements of the 6 Solos and listed in DOB order.

Performer, Release Date	HIP										MSP							
	Phrasing	Accenting	Bowing	Multiple stops	Ornamentation			Rhythm	Dynamics	Tone (Vibrato & Intensity)	Phrasing	Accenting	Bowing	Multiple stops	Tempo Rubato	Rhythm	Dynamics	Tone (Vibrato & Intensity)
	Short units	Hierarchical; small motives	Inflected, short	Arpeggio light-together	Graces	Embellished	Improvisational	Inflected, grouped	Local, rapid result of bowing	Light, varied inconspicuous	Long melody	Even, regular	Even, smooth intense	Together heavy accent	Phrase length	Accented	Terraced, graded long-range	Intense, even pronounced
Shumsky '83	2	0	0	0	1	0	1	1	0	0	9	8	9	9	9	8	9	9
Ricci '81†	0	0	0	0		0	1	0	0	0	9	10	10	8	9	7	8	9
Schröder '85	8	7	3	6	5	0	3	6	1	7	2	3	7	2	5	5	5	5
Poulet '96	5	4	2	1	1	0	2	3	1	1	6	5	8	8	3	7	7	7
Luca '77	9	8	8	9	8	7	7	8	7	6	0	1	3	0	1	5	2	3
Kuijken '83	5	5	6	7	3	0	2	4	1	7	7	7	5	2	5	6	3	4
Kuijken '01	5	5	6	8	3	1	2	4	1	6	6	7	4	2	5	6	3	5
Perlman '86	0	0	0	0	0	0	0	1	0	1	9	9	9	9	7	2	8	9
Van Dael '96	9	9	9	6	4	2	9	9	9	9	0	0	0	3	1	1	1	1
Kremer '80	1	0	0	1	0	0	1	1	0	1	8	9	9	9	8	6	7	9
Kremer '05	8	6	4	0	0	1	1	4	1	5	4	7	7	9	5	8	7	7
Holloway '04	9	8	9	9	2	0	8	9	6	9	1	2	1	1	1	4	0	0
Wallfisch '97	9	8	9	9	3	1	6	8	9	8	1	1	1	1	2	3	1	1
Huggett '95	10	10	10	10	4	5	9	10	10	8	0	0	0	0	6	5	0	0
Mintz '84	0	0	0	0	0	0	0	1	0	2	9	9	9	10	5	4	8	9
Mullova '87*	1	0	0	0	0	0	0	0	0	0	8	9	9	7	3	3	2	8
Mullova '94†	3	6	4	5	1	1	2	4	3	7	6	1	5	3	0	6	4	2
Mullova '09	8	9	9	8	8	8	9	9	8	9	2	1	3	4	3	3	2	0
Lev '01†	6	7	2	3	0	0	1	5	2	3	3	3	7	4	6	7	2	6
Buswell '94	2	4	3	2	1	0	3	2	1	6	7	6	6	5	1	6	7	3

3. Violinists, Violin Schools and Emerging Trends

Performer, Release Date	HIP										MSP							
	Phrasing	Accenting	Bowing	Multiple stops	Ornamentation			Rhythm	Dynamics	Tone (Vibrato & Intensity)	Phrasing	Accenting	Bowing	Multiple stops	Tempo Rubato	Rhythm	Dynamics	Tone (Vibrato & Intensity)
	Short units	Hierarchical; small motives	Inflected, short	Arpeggio light-together	Graces	Embellished	Improvisational	Inflected, grouped	Local, rapid result of bowing	Light, varied inconspicuous	Long melody	Even, regular	Even, smooth intense	Together heavy accent	Phrase length	Accented	Terraced, graded long-range	Intense, even pronounced
Brooks '01	7	4	5	2	1	0	7	6	7	9	0	5	3	4	2	5	4	0
Bcznosiuk '11	2	4	5	4	7	4	3	4	2	8	8	5	2	2	1	6	7	0
Zehetmair '83	8	9	8	1	0	0	8	9	9	6	3	0	2	8	7	5	3	6
Tognetti '05	8	8	8	7	8	5	6	8	6	8	1	1	0	5	0	1	1	1
Tetzlaff '94	8	9	8	6	4	0	5	7	2	7	5	0	1	4	7	7	5	0
Tetzlaff '05	7	8	7	5	4	1	6	8	4	2	6	6	8	5	6	6	7	8
Matthews '00	8	9	9	8	0	1	7	8	9	10	1	0	1	2	0	2	1	0
Schmid '00	8	9	9	2	1	1	8	9	9	9	2	0	1	8	3	2	1	1
Podger '98	8	9	9	8	7	4	8	9	9	8	3	0	1	2	3	1	2	1
St John '07	3	7	7	6	0	0	3	5	3	8	4	1	1	1	1	2	5	1
Faust '10†	9	8	7	9	9	8	9	9	9	9	0	1	5	1	1	1	1	0
Barton Pine '99	6	8	7	8	3	1	2	9	8	4	4	2	3	2	6	2	2	2
Barton Pine '04†	8	8	8	5	2	0	3	8	9	9	0	0	1	0	0	1	1	0
Barton Pine '07	8	8	8	8	1	1	5	8	9	8	2	1	1	0	2	2	1	0
Ehnes '99	1	0	0	0	0	0	0	1	0	0	9	8	9	9	5	1	8	10
Hahn '97†	0	0	0	0	0	0	0	1	0	0	9	9	10	9	1	2	8	10
Gringolts '01†	9	9	8	8	8	9	8	8	4	8	1	1	1	1	1	5	1	0
Fischer '05	5	5	3	1	0	0	1	1	2	3	6	7	7	8	7	7	7	7
Khachatryan '10	4	3	1	5	0	0	1	3	1	3	8	8	8	3	8	2	9	9
Ibragimova '08	9	9	9	10	0	0	8	9	9	9	0	1	0	0	3	2	2	0

* In 1987 Mullova only recorded the B minor partita.
† Only 3 or fewer works recorded by these violinists. For detail refer to Discography.

The overall results listed in Table 3.3 are presented graphically in Figures 3.1. This shows the outcome of the subjective rating of performance features expressed as a percentage of the total score. This way it is easy to see the relative presence of MSP and HIP characteristics in each version and to place the recordings of the past thirty years along the continuum of ever changing performance styles. Ordering the data according to the violinist's date of birth assists seeing the relationship between the age of the artist and stylistic trends and shows both similarities and differences across generations.

3.5. Overall Findings and Individual Cases

Looking at the results for particular violinists (Figure 3.1), the following recordings show the greatest mixture of styles: Schröder, Kuijken (both), Schmid, Kremer 2005, Mullova 1993, Beznosiuk, Zehetmair, Tetzlaff (esp. 2005), Khachatryan, and to a lesser extent Lev, Buswell, Brooks, and Fischer. Although Table 3.3 provides the information regarding which performance features contribute most strongly to this overall result, it is worth commenting on these recordings further.

In the case of Schröder, his phrasing, articulation and delivery of multiple stops are the clearest signs of HIP, whereas his bowing and use of tempo rubato tend to be closer to the MSP style. The table also indicates that in terms of rhythm and tone his performance is neither MSP nor HIP. Kuijken's two recordings do not seem to differ much according to the rating in Table 3.3. Most of the scales show a fairly even distribution between the two styles, with ornamentation, the delivery of multiple stops, and a tendency to curtail the use of vibrato being the three main HIP features.

At times aspects of Kremer's (2005) and Schmid's recordings, but also Lev's and Zehetmair's, sound like a somewhat mannered imitation of the HIP style. This impression comes about because of the exaggerated tempos, dynamics, heavy accents and a squarer, less well-integrated rhythmic flexibility and phrasing. Although Kremer's two versions show many similarities, the ratings in Table 3.3 clearly indicate a shift towards this self-styled HIP phrasing and articulation. These ratings need to be qualified: In his second recording Kremer's use of nominally HIP characteristics (such as the locally nuanced rhythmic flexibility) sound mannered and unintegrated. I do not perceive the many forceful accents and tempo fluctuations as natural, but almost like a parody of HIP.⁹⁷ Just like Kremer, Schmid's style is also rather "hybridized." His interpretation offers strong pulse, detailed articulation and varied bowing. However, dynamics and tone often sound overtly expressive, especially in slower movements where extremes of soft or intense playing and vibrato are common. In Lev's recording, it is again primarily phrasing and articulation that makes it sound HIP-like at times. The mixture of styles in Zehetmair's recording is due to his vibrato, playing of chords, and use of tempo rubato on the one hand, and his HIP-like phrasing, articulation, bowing, rhythm and dynamics, on the other.

Mullova still tends towards longer phrases in 1993 but her articulation and tone are rated as closer to HIP than MSP. Her bowing has also become shorter, her rhythm more inflected and she started adding embellishments. Importantly, there are no signs of tempo rubato. Instead, her playing has gained an improvisatory feel.

Interestingly, Brian Brooks, a young period violinist who has worked with several British period orchestras, has a fairly neutral style, leaning towards the HIP because of his non-vibrato tone, locally nuanced articulation and dynamics.⁹⁸ In contrast, in the playing of another period violinist and orchestra leader, Pavlo Beznosiuk, it is phrasing and dynamics that contribute the most to the MSP effect, whereas his articulation and delivery of rhythm utilize elements of both styles. However, he also plays without vibrato, his bowing tends to be inflected (given his baroque bow, this is not surprising), and he renders ornamental rhythmic gestures in a flexible manner while also adding ornaments and embellishments here and there. An approximate contemporary of Beznosiuk, James Buswell is a mainstream violinist scoring only somewhat higher on those scales than Beznosiuk. Buswell's playing shows considerable influence of HIP, especially in terms of articulation and tone but also because of his gestural playing of ornamental rhythmic groups.

The ratings for Tetzlaff's two recordings show his turning away from the earlier influence of HIP in 2005. In 1994 his phrasing, articulation,

---

97 Some reviewers registered similar criticism. See, for instance, Jed Distler, 'Review: Bach 3 Sonatas and 3 Partitas, BWV1001-BWV1006, Gidon Kremer *vn*, ECM New Series 4767291 (131 minutes: DDD),' *Gramophone*, 83/1001 (January 2006), 63.

98 Apparently he studied at the Royal Academy of Music and also with Szymon Goldberg before enrolling in the doctoral programme at Cornell University. In his native England he performed with leading period ensembles such as the English Baroque Soloists, the London Classical Players, and the English Concert. Available at http://www.sarasamusic.org/aboutus/musician-bios/BrianBrooks.shtml

bowing and tone were all closer to what is considered the period style than in the later version. Tetzlaff's second recording offers a return to longer phrases, waving dynamics, vibrato tone, weak pulse in slow and dance movements, while the faster movements are often played too fast to keep HIP attributes obvious. The only aspect of his interpretation that may be regarded more HIP-like in 2005 is ornamentation, especially the addition of embellishments and a slightly greater sense of improvisational delivery of rhythmic groups.

Fischer's and Khachatryan's interpretations have many similarities in phrasing, articulation, bowing, dynamics, tone and the use of tempo rubato. However, Khachatryan tends to play chords more lightly, often with arpeggiation, and inflects rhythmic cells more strongly, thus gaining HIP attributes. At the same time his vibrato is more conspicuous. In contrast, Fischer's blended MSP style is reinforced by a lack of rhythmic projection and the chordal playing of multiple stops. How these attributes influence the styles of particular movements in these recordings is summarized in Table 3.2.

Trends in Particular Movements

Although I have already mentioned some general observations regarding trends in individual movements, it may be useful to communicate further detail because these are not decipherable from the tables and figures. The performance style of the Fugues, the fast sonata finales (Presto, Allegro and Allegro Assai), the E Major Preludio as well as the D minor Allemanda and Corrente and also the E Major Gavotte tend to converge: HIP players may also play with accents and MSP players also highlight harmonic groups at times through agogic stress. This can be true of the two gigues as well (D minor, E Major). The B minor Tempo di Borea may also be primarily accented rather than inflected. The *Doubles* in the B minor Partita are often played very similarly, too; just lightly accented and mostly shaped through dynamics. However, HIP versions use more agogic stresses to inflect harmonically important moments.

The dotted rhythm as well as the texture and tempo of the C Major Adagio and to a (much) lesser extent the B minor Allemanda provide for very similar readings across the recordings. The C Major Adagio tends to be played very legato, sustained and with a gradual building of dynamics and intensity (tension) which starts anew in bar 15 and again in bar 27 although this time not quite from the previous low point. The real difference among the versions seems to be found in the performance of the chords (together or lightly arpeggiated) and the linear-ornamental bars (bb.12-14; 39-47), namely, whether these gestures are delivered literally or in a more improvisatory manner. Very few violinists emphasize, or make audible, the paired slurs Bach wrote out on every dyad in thirteen similar bars. Likewise, there seems to be little differentiation between the dotted dyads and those of equal quavers slurred in pairs. The legato style as well as the multiple stops for the first notes of each pair make those notes longer and more weighted, whether dotted or not.

In contrast, the A minor Andante, C Major Largo, and especially the E Major Loure tend to diverge: MSP players perform them more lyrically and "phrased," often at a slower tempo and with more use of long-range dynamics. The two Sarabandes show this trend as well, with HIP and HIP-inspired violinists delivering lighter, freer, more forward-moving music than the slower, more measured, intense, and sustained style of MSP players. Other dance movements (esp. the E Major Menuet I and II) may also show clear differences, as HIP violinists tend to play around with the rhythm and pulse much more.

The style of the opening slow movements (G minor Adagio, A minor Grave) seems to depend on bowing (sustained, weighted or inflected, lifted), dynamics, and tone (combination of bow pressure and vibrato, choice of fingering impacting on timbre).[99] These features become crucial in creating differences because the basic interpretative approach is similar: most of the younger violinists play these movements with a degree of "improvisatory" freedom rather than literally as was the MSP custom until the 1990s. Nevertheless, and even though the somewhat fragmented nature of the musical material may also foster a freer interpretation, the versions by MSP players tend to have longer lines and phrases created through dynamics and sustained or longer bow strokes. These become particularly noticeable when bowing is weightier and the timbre more intense and uniform. In contrast, HIP players allow more decay between the first and last notes of the bar or half-bar-long gestures. They also seem to limit dynamic variation to the length of such gestures through bowing inflection; they do not link

---

99 Period violinists tend to choose lower positions which requires more string crossing than when a violinist opts for shifting and thus remaining on the same string for a unified tone of a given melody.

these gestures into longer phrases by progressively building dynamics or intensity but use lifted bow strokes, creating uneven timbre and dynamics.

In the following chapters I will discuss further the reasons for these ratings and evaluate the lessons that can be gained from inspecting the scores in Table 3.3 or the graph in Figure 3.1. Ultimately they provide evidence for the complex interactions of performance features demonstrating stylistic and interpretative diversity. They support my theory that music performance is a dynamical system that needs to be analysed in a complex, non-linear way. There is only one more point I need to highlight here as an important finding of this overview.

The Importance of Ornamentation

In my earlier work on Bach performance practice in the twentieth century I argued that ornamentation, together with the use of period instruments, was a less important matter in establishing the style of a performance than rhythmic projection and articulation.[100] I came to this conclusion in relation to performances from the 1950s to the 1970s and to that extent I still stand by my opinion. However, in the examination of the current body of recordings, ornamentation turned out to be one of the most rewarding aspects of study. Not just in terms of providing thrill and pleasure while listening but also because it emerged as an important indicator of how far the HIP movement has developed. In effect I am now inclined to claim that ornamentation is perhaps the most obvious signifier of advanced HIP style.

I have already discussed why the choice of apparatus and specialising in baroque repertoire may not be adequate criteria for categorizing violinists into stylistic camps. This was true for most recordings of Bach's music up to the 1980s as well. In performances from the 1950s to the 1980s articulation (phrasing) and approach to rhythm and pulse proved most useful in distinguishing between styles. The current analyses indicate that by now these and several other aspects of the two basic interpretative approaches may converge (e.g. the use of accents and metrical stresses; dynamics and bowing; tempo and rhythmic rubato), making it difficult to distinguish between the HIP and MSP styles (cf. Tables 3.2, 3.3 and Figure 3.1).

In this situation ornamentation becomes crucial in establishing a possible dividing line. To be precise, it is the level and kind of ornamentation,

---

100 Fabian, *Bach Performance Practice*.

the way it is delivered, that makes the difference. Actually it is not even accurate to call it simply ornamentation because this word is supposed to refer to grace notes: trills, appoggiaturas and various other types of short figures eighteenth-century sources indicated (or not) by signs. Although it is pleasing and certainly in line with historical practice to add such decorations at cadence points, on accented notes and at other appropriate moments, their occasional use does not make a huge difference to the overall effect of a performance. In contrast, when smaller note values are played with quasi improvisatory freedom; when such smaller notes are added as embellishments to smooth out or decorate melodic lines; to fill or emphasize larger leaps and dissonances; to add energy or weight to structurally important notes; or to vary oft repeated melodic turns, then the music gains stylistic affiliation and character because it sounds freer, more gestural, affect-centred, impulsive, possibly improvised—all desirable characteristics as theorized in eighteenth-century treatises. The richer such details are and the more spontaneous-sounding their delivery, the more they appear to match eighteenth-century performance aesthetics as we understand them today.[101]

It is clear from the scores in Table 3.3 that there is still a long way to go to resurrect the baroque practice of embellishing during performance and to make it common in our contemporary practice. The whitest section (i.e. lowest scores) in Table 3.3 are the three columns relating to ornamentations. Apart from Luca only fellow HIP specialists, Huggett and Podger go some way in this regard and only in a few select movements during the twentieth century (for a list of embellished movements and the violinists involved, see Table 4.5).[102] What is even more significant is the finding that since the mid-2000s, non-specialist violinists are leading the way (e.g. Barton Pine, Gringolts, Tognetti, Tetzlaff), with Isabelle Faust's and Viktoria Mullova's very recent recordings taking the palm.

---

101 What the historical treatises say and whether Bach's music differs from that of his contemporaries in this regard will be discussed in the Ornamentation section of chapter four.

102 Obviously this book lists only violinists who issued recordings of the Bach Solos. Therefore it may be that many more names could be added if recent recordings of the entire baroque violin repertoire were considered. However, my casual listening to cello suite recordings does not indicate this; there are hardly any where added graces can be heard and basically none with added embellishments (e.g. Angela East on Red Priest Recording RP006 from 2009 [Rec 2001-2004]) and David Watkin on Resonus RES10147 from 2015 [Rec.: 2013]).

3.6. Conclusion

Although the recordings differ in myriads of details (to be discussed specifically in the next chapter), two overarching trends can be established already at this point: the influence of HIP on MSP performance practices (and *not* vice versa), and a gradual shift towards a more flexible way of playing. As we progress from the 1980s to the end of the new millennium's first decade the pluralism of the era leaves its indelible mark on recordings of Bach's Solos as well. In the context of a saturated and shrinking classical music market and the healthy cross-fertilization of musical styles readily available to all who are interested, young players are looking for individual distinguishing features, their own voice, rather than some authoritative tradition that is not only stultifying but has ceased to offer opportunities for "sticking out of the crowd." Furthermore, with the decline of the large classical record labels the industry is undergoing major change. The mushrooming small or specialist labels many young performers use might actually foster a different mentality, one that embraces and encourages experimentation, individuality and risk taking.[103]

This preliminary discussion shows similar results to Ornoy's study conducted between 1996 and 2000.[104] Through his survey of over two-hundred HIP musicians from across Europe and the Americas he found that most time is spent on fine-tuning technical-idiomatic factors rather than related concepts, including formal analysis. This perhaps explains the similarities across the recordings. Differences on the other hand could stem from the diverse attitude to reading historical sources and learning about / practising ornamentation. More pertinently for my purposes here, Ornoy also found that older, more senior participants showed more "positivistic" traits (e.g. being "pedantic" about instrument choice, researching repertoire, scores / manuscripts etc.). They were more inclined to "claim the transmission of 'objective' messages than those who view[ed] their role as enabling the transmission of individual messages."[105]

---

103 Working with small labels often means the musicians having to invest their own money in the recording and running financial risks. However, they have more say in what they want to record and with whom. If the label secures good distribution it can be a win-win situation, as Viktoria Mullova explains in relation to her work with the Onyx label, "I own all the rights and get much more in return" (Mullova and Chapman, *From Russia to Love*, p. 237).
104 Ornoy, 'In Search of Ideologies and Ruling Conventions.'
105 Ibid., p. 17.

The fact that the influence of a more flexible HIP is observed at the turn of the twenty-first century rather than the opposite flow from "modernist" MSP adds an important layer to the debate regarding the similarities and differences between HIP and MSP. Even if HIP is a twentieth-century aesthetic invention it is the newer, the alternative to the "modern," and as such it "wins out" because ultimately it reflects better our accumulated hunger for "vitalist" music making.

The investigation also shows the passing of time and arrival of newer generations and trends: HIP and MSP versions of late are more interventionist and idiosyncratic than before. This gives rise to differences within the respective groups of performing styles as well as across styles. The expressive vocabulary is enlarged; extreme dynamics, extra strong accents and inflections, copious ornamentation and other flexibilities are part and parcel of most recordings since the mid-1990s (Huggett, Podger) but especially since 2005 and in HIP-inspired MSP versions (Gringolts, Tognetti, Tetzlaff, Barton Pine, Faust, Mullova), as the parenthetical list of names indicates. The importance of pulse and metric hierarchy has been recognized just as much as the significance of harmony and harmonic goals. The variation in interpretation now tends to stem from how these elements are treated and used to shape the various movements on the small as well as large-scale. And since both the harmony and meter tend to be localized in baroque music (i.e. they affect the bar, half-bar or pairs of bars rather than eight or sixteen-bar periods as in later music), the differences in interpretation are also localized and subtle, observable in the degree of nuance and detail (cf. examples from G minor Fuga, for instance, or differences between Huggett's and Gringolts' E Major Menuet II discussed in subsequent chapters).

These results resonate with the point Deleuze and Guattari make when discussing "refrain" and what they call the "deterritorialising impulse": The moment a territory [in our context a "style of performance"] is established it is already in the process of changing and transforming itself.[106] As soon as HIP became established and formulised by the 1990s it has started to deterritorialise, to move away from order and rules. This process of transformation is clearly audible in the recordings studied here and even more strongly in evidence in performances since the mid-2000s. Instead of molar lines (whether MSP or HIP) we find increasing signs or examples

---

[106] Gilles Deleuze and Felix Guattari, *A Thousand Plateaus: Capitalism and Schizophrenia* (London: Bloomsbury, 2013), pp. 311-350.

of "rhyzomic molecular lines" and "lines of flight." These break up the mould of the "One," the accepted and expected standards of performance characteristics when playing Bach's Violin Solos. Their "minoritarian tendencies" have a "deterritorialising" effect creating the current mix of styles that is infused with personal subjectivities and inconsistencies. Therefore the changes observed are *not* a pendulum swing! Rather, they occupy the "space in-between" and are the engines of the process of change. They are witnesses of becoming, of transformation. Through them we encounter new ways of thinking-hearing and doing.

Perhaps it is just a skewed effect of available recordings, but in the current sample non-specialist violinists seem to be more daring in their freedom of interpretation than period instrument players.[107] If one compares Brooks' recording with Gringolts's, for example, one is tempted to agree with the results in Ornoy's above mentioned study that HIP ideology has remained somewhat rigid and normative in spite of the more relaxed narrative that has developed in the wake of criticism by Richard Taruskin and others.[108] The fact that ornamentation and embellishment are much more abundantly found in recordings of non-specialists (Gringolts, Tognetti, Mullova, Faust) is another indicator. These players seem to choose to play how they like—to the extent of changing to a baroque bow and freely nit-picking effects and HIP conventions of their liking. Is it possible that many baroque specialists are still weighed down by rules and musicological prescriptions? That they all believe Bach wrote out the ornaments he wanted so nothing more should be added even when all repeats are performed, often without any change? The point that "As soon as it becomes acceptable to dislike what Bach might have done it is easier to allow [choices]"[109] may be a greater liberating force among MSP violinists inspiring them to cross over and embrace what they like about HIP without feeling the need to become

---

[107] Bernard Sherman lists twenty-six complete set recordings of the Bach Solos just from the period between 2000 and 2010. Out of these there are eleven (two HIP and nine MSP) that I have not heard. See http://bsherman.net/BachViolinGlutofthe2000s.htm. Other recordings might have been re-issued but not made during this period (e.g. Paul Zukovsky's 1971-1972 Vanguard [VSD 71194/6] recording remixed and remastered for release by Musical Observations in 2005).

[108] Taruskin, *Text and Act*; Daniel Leech-Wilkinson, 'What We Are Doing with Early Music is Genuinely Authentic to Such Small Degree that the Word Loses Most of its Intended Meaning,' *Early Music*, 22/1 (1984), 13-25; *Authenticity and Early Music*, ed. by Nicholas Kenyon (Oxford: Oxford University Press, 1988). One of the first to note a relaxation of rhetoric was Michelle Dulak, 'The Quiet Metamorphosis of "Early Music",' *Repercussions*, 2/2 (1993), 31-61.

[109] Butt, 'Bach Recordings since 1980,' p. 191.

experts and dogmatic about it. Their playing certainly sounds as if they "owed" the music, rather than simply transmitting it with due reverence for composer, work and style. Although most of them collaborated with and learnt from period specialists,[110] they are essentially MSP soloists. Yet it is often in their playing that the HIP style has gained depth through liberation from dogmatic views so typical until at least the 1990s.

---

110 Mullova writes in her liner notes to her 2009 album (Onyx 4040, recorded 2007-2008): "The injection of trust from other Baroque musicians has led me to study intensely and to make the Baroque repertoire central to my artistic life." (Also cited in Mullova and Chapman, *From Russia to Love*, p. 253). She has worked and made recordings with Il Giardino Armonico, Venice Baroque Orchestra, Ottavio Dantone, and the Orchestra of the Age of Enlightenment, among others. In the same Onyx album she acknowledges the initial inspiration and encouragement coming from the bassoonist and continuo player Marco Postinghel (Liner Notes, p. 1).

4. Analysis of Performance Features

Having focused on overall trends and the inter-relationship between HIP and MSP characteristics in the previous chapter, here I provide a systematically detailed account of performance features. My aims are, however, the same as throughout the book: 1) to investigate the claim that performances have become more uniform and homogeneous both technically and stylistically; 2) to examine how different performance features interact to create particular interpretations and aesthetic constructs; 3) how these relate to time and place as well as musical sensibilities and knowledge; and 4) what all this tells us about musical performance. Ultimately I aim to provide empirical evidence for the complex nature of performing western classical music and a model for an integrated analytical approach.

The recordings testify to a fascinating palette of interpretative possibilities. It is quite staggering to contemplate how Bach managed to compose such pieces that speak to us almost exactly 300 years later with such directness and wealth of potential that all violinists wish to perform and record them, one generation after another. In the previous chapter I have quoted several violinists of varied background and ilk who all discussed, explicitly or implicitly, the emotional pull and instrumental challenge of Bach's Violin Solos. They mentioned the honesty, awe, curiosity, puzzle and bewilderment these works represent for them. So what is their answer? How do they solve the problems? How do they respond to Bach's invitation? What conversations may we, listeners,

© Dorottya Fabian, CC BY   http://dx.doi.org/10.11647/OBP.0064.04

witness between composer and performer 300 years apart? How is the age of the musician reflected in his or her dialogue with the music? Are youthful players drawn to different aspects of the music then older ones? Are cultural pre-conceptions more dominant than personal age and psychological-musical maturity? The spectrum offered by Bach from timeless contemplative music to period-bound genre pieces is wide open.

Musicians and listeners find the seemingly endless ways of engaging with the Solos unquestionably rewarding. As a listener one often has a sense that quite a few violinists must also enjoy facing the technical challenges inherent in them. Otherwise they wouldn't be returning to the pieces and performing and recording them over and over again. The sheer sonority, physicality, virtuosity of certain movements is so imminent and the performance of them so abundantly brilliant that one is reminded of musicians confiding off-record, "Yes, wasn't that great, playing so fast? I can do it!" — echoing Horowitz, who, when asked once why he had played so fast, responded simply: "Because I can." The reward is not exclusively the musician's. Listeners are enchanted as well; otherwise the market would have long relegated the works back to the pile of forgotten music or the practice studio. I for one certainly love listening to this music and find something beautiful, interesting, or novel in most versions and even those I don't much enjoy can envelop me in Bach's sound world in ways that lift me into another sphere. It is therefore an exciting challenge for me to explain how they do it and why I may prefer one over another when most are truly wonderful and of exquisite standards.

I have organized my analysis along performance features, moving from the most factual towards the more subjective measures. First I look at tempo choices, vibrato and ornamentation. This is followed by the discussion of rhythm and timing which entails an analysis of playing dotted rhythms and the topic of inégalité as well as the expressive timing of notes, including tempo and rhythmic flexibility. Subsequently I discuss matters that are even harder to describe in words, such as bowing (including the playing of multiple stops), articulation, and phrasing. Wherever possible I compare performance choices to musicological opinion, as found in both historical sources and modern pronouncements. The points I make are supplemented by further observations presented in tables, graphs and transcriptions as well as descriptions of particular moments in recordings. The more detailed or specific analytical observations and descriptions appear in boxed texts shaded grey for ease of navigation.

It is a daunting task to provide an honest account when analysing forty-odd recordings of Bach's *Six Sonatas and Partitas for Solo Violin*. Each complete set entails about two hours of music. Given my position regarding the problems of the current state of music performance studies that I outlined in chapters one and two, my conclusions cannot be based on a case study. The main challenge is, therefore, to find a balance between sampling a judiciously appropriate cross-section of movements and violinists for each performance feature under investigation without getting lost in detail. Perhaps an eclectic approach will help: At times, like in the case of tempo choice and ornamentation, I provide comprehensive coverage with numerous tabulated summaries and transcriptions. Other times, like in the case of vibrato, I illustrate my claims through measurement of specific moments in a select few movements. In both cases I aim to highlight the potential for misinterpretations and misrepresentations; how the data, masquerading as objective, can nevertheless be manipulated to support whatever argument the researcher wishes to make.

Certain performance features, like the performance of dotted rhythms or multiple stops, self-determine what excerpts I have to focus on as only certain movements feature such material. What is of special interest here is the obvious slippage that readers will notice: ostensibly about dotting or the delivery of multiple stops, the discussion will actually shift to various other performance features, namely articulation, dynamics, timing, bowing, and tempo (again)—illustrating the workings of a complex, non-linear system of interactions that give rise to musical character, the affective-aesthetic dimension of the performance. Overall, it is probably inevitable that certain movements will feature more frequently because they offer more for discussion. In particular, the E Major Partita somehow emerged as a focal point, but the two Sarabandes, the A minor Andante and the G minor Adagio and Fuga also receive much attention. At the same time, the famous Ciaccona is conspicuous for its absence. It deserves a separate study.

4.1. Tempo Choices

Right here at the start and in relation to an apparently straightforward matter, a difficulty has to be noted: it is near impossible to generalize tempo trends as each movement provides something different (Tables 4.1-4.3). Furthermore, and perhaps contrary to expectations, period specialists have slower averages than MSP players, except in the slow movements, allemandes and courantes. Therefore, the once commonly held view that performances, especially HIP versions, of baroque music have become faster as we progress through the twentieth century is questionable.[1]

But let us stop for a minute and take a closer look. First, how should one group violinists into MSP and HIP categories if there is such confluence between approaches as discussed in the previous chapter? Readers are invited to consult Table 4.1 to see the results of grouping violinists simply on the basis of specialist / non-specialist. Table 4.2 takes into account a larger pool of players including recordings made since the beginning of the twentieth century. The top row presents the same simple subdivision (specialist / non-specialist) while the bottom row re-configures the grouping by adding the HIP-influenced players to the specialist group

---

[1] The "breathless tempi of much early music" is an opinion generally expressed rather casually, as in Bernard D. Sherman (ed.), *Inside Early Music: Conversations with Performers* (New York: Oxford University Press, 1997), p. 292. Taruskin noted both the acceleration of tempo choices over time and some slower than historically documented tempos chosen by HIP performers, although in relation to orchestral or ensemble music (Richard Taruskin, *Text and Act: Essays on Music and Performance* (New York: Oxford University Press, 1995), pp. 134-135, 214-217, 293-294, 232, etc.)). From his discussions it transpires what other, less often cited writers also note, namely that some early twentieth-century musicians often chose much faster tempos than what we are accustomed to today. See Vera Schwarz, 'Aufführungspraxis als Forschungsgegenstand,' *Österreichische Musikzeitschrift*, 27/6 (1972), 314-322. Among the 55 versions of the E Major Preludio in my collection the fastest was recorded in 1904. The performer is nineteenth-century virtuoso Pablo Sarasate. Just how much faster than anybody else he plays is indicated by his Standard Deviation score: 3.27 (see fn. 5 for an explanation of Standard Deviation values). Sarasate's E Major Preludio recording remains the fastest among Dario Sarlo's larger sample set as well (Dario Sarlo, *The Performance Style of Jascha Heifetz* (Farnham: Ashgate, 2015)). In Sarlo's collection the next fastest is by Deych (1999) and then Brooks (2001), followed by Szigeti in 1908 and Wallfisch in 1997. Another nineteenth-century violinist, Eugène Ysaÿe is also noted for his incredibly speedy interpretation of the third movement of Mendelssohn's Violin Concerto. See Dorottya Fabian, 'The Recordings of Joachim, Ysaÿe and Sarasate in Light of their Reception by Nineteenth-Century British Critics,' *International Review of the Aesthetics and Sociology of Music*, 37/2 (2006), 189-211.

and contrasts them to the "hard-core" MSP cluster. Finally, in Table 4.3 I present the average tempo values of all recorded performances selected for the present study against the pre-1977 average.

In each Table the results are slightly or strikingly different! This is extremely important to note because it highlights how easy it is to draw incorrect conclusions. Even if one is interested in overall trends only (Table 4.3), caution is warranted: only 19 out of 28 movements (68%) show a slight increase in tempo. It is noteworthy that the Fugues, the E Major Preludio, as well as the D minor Allemanda and Giga have become slower. Moreover, the size of the pool of recordings examined also has to be kept in mind. Many more recordings may exist and although I believe I have examined a fairly exhaustive portion of the most readily available versions, additional versions could change the results reported here.[2] Furthermore, the perceptual difference between one or two metronome marks is unlikely to be significant, especially since these values are averages based on overall tempo calculated from duration.

However honestly one reports averages, such a presentation hides what I believe to be the case: that tempo is a personal thing. My investigations over the years indicate that there are musicians who like to play fast and there are those who prefer it slower. Alternatively, some tend to play fast movements really fast and slow movements quite languidly (e.g. Ibragimova in the current data set), while others prefer less extreme tempo choices regardless of movement type (most HIP violinists). This lesson can be drawn from the examination of pre-1980 recordings as well and seem to hold true in other repertoires too.[3]

---

[2] Dario Sarlo studies over 130 recordings of the E Major Preludio in his forthcoming book, *The Performance Style of Jascha Heifetz* (Farnham: Ashgate, 2015) and refers to James Creighton's *Discopaedia of the Violin, 1889-1971* (Toronto: University of Toronto Press, 1974). This indicates that "by 1971 there were at least 320 complete and partial recordings from the solo works" (Sarlo, *Heifetz*, 2015, chapter eight).

[3] Dorottya Fabian, *Bach Performance Practice, 1945-1975: A Comprehensive Review of Sound Recordings and Literature* (Aldershot: Ashgate, 2003), pp. 97-124. Another issue is the *perception* of tempo. As Harnoncourt pointed out many years ago, well-articulated music will always sound faster. Nikolaus Harnoncourt, *Baroque Music Today: Music as Speech* (Portland, Oregon: Amadeus Press, 1988), p. 52. *Musik als Klangrede*, trans. by M. O'Neill (Salzburg: Residenz, 1982).

Table 4.1. Summary of tempo trends 1977-2010 (For change to be noted $R^2 = >0.001$)[4]

Performing style	Speeding up	Slowing down	No change
MSP (all non-specialist)	**Am** Grave, Fuga **CM** Adagio, Allegro assai **Bm** Allemanda (v. slightly); Corrente Double, Borea & Double **Dm** Corrente, Giga **EM** Preludio, Loure, Bourée	**Gm** Fuga, Siciliano, Presto **Am** Andante, Allegro **CM** Largo **Bm** Allemanda Double; Corrente, Sarabande & Double **Dm** Sarabanda **EM** Menuets	**Gm** Adagio **CM** Fuga **Dm** Allemanda, Ciaccona **EM** Gavotte, Gigue
HIP (all period specialists; Gähler not regarded as such)	**Gm** Siciliano, Presto **Am** Fuga **CM** Allegro assai **Bm** Corrente, Borea & Double, **Dm** Corrente, Giga **EM** Preludio, Gavotte, Menuet 2 & da Capo, Gigue	**Gm** Adagio, Fuga **Am** Grave, Andante, Allegro **CM** Adagio **Bm** Allemanda & Double, Sarabande & Double **Dm** Allemanda, Sarabanda, Ciaccona **EM** Loure, Bourée	**CM** Largo, Fuga **Bm** Corrente Double, **EM** Menuet 1,

Table 4.2. Average MSP and HIP tempos across all studied recordings made since 1903 (Joachim). Violinists who were added to HIP are: Zehetmair, Tetzlaff (both), Tognetti, St John, Barton Pine, Gringolts, Mullova (1993, 2008), Faust, and Ibragimova.

G minor Sonata:

Adagio		Fuga		Siciliano		Presto	
HIP	MSP	HIP	MSP	HIP	MSP	HIP	MSP
25	22	66	72	26	25	69	76
Recalculate adding "cross-over" to HIP							
25	21	69	72	27	24	74	75

---

4   R-squared is a statistical measure of how close the data points are to the fitted regression line. It is a measure of variance explained. See Timothy C. Urdan, *Statistics in Plain English* (New Jersey: Lawrence Erlbaum Associates Inc., 2005), p. 155. I calculated a simple linear regression of tempo choices over time.

4. Analysis of Performance Features

A minor Sonata:

Grave		Fuga		Andante		Allegro	
HIP	MSP	HIP	MSP	HIP	MSP	HIP	MSP
26	23	70	77	31	29	41	43
Recalculate adding "cross-over" to HIP							
26	22	76	75	32	28	43	42

C Major Sonata:

Adagio		Fuga		Largo		Allegro assai	
HIP	MSP	HIP	MSP	HIP	MSP	HIP	MSP
38	32	65	70	28	26	120	126
Recalculate adding "cross-over" to HIP							
37	31	69	69	28	26	126	123

B minor Partita

Allemanda		Double		Corrente		Double		Sarabande		Double		Borea		Double	
HIP	MSP	HIP	MSP	HIP	MSP	HIP	MSP	HIP	MSP	HIP	MSP	HIP	MSP	HIP	MSP
38	36	35	34	127	138	131	136	57	54	73	79	79	79	82	86
Recalculate adding "cross-over" to HIP															
39	35	35	34	141	134	137	133	56	54	72	83	82	77	85	85

D minor Partita

Allemanda		Corrente		Sarabanda		Giga		Ciaconna	
HIP	MSP	HIP	MSP	HIP	MSP	HIP	MSP	HIP	MSP
59	56	125	118	40	40	76	79	60	55
Recalculate HIP adding "cross-over"									
58	56	122	114	41	39	79	78	60	54

E Major Partita

Preludio		Loure		Gavotte		Menuet 1		Menuet 2		Bourée		Gigue	
HIP	MSP	HIP	MSP	HIP	MSP	HIP	MSP	HIP	MSP	HIP	MSP	HIP	MSP
115	121	26	22	73	73	119	117	122	118	50	51	71	72
Recalculate HIP to add cross-over players													
119	120	26	21	75	71	122	114	124	117	52	48	74	71

134 A Musicology of Performance

Table 4.3: Average tempos in recordings made pre and post 1978 (before or after Luca).
MSP and HIP versions are combined.

4.3a: Tempo averages in slow movements

	Gm Adagio	Am Grave	CM Adagio	Gm Siciliano	Am Andante	CM Largo	Dm Sarabanda	Bm Sarabande (Double)	EM Loure
Pre-1980	20	21	31	23	28	24	39	55 (87)	20
Post-1980	23	24	34	26	31	27	40	55 (74)	24

4.3b: Tempo averages in fugues and final allegros

	Gm Fuga	Am Fuga	CM Fuga	Gm Presto	Am Allegro	CM Allegro assai	EM Preludio
Pre-1978	72	77	69	73	42	121	121
Post-1978	70	75	68	74	42	126	118

4.3c: Tempo averages in other movements

	Bm Allemanda (Double)	Dm Allemanda	Bm Corrente (Double)	Dm Corrente	Dm Giga	EM Gigue
Pre-1978	34 (34)	59	132 (130)	112	79	70
Post-1978	37 (35)	56	139 (137)	122	78	73
	EM Gavotte	EM Menuet I	EM Menuet II	EM Bouree	Bm Borea (Double)	Dm Ciaconna
Pre-1978	72	110	113	48	77 (87)	55
Post-1978	74	120	120	51	80 (84)	56

A focus on individual differences in tempo choices makes overall trends recede and diversity emerge. Some basic statistics may assist us to better understand the extent of this diversity. Standard Deviations (SD) are useful in determining global relationships. They show that there are examples in every movement of every work where the tempo difference is above two or close to three SD.[5] Almost any violinist, irrespective of age, may

---

5 The Standard Deviation (SD) is defined as the average amount by which scores in a distribution differ from the mean. It shows how much variation there is from the mean. Generally three standard deviations account for 99.7% of the studied data. One SD accounts for about 68% of the data set while two SD about 95%. When SD is close to 0 this indicates that the data points are very close to the mean. In the current

be performing above one SD in any given movement, indicating fairly wide-spread tempo choices. This is also true when HIP and HIP-inspired players are grouped together against "hard-core" MSP players as well as when tempo choices are pooled into groups of non-specialist versus period violinists.

One overall observation that can be made reasonably safely, I believe, is that extreme tempos (i.e. SD values well above ±2) are more typical among MSP players: First and foremost Zehetmair, Tetzlaff, Kremer (in 2005) and Gringolts who all tend to play fast, but also Edinger and Gähler who tend to choose tempos at the slower end of the spectrum. In contrast, when compared to the entire pool of the studied recordings, only two HIP violinists stand out with frequently higher than ±2 SD scores: Monica Huggett and, to a lesser extent, Brian Brooks. Hers are often among the slowest whereas Brooks' are among the faster versions. Other HIP violinists might deviate much in just one movement, like Beznosiuk who plays the C Major Allegro assai much slower than the norm (-2.04 SD). Among HIP-inspired violinist a similar example is Tognetti who takes the A minor Fuga very fast (2.84 SD) and the Double of the B minor Sarabande rather slow (-1.82 SD). Otherwise his tempos are close to the average found in recordings issued since the beginning of the twentieth century.

So what have we learned about tempo that was worth the trouble and informs the main goals and argument of this book? We gained three significant insights: First, there is great plurality in tempo choice among the examined recordings which may be overlooked when reporting only averages. This diversity seems to be relatively independent of the performer's age and generation; it is related, rather, to individual preference. Nevertheless closer study may indicate the impact of advances in musicology and performance practice in terms of knowledge about baroque dances and determining the right tempo of these and other movements (e.g. through an understanding of the meaning of eighteenth-century time signatures and notation practices).[6] Blanket statements that

---

study negative values indicate a deviation slower than the mean score while positive values are faster than average. I did not include a tabulation of SD values here but the information can be provided upon requests.

6   Key sources for an understanding of the role of meter and its relationship to tempo are Johann Kirnberger's treatise, *Die Kunst des reinen Satzes in der Musik* (*The Art of Strict Composition in Music*, 1774, especially Book II, part IV, pp. 105-153) and George Houle, *Meter in Music, 1600-1800* (Bloomington: Indiana University Press, 1987). The tempo of dance movements are discussed in many recent books on baroque music, including David Ledbetter, *Unaccompanied Bach: Performing the Solo Works* (New Haven: Yale University Press, 2009) and Jaap Schröder, *Bach's Solo Violin Works: A Performer's Guide* (London: Yale University Press, 2007).

the performance of baroque music has become faster over time hide these important reasons and may lead to unwarranted explanations privileging broader cultural or social forces.

Second, although the average tempo of HIP-inspired players is often closer to the average of HIP violinists, the *range* of tempos found in the former group is nevertheless more in line with the spread found among "hard-core" MSP players (evidenced in the reduction of SD values when these players are grouped with MSP versions). This, in turn, points to the third insight, namely the greater congruence of tempo (i.e. less diversity) among HIP versions.

Period violinists tend to choose less extreme tempos in every movement. This means that the tempo contrast between faster and slower movements is also less significant in these versions, reflecting historically informed tempo choices. Current readings of historical treatises encourage moderate tempos across the board; the idea being that extreme tempos are a feature of nineteenth-century romantic conceptions of music. Perhaps this belief impacts primarily on the slower movements where musicians may feel that an overtly slow Adagio or Largo may foster a romantic emotion. The resulting faster pace of ostensibly slow movements may foster the public impression that performances have become faster. Even if this was upheld by an examination of a large corpus of recorded performance, a tendency for faster tempos in all movement types may have more to do with historical performance practice research than modernist aesthetics: playing Bach's music fast is congruent with Philip Emmanuel Bach's edict, reported by Forkel, that "in the execution of his own pieces [his father] generally took the time very brisk." However, the sentence continues by stating that "besides this briskness [Bach contrived] to introduce so much variety in his performance that under his hand every piece was, as it were, like a discourse."[7] The more moderate speeds found in HIP versions often serve a more closely articulated performance that is richer in nuance and agogic-rhetorical detail.

Finally, the subjectivity of tempo is also underlined by a comparison of recommendations found in the literature and actual practice. For the Preludio of the E Major Partita, for instance, Schröder recommends a

---

7   *The New Bach Reader—A Life of Johann Sebastian Bach in Letters and Documents*, ed. by Christoph Wolff (London and New York: Norton, 1998), p. 436.

"relaxed [crotchet] = 110, approximately."[8] Most violinists tend to opt for a faster tempo with the average being around 118 (see Tables 4.2 and 4.3c). Schröder's own version is considerably slower; in fact it is the second slowest at 99 crotchet beats per minute (Beznosiuk's tempo is 98 bpm).

4.2. Vibrato

Apart from tempo and dynamics, vibrato is perhaps the most often studied parameter, especially in empirically orientated studies of vocal and violin performance.[9] Being a very personal matter, a whole study could be dedicated to analysing and comparing the nature and characteristics of different violinists' vibrato. Although of potential interest to other violinists, it is doubtful if written accounts and objective measurements provide meaningful information regarding this particular matter. Visual inspection of players in action, reflecting on resulting sound qualities and pondering their affective dimension may be more productive. Engaging with bodily, kinaesthetic actions and musical-emotional gestures are likely to be more useful than thinking in terms of vibrato width (depth) or rate.

In this regard my data set shows that period and HIP-inspired players vary their vibrato more, often combining it with "hair-pin" swells (i.e. rapid crescendo on a single note) or *messa-di-voce* effects (i.e. adding or increasing vibrato in the middle of a rapid crescendo-decrescendo). Longer notes starting straight and being vibrated from half-way through are also quite common. Other times the vibrato might be tapered off into straight notes either in combination with a diminuendo or without. Quite clearly, for these violinists vibrato is an expressive device whereas "hard-core" MSP players use it as a part of basic tone production. Their well-regulated, near-continuous, and uniform vibrato indicates this (Figure 4.1a-c).

---

8   Schröder, *Bach's Solo Violin Works*, p. 168.
9   Most violin tutors discuss vibrato at length. Many modern studies could also be mentioned that provide a historical context for the aesthetic ideals behind its use and discussion of individual characteristics. The reader is pointed to three key publications that report, among others, vibrato in recorded violin performances: David Milsom, *Theory and Practice In Late Nineteenth-Century Violin Performance: An Examination of Style in Performance, 1850-1900* (Aldershot: Ashgate, 2003); Mark Katz, *Capturing Sound: How Technology has Changed Music* (Berkeley and Los Angeles: University of California Press, 2004) and Daniel Leech-Wilkinson, *The Changing Sound of Music: Approaches to Studying Recorded Musical Performance* (London: CHARM, 2009).

(a) Hahn

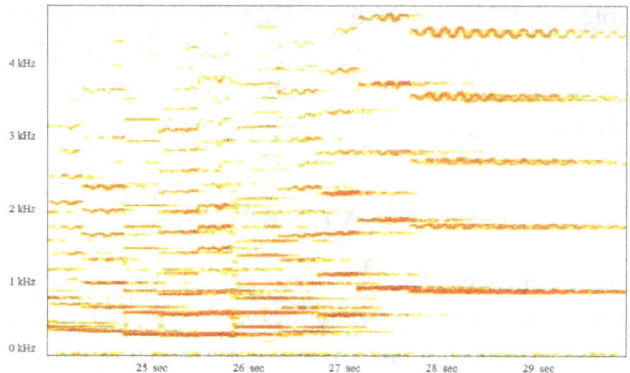

(b) Shumsky

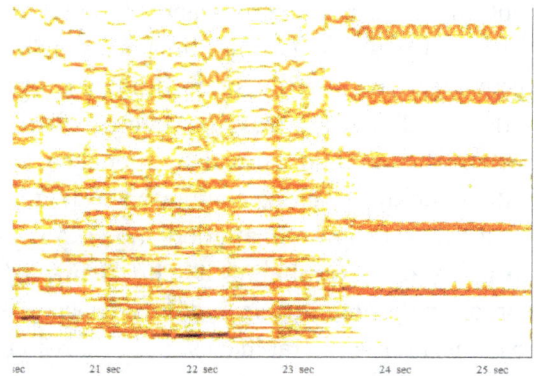

(c) Podger

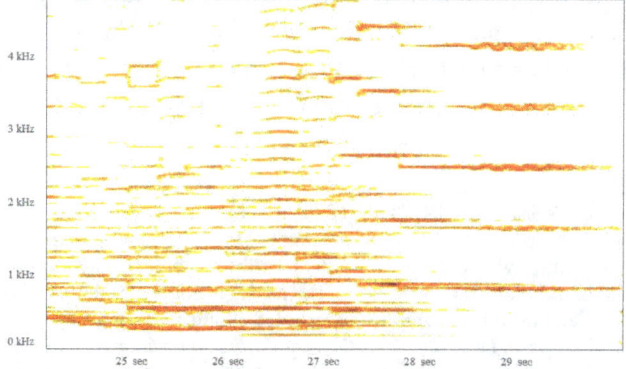

(d) Tognetti

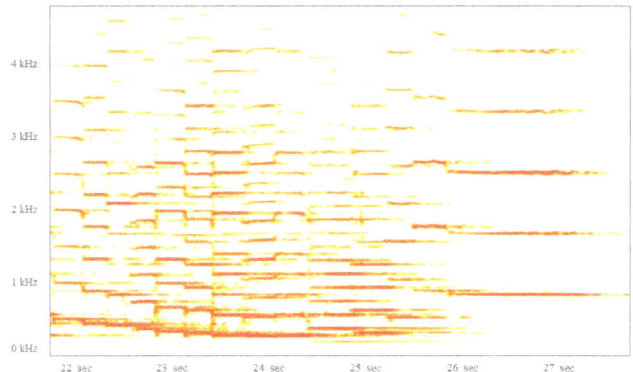

(e) Ibragimova

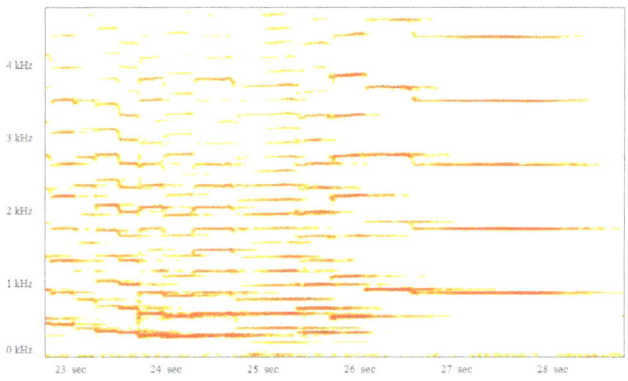

(f) Mullova 2008

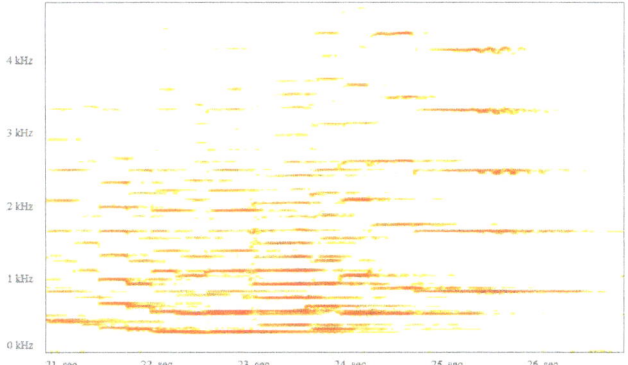

Figure 4.1a-f. Spectrograms of bars 5-6 of the D minor Sarabanda performed by (a) Hahn, (b) Shumsky, (c) Podger, (d) Tognetti, (e) Ibragimova and (f) Mullova in 2008. [Spectrogram parameters: High band Hz: 4800; Window size / Display width: 6 sec; Colour Spectrum Level Minimum: -80dB; Frequency resolution: 12.5 Hz.]

Exceptions among MSP players include Buswell. He plays many notes non-vibrato, using it instead to intensify certain longer notes, such as melodic high-points. Mullova is an interesting case as her vibrato often starts from below; in other words with a downward fluctuation of pitch (especially in 2008). In her later recordings she limits vibrato to function only as decoration, often simply a fast single quiver on a short or long note. On the basis of visually inspecting the spectrograms of her recordings I believe that it might be more bow (and / or finger) pressure fluctuation that contributes to a vibrato effect rather than change in the width of the pitch's frequency range achieved through finger or wrist movements. Her practice of lifted bowing (quick decay) allows more room for changes in dynamics (intensity of sound level) than for vibrato.

Such a conflation of bowing and vibrato underscores the multiplicity of elements contributing to the acoustic-aesthetic stimulus we listeners perceive. Tonal colouring enriches the expressive content musical moments communicate. The greater the blend of elements from bowing, phrasing, timing, dynamics, tone colour, harmony and melody, the stronger the "Gestalt" experience: we are less inclined to say "oh, did you hear that vibrato?" or "what exquisite bowing!" and more inclined to respond globally: "ah, that was beautiful!" When one or another performance element comes to the fore our analytical mind may interfere with our holistic perception. We may relish the fact that we can pick out the cause of an effect, "ahah, she used vibrato here to highlight that note"; or "gosh, that was a wide vibrato!" But if such analytical recognition happens too often, the overall verdict may be that the performance is "idiosyncratic" or "mannered."[10] So it is really doubtful what purpose the attention to measuring vibrato (or indeed looking at performance features in an itemized fashion as I do here in this chapter) serves.

Furthermore, quantitative results are also silent about additional characteristics of approaches to vibrato use. For instance, quite a few violinists reduce their vibrato during repeats (e.g. Buswell, Huggett, St John, Mullova in 1993). Fischer is the only player who vibrates more notes

---

10 To the extent something jarring may create negative emotions, this is corroborated by Juslin when he posits that "[a] possible effect of emotion on aesthetic processing is that positive emotions can lead a listener to process the music more 'holistically,' whereas negative emotions will him or her to process it more 'analytically.'" Patrik N. Juslin, 'From Everyday Emotions to Aesthetic Emotions: Towards a unified theory of musical emotions,' *Physics of Life Reviews*, 10 (2013), 235-266 (pp. 256-257). I thank Daniel Bangert for alerting me to this recent paper by Juslin.

in repeats but the depth is extremely narrow, making the vibrato sound more like a fast, enhancing quiver or extra vibration. Nevertheless, for those who are interested in quantitative measures I offer Table 4.4 and a brief commentary on the four overarching information that can be deduced from the data: 1) a steep decline in use of vibrato since around 1995; 2) a fairly standard vibrato rate; 3) a narrower vibrato depth among HIP and younger players; and 4) a lack of noteworthy change in vibrato style in subsequent recordings of the same violinist.[11]

Table 4.4. Vibrato rate, width (depth) and frequency of use measured on selected notes in different movements and averaged across each selected violinist. (Rate is expressed in cycles per second (cps); Width in semitones (sT). Frequency refers to occurrence of vibrato on the selected pitches). Standard Deviation (SD) indicates the evenness of each player's vibrato (the smaller the number, the more regular the vibrato).

Performer, date	Rate (in cps) (SD)	Width (in sT) (SD)	Frequency of use
Barton-Pine 1999	6. (SD: 0.9)	0.21 (SD: 0.12)	62%
Barton-Pine 2004	nil		
Barton-Pine 2007	6.1 (SD: 0.9)	0.12 (SD: 0.03)	14%
Besnosiuk 2007 (HIP)	Very little	not measurable	<5%
Brooks 2001	6.9 (SD: 1.08)	0.12 (SD: 0.03)	67%†
Buswell 1987	6.5 (SD:0.08)	0.19 (SD: 0.08)	89%
Ehnes 1999	6.3 (SD:0.6)	0.2 (SD: 0.05)	100%
Faust 2010	Fast quivers	<0.1	<1%
Fischer 2005	6.4 (SD: 0.5)	0.14 (SD: 0.04)	50%
Gähler 1998	6.3 (SD:0.37)	0.15 (SD: 0.06)	>60%*
Gringolts 2001	6.9 (SD:0.28)	0.16 (SD: 0.04)	<3%
Hahn 1999	6.6 (SD: 0.3)	0.23 (SD: 0.1)	100%
Holloway 2006 (HIP)	6 (SD: 0.5)	0.17 (SD: 0.04)	39%
Huggett 1995 (HIP)	5.8 (SD: 0.5)	0.12 (SD: 0.06)	46.3%
Ibragimova 2009	Nil to measure	nil	0%

---

11 Vibrato measurements were taken on thirty-eight selected notes in the A minor Sonata's Andante (number of violinists = 29) and the D minor Partita's Sarabanda (n = 9) movements or the E Major Partita's Loure (n = 9) when there was no recording of the D minor Partita by a given violinist. Frequency of vibrato use was calculated by noting how many of these notes were played with vibrato. The software program *Spectrogram 14* was used to measure vibrato. The program displayed a spectrogram of the audio file using the following parameters: High band Hz: 4200; Window size / Display width: 4 sec; Frequency resolution: 18.7 Hz; Colour spectrum range: 0 to -80 dB. To calculate vibrato speed / rate the number of undulations were counted relative to the note duration in milliseconds. Vibrato depth / width was calculated from the frequency (Hz) difference between the inner bottom and top edges of undulations (as read off the screen by manually placing the pointer to the relevant position). All depth measurements were carried out twice to check for possible errors and adjust if necessary.

Table 4.4., cont. Vibrato rate, width (depth) and frequency of use measured on selected notes in different movements and averaged across each selected violinist. (Rate is expressed in cycles per second (cps); Width in semitones (sT). Frequency refers to occurrence of vibrato on the selected pitches). Standard Deviation (SD) indicates the evenness of each player's vibrato (the smaller the number, the more regular the vibrato).

Performer, date	Rate (in cps) (SD)	Width (in sT) (SD)	Frequency of use
Khachatryan 2009	6.8 (SD: 0.6)	0.17 (SD:0.05)	89-94%
Kremer 1980	6.3 (SD: 0.36)	0.26 (SD: 0.07)	91%
Kremer 2005	6.2 (SD: 0.8)	0.2 (SD: 0.15)	44%
Kuijken 1983 (HIP)	5.9 (SD: 0.6)	0.15 (SD: 0.07)	63.3%
Kuijken 2001 (HIP)	5.9 (SD: 0.8)	0.16 (SD: 0.9)	60%
Lev 2001	6.8 (SD: 0.29)	0.12 (SD: 0.04)	61%
Luca 1977 (HIP)	6.7 (SD: 0.1)	0.14 (SD: 0.08)	39.5%
Matthews 1997	Rarely measurable; end of trills		<1%
Mintz 1984	5.9 (SD: 0.4)	0.3 (SD: 0.04)	90%
Mullova 1993	6.8 (SD: 0.5)	0.16 (SD: 0.06)	44%
Mullova 2008	6.8 (SD: 0.26)	0.12 (SD: 0.03)	11%
Perlman 1987	6.6 (SD: 1.7)	0.33 (SD: 0.15)	76%
Podger 1999 (HIP)	6 (SD: 0.7)	0.14 (SD: 0.09)	27%
Poulet 1996	6.2 (SD: 0.3)	0.19 (SD: 0.06)	72%
Ricci 1981	6.0 (SD: 0.5)	0.3 (SD: 0.17)	76%
Schröder 1985 (HIP)	6.5 (SD: 0.6)	0.15 (SD: 0.06)	55%
Shumsky 1983	6.4 (SD: 0.27)	0.21 (SD: 0.05)	100%
St John 2007	6.7 (SD: 0.6)	0.23 (SD:0.02)	22%
Szenthelyi 2002	6.4 (SD: 0.28)	0.3 (SD: 0.1)	82%
Tetzlaff 1994	6.2 (SD: 1.1)	0.16 (SD: 0.12)	73%
Tetzlaff 2005	6.5 (SD: 0.43)	0.21 (SD: 0.48)	91%
Tognetti 2005	5.9 (SD: 0.3)	0.1 (SD: 0.03)	39%
Ughi 1991	(quite fast)	Not wide	100%
Van Dael 1996 (HIP)	6.3 (SD: 0.8)	0.13 (SD: 0.04)	17%
Wallfisch 1997 (HIP)	5.8 (SD: 0.5)	0.06 (SD: 0.14)	45.5%
Zehetmair 1983	4.8 (SD: 0.5)	0.44 (SD: 0.16)	14%

† Brooks' vibrato is often very fast and extremely narrow; hard to measure at all let alone accurately. Therefore the frequency percent is an estimate based on where rate could be measured but width not and where width was measurable but not the rate (signal showing a thick line with fluctuating intensity).

* Gähler's vibrato is basically continuous but when playing full chords it is not easily executed or measured. Measurements were possible for more than 60% of the selected notes. His vibrato tends to be slow but not too wide except on single longer notes. On these occasions it becomes faster.

First, the steep decline in the use of vibrato since around 1995 is also indicated by the considerable drop in vibrato use in subsequent recordings of the same violinist (see Kremer 91% to 45.3%, Barton Pine 62% to 14%). The exceptions are Tetzlaff, who vibrated more frequently in 2005 and Kuijken, whose approach remained steady, around 60%, the highest among HIP versions.

Second, according to various researchers, a well-regulated vibrato has around six to six-and-a-half cycles per second (cps).[12] Table 4.4 shows most violinists' vibrato rate to hover around this value. The vibrato speed of HIP players is slightly slower (except for Brooks). I believe this slower rate to be related to the idea of vibrato being an ornament because a slower vibrato tends to be more audible and to sound more like an expressive decoration or a change in tone colour. A fast vibrato sounds more like a quiver, at times a sign of tension, although it could also tend towards a shake or trill.

Third, vibrato depth (or width) is shallower in HIP (up to 0.15 of a semitone [sT]) than in MSP versions (up to around 0.3 sT). This may also be related to the aim of avoiding vibrato altogether: In a stream of straight notes a very shallow vibrato may create enough tonal nuances to signify certain musical moments.

Fourth, multiple recordings of violinists show no substantial change in their vibrato style. One may speculate that no change in vibrato width and rate in these multiple versions is evidence that the technical delivery of vibrato is a personal signature and when players control it unconsciously it reflects their ingrained technical style. Of course at their level of professionalism it is perfectly within their conscious control to vary vibrato for expressive effect—or to eliminate its use entirely.

Table 4.4 also provides information about variety of vibrato. This can be deduced from the SD values. Standard Deviation values indicate the variability in the measurement of each player's vibrato. According to this, the depth varies much less than the rate. Brooks, Perlman and Tetzlaff in 1994 have the least regular vibrato rate, having greater than 1 SD. The results for Zehetmair's vibrato are also worth pointing out: they are extreme and indicate one aspect of his highly idiosyncratic style. He used vibrato infrequently and also varied it quite a bit. At significant high notes it tended to be wide and slow—very noticeable, indeed.

---

12 Richard Miller, *The Structure of Singing: System and Art in Vocal Technique* (London and New York: Schirmer Books, 1986). See also Leech-Wilkinson, *The Changing Sound of Music*.

144   A Musicology of Performance

Finally it is worth picking out some violinists from the roster for individual attention. This may help to unpack the interaction of vibrato with other performance features or to explain seeming anomalies in Table 4.4.

> Looking at players with narrow vibrato width, Kachatryan should be mentioned first. When he is playing softly, it becomes almost impossible to measure due to lack of visible signals. Hence the range of percentage for him in Table 4.4: the lower number excludes notes where only rate could be measured. Brooks' vibrato is also often extremely narrow and quite fast, making accurate measurements difficult. Therefore the percentage of frequency of use is an estimate only; a combination of where rate could be measured but depth not (i.e. signal showing a thick line with fluctuating intensity) and where depth was measurable but not the rate. Ehnes' vibrato is audible primarily because it tends to be rather slow. At the same time it is quite narrow (and therefore hard to measure) and it tapers off on longer notes. Lev's vibrato seems often to be a result of bow pressure fluctuation, a consequence of strong down-bows followed by quick decay. At other times it might be a short quiver creating emphasis. Barton Pine has no measurable vibrato in 2004 (only the D minor Sarabanda was available). Bowing (e.g. swell and reverse swell / down-bow) shows some fluctuation but as it is not vibrato but an effect of bowing, it is rather pointless to measure.
>
> In Gringolts' A minor Andante there is nothing measurable. What one may hear as vibrato seems to be an effect of his bowing (pressure, speed) that creates a kind of "gliding," rapidly fluctuating sound. However, it is hardly possible to call that vibrato: not a single vibrato curve can be seen in the spectrogram, just some unsteadiness in the intensity of the signal. In his interpretation of the E Major Loure, quivers (or just a single quiver) are more audible when "leaning-on" with bowing (down-bows). Proper vibrato curves are still hard to detect and often turn out to be trills. The two notes where vibrato could be measured in the Loure were the B crotchet on the down-beat of bar 8 and the A crotchet on the forth beat of the same bar. The vibrato rate of the two notes was 6.4 and 7.1 cps, respectively, while the depth measures were 0.13 and 0.19 sT.
>
> Among older MSP players, who are inclined to regard vibrato as integral to tone production, Poulet's vibrato is quite slow but not too wide. It becomes more prominent on melodically or harmonically important notes. Shumsky's vibrato is wider than the younger players' and at times slower as well. Gähler's vibrato is basically continuous but when playing full chords with his curved "Bach-bow," it is not easily executed creating blurred signals. Measurements were possible for more than 60% of the selected notes. His vibrato tends to be slow but not too wide except on single longer notes. On these occasions it was faster or sped up after a slower beginning.

All this speaks particularly to two of my main aims in this book. Firstly, it shows that even vibrato has again become less homogeneous during the past thirty years; it has started to sound similarly varied to what one hears on early twentieth-century recordings. This is true on several levels: at the level of contrasting MSP and HIP approaches to vibrato along a continuum of frequency of use and tone production, and at the level of varying vibrato "style" or quality. Secondly, it shows the interaction of performance elements contributing to tone production and musical expressivity.

Diversity in vibrato is interesting first and foremost for *how* it is varied, not whether it is used at all. It is fascinating to realize that vibrato has again become part of expression rather than tone production. And not just in this special repertoire as might be objected. I have studied many recordings of Beethoven and Brahms violin sonatas as well, for instance, and can confirm that variation in vibrato for expressive tonal effects is on the rise among players as different as Anne-Sophie Mutter, Viktoria Mullova, Rachel Barton Pine, Isabelle Faust or Daniel Sepec.[13]

Why is variety in vibrato an important finding? Because a fundamental piece of evidence that supports the criticism of uniformity in performance is uniformity of sound—homogeneous, undifferentiated tone achieved through seamless bowing of equal pressure throughout and perfectly controlled, even vibrato, as exemplified by Hilary Hahn's playing, for instance. Joseph Szigeti complained already in the 1950s that players have lost the "speaking quality" of their bowing, that too much emphasis has been put on right hand technique and power of tone. He pointed out that without varied bow strokes the musical characters are ironed-out.[14] Alternatively people blamed the recording industry and oversized concert halls for needing big sounds that carry into the farthest corners and

---

13 Beethoven Violin Sonatas with Sophie Mutter and Lambert Orkis on Deutsche Grammopon 457 623-2 (1998); Viktoria Mullova and Christian Bezuidenhout on Onyx 4050 (2010); Rachel Barton Pine and Matthew Hagle in concert on Chicago's WFMT Radio (2005); Isabelle Faust and Alexander Melnikov on Harmonia Mundi 902025-27 (2009); Daniel Sepec and Andreas Staier on Harmonia Mundi 901919 (2006). However, a cursory listening to about ten recordings of Mozart's Violin Concerto No. 5 made since the 1980s did not show much diversity in tone (or in other features, for that matter). For instance, the nominally HIP version of Andrew Manze (Harmonia Mundi 2006 HMU 807385) has a fairly vibrato-less tone while Hilary Hahn's 2015 recording (Deutsche Grammophon 0289 479 3956 6 CD DDD GH) displays all the hallmarks of MSP and evenly regulated, continuous vibrato.

14 Joseph Szigeti, *Szigeti on the Violin* (New York: Dover Books, 1979), especially pp. 38-43.

balance well with the might of large orchestras. We have seen, in chapter three, how famous teachers contributed to this development and Table 4.4 clearly shows that violinists of the Juilliard / Curtis School continue this tradition. The continuous vibrato, allegedly developed to counteract the depersonalized nature of sound recordings,[15] became a vehicle for an idealized aesthetic of perfect control manifest in consistent tone. Perhaps it is a saturated market calling on musicians to differentiate themselves, perhaps it is the opportunity offered by smaller independent record labels, perhaps it is the musicians' need to do something new, perhaps it is our pluralistic time that *allows* musicians to interpret, to *play* and not be bound by rules and the tyranny of perfection that resulted in the return of varied vibrato. Most likely it is a combination of all this that calls on violinists to question the nature of perfection by creating performances full of tonal shades, uneven bow strokes and variously vibrated notes.

4.3. Ornamentation

Much has been written about ornamentation in baroque music and I focus only on those matters that relate to the broader concerns of this book. Pertinent among these is the aesthetic effect achieved. Therefore, first I will discuss some of the scholarly opinions that highlight essential aesthetic problems and then will aim to analyze the recordings in this context.

Problems of Aesthetics and Notation Practices

One of the most difficult problems of ornamentation and improvisation in baroque music is deciding not so much how but *when* and *how much* to do it.[16] There are countless charts providing solutions to symbols of graces

---

15   Katz, *Capturing Sound*, pp. 85-98, esp. 93, 95-96.
16   Basic and detailed information on ornamentation practices, including the differences between national styles are readily and abundantly available in modern publications. The best known are Arnold Dolmetsch, *The Interpretation of the Music of the Seventeenth and Eighteenth Centuries* (London: Novello, 1949/1915 [R1969]); Robert Donington, *The Interpretation of Early Music* (London: Faber, 1963 [rev. edn 1989]); Putnam Aldrich, *Ornamentation in Bach's Organ Works* (New York: Coleman-Ross, 1950), Frederick Neumann, *Ornamentation in Baroque and Post-Baroque Music* (Princeton: Princeton University Press, 1978). Therefore, I restrict discussion to issues that are relevant to my project at hand.

and many examples of figurative embellishments.[17] However, in the end all sources, modern and historical alike, reiterate that it is a matter of good taste to know when and what, or how much, is appropriate. What's more, it is obvious that the sensibility of this infamous *bon goût* changes with the passing of generations.

Take Pier Francesco Tosi (1653-1732), for instance. Writing in his old age, when the much younger Farinelli (alias Carlo Maria Broschi, 1705-1782) and other popular singers are admired for their ability to lavish simply sketched melodies with *passagi* and *roulades*, he decries them as "modernists" who are lacking in true taste, scorning them for "their offences against the true art of singing."[18] At the same time, Johann-Joachim Quantz (1697-1773), a contemporary of Farinelli, enthusiastically praises the 1720s-30s when, in his view, the art of singing reached its greatest height.[19] However, reading both Tosi and Quantz further, one encounters statements from the former: "whoever cannot vary and

---

17 Bach himself prepared such a table for his eldest son (see "Explication unterschiedlicher Zeichen, so gewisse Manieren artig zu spielen, andeuten" in *Clavierbüchlein für Wilhelm Friedemann Bach*, ca. 1720; manuscript in School of Music Library, Yale University) that has often been reproduced and transcribed. Examples of figurative embellishments can be found, for instance among Handel's scores (performance copies he created for some of his singers) or, famously, Roger's 1710 Amsterdam edition of Corelli's violin sonatas Op. 5. In my discussion, I aim to distinguish between the French practice of *agréments* and the Italian melodic embellishment. The former comprises short grace notes either notated in small font or indicated by symbols, such as trills, mordents, appoggiaturas, slides and turns. Melodic embellishments are basically diminutions or divisions where written notes are broken up into smaller denominations, providing figuration on the melody and harmony. To confuse matters further, Bach often uses a combination of signs and normal font in his notation practices, although he often omits the sign itself while still notating out a part of the grace. A common example is a long note followed by two short notes in a suffix melodic shape. Even without the trill sign on the long note, the two short notes may in effect be the written-out ending of a trill. Similarly, appoggiaturas are often written out, masking the context and erroneously inviting added appoggiaturas (for starting a trill, for instance). I have shown such examples in my paper 'Ornamentation in Recent Recordings of J. S. Bach's Solo Sonatas and Partitas for Violin,' *Min-Ad: Israel Studies in Musicology Online*, 11/2 (2013), 1-21, available at http://www.biu.ac.il/hu/mu/min-ad/. Literature on ornamentation in Bach's music is vast. For a comprehensive review of such specialized literature see Fabian, *Bach Performance Practice*, chapter five.
18 Pier Francesco Tosi, *Opinioni de cantori antichi sopra il canto figurato* (1723), cited in Frederick Neumann, *Performance Practices of the Seventeenth and Eighteenth Centuries* (New York, Schirmer 1993), p. 521.
19 Johann-Joachim Quantz, *On Playing the Flute* [*Versuch*], trans. by E.R. Reilly (New York: Schirmer, 1975/1752), chapter eighteen, par. 58.

thereby improve what he has sung before is no great luminary";[20] and from the latter: "all-too-rich diminutions will deprive the melody of its capacity to 'move the heart.'"[21] So how do we know what is "all-too-rich" and what may be an "improvement" on what has already been sung?

Among modern writers on the matter Neumann provides an open-ended basic framework when he distinguishes between first- and second-degree ornamentation:

> As a rule of thumb [...] an adagio is skeletal if it contains no, or only very few, notes smaller than eighths; it has first-degree diminutions if it contains many sixteenth notes; it has second-degree diminutions if it contains a wealth of thirty-second notes or smaller values. The skeletal types were always in need of embellishment; the first-degree types may fulfill stylistic requirements in the lower range [...] further ornamental additions are optional and often desirable on repeats; the second-degree designs were in no need of further enrichment but on repeat could be somewhat varied.[22]

Bach's notation practices tend to fall into the third category (i.e. second-degree design). Deciding on ornamentation in his music is often complicated as he was in the habit of notating out diminutions, even graces that others indicated with symbols (see fn. 17 above). John Butt considers it likely that this practice of Bach, that he notates everything that is to be played, might be the key reason for the lasting appeal and value of his music.[23] Bach was chastised for it in his own time by Johann Adolf Scheibe (1708-1776) and defended by Johann Abraham Birnbaum (1702-1748) in a public debate that seems to rehearse the familiar problem of taste, the composer's "honour" and the performer's "prerogative" that are voiced also in other historical sources.[24]

---

20 Cited in Neumann, *Performance Practices*, p. 521.
21 Ibid., p. 538, citing Quantz, *Versuch*, chapter thirteen, par. 9.
22 Neumann, *Performance Practices*, p. 529.
23 Butt, *Bach Interpretation: Articulation Marks in Primary Sources* (Cambridge: Cambridge University Press, 1990), pp. 207-208.
24 For instance, compare Birnbaum's text (published in *The New Bach Reader*, pp. 338-348) with Giovanni Bononcini's complaint in the Preface to the publication of his *Sonate da Chiesa a Due Violini* (Venice: [n.p.], 1672): "because today there are some [performers] so little informed of that art of tasteful embellishment that in singing or in playing they want with their disorderly and indiscreet extravagances of bow or of voice to change, indeed to deform, the compositions (even though these were written with every care and conscientiousness) in such a manner that the authors have no choice but to beg those singers and players to content themselves with rendering the works plainly and purely as they are written" (cited in Neumann, *Performance Practices*, 570). François Couperin (Preface to *Pièces de Clavecin*, Book 3) is also on record demanding performers to be faithful to his notation whereas Michel de Saint Lambert, like Scheibe, defended

Scheibe (1737) reproached Bach for writing out all the melodic embellishments (figures or divisions) and for not leaving space for the performer's improvisation: "Every ornament, every little grace, and everything that one thinks of as belonging to the method of playing, he expresses completely in notes."[25] In Bach's defense, Birnbaum observed that it was a fortunate situation when a score where embellishments are added by the composer was available, for he knew best "where it might serve as a true ornament and particular emphasis of the main melody." Birnbaum considered it "a necessary measure of prudence on the part of the composer" to write out "every ornament ... that belongs to the method of playing." He asserted that improvised embellishments "can please the ear only if it is applied in the right places" but "offend the ear and spoil the principal melody if the performer employs [embellishments] at the wrong spot." To avoid attributing errors of melody and harmony to the composer, Birnbaum posited the right of "every composer [...] to [...] [prescribe] a correct method according to his intentions, and thus to watch over the preservation of his own honor."[26]

The Role of Delivery

The mid-twentieth-century Bach scholar and conductor Arthur Mendel (1905-1979) pointed out the crucial lesson in this debate, which turns the attention away from petty point scoring and the matter of taste toward the fundamental issue in twentieth-century Bach performance and playing baroque music in general. He suggested that Scheibe's objection was perhaps due to the difficult rhythmic patterns that arise from written-out turns and other embellishments:

> Because of the essentially improvisatory character of trills, appoggiaturas, and other ornaments, the attempt to write out just what metric value each tone is to have can never be successful. I think this may be partly what Scheibe meant in criticizing Bach for writing out so much [...] The attempt to pin down the rhythm of living music at all in the crudely simple arithmetical ratios of notated meter is [hardly ...] possible.[27]

---

    the rights of the performers "to add new ornaments [and] leave out those that are prescribed [or] to substitute others in their stead" (*Principes du Clavecin* [1702], p. 57, cited in Neumann, *Performance Practices*, p. 514).
25 *The New Bach Reader*, p. 338.
26 *The New Bach Reader*, pp. 346-347.
27 Arthur Mendel (ed.), *Bach: St John Passion—Vocal Score* (New York: Schirmer, 1951), xxii.

In their concern for the text, the notated score of a composition, and its technically correct rendering, modern musicians are easily misled by the visual representation of music. Notes of equal significance in print will likely be played with equal importance. Recognizing the ornamental nature of Bach's notation practices is a first step toward rendering rhythmic patterns and melodic groups with some freedom.

The G minor Adagio is a good example of this problem. The opening bars of it would likely have been notated as in the top system of Figure 4.2 by most other baroque composers, especially those of the Italian tradition.[28] Instead, Bach wrote out a possible embellished performance version. Playing the notes rhythmically accurately is therefore a mistake, because spontaneous ornamentation is never rhythmically stable or exact. As Lester points out, "Thinking of the *Adagio* as a prelude built upon standard thoroughbass patterns can [help] the melody [be] heard not so much as a series of fixed gestures, but rather as a continuously unfolding rhapsodic improvisation over a supporting bass."[29]

Figure 4.2. Bars 1-2 of Bach's G minor Adagio for solo violin (BWV 1001). The top system is a hypothetical version that emulates the much sparser notation habits of Italian composers such as Corelli, who tended to prescribe only basic melodic pitches that the musicians were supposed to embellish during performance. The middle stave is Bach's notation, reflecting one possible way of ornamenting the passage. His original slurs indicate ornamental groups to be performed as one musical gesture. The lowest stave shows the "standard thoroughbass" that players might conceptualize for a "rhapsodic improvisation" to unfold.

---

28 Noted also by Jaap Schröder in 'Jaap Schröder Discusses Bach's Works for Unaccompanied Violin,' *Journal of the Violin Society of America*, 3/3 (Summer 1977), 7-32; and Ledbetter, *Unaccompanied Bach*, p. 95ff.
29 Joel Lester, *Bach's Works for Solo Violin: Style, Structure, Performance* (Oxford-New York: Oxford University Press, 1999), p. 38.

4.1. Literal versus ornamental delivery of small rhythmic values in J. S. Bach, G minor Sonata BWV 1001, Adagio, extract: bars 1-2. Six versions: Monica Huggett © Virgin Veritas, Oscar Shumsky © Musical Heritage Society, Shlomo Mintz © Deutsche Grammophone, Julia Fischer © PentaTone Classics, Sergey Khachatryan © Naïve, Alina Ibragimova © Hyperion. Duration: 2.08. See also Audio examples 5.22, 5.23 and 5.24.

To listen to this extract online scan the QR code
or follow this link: http://dx.doi.org/10.11647/OBP.0064.07

Tracing flexibility (or lack thereof) in performances of the G minor Adagio throughout the course of the work's recorded history provides an excellent window into the trajectory of Bach performance practice since the beginning of the twentieth century.[30] Among the recordings under examination here, Huggett, Wallfisch, Barton Pine, Ibragimova, Mullova and others, including Schröder and Buswell, play with enough flexibility to create the impression of free ornamentation. Shumsky, Fischer, Khachatryan, Ehnes, Mintz, among others, provide much more literal and measured readings (Audio example 4.1 at Figure 4.2).

The difference in performance style also impacts on the perceived affective dimension of the piece. This movement is clearly melancholic-meditative since it contains many dissonances, displays descending melodic tendencies, and is in the minor mode;[31] a soliloquy that perhaps sounds less sad and personal when played in a measured style and sounds more as a self-reflective monologue passing through passionate outbursts and calming-tenderness when performed with fluid, rhapsodic freedom. Pondering the perceived affective dimensions of various versions is fascinating, especially since fairly small variations in particular details can

---

30   For trends in earlier recordings, see my 'Towards a Performance History of Bach's Sonatas and Partitas for Solo Violin: Preliminary Investigations,' in *Essays in Honor of László Somfai*, ed. by László Vikárius and Vera Lampert (Lanham, Maryland: Scarecrow Press, 2005), pp. 87-108. For a short summary of how the opening chord is played by various violinists in the current selection of recordings see section "Multiple Stops" later in this chapter.

31   Michael Spitzer and Eduardo Coutinho, 'The Effect of Expert Musical Training on the Perception of Emotions in Bach's Sonata for Unaccompanied Violin No. 1 in G minor (BWV 1001),' *Psychomusicology: Music, Mind and Brain*, 24/1 (2014), 35-57. I will discuss this movement and diverse affects generated by different interpretations in chapter five.

lead to quite diverse overall impression. I will come back to this in the next chapter where I consider individual differences and affective response.

Given Bach's notation practices, it might seem enough for the contemporary musician and listener to adopt a quasi-improvisatory style of playing when faced with performing Bach's written-out ornaments. However, there are also movements that are less clearly decorated, where the quantity and place of additional ornaments and embellishments are worth contemplating. Although Bach habitually wrote out more figuration than his contemporaries, including elaborate ornamental figures as we have just seen, as well as appoggiaturas and terminations of trills that need to be recognized and performed as such, he indicated graces such as trills, slides, and mordents relatively sparingly. In addition, surviving successive versions of pieces, for instance the *Inventions and Sinfonias* (BWV 772–801) or the reworking for lute of the E Major Partita for Solo Violin (BWV 1006a), show different degrees of ornamentation. According to contemporary records, Bach was also in the habit of improvising richly textured, polyphonic continuo parts instead of the apparently more common simple chordal style. So what is a performer supposed to do? What might be within "good taste"?

There seems to be "a fairly broad range of legitimately possible levels of ornamentation, extending from a desirable minimum to a saturation point."[32] Moreover, "informed" subjectivity is encouraged by Neumann when he recommends Georg Friedrich Telemann's published embellishments to his *Sonate metodiche for violin or flute* (Hamburg: [n.p.], 1728) as "helpful [...] to late Baroque diminution practice because they strike a happy balance between austerity and luxuriance."[33]

As always, performances are judged ultimately for their expressive affect and, in this regard, Quantz's reasons for his admiration of "Italian singing style [and] lavishly elaborated Italian arias" are perhaps the most useful guide. His praise is earned because they are profound and artful; they move and astonish, engage the musical intelligence, are rich in taste and rendition, and transport the listener pleasantly from one emotion to another.[34] In the footsteps of Quantz we should feel liberated to speak of the

---

32 Neumann, *Performance Practices*, p. 528. I would not even use the word "legitimate" since the range is so broad the word loses its meaning, if it is a useful concept / adjective at all.
33 Neumann, *Performance Practices*, p. 536.
34 Quantz, *Versuch*, chap. 18, par. 76, as paraphrased from Neumann, *Performance Practices*, p. 536.

subjective, to use metaphor, to allow our holistic and affective mind-body to sort out what "works." Such a reporting goes against my scientifically trained brain but feels valid to my listening, music-loving persona. I aim to balance the two by recognizing that both the performer and the analyst are confronted with a multitude of musical puzzles and possibilities with no hard and fast rules, but only "sufficiently developed taste," culturally and historically conditioned expectations, and subjective boundaries regarding what *feels* appropriate as aids and foundations for aesthetic judgment. Importantly, I hope to have demonstrated that none of this ought to be a moral issue, not even in the music of the "great" Johann Sebastian Bach. Performance is not about absolutes but about conviction and affect, nowhere more so than in relation to ornamentation and embellishment.

The Performance of Embellishments

So what do we find in the recordings? In this repertoire the past thirty years seem to demonstrate that we have reached a stage where quite a few violinists *dare* ornament several movements quite lavishly, especially in most recent times. However, ornamentation happens less in the slow movements that are already embellished by Bach and more in the lighter dance movements. Furthermore, adding short graces and altering articulation, rhythm or dynamics, or, as we have seen, using vibrato to ornament special notes are more common than melodic embellishment.[35] Nevertheless, there are also significant instances of sumptuous embellishing, even complete rewriting of bars and passages, and even in movements containing written-out figuration.

Again we can note the difference between what the factual information tells us and what it hides. Table 4.5 lists the most ornamented movements and the violinists involved in order of the amount of ornamentation and / or embellishment observed. It is immediately apparent that the E Major Partita features prominently and, although slow movements are represented, none of the opening adagios of the sonatas is listed (to my knowledge only Montanari adds embellishments in the G minor Adagio and this 2013 recording was made after the designated three decades of

---

35 A striking exception to this generalisation is Stefano Montanari's 2011 recording of the works (Amadeus Elite Paragon, 2012 DDD AMS 108/109-2 SIAE) that I first heard when revising this chapter. He embellishes practically every movement, including the opening Adagios, fast finales and fugues, and not just sparingly.

1980-2010 under discussion here). The table also makes it apparent that ornamentation is more frequently practiced by non-specialist than HIP violinists—only Luca, Huggett, van Dael, Wallfisch, Beznosiuk and Podger represent period instrumentalists, and only Luca's name can be seen in the columns of the slow movements. Huggett adds beautifully haunting ornaments in the D minor Sarabanda but only during the repeat of the first half (bb.1-8) and in none of the other slow movements. It is also obvious from Table 4.5 that less than one third of the forty-odd violinists studied here add ornaments and only four (Luca, Mullova, Gringolts, and Faust) to a significant extent.

Table 4.5. Most embellished movements listed in order of amount of ornamentation. The named violinists add graces and embellishments extensively, decreasingly so as moving downward in each column. Others not listed here may also add a few graces here and there.

EM Gavotte	EM Menuet	EM Loure	Bm Sarabande	Am Andante	Dm Sarabanda
Huggett	Faust	Gringolts	Gringolts	Gringolts	Faust
Podger	Mullova '08	Faust	Mullova '92	Luca	Beznosiuk
Gingolts	Gringolts	Mullova '08	Mullova '08	Tognetti	Huggett (1st half)
Mullova '08	Podger	Luca	Luca	Faust	(Barton Pine 2004)
Faust	Wallfisch	van Dael	Faust		(Luca)
Tognetti	(Tognetti)	Wallfisch	Tetzlaff 2005		
Beznosiuk		Tognetti	(Tognetti)		
(Matthews)			(Kuijken)		
(Barton Pine)					
(van Dael)					

What we cannot see from the table is the fact that the solutions of different violinists tend to vary widely in terms of type, place and frequency of added ornaments. I discussed more of this fascinating detail in a separate paper so here I only provide some additional observations, transcriptions and Audio examples.[36] My current concern is rather to explore further the meaning and affective dimensions of ornamentation and embellishment.

In the slow movements (including the E Major Loure) what I find most important to highlight is the sharp contrast between Gringolts's almost

---

36 Fabian, 'Ornamentation in Recent Recordings.'

constant ornamentation and the more selectively added melodic passing notes and occasional flourishes or compound graces in Luca's, Tetzlaff's, Tognetti's, Mullova's and Faust's or Beznosiuk's versions. Kuijken tends to add only trills and approggiaturas. Furthermore, compared to Gringolts, these versions maintain a greater sense of rhythm and basic pulse and they also manage to keep the original melody intact.

In the A minor Andante, for instance, Gringolts bows very smoothly and swiftly, adding many twists and turns throughout. In contrast Luca's embellishments are more selective, filling in or varying certain well-recognizable melodic motives in a pattern-like manner, keeping with the movement's steady style of harmony and rhythm (Audio examples 4.2).

4.2. Ornamentation in J. S. Bach, A minor Sonata BWV 1003, Andante, extract: repeat of bars 1-11. Two versions: Sergiu Luca © Nonesuch, Ilya Gringolts © Deutsche Grammophon. Duration: 1.07.

To listen to this extract online scan the QR code
or follow this link: http://dx.doi.org/10.11647/OBP.0064.08

The difference in affect is palpable: the Andante in Luca's hand is a simple, direct, beautifully balanced little aria, an intimate song. In Gringolts' interpretation it sounds more like an over-cultivated flower that delights with its intricacies and quasi magical unfolding (as if on a sped-up film showing the opening of a bud) but somehow leaves the heart detached; calling forth a captivated outside observer rather than an intent listener enchanted by the serene beauty of the song. Overall I find Gringolts' embellishments and bowing curiously unusual and intriguing. It surprises me that my students are quite categorically dismissive of this performance. I have always found them to prefer Luca's version and in the ensuing discussion I will eventually offer reasons for this fairly constant aesthetic response.

Interestingly, while reviewers of Gringolts' disk comment on its "swaggering individuality and abundant fantasy"[37] and find that his

---

[37] Robert Maxham, 'Bach Violin Partitas: No. 1 in b; No. 3 in E. Solo Violin Sonata No. 2 in a. Ilya Gringolts (vn). Deutsche Grammophon B0000315-02 (58:56),' *Fanfare*, 27/2 (November 2003), 111-112.

"readings are remarkably elastic, and many figures are played with capricious fleetness,"[38] they hardly mention ornamentation.[39] Most surprisingly Robert Maxham opines that "movements like the Second Sonata's Andante ([...]) come closer to the interpretive canon," meaning, I guess, the playing of violinists like Szigeti and Milstein! Apart from the aural experience, my transcription of Gringolts' lavishly embellished performance of the Andante's second half shows that this can hardly be the case (Figure 4.3).

Figure 4.3. A minor Andante, bb. 12-24. Transcription of melodic embellishments in Gringolts' performance during repeat.

Similar observations could be made in relation to the E Major Loure or B minor Sarabande as well. The Loure is a particularly good example of the idiosyncratic nature of Gringolts' ornamenting. In light of Schröder's recommendation that the movement should never sound busy and should always retain a sense of "quiet nobility," Gringolts' reading seems a-historical.[40] It sounds busy, indeed. The near constant addition of notes, trills, slides, scalar figures and appoggiaturas requires him to play with very light, uneven bowing, creating continuous chiaroscuro effects as he glides up and down and across the strings. Nevertheless he maintains some of the key rhythmic elements and pulse of the Loure (Audio example 4.3).

---

38 Joseph Magil, 'Bach Solo Violin Partitas 1+3, Sonata 2. Ilya Gringolts DG 315,' *American Record Guide*, 66/6 (Nov 2003), 75-76.
39 Maxham does when he refers to the "jazzy ornamentation" of the Tempo di Borea Double.
40 Schröder, *Bach's Solo Violin Works*, p. 171.

4.3. Ornamentation in J. S. Bach, E Major Partita BWV 1006, Loure, extract: repeat of bars 5-20. Ilya Gringolts © Deutsche Grammophon [edited sound file, first time play of bars 12-20 eliminated to show only the repeats]. Duration: 0.58.

To listen to this extract online scan the QR code
or follow this link: http://dx.doi.org/10.11647/OBP.0064.09

The special quality of his playing becomes particularly clear when compared to other versions (cf. Audio examples 4.7, 4.12, 5.1 and 5.2). Although in the Sarabande Gringolts' embellishing contains a few more metrically well-defined moments (for instance b. 7), elsewhere it again tends to sound overelaborated (e.g. b. 11) as I will discuss in more detail below. Here too the overall effect is created by the "gliding" bow strokes and the many smooth, sliding filler notes that grace not just larger melodic leaps but stepwise motions as well (cf. Audio example 4.4 contrasting Mullova, Gringolts and Luca, below).

While transcriptions convey well the differences between Luca's and Gringolts' ornamentation of the A minor Andante, with the B minor Sarabande the situation is different. Here the visual information can be deceptive because the transcription of Mullova's decorations may seem just as lavish as Gringolts' (Figure 4.4a, b). Furthermore, some of her solutions resemble those of Gringolts in terms of placement and shape or pitch content. Yet the delivery, the *sound* of their respective performances is very different, highlighting the difficulty in finding academically meaningful (and printable) presentations of critical observations—or rather, it underscores the difficulty in making the object of study (aurally perceived sound) readily available for analysis, for visual and verbal dissection.

One of the similarities between the transcriptions is found in measure 17. Both musicians grace the E dotted crotchet with an upper neighbour motion, but Mullova plays the two semiquavers ornamentally (i.e. soft, light), like Luca, not melodically as Gringolts does. In the transcriptions I aimed to convey this by using smaller notes for Mullova and normal semiquavers for Gringolts. Similarly, she plays the upward runs in bars 32

158 A Musicology of Performance

and 10 before the beat, giving emphasis to the downbeat and not affecting the basic pulse. Gringolts, on the other hand, while using a practically identical type of embellishment in b. 10, plays it in a less dotted and rhythmical manner. It sounds more like a gracing of the high B that he introduces as anticipation at the end of the previous bar (Figure 4.5a).[41] Through his constant diminution of rhythm and anticipation or delay of harmonic notes Gringolts loosens the sarabande pulse that Bach so clearly outlined with harmonic, melodic and rhythmic structures. Mullova's performance remains close to the implications of the score and is metrically steadier, with a less altered melody line. As one reviewer put it, "she adorns the 'open spaces' of the Sarabande of the B minor Partita in a delightful fashion" and "with discretion."[42] Her embellishments fulfill their supposed historical function as they *heighten* the rhythmic-melodic-harmonic character of the music. Gringolts' constantly flowing, light flourishes cover up these underlying structures. To better appreciate the differences and to exemplify Mullova's own interpretative trajectory, I have included the same section in all three of Mullova's commercial recordings (in chronological order), followed by Gringolts' performance and then Luca's discussed below (Figure 4.4c). Mullova's 1987 recording (the first example heard in the audio) has no ornaments and thus establishes the reference for Bach's score (Audio example 4.4: repeat of bb. 9-17 Mullova 1987, 1993, 2008 followed by Gringolts then Luca. For other, unembellished versions see Audio example 4.17).

4.4. Ornamentation in J. S. Bach, B minor Partita BWV1002, Sarabande, extract: repeat of bars 9-16. Five versions: Viktoria Mullova 1987 © Philips, 1992 © Philips, 2008 © Onyx, Ilya Gringolts © Deutsche Grammophon, Sergiu Luca © Nonesuch. Duration: 2.31.

To listen to this extract online scan the QR code
or follow this link: http://dx.doi.org/10.11647/OBP.0064.10

---

41 Ideally one should have a tie or slur between the two high Bs at either ends of bars 9-10 in the transcriptions and place the ornament over the bar line under this tie / slur, as per dotted curve.

42 J[ohn] D[uarte], 'Bach Partitas—No. 1 in B Minor, BWV 1002; No. 2 in D minor, BWV 1004; No. 3 in E, BWV 1006, Viktoria Mullova (vn). Philips 434 075-2 PH (77 minutes DDD),' *Gramophone*, 72/853 (June 1994), 80.

4. Analysis of Performance Features   159

Figure 4.4a. B minor Sarabande—Transcription of embellishments in Gringolts' performance of the repeats.

160   A Musicology of Performance

Figure 4.4b. B minor Sarabande—Transcription of embellishments in Mullova's 2008 performance of the repeats.

In comparison to these highly ornamented versions I offer a transcription of the more sparsely embellished performance of Luca, bars 9-17 of which are heard at the end of Audio example 4.4 (Tognetti, Tetzlaff and Holloway embellish the movement so sparsely that it is not worth commenting on; it is enough just to enjoy!). What is interesting about Luca's performance is the way he also varies accenting, articulation and rhythm during the repeats (e.g. both the dotting in bb. 8, 16 and the paired slurs in b. 15 are heard only during repeat). Although the added decorations often fall on the downbeat, their shape, rhythm and delivery tend to function so as to give impetus to the second beat of the measure, which is traditionally accented in sarabandes (e.g. bb. 2, 3, 10).

Figure 4.4c. B minor Sarabande—Transcription of embellishments in Luca's performance of the repeats.

The E Major Menuet is another movement worth considering briefly. Being in the French style some players (e.g. Schröder, Podger, St John) introduce slight dotting or lilted playing of the quavers. Podger also adds short graces, trills and mordents, during repeats. Given its simple structure and many repetitions (especially if Menuet I is played again as a da capo after Menuet II and with all repeats), it seems quite reasonable to expect HIP performers to add decorations. This is not really the case. Apart from Podger and Wallfisch it is again the HIP-inspired MSP violinist who ornament the most, in particular Isabelle Faust (cf. Table 4.5). She performs all repeats in the da capo as well and not twice the same way. What is wonderfully playful about her rendering is that she uses ideas and figures from different parts of the movement to vary other bars. It teases the ear and brings a smile on the listeners' face, as I have often found in conference and class presentations. The Audio example offers one straight and two slightly lilted interpretations of the first 8 bars—with St John's an instance of the latter. This is followed by Faust's recording edited so that only repeats are played taken from her performance of Menuet I and the Da Capo of Menuet I (Audio example 4.5).

> 4.5. Ornamentation and lilted rhythm in J. S. Bach, E Major Partita BWV1006, Menuet I, four extracts: bars 1-8. Jaap Schröder © NAXOS; bars 1-8 with repeat. Rachel Podger © Channel Classics; bars 1-8. Lara St John © Ancalagon; embellished repeats from Menuet I and its Da Capo. Isabelle Faust © Harmonia Mundi [edited sound file to show repeats only]. Duration: 2.31.
>
>
>
> To listen to this extract online scan the QR code
> or follow this link: http://dx.doi.org/10.11647/OBP.0064.11

I identified and discussed several similar findings in relation to the other ornamented movements in my 2013 paper (see fn. 17), to which the interested reader is referred. However, I need to make one amendment to the data presented in that paper. There I state that "except for Luca adding two graces in measures 6 and 21, Faust is the only violinist who embellishes the D minor Sarabande, although I have heard it embellished by others in live concerts" (p. 18). Since publication I have noticed that Huggett adds soulful embellishments during the first repeat while Beznosiuk and Barton Pine add grace notes and short ornaments in a few bars: Beznosiuk in bars 1, 2, 6 and 21; Barton Pine (only on the commercial disk from 2004) in bars 4, 6, 11-12 and 18-19.[43] What Beznosiuk does is simpler but at times similar to Faust's solutions in that he plays around with adding mostly appoggiaturas. Barton Pine adds an appoggiatura in bar 6 and light-fast turn-like graces and trill elsewhere. Overall Beznosiuk's playing is not just less embellished but also much more reserved and measured than Faust's or Barton Pine's. In addition Huggett

---

43 In 1983 Kuijken also adds a trill with appoggiatura on the downbeat of bar 12 and a trill on the high G in bar 16. In the 2001 recording he graces the second beat (B of the upper voice) in bar 10, does the same in bar 12 as in 1983. The trill in bar 16 is not properly executed, sounds more like just a fast lower appoggiatura.

plays most of the semiquavers in the second half, but in particular the coda (bb. 25-29), as if she was improvising (Audio example 4.6).

> 4.6. Ornamentation in J. S. Bach, D minor Partita BWV 1004, Sarabanda, six extracts: repeat of bars 1-8. Two versions: Pavlo Beznosiuk © Linn Records, Isabelle Faust © Harmonia Mundi; repeat of bars 16-21. Two versions: Isabelle Faust, Pavlo Beznosiuk; repeat of bars 4-21. Rachel Barton Pine 2004 © Cedille [edited to show only repeats]; repeat of bars 1-8 and 25-29. Monica Huggett © Virgin Veritas. Duration: 5.05.
>
>
>
> To listen to this extract online scan the QR code
> or follow this link: http://dx.doi.org/10.11647/OBP.0064.12

Otherwise enough has already been said here regarding the fundamental aesthetic issue: whether the added ornaments fit well with the pulse and overall musical character of the movement or go somewhat against these. Other details, such as the appropriateness of choosing upper or lower appoggiaturas, compound ornaments, and so on (discussed in my above mentioned paper) seem like moot points. Few listeners are acutely aware of eighteenth-century rules and even fewer would register such minor details when listening to the recordings. The speed with which such ornaments pass by is frequently quite fast. Accurate transcription is often only possible by repeated close listening and slowing down the recording to half or slower speed with the aid of computer technology: useful for creating accurate data but of little ecological value. So to conclude this exploration of ornamented-embellished examples I rather just recommend listening to the brilliant and playful passage work that varies statements (usually but not always the last) of the Gavotte and Rondeau's theme (Figure 4.5; see also Audio example 5.6 illustrating Gringolts' embellishing recurrences of the theme) and the many graces and melodic alterations in the Loure (Figure 4.6 and Audio example 4.7). In the Loure the differences in sound effect, in *delivery*, are hard to convey in transcription. The scale up to the top B in bar 1, for instance, is played quite differently by all 3 violinists who introduce it (van Dael, Wallfisch and Mullova). And this is so even though all three of them use the gesture to create a spritely effect, to point up the rhythm and create energy! Speed, bowing, timing, and articulation contribute to the clearly perceivable aural difference.

164 A Musicology of Performance

Figure 4.5. Gavotte en Rondeau, E Major Partita: theme and its major variants.

4. *Analysis of Performance Features* 165

Figure 4.6. Transcription of 7 different ornamentations during the repeat of bars 1-3 of the Loure, E Major Partita WITH audio 4.7.

4.7. Ornamentation in J. S. Bach, E Major Partita BWV 1006, Loure, extract: repeat of bars 1-3. Seven versions: Ilya Gringolts © Deutsche Grammophon, Isabelle Faust © Harmonia Mundi, Viktoria Mullova 2008 © Onyx, Lucy van Dael © NAXOS, Elizabeth Wallfisch © Hyperion, Sergiu Luca © Nonesuch, and Richard Tognetti © ABC Classics. Duration: 1.53.

To listen to this extract online scan the QR code
or follow this link: http://dx.doi.org/10.11647/OBP.0064.13

Diversity — Once More

Moving on from added ornaments and returning to questions of understanding the meaning of notation, one particular moment of the set needs our attention: the final two bars of the A minor Grave (Figure 4.7). This excerpt illustrates spectacularly the rich variety of interpretations and individual solutions currently available on record. At least eighteen different solutions can be identified among the thirty-one examined recordings (Table 4.6). Such diversity challenges the claims that today's performances occupy a uniform scene with very few real individuals compared to the "golden age" of the early recording era.

How to render the notation of the two double stops in the penultimate bar is open to debate (Figure 4.7), although Neumann asserts, on the basis of considerable evidence and concurring with several other authors, that the wavy line Bach notated indicates vibrato.[44] According to Neumann a combination of bow and finger vibrato should be used followed by a trill starting on the main note.[45]

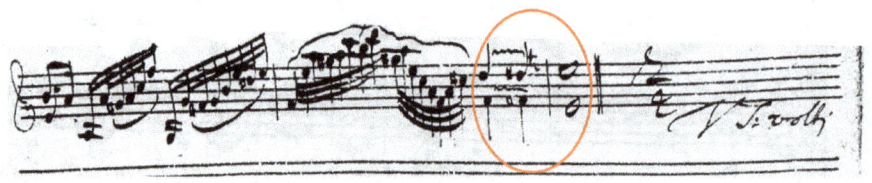

Figure 4.7. Grave, A minor Sonata: facsimile of final bars.

Older MSP versions tend to trill the top notes or just the D♯, more recent and HIP versions (except for Huggett and Ibragimova) seem to opt for a kind of tremolo effect achieved through "bow vibrato." This is a term used by several authors and is related to what Moens-Haenen calls "measured vibrato."[46] She explains it as playing with "controlled pressure changes of the bow" and states that the "beats should be strictly in time" because "measured vibrato is as a rule written out by the composer" (in eighth or

---

44 Neumann, *Ornamentation in Baroque and Post-Baroque Music*, pp. 519-520.
45 Frederick Neumann, 'Some Performance Problems in Bach's Unaccompanied Violin and Cello Works,' in *Eighteenth-Century Music in Theory and Practice: Essays in Honour of Alfred Mann*, ed. by Mary Parker (Stuyvesant, NY: Pendragon Press, 1994), pp. 19-48 (pp. 29-30).
46 Greta Moens-Haenen, 'Vibrato,' Grove Music Online. Oxford Music Online.

sixteenth-notes that are indicative of speed). The resulting pulsating sound is said to emulate the tremulant stop on the organ. Other authors use the term "bow vibrato" and discuss its possible context and execution a little less categorically. They seem to agree that the wavy line here may be a sign for this tremolo-vibrato effect. Stowell cites Baillot's treatise identifying "a wavering effect caused by variation of pressure on the stick";[47] Neumann claims that "in the Italo-German tradition vibrato was often done by bow pulsation,"[48] whereas Ledbetter suggests vibrato or a "sort of bow vibrato."

> Since [the pair of wavy lines] seems to have something to do with going up a semitone, one obvious possible interpretation is the vibrato (*flattement*) followed by glissando up a fret (*coulé du doigt*) common in French viol repertory. The *flattement* can be either a finger vibrato (striking lightly, repeatedly, and as closely as possible to the fixed finger with the finger adjacent to it), or it can be a wrist vibrato. Marais and others use a horizontal wavy line for this. […] In the Brandenburg Concerto the solo parts [from measure 95] are accompanied in the ripieno by a sort of bow vibrato (repeated notes under the slur), and that also is a possible interpretation of the wavy line. J.J. Walther (1676) uses repeated notes with a wavy line to indicate this.[49]

Basically, the accelerating frequency of energy pulsation creates an effect that is similar to what Caccini (1602) and others of the early baroque period called the trillo (rapidly repeated pitch) and that is indeed very similar to the tremulant stop on the organ. Since in the A minor Grave the effect is not written out in small note values but simply indicated by a wavy line connecting two held notes, the choice between finger and bow vibrato remains open and thus the term "bow vibrato" seems more appropriate than "measured vibrato." Bow vibrato is also distinct from "tremolo" which is achieved by rapid up-down bow movements rather than change in bow pressure.

Other possibilities for variety include the shape and speed of trills and tremolos, choice of dynamics and articulation (e.g. slurring the dyads), and the decisions whether to add short or long, lower or upper appoggiaturas and / or terminations to the trill(s), to play the final octave with or without anticipation, and whether to emphasize either note of the final octave. Altogether approximately eighteen different solutions were found in thirty-one examined recordings; some more subtle than others.

---

47 Robin Stowell, *The Early Violin and Viola* (Cambridge: Cambridge University Press, 2001), p. 66.
48 Neumann, 'Some Performance Problems,' p. 29.
49 Ledbetter, *Unaccompanied Bach*, p. 121.

Table 4.6 provides a summary of the main choices without differentiating all the nuances that are clearly audible and make each version slightly different from the other. These nuances are illustrated through a selection of audio excerpts (Audio example 4.8).

> 4.8. Interpretations of the notation at the end of J. S. Bach, A minor Sonata BWV 1003, Grave, extract: bars 22-23. Eight versions: James Ehnes (© Analekta Fleurs de lys) trilling both notes in both dyads; James Buswell (© Centaur) trilling the top notes of the dyads; Miklós Szenthelyi (© Hungarton) strongly vibrating the first dyad and then trilling the top note; Lara St John (© Ancalagon) trilling the top note and then both notes; Pavlo Beznosiuk (© Linn Records) producing a trillo (bow-vibrato) on the first dyad followed by a trill on the second; Brian Brooks (© Arts Music) performing a less obvious bow vibrato; Benjamin Schmid (© Arte Nova) playing a crescendo with increasing vibrato leading to trill on second dyad followed by decrescendo; Alina Ibragimova (© Hyperion) playing without vibrato, creating a small mezza-di-voce on the first dyad then a trill with diminuendo on the second. Duration: 2.43.
>
>
>
> To listen to this extract online scan the QR code
> or follow this link: http://dx.doi.org/10.11647/OBP.0064.14

Table 4.6. Summary of solutions in the penultimate bars of the A minor Grave

Both notes trilled in both dyads	Top note trilled in first and both trilled in second dyad	Top note trilled in both dyads	Top note trilled in second dyad	Both dyads with vibrato (tremolo) followed by trill†	Vibrato and / or crescendo followed by trill	Straight (with crescendo or messa di voce) followed by trill*
Huggett Ehnes Kremer '05	St John	Ricci Perlman Mintz Buswell	Shumsky Poulet Kremer '80	Luca Kuijken Schröder van Dael Barton Pine Brooks Tetzlaff Tognetti Holloway Beznosiuk Mullova	Szenthelyi Zehetmair Wallfisch	Podger Ibragimova Fischer Schmid Gringolts Khachatryan

† Brooks's and Tetzlaff's delivery seems to be a combination of bow and finger vibrato perhaps closer to tremolo.

* Fischer and Schmid create a crescendo-decrescendo over the duration of the two dyads (accompanied by increasing-decreasing vibrato) whereas Ibragimova performs a messa di voce proper on the first dyad alone without any vibrato and articulates the second dyad quite separate from the first. There is hardly any crescendo-decrescendo in Podger's and Khachatryan's versions; straight-held dyads with trill on D# although one can perhaps detect a very slight tremolo/vibrato in Podger's.

Ornamenting or Improvising?

Our discussion of ornamentation started with the need to understand what Bach's notations mean; to render the many small note values as if spontaneously unfolding improvisations over an imagined melody. Circling back to such broader issues, the contention that ornamentation should always be improvised is worth unpacking. So far I have argued that the performance should *sound* as if improvised. How are we to know, really, whether or to what degree an added ornament is pre-planned or spontaneous? Musicians intimately familiar with a particular style are able to play extempore, they just have not been encouraged much to do so until recently.[50]

People, including musicians, used to say that ornamentation in recorded performance is not desirable because of the repeatability offered by the medium. The idea being that the listener will not be able to hear it as improvised, or as an added ornament, because it will recur unchanged in each playing of the record. It may even become annoying to hear it over and over again instead of "the music proper." Christopher Hogwood apparently advised his players against ornamenting in the recording studio

> because he felt that risk-taking, 'wild risks' and 'fantastic cadenzas,' improvisatory élan, spontaneity and dangerous living which would certainly elicit cheers in a live performance 'nearly always pall on repeated hearings.'[51]

A debatable position, indeed! Yes, perhaps I hear some of these embellishments as if part of the composition—especially when they seem as fitting and enriching as in Mullova's and Faust's recordings. But I certainly don't get tired of hearing them and due to the style of delivery, always hear them as embellishments.

However, there is one recording where I think the listener is surely witnessing improvised (rather than potentially pre-meditated) graces: Richard Tognetti sometimes adds graces during first play and different ones during repeat.[52] This habit and the way he plays the ornaments create

---

50 This has started to change as evidenced in courses and masterclasses in improvisation for classical musicians. David Dolan et al., 'The Improvisatory Approach to Classical Music Performance: An Empirical Investigation into its Characteristics and Impact,' *Music Performance Research*, 6 (2013), 1-38. See also Aaron L. Berkowitz, *The Improvising Mind: Cognition and Creativity in the Musical Moment* (New York: Oxford University Press, 2010).

51 Timothy Day, *A Century of Recorded Music: Listening to Musical History* (New Heaven and London: Yale University Press), p. 158 citing Christopher Hogwood in James Badel, 'On Record: Christopher Hogwood,' *Fanfare*, 9/2 (November-December 2005), 90.

52 I am aware that this could be a result of post-performance editing (patching up two different play-throughs where the embellishments may have been the same in repeats

an impression of *ad hoc*, possibly improvised-on-the-spot performance. Often ornaments are added at less obvious places as well and occasionally they sound jolted rather than smoothly integrated. For me this indicates a spontaneous gesture, *not* something fully thought through, practised and polished. Such instances are the added trills in bb. 7-8, 21, 30-31 during the first play of the B minor Sarabande rather than in the repeat, whereas during repeats there is only one embellishment on the last beat of bar 3. Another example is the added embellishment during the repeat of bar 1 of the Sarabande Double. Given the structure of the music, this gracing could become a pattern but it doesn't; none of the other analogous bars has any ornamentation. All this suggests spontaneity rather than relying on premeditated solutions, even if it happens to be a coincidence resulting from post-production editing and selection of takes. If takes are so different, then there must have been spontaneity. That such improvisation can be witnessed in a studio recording goes some way against the much heard assertions that the studio inhibits players, that recordings are not performances and that the spontaneous nature of ornamentation is against the repeatable nature of sound recordings.

In my experience repeated listening does not diminish the aesthetic value and spontaneous effect of the embellishments observed in these versions of Bach's *Six Sonatas and Partitas for Solo Violin*. I also question the reality of people commonly listening to the same recording repeatedly, especially now, when there is an abundance of music at one's fingertips to download instantly.

Summary

Ornamentation is a performance feature that could be seen as independent from most other aspects. You either add a trill, grace note, melodic embellishment or you do not. Simple. End of story. No wonder that during the early decades of the early music movement an enormous emphasis was placed on discussing the importance of *adding* graces to create a "stylish" baroque performance. But what is "stylish"? The decision to add a trill rather than a mordent? To trill from above rather than from the note? To play a trill with or without termination? Or to correctly decide whether the

---

but different in the two takes). However, I was actually present when these recordings were made and I remember that Tognetti did vary the graces he was adding during first plays and in the repeats.

appoggiatura should be short or long? If this were true, my discussion of the recordings would have completely missed the point!

I did not engage with any of such fussy detail because the real issue in ornamentation, as I see it, is indeed style; the musician has to demonstrate *bon goût* not just through the choices of ornaments but through their placement and frequency. Most importantly, they have to *perform* the embellishments in a way that truly decorates the music, enhances its character, rhythmic, melodic, and harmonic potential. As soon as we start talking about these aesthetic issues it becomes all too obvious that ornamentation is also interacting with several other performance features in achieving its effect. It is not a simple matter, not an independent element but combines with articulation, rhythm, dynamics, timing as well as bowing and tone production. Throughout my commentary I repeatedly drew attention to the differences between what transcriptions can convey and what one actually hears. I tried to describe the sound effect, the perceived gesture rather than evaluate the content or type of an ornament and embellishment.

The discussed examples confirmed an increasing liberty in performing these works—once regarded monumental and untouchable—that brings forth a playful attitude. Violinists as diverse as Luca, Mullova, Podger, Tognetti, Faust and Gringolts seemed especially to delight in manipulating the material through added trills and slides, appoggiaturas and other graces or even changes in melodic turns, filling in gaps between notes, ornamentally highlighting gestures and, ultimately, re-writing measures and entire passages, as in the Gavotte an Rondeau. Most importantly, the graces and flourishes, whether written out by Bach or added by the player were delivered "gesturally," with a sense of play, abandon, and improvisatory freedom. In this regard Mullova, Faust and Luca have excelled especially, but all of them displayed a confident "ownership" of the pieces conveyed by a sense of exuberance, daring fervour and convincing personal authenticity.

If we now reconsider Quantz's opinion, namely that he saw a danger that all-too-rich diminutions will deprive the melody of its capacity to "move the heart" and recommended that instead of indulging too freely in diminutions, players should render a simple melody nobly, clearly, and neatly,[53] then this examination should perhaps conclude with the verdict that Gringolts may have gone too far. His performance can still strike as appealing and musical— especially if somebody has never heard the pieces before—but not quite

---

53 As recalled in Neumann, *Performance Practices*, p. 538.

appropriate *if* we desire to preserve the style and compositional aesthetics of Bach as we currently understand these.[54] In Gringolts' performance, the lack of rhythmic definition and pulse and constantly shifting dynamics and timbre make his embellishments sound restless and over-elaborate, perhaps more rococo in style, bringing to mind the aesthetic reactions of seventeenth-century commentators who originally used the word *barocco* in a pejorative sense to denigrate an over-elaborate piece by comparing it to a misshapen pearl.

Although it is undeniable that the embellished versions represent a minority group among the thirty-odd recordings studied here, the variety and creativity of solutions found in them proves that there are violinists today who are not afraid of putting their personal stamps on Bach's works. Interestingly, MSP violinists outnumber HIP players among those who frequently introduce sumptuous embellishments (Table 4.5). The sheer fact that embellished versions appear to proliferate as we pass through the decades (think also of Montanari's 2013 recording not studied here) provides ground for hope that performers are leaving behind the modernist "Urtext-mentality" of the 1950s to 1980s period. As they reclaim their prerogative to bring compositions to live rather than just "letting [them] speak for themselves,"[55] these violinists offer listeners diverse and individual interpretations. The choice is wide and the differences among them are as good as ever.

4.4. Rhythm

As I have mentioned earlier, there are several issues one should consider under the umbrella of rhythm. Broadly speaking the topic involves anything to do with the timing of notes and thus it is linked to articulation as well as

---

54 Tellingly reviewers are ambivalent although tending towards the positive: Maxham ('Ilya Gringolts,' 111-112) states "Almost everybody will find something to choke on—but only for a few seconds"; and concludes by saying "it could easily turn out to be either the best or the worst recording of the piece ever made." David Denton on the other hand finds the quality of playing "quite superb" but a "harsh element introduced in the E Major Preludio and the rather cut up of the following Loure" are "not welcome." In this very short review Gringolts' presentation of the Gavotte is acknowledged to be "humorous" and the two Menuets "charming." (David Denton, 'Bach Partitas no. 1 in B minor BWV 1002 and no. 3 in E Major BWV1006, Sonata no. 2 in A minor BWV1003. Ilya Gringolts (violin) Deutsche Grammophon 474-235-2,' *Strad*, 114/1363 (November 2003), 1269.

55 Richard Taruskin, 'On Letting the Music Speak for Itself: Some Reflection on Musicology and Performance,' *Journal of Musicology*, 1/3 (July 1982), 101-117.

bowing. In baroque music, rhythm is organized around metrical hierarchies and the underlying harmony.[56] A projection of these through micro variations in rhythmic delivery may also impact on local tempo. And, as we have just seen while exploring ornamentation, performances that sound improvisatory are achieved through flexible-gestural rendering of notated rhythmic values. Speaking more specifically, the playing of dotted rhythms and the French convention of *notes inégales* are particularly noteworthy when baroque performance conventions are considered. First I will focus on these, leaving the broader, more qualitative matters of rhythmic flexibility for later. However, it will transpire that even the seemingly straightforward matter of playing dotted rhythms is impossible to discuss without reference to tempo and articulation or bowing. Neither close listening nor quantitative measurements can tell the full story on their own as cause and effect are not veridical.

Dotted Rhythms

The performance of dotted rhythms in baroque music has received much attention during the second half of the twentieth century. Most researchers advocated double or over-dotting in pieces where such rhythms prevail. For long, the late Frederick Neumann was the only author voicing an opposition.[57] Case studies of recorded performances generally confirmed over-dotting in Bach repertoire.[58]

In the Violin Solos, three movements offer opportunity for studying the delivery of dotted rhythms: The D minor Corrente, B minor Allemanda, and the C Major Adagio. Table 4.7 provides the quantitative results showing slight under-dotting in the D minor Corrente and over-dotting in the other two movements.[59]

---

56 Houle, *Meter in Music*.
57 The literature on rhythmic alteration in baroque music is too large to be cited here. Comprehensive recent summaries include Stephen Hefling, *Rhythmic Alteration in Seventeenth- and Eighteenth-Century Music* (New York: Schirmer, 1993) and Neumann, *Performance Practices*. A detailed review of this literature is provided in Fabian, *Bach Performance Practice*, pp. 169-185.
58 For instance in relevant movements of the two Passions, the Brandenburg Concertos and the Goldberg Variations as reported in Fabian, *Bach Performance Practice*, pp. 170-179 and Dorottya Fabian and Emery Schubert, 'A New Perspective on the Performance of Dotted Rhythms,' *Early Music*, 38/4 (2010, November), 585-588.
59 The dotting ratio in this discussion is expressed as percentage of the duration of the dyad. In other words a literal (or mechanical) dotting is achieved by a ratio of 0.75:0.25 between the dotted and the short note. I calculated these ratios from note on-sets and off-sets. Note on-sets and off-sets were identified by aural and visual inspection of

Table 4.7. Average dotting ratios in 3 movements where such rhythms prevail; selection of recordings, listed in order of release date.

Violinist	Dm Corrente	CM Adagio	Bm Allemanda
Luca 1977	0.74	0.8	0.85
Kremer 1980	0.76	0.8	0.73
Ricci 1981	0.76	n/a	n/a
Kuijken 1982	0.71	0.86	0.75
Zehetmair 1983	0.70	0.85	0.78
Shumsky 1983	0.73		
Mintz 1984	0.78	0.81	0.78
Schröder 1985	0.72	0.78	0.77
Perlman 1987	0.65	0.8	0.75
Mullova 1987	n/a	n/a	0.79
Buswell 1989	0.75	0.79	0.78
Ughi 1991	0.77		
Mullova 1993	0.74	n/a	0.8
Tetzlaff 1994	0.77	0.78	0.77
Huggett 1995	0.69	0.79	0.71
Van Dael 1996	0.73	0.81	0.74
Poulet 1996	0.71	0.80	0.82
Rosand 1997	0.75	n/a	n/a
Wallfisch 1997	0.72	0.85	0.78
Hahn 1997	0.78	0.81	n/a
Gähler 1998	0.74	0.73	0.74
Ehnes 1999	0.8	0.81	0.75
Podger 1999	0.72	0.77	0.77
Schmid 1999	0.77	0.77	0.82
Barton Pine 1999	0.76	0.81	0.77

audio signals using spectrographic displays in the software programs *Adobe Audition 1* and *Sonic Visualiser 3.2* ("Nevermore spectral transform" option of the "Mazurka" plug-in). The window size for visualization in Adobe Audition 1 was between 0.5 and 2.7 milliseconds which provided magnification that countered the possibility of errors occurring within the range of human perception. (Roughly speaking the threshold is 20 milliseconds [mS], but below 200 mS sounds can be lost depending on their level of intensity; see Stanley Gelfand, *Hearing: An Introduction to Psychological and Physiological Acoustics*, 2nd edn (New York and Basel: Marcel Dekker, 1990)). In the D minor Corrente note on-sets and offsets were identified in bars 3-4 and 6. In the B minor Allemanda the first 7 bars were studied but only dotted dyads were measured (i.e. dotted figures where the short note was replaced by a series of shorter values were not included). In the C Major Adagio bars 1-4 and 6 were studied (there are no dotted rhythms in bar 5). The identification of note on-sets and note off-sets in each studied recording was prepared twice, once each by the author and a research assistant to ensure accuracy. All marking points were confirmed aurally through the clicking device in *Sonic Visualiser*. In particularly difficult-to-hear recordings the audio files were slowed down to half speed (e.g. Huggett, B minor Allemanda). *Sonic Visualiser* is a free computer program for audio analysis, see http://www.sonicvisualiser.org/ or Cannam, Chris, Landone, Christian, and Sandler, Mark, 'Sonic Visualiser: An Open Source Application for Viewing, Analysing, and Annotating Music Audio Files,' in *Proceedings of the ACM Multimedia 2010 International Conference* (Florence: October 2010), 1467-1468.

Matthews 1997 (2001 issue)	0.73	0.79	0.79
Brooks 2001	0.72	0.89	0.75
Gringolts 2001	n/a	n/a	0.76
Lev 2001	0.75	0.74	n/a
Kuijken 2001	0.71	0.86	0.76
Poppen 2001	0.76	n/a	n/a
Szenthelyi 2002	0.74		0.82
Barton Pine 2004	0.74	n/a	n/a
Holloway 2004	0.75	0.75	0.80
Kremer 2005	0.76	0.85	0.73
Tetzlaff 2005	0.78	0.82	0.73
Tognetti 2005	0.72	0.81	0.8
Fischer 2005	0.78	0.81	0.79
Beznosiuk 2007 (2011 issue)	0.66	0.76	0.74 (v. kerned)
Barton-Pine 2007	0.7	0.82	n/a
St John 2007	0.67	0.77	0.78
Mullova 2008	0.71	0.78	0.78
Faust 2009	0.73	0.79	n/a
Ibragimova 2009	0.70	0.84	0.75 (kerned)
Khachatryan 2010	0.74	0.78	0.81
Average	0.73	0.80	0.77

Compared to earlier recordings and published views of some violinists, the tendency to under-dot in the Corrente is striking. It is also stronger among HIP (average length of dotted note = 0.716) than MSP versions (average = 0.742). Earlier selective measurements of recordings made between 1930 and 1970 showed over-dotting becoming the dominant practice by the 1950s, excepting Heifetz.[60] In an interview Luca talks about over-dotting and suggests that the D minor Corrente "is most effective played very short on the sixteenths."[61] His delivery of both the dotted and the short notes is indeed very staccato. Nevertheless even his average dotting is slightly under-dotted (0.74). This overall trend towards under-dotting may reflect the view that dotted rhythms within fast triplet motion are to be assimilated into long-short swings because the notation of dotting in such context represents the eighteenth-century way of expressing what later became notated as crotchet-quaver with a triplet bracket over the two notes.[62] (Audio example 4.9)

---

60 Data is reported for the 1930s-1950s period in Dorottya Fabian and Eitan Ornoy, 'Identity in violin playing on records: interpretation profiles in recordings of solo Bach by early twentieth-century violinists,' *Performance Practice Review*, 14 (2009), 1-40 (p.22).
61 Samuel Applebaum, *The Way they Play*, Book 4 (Neptune City, N.J., Paganiniana Publications, 1975), p. 261. I thank Daniel Bangert for this reference.
62 Neumann, 'Some Performance Problems,' p. 25.

4.9. Dotting and accenting in J. S. Bach, D minor Partita BWV 1004, Corrente, extract: bars 1-6. Three versions. Sergiu Luca © Nonesuch, Ingrid Matthews © Centaur, Julia Fischer © PentaTone Classics. Duration: 0.30.

To listen to this extract online scan the QR code
or follow this link: http://dx.doi.org/10.11647/OBP.0064.15

In contrast, both the B minor Allemanda and the C Major Adagio tended to be over-dotted. However, these movements also show differences between HIP and MSP versions in the extent of over-dotting. Compared to MSP violinists, HIP players used a lesser over-dotting in the Allemanda and a stronger over-dotting in the Adagio (cf. Table 4.7). Additionally, one could observe a progressively more staccato delivery of dotted patterns in the Allemanda and Corrente while the slower Adagio tended to be played legato. In this movement the dotted notes form multiple stops. The time needed to sound each note of the three or four-part chord has likely contributed to the elongated delivery.

Mentioning articulation and tempo in relation to dotting is crucial as research shows their impact on the perception of dotting.[63] Dotted rhythms sound sharper, more over-dotted when played in a detached style with "air" (i.e. silence) between the long and the short note. They also tend to sound more dotted when the tempo is fast. In other words, the desired effect or musical character can be achieved without much over-dotting, explaining the lesser average ratios found in the B minor Allemanda compared to the C Major Adagio. Listeners, and performing musicians are also listeners, "may believe they respond to the 'dottedness' of a rendering" but "their judgement seems to reflect [...] a higher order construct," a holistic perception of performance features that "incorporates tempo and articulation" as well as dotting.[64] Musicians focusing on projecting a particular character or mood seem to intuitively adjust the interacting

---

63 Fabian and Schubert, 'A New Perspective.'
64 Dorottya Fabian and Emery Schubert, 'Musical Character and the Performance and Perception of Dotting, Articulation and Tempo in Recordings of Variation 7 of J.S. Bach's *Goldberg Variations* (BWV 988),' *Musicae Scientiae*, 12/2, 177-203 (p. 198).

elements. But when trying to explain what to do, they may incorrectly emphasize one or the other component as seen in much of the above mentioned literature on dotting in baroque music. As Nicholas Cook noted, there are musical situations when "close listening may correctly identify the effect, yet fail to proceed from effect to cause."[65]

This auditory illusion may also explain why we hear most recordings of the D minor Corrente to be well dotted in spite of the measured under-dotted ratios. The fast tempo most performers chose in this movement compensates for the smoother ratio between the dotted and short notes. In the flow of running triplets the airy (or "kerned") delivery of the dotted notes and the staccato articulation of the short notes create a floatingly skipping effect.[66] Importantly, the dotting ratio tends to be sharper on downbeats and most under-dotted on the last pairs before the return of the running triplets (i.e. last beat of bars 4 and 6, for instance). In other words a strong sense of pulse propels the skipping effect forward to the next flight of triplets (cf. Audio example 4.9).

A comparison of Kremer's two recordings of the B minor Allemanda illustrates the auditory illusion at play (Figure 4.8; Audio example 4.10). The more sustained style of the earlier version sounds less dotted even though the measured ratios produce identical average dotting in the two recordings. In the later version Kremer plays both the dotted notes and their short pair staccato, in a "lifted" way, allowing the decay of the tone to start on average around 66% of the notated nominal duration. This "kerning" is stronger in case of the long notes, when the decay starts already around 56%. Shorter note values are held on average to 76% of their written value.[67] The different delivery shows up very clearly in the spectrogram of the audio file (Figure 4.8).

---

65 Nicholas Cook, *Beyond the Score: Music as Performance* (New York: Oxford University Press, 2014), p. 144.
66 Research into jazz swing has shown that the ratio reduces as the tempo increases (i.e. the length of the dotted note becomes shorter with respect to the beat with increased tempo) until it plateaus around 200 beats per minute to a more or less even 0.5:0.5. Anders Friberg and Andreas Sundström, 'Swing Ratios and Ensemble Timing in Jazz Performance: Evidence for a Common Rhythmic Pattern,' *Music Perception*, 19/3 (2002), 333-349.
67 The term "kerning" was introduced by Schubert and Fabian to denote the gap or silence between notes. See Emery Schubert and Dorottya Fabian, 'Perception and Preference of Dotting in 6/8 patterns,' *Journal of Music Perception and Cognition*, 7/2 (2001), 113-132.

178 A Musicology of Performance

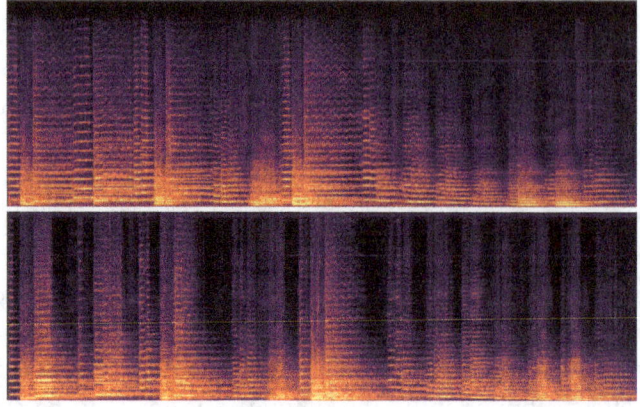

Figure 4.8. Adobe Audition screenshots of spectrograms showing bars 1-3 of the B minor Allemanda in Kremer's two recorded performances. The 2005 version (bottom pane) shows more gaps between note onsets indicating staccato playing.

4.10. Articulation and perceived dotting in J. S. Bach, B minor Partita BWV 1002, Allemanda, extract: bars 1-3. Two versions. Gidon Kremer 1980 © Philips, 2005 © ECM. Duration: 0.26.

To listen to this extract online scan the QR code
or follow this link: http://dx.doi.org/10.11647/OBP.0064.16

Mullova is also an interesting case. She has 3 recordings of the B minor Allemanda (Figure 4.9; Audio examples 4.11). The earliest, 1987 version is slow, the bow strokes are long and even, giving it a sustained and broad feel. The 1992 version is more staccato but not much faster. It sounds a little more dotted overall, partly because of the shorter bowing and more detached style. The most recent, 2008 version is faster, even more staccato and sounds the most dotted. Inspection of spectrograms shows lots of kerning; both the dotted and the short notes are sharply articulated with clear gaps between note onsets (Figure 4.9). When one compares the measured dotting ratios of the three recordings the difference is very little, with the averaged dotting ratio found to be the least over-dotted in the most recent version: 0.79 in 1987, 0.8 in 1992, and 0.77 in 2008. It must be the faster tempo and staccato delivery that contribute significantly to nevertheless perceiving this last recording as the most dotted of the three.

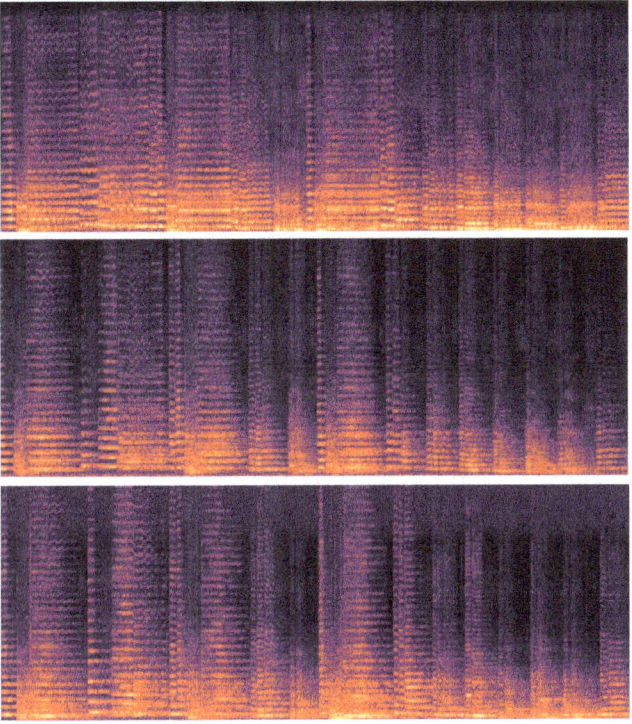

Figure 4.9. Adobe Audition screenshots of spectrograms showing bars 1-3 of the B minor Allemanda in Mullova's three recorded performances. The 1992 (middle pane) and 2008 (bottom pane) versions show increasing gaps between note onsets indicating progressively more staccato playing.

4.11. Articulation and perceived dotting in J. S. Bach, B minor Partita BWV 1002, Allemanda, extract: bars 1-3. Three versions. Viktoria Mullova 1987 © Philips, 1992 © Philips, 2008 © Onyx. Duration: 0.42.

To listen to this extract online scan the QR code
or follow this link: http://dx.doi.org/10.11647/OBP.0064.17

A slightly different case to the movements discussed so far (Table 4.7) is the E Major Loure. Dotted rhythms are frequent here too, but they rarely form a "running" pattern. Instead they occur in isolation but at prominent melodic or metrical moments. Furthermore, both the dotted crotchet—quaver and the dotted quaver—semiquaver combinations are common. Importantly, the Loure is perhaps the most diversely performed movement of the whole set of the Six Solos. As will be discussed in chapter five, the Loure was considered to be "the slow movement" of this partita for a long time. The many languid, lyrical, and melodically conceived interpretations evidence this approach. With the HIP movement in full swing by the 1980s, the Loure's dance character has become recognized, giving impetus for a less lyrical and more rhythmical delivery in recent versions. However, long-held traditions die hard and performances of the Loure seem to occupy an open field: tempo often remains slow but rhythm more sharply shaped, or tempo faster but articulation legato and phrasing melodically orientated. What is interesting to note therefore is not so much the dotting ratio *per se*, but the interconnection of tempo, articulation, phrasing and dotting.

Contrary to what we observed in relation to the D minor Corrente, B minor Allemanda and C Major Adagio, here the slower, more legato versions (e.g. Hahn, Khachatryan, Fischer) tend to be *less* over dotted, with the average dotting ratio being somewhere between 0.75 and 0.77. The more staccato versions of the Loure, whether faster or similarly slow, have a sharper average dotting ratio, around 0.80 (Audio example 4.12, see also Audio examples 4.7, 4.3, 5.1 and 5.2).

4.12. Tempo, articulation and musical character in J. S. Bach, E Major Partita BWV 1006, Loure, extract: bars 1-8. Four versions: Hillary Hahn © Sony, Miklós Szenthelyi © Hungaroton, John Holloway © ECM, Alina Ibragimova © Hyperion; repeats of bars 1-8: Jaap Schröder © Naxos. Duration: 3.13.

To listen to this extract online scan the QR code
or follow this link: http://dx.doi.org/10.11647/OBP.0064.18

I was puzzled enough by this finding to look closer. First I found that the dotted quavers tended to be played less dotted than the dotted crotchets (except for Khachatryan and Fischer, among a few others). Score analysis revealed the reason (Figure 4.10): these dotted quavers in, for instance, bb. 4, 6-7 are preceded by a long written-out appoggiatura (or suspension) on the downbeat and so played with emphasis by most players, blurring the onset of the dotted note. Since the dotted notes are in essence the resolution of the dissonance, they are delivered softly and under the same bow as the suspension (note that these two notes are slurred throughout by Bach). Furthermore, since in terms of harmony these dotted quavers are concluding points, their semiquaver pair actually functions as an anacrusis to the following note. So it is not so much the dotted note that catches the ear but the short note as it leads quickly into the next main note. This explains why these patterns are not particularly over-dotted; rather they are articulated in a manner that highlights melodic direction and adds rhythmic momentum.

Figure 4.10. Loure, E Major Partita, bars 4-7.

Rhythmic Alteration

Apart from dotting, alteration of rhythm occurs in other context as well. In particular, a lilted-dotted manner of performing the quavers in the two E Major Menuets (e.g. Podger, Matthews, Tognetti, Holloway) and the B minor Sarabande (e.g. Luca and Mullova in 1992 during repeats) are noteworthy. Although the French convention called *notes inégales* was supposed to be used in pieces where strings of evenly notated quavers were common, the slightly lilted delivery of quaver pairs in these French dance movements is stylistically reasonable and certainly effective. In Menuet I of the E Major Partita there are complete bars with only quavers (bb. 4, 6) and the swinging interpretation gives them energy and a stronger sense of pulse. This lilting also adds variety and contrasts well with the shifted accentual pattern Bach creates through the prescribed slurs from bar 20 onwards. These indicate slurring the first three quavers in each figure, effectively going against the 3/4 metre and earlier paired quavers, although still highlighting most down-beats (cf. Audio example 4.5; see also Figure 5.3).

In the B minor Sarabande the quavers that are played in a slightly swung manner by Mullova in 2008, for instance, tend to have a melodic pattern that resembles "sigh motifs" (b. 15, cf. Figure 4.4b; Audio example 4.4). In bars 21 and 23 Bach even marks them with the indicative slur (descending pairs of slurred notes). If a performer intends to project the sarabande's characteristic pulse and the harmonic-melodic design of the movement, lilting the rhythm in these bars is almost inevitable. For instance, technical constrain caused by the triple stop crotchets in bar 15 together with the emphasis on the musical content of descending pairs of suspension-resolution quavers ("sigh motif") in the melody will make the on-beat notes sound longer and stressed and the off-beat quavers lighter and shorter. So here we have an example when score and performance analyses go hand in hand rather than being in a hierarchical relationship. The cause and effect are reciprocal.

As discussed earlier in relation to ornamentation, Luca's interpretation of the B minor Sarabande defers from these more subtle and general rhythmic flexibilities because he plays several of the quaver patterns in a strongly dotted manner during repeats, especially in the first half of the movement. Dotting is first introduced in the *prima volta* bar 8 where he plays the first quaver short and then the next two as a dotted dyad. However, he doesn't apply this alteration in a uniform manner. For instance, the similar gesture in bar 2 is played as written but in bar 4 it is dotted again. The first four quavers in bar 3 are played straight but the last two are dotted, and so on. This constant variation and fluidity lends an ornamental quality to these rhythmic alterations. Mullova also plays notes in a dotted manner in 1992 (in b. 8 *prima volta,* and the repeat of bb. 1, 7 (beats 2-3), 10 (beats 2-3), 16, 21 (beat 2), 23 (beats 2-3), 30 (beat 2)) as can be heard in Audio example 4.4.

Finally, there are also those alterations that affect a whole group of notes. In these movements, like elsewhere, the difference in interpretation may largely depend on how flexible a violinist may shape certain gestures, how she or he may project the pulse of the dance, the harmonic architecture of the piece. When Menuet I is played in a "sturdy" style, with equal emphasis on all chords, the dance character is weakened because the 3/4 pulse is hard to perceive.

4.13: Sturdy style of evenly emphasized beats in J. S. Bach, E Major Partita BWV 1006, Menuet I, extract: bars 1-8. Rudolf Gähler (curved "Bach-bow") © Arte Nova Classics. Duration: 0.13

To listen to this extract online scan the QR code
or follow this link: http://dx.doi.org/10.11647/OBP.0064.19

When notes are grouped to highlight metrical units, like, for instance, Tognetti's or Holloway's delivery of the slurred four semiquavers in bar 14 of the B minor Sarabande (heard in Audio example 4.17), then there is a different sense of phrasing and movement, as we can hear in many examples used throughout this book. Slightly stressing moments by holding over harmonically or metrically important notes, or the first note under a slur and then slightly hurrying the remaining notes within the same beat or until the next significant harmonic-metric moment occurs, creates subtle nuances and local ebb and flow.

Rhythm and Musical Character

Beyond dotting ratios, formal *notes inégales* convention, and other quantifiable matters it is the character of these timing flexibilities that underlie the perceived differences between the studied recordings. It is not just how the dotted rhythms are delivered in the D minor Corrente that catches the attention. But whether the running triplets are grouped by metric units (i.e. by bar or pairs of bars) or played-out in a literal fashion; whether certain notes are accented through staccato or stressed by dynamic or timing accents, or not highlighted at all.

Matthews' version starts differently to many others because she accents not just the down-beat chord but also the first note of the first triplet group in both bars 1 and 2. Playing these notes staccato makes them sound almost linked to the previous crotchets; as if they were slurred to the down-beat. This feature of her interpretation is more striking and memorable than the question of how she delivers the dotted notes (cf. Audio example 4.9).[68] St John's E Major Menuet is similarly unique in that she really hurries the second beat (the quavers sound almost short-long) but takes the first beat rather leisurely, enabling a strong sense of down-beat but an unusual, slightly limping 3/4 pulse. This slight hurrying towards the end of bars is also perceptible in bars 4 and 6. The strings of six quavers of these bars in St John's performance move rapidly towards the next bar, but not before a momentary hesitation on the first note in each group of six. The effect is assisted by minor shifts in dynamics. As discussed under ornamentation, an even more playful Menuet is created by Faust who makes many alterations both rhythmic and ornamental (cf. Audio example 4.5).

Innumerable other examples could be mentioned, of course, that have unique features and I will discuss some more as I progress towards a holistic analysis of these recorded performances. Although many interactions of performance features have already been pointed out in

---

68 Schmid performance shows some similarity but he seems to just stop the bow after the downbeat and then accent the first note of the triplets.

this chapter, the topic of playing rhythm "gesturally," grouping notes according to pulse, harmony or melodic contour is the first that cannot be separated out properly and is best discussed in terms of bowing, phrasing and articulation, the next big topic of this chapter.

4.5. Bowing, Articulation and Phrasing

Bowing and Timbre

One of the most commonly noted differences between HIP and MSP violin playing rests with bowing. Older and MSP violinists use a broadly uniform, seamless bowing with mostly even portato strokes, (e.g. Shumsky, Poulet, Perlman, Hahn, Ehnes, Fischer, Khachatryan). HIP violinists tend to use shorter bow strokes and the uneven distribution of weight of their period bows makes the difference between up and down strokes more prominent. Accordingly, the performances of the younger and HIP-inspired players and especially those using a baroque apparatus display a less on-the-string bowing and less even tone. They use a great variety of strokes and a more articulated style with faster note decay. In these recordings one can hear more rhythmic projection, a greater emphasis on the dance character, on meter and pulse. This is achieved primarily through the more lifted bowing; the uneven bow-strokes delineate metric-harmonic groups. The effect can be emulated, to a certain degree, with a modern bow as demonstrated by Lev, Buswell, and more obviously by Zehetmair, Schmid, Tetzlaff, St John, and others (cf. Table 3.3). In the liner notes to her 2008 recording Mullova captured this shift from long, even strokes to a bouncier, metrically orientated bowing eloquently, as cited earlier (chapter three).

Fingering choices involving lower positions and use of open strings are also more commonly observed in the recordings of specialist and HIP-inspired players.[69] This impacts on timbre as lower positions involve

---

69 Bowing observations were made by careful repeated listening and two experienced violinists with tertiary music degrees acted as research assistants to aid the interpretation of the aural analyses. Fingering was not analyzed in detail. The use of avoidable open strings was interpreted as evidence for fingering choices favoring lower positions, as was common during the baroque period. Comments regarding dynamics are also based on aural analyses. References to various dynamic levels should be understood as relative to the specific recording under discussion or occasionally in comparison with other versions. In this latter case the amplitudes of the recordings were normalized for the purpose of comparison.

more string crossing creating timbrel variety as each string has its own character. In contrast to HIP practice, the MSP style's focus on melodic unity encourages shifting to remain on the same string and create a unified tone for the melodic phrase. These two opposing aesthetic views contribute to considerable aural differences. However, recording technology cannot be ignored when wondering about timbre. The acoustics of the recording venue, the placement and choice of microphones, as well as post-production editing such as the addition of reverbs can alter the overall sound to such a degree that it is simply not possible to make sound comparative judgements regarding the players' actual tone. What is possible is to comment on certain local effects within the same recording. These are most likely achieved through bowing and thus reflective of interpretative decisions rather than technological artefact.

Importantly, by now we have had at least three decades of training and performance with period apparatus, and many violinists use relatively longer baroque bows that enable Italianate cantabile playing as much as French-style "thundering" down-bows. It is therefore interesting to note the many nuanced differences in bowing among HIP players alone. Not surprisingly age seems to matter in this regard. Generally speaking, among HIP violinists Schröder seems to have used the most "conventional" bowing. Beznosiuk has also tended to use longer bow strokes, especially when performing multiple voices.

To provide some specific information I discuss just one example, the beginning of the G minor Fuga (Audio example 4.14). The differences among HIP versions are quite palpable even though all period violinists play the opening in a detached style. Still, the length of bow strokes varies across players who also often stress different notes or stress the same ones but to a different degree.

4.14. Different bowings within HIP style in J. S. Bach, G minor Sonata BWV 1001, Fuga, extract: bars 1-6. Six versions: Sigiswald Kuijken 1983 © Deutsche Harmonia Mundi, Rachel Podger © Channel Classics, Elizabeth Wallfisch © Hyperion, John Holloway © ECM, Pavlo Beznosiuk © Linn Records, Monica Huggett © Virgin Veritas. Duration: 2.11.

To listen to this extract online scan the QR code
or follow this link: http://dx.doi.org/10.11647/OBP.0064.20

Kuijken uses the shortest, crispiest strokes in both of his recordings until b. 4, but in the thicker textures of bb. 4-6 the strokes sound longer. Luca's are also short but sounding less staccato. Podger and Huggett play in a detached manner but with somewhat longer strokes. While Podger tends to emphasize, through longer strokes, the third beat of bars, Wallfisch often stresses the first as well as the third beats. Huggett tends to lean on more notes than anybody else (not necessarily in the first six bars). Holloway plays slower than others but his accenting is similar to Beznosiuk's. They tend to emphasize the first and third crotchet beat of bars. Wallfisch arpeggiates the chords in bars 4-6, the others tend to play the triple stops in a fast bow-stroke.

Bars 35-42 also show differences within a basically detached style in each recording. Huggett and also Matthews always emphasize the main (bottom) note or part, whereas Schröder and Kuijken (2001) change this pattern in b. 38 to bring out the top line. Podger plays the top notes much shorter, with less resonance than the pedal note. Luca's strokes are relatively longer, Wallfisch's fairly off the string and Kuijken's almost spiccato, especially in 1983.

Variety of bowing and articulation could also lead to major differences in interpretation. The performance solutions of bars 35-42 of the G minor Fuga are strikingly varied because of the ambiguities in Bach's notations. Table 4.8 lists the main types of delivery. Indicative transcriptions are provided in Figure 4.11. The first thing to note is the lack of obvious preference for particular solutions among HIP or MSP musicians.

The score has triple stopping between bb. 35-37 which is followed by double stops over a D pedal in bb. 38-41. Most commonly the first two and a half bars are played in an arpeggiated manner while the double stops over the D pedal as written or with playing the D after every double stop (forming semiquaver groups). Other solutions include playing the minims as chords (Kremer 1980, Gähler, Szenthelyi, Luca, Mullova) or arpeggiating the entire section (e.g. Barton Pine, Tetzlaff, and most HIP violinists). Van Dael, Huggett, Holloway and Tognetti introduce a different arpeggiation at bar 38: by re-articulating the top note and repeating the pedal D at the end of each group they create sextuplet patterns slurred in threes.

Table 4.8. Summary of *basic* differences in executing bars 35-41 of G minor Fuga

Section	Arpeggiated demi-semiquavers	Chords and quavers	Semiquavers	Soft	Loud
Bars 35-37	Zehetmair Schröder Huggett van Dael Schmid Wallfisch Tognetti Khachatryan	Perlman Shumsky Buswell Kremer '05 St John	Ibragimova	Wallfisch Mintz Ibragimova Matthews Holloway (descres.)	Poulet Zehetmair Kremer '05 Khachatryan
Bars 38-41	Huggett, van Dael & Tognetti (sextuplets slurred in groups of three notes) Buswell St John Ibragimova		Zehetmair Shumsky Perlman Schröder Wallfisch Schmid Kremer '05	Poulet, Zehetmair Kremer '05 Matthews (cresc.) Khachatryan (cresc.) Holloway (cresc.)	Wallfisch Mintz (cresc.) Ibragimova (cresc.)
Whole passage (35-41)	Barton Pine Brooks Tetzlaff (both) Kuijken (both) Podger Matthews Holloway Beznosiuk	Luca Szenthelyi Gähler Kremer '80 Mullova	Ehnes Poulet Mintz Fischer Khachatryan	Barton Pine Brooks Huggett Kuijken Schmid (cresc.)* Tetzlaff Tognetti van Dael (cresc.)*	Szenthelyi Shumsky Perlman Gähler, Ehnes Luca, Buswell Kremer '80 Schröder Beznosiuk St John Mullova (p)* Fischer (p)*

* Crescendo usually starts in the second half of b. 39, or in b. 40; there is a *subito p* in b. 38 after which loud dynamics resume.

188 A Musicology of Performance

[Musical notation: Bach's original scoring of bars 35-41]

Bars 35-37 (or to 41), Perlman, Shumsky, Kremer

Bars 35-41 like that by e.g. Luca, Szenthelyi

Bars 35-41, Ehnes, Poulet, Mintz, Fischer

Bars 38-41, e.g. Wallfish, Schröder, Zehetmair

Bars 38-41, e.g. Huggett, Holloway, Tognetti

Bars 35/38-41, e.g. Matthews, Podger, Barton-Pine, Tetzlaff; bb.35-38 arpeggiated by Schröder

Figure 4.11. Bach's original scoring of bars 35-41 of the G minor Fuga and transcriptions of performed interpretations (cf. Table 4.8).

4.15. Different interpretations in J. S. Bach, G minor Sonata BWV 1001, Fuga extract: bars 35-42. Seven versions: Ingrid Matthews © Centaur, Rachel Podger © Channel Classics, Jaap Schröder © NAXOS, Sergiu Luca © Nonesuch, Elizabeth Wallfisch © Hyperion, Sigiswald Kuijken 1983 © Deutsche Harmonia Mundi, John Holloway © ECM. Duration: 3.09.

To listen to this extract online scan the QR code
or follow this link: http://dx.doi.org/10.11647/OBP.0064.21

Within these basic similarities among groups of violinists there were many important differences. A comparison of Podger's and Matthews' recording, for instance, shows Podger to approach the section with virtuosity creating a richly sonorous recording. In contrast, Matthews' reading has a dreamy quality, especially from bar 38 onwards. Here she drops the dynamics to very soft levels and starts the new arpeggiation pattern slowly and gradually, giving it a tentative feel (cf. first two examples in Audio example 4.15).

Others have also played around with the dynamics of this episode. Quite a few violinists (e.g. Kremer, Tetzlaff) chose to drop the volume to *p* or *pp* in b. 38 either gradually from bar 37 or 36 or quite abruptly so as to coincide with the new figuration in b. 38. A *crescendo* often ensued from half-way through b. 40. Perlman, in contrast, played the whole passage *forte* while others started *mf* and gradually built up the volume to the beginning of b. 42.

As mentioned earlier, and illustrated through Audio example 4.15, variety also involved matters like stressing certain harmonies, holding over downbeats, accenting every half-bar, playing the pedal note louder or softer than the other notes, adding slurs to the double stops from b. 38 onward, or suddenly slowing and then slightly speeding tempo to mark bars 38 or 42. But of course the most striking difference comes from whether the passage is arpeggiated or not and if so how.

Neumann states that "Bach invariably writes 'arpeggio' or 'arp' when he wants chords so treated," for instance in the D minor Ciaccona (bb. 89-120).[70] These bars of the G minor Fuga are not marked like that. If Neumann is right about Bach's notational practices, it becomes questionable whether the arpeggiation one hears in the recordings has any historical validity. More pertinently, the question arises *when* such a playing tradition may have started. The recorded history of the works indicates no arpeggiation in this episode until the 1980s. In my collection of over 60 versions, proper arpeggiation is found only in those listed in column 1 of Table 4.8. Except for Sándor Végh (1971), Arthur Grumiaux (1961) and Emil Telmányi (1954), who play the passage as written (i.e. like Luca et al.), all others tend to play it as semiquavers, although some start this at b. 38 only.

Interestingly, a few paragraphs later Neumann acknowledges the existence of passages where "arpeggiation is not ornamental in nature, but necessitated by the technical limitations of the instruments."[71] Given

---

70 Neumann, 'Some Performance Problems,' p. 27.
71 Ibid.

that these measures are played as written by at least eight violinists on record (although Telmányi and Gähler are using a curved bow), it remains arguable what might be considered a "technical necessity."

Multiple Stops

Looking at the delivery of multiple stops more generally it is perhaps not surprising to find that MSP violinists tend to play four-note chords as three plus one or two plus two notes, giving emphasis to the melodic pitch, particularly if it is the top note. The alternative among these versions is a rapid delivery, making the notes sound more chord-like. In such cases a noticeable sound quality results, especially in the fugues: the greater bow pressure and stronger attack of older players create a "whipping" effect (Kremer, Shumsky). In more recent recordings of younger violinists the bowing is lighter and the sound less forceful (Mullova, Faust, Barton Pine, St John, Gringolts, Ibragimova). Of course some of these violinists use gut strings and / or a baroque bow which may assist in achieving the effect because of the lower tension in both the strings and the bow hair. The lower bridge of the baroque violin also makes string crossing easier. HIP players (less so Kuijken) and those influenced by historical performance practice research are more likely to arpeggiate three and four-note chords to a varying degree. Tognetti and Tetzlaff, for instance, tend to break chords faster while Huggett and Wallfisch slower. Depending on the musical context, they highlight the bottom, the top, or none of the notes. Finally, in polyphonic textures with the subject in the lowest voice some violinists play the chords from top note down (e.g. A minor Fuga bb. 40-43 and 92-93 in Kremer 2005).

A good example to look at more closely is the famous opening chord of the G minor Adagio. Its delivery illustrates at least three basic differences in approach: Huggett and Holloway play the opening chord with emphasis on the low G followed by a moderately slow arpeggiation and then a pause on the high G. Wallfisch and others (especially HIP violinists but Zehetmair, Tognetti, Mullova, Ibragimova, etc. as well) also arpeggiate but faster and in one gesture, holding out (or not) the top G at the end. The third type of delivery aims to make it sound like a chord, generally with a fast break between the bottom and top two notes (e.g. Perlman, Shumsky, Buswell, Ehnes, Fischer) and holding out the top dyad. St John's delivery sounds more like one plus one plus two. Matthews plays the bottom two notes then the Bflat and eventually the top G; these last two notes are delivered in a slowly arpeggiated manner (Audio example 4.16, for further versions see Audio examples 4.1, 5.22, 5.23 and 5.24).

4.16. Performance of multiple stops in J. S. Bach, G minor Sonata BWV 1001, Adagio, extract: bar 1, chord 1. Four versions: James Ehnes © Analekta Fleurs de lys, Ruggiero Ricci © One-Eleven, Ingrid Matthews © Centaur, John Holloway © ECM. Duration: 0.18.

To listen to this extract online scan the QR code
or follow this link: http://dx.doi.org/10.11647/OBP.0064.22

Turning now to the interaction between bowing, articulation and dynamics in relation to multiple stops, I again consider the Sarabande from the B minor Partita. It provides a good example of how these features combine to create differences within broadly similar interpretative approaches (Table 4.9; Audio example 4.17).

Table 4.9: Summary of modifications in the B minor Sarabande within the two essentially differing approaches.

Summary of differences within the Sustained bowing / Legato style		Summary of Differences within the Lifted / uneven Bowing style	
Performance feature	*Performer*	*Performance feature*	*Performer*
Chords are soft, short fast	Kremer, Buswell, Fischer, Poulet	Chords arpeggiated	Wallfisch, Tognetti, St John, Luca
Articulating chords separately (e.g. bb. 1, 9)	Kremer, Fischer	Fast chords	Tetzlaff, Szenthelyi, van Dael
Chords very soft	Fischer		
Chords louder	Kremer, Perlman, Mintz		
Chords almost arpeggiated	Mintz		
Chords broken 2+2	Perlman		
Even dynamics	Perlman, Mintz		
More legato when loud	Kremer		
More legato during repeat	Fischer		
Soft (gentle) arpeggio	Tetzlaff (2005)		
Use of tempo rubato (for phrasing)	Tetzlaff (2005)		

> 4.17. Increasingly lighter bowing, less legato articulation and stronger pulse in J. S. Bach, B minor Partita BWV 1002, Sarabande, extract: bars 9-17. Eleven versions: Ruggiero Ricci © One-Eleven, James Ehnes © Analekta Fleurs de lys, Sergey Khachatryan © Naïve, Gerard Poulet © Arion, Julia Fischer © PentaTone Classics, Benjamin Schmid © Arte Nova, Richard Tognetti ©ABC Classics, John Holloway © ECM, Lara St John © Ancalagon, Ingrid Matthews © Centaur, Elizabeth Wallfisch © Hyperion. Duration: 5.46.
>
>
>
> To listen to this extract online scan the QR code
> or follow this link: http://dx.doi.org/10.11647/OBP.0064.23

Overall, MSP players tend to emphasize the melody through a sustained, over-legato style, where the top notes are held over while the chords of the next note are played softly and unobtrusively (e.g. Ehnes, Khachatryan, Perlman, Shumsky). Fast chords, soft and short lower notes can also be observed in many other versions, including some HIP, where the melody is foregrounded (Matthews, Holloway, Barton Pine). But as one can hear in the Audio examples, there are many subtle variations within this general legato style.

A real difference is achieved only by adopting a radically different bowing style, one that is more lifted and uneven, resulting in a constant fluctuation of timbre and dynamics. In these versions there are slight swells up to the melody note and then a decay or "reverse swell" before the next multiple stop. This bowing creates a little accent on the lower pitches at the beginning (whether played arpeggio or as fast chord / "sliding-up" to the top note) and thus integrates the harmony more (Huggett, Schmid, Ibragimova, Zehetmair). The gaps between the chords make the melody sound less legato while the fluctuation of the dynamics enhances the sense of pulse. At times there seems to be a slight pushing forward of tempo; just moving on rather than speeding up. As we have seen earlier (Audio example 4.4), Mullova's three recordings show the trend from the "fast chords, even tone, legato melody, over-held top notes" style of playing to a lighter, more detached articulation, arpeggiated or almost arpeggiated delivery of multiple stops, constantly fluctuating dynamics, and stronger projection of pulse. As was noted earlier, she alternates the rhythm by adding dotting (like Luca) in her 1993 recording and delivers increasingly flexible, expressive, and ornamented versions in 1993 and 2008.

Phrasing and Dynamics

A telling instance of interacting performance features is the phenomenon that differences in phrasing can be captured by observing the use of dynamics. Terraced dynamics was quite common, especially for repeats or between the A and B materials of binary form movements (e.g. Khachatryan in D minor Giga). Zehetmair also used terraced dynamics but for sections *within* the A and B parts of these movements. On the other hand, violinists like Faust or St John, would start these movements soft and play them gradually louder, more "defined," especially for the repeats. Fugues also tended to be structured through dynamics. Apart from large-scale crescendos, violinists, especially MSP musicians, quite commonly played episodes or certain fugal statements softer or louder than the surrounding material (e.g. Shumsky, Kremer, Ehnes in the G minor Fuga). HIP players used less contrastive dynamics; their volume generally stayed within a narrower band than those of older MSP violinists. Dynamics could also reflect the thickness and register of the musical texture with higher or denser material tending to sound louder. The prescribed terraced dynamics in movements such as the A minor Allegro, E Major Preludio, and the gigues were generally observed by all studied performers to a greater or lesser extent probably contributing to a potential sense of uniformity of interpretation in certain movements.

An aspect of dynamics even more clearly linked to phrasing is the convention of so-called phrase-arching; whether a performer plays louder and faster as they progress towards the middle of the phrase and then softer and slower as they conclude it, and to what extent (cf. Table 3.3).

Nicholas Cook dedicated a whole chapter to this issue in his recent book.[72] Stravinsky railed against and ridiculed such performances. In his Harvard Lectures in 1939 he jibbed:

> The sin against the spirit of the work always starts with the sin against its letter and leads to the endless follies [...] Thus it follows that a *crescendo*, as

---

72   Cook, *Beyond the Score*, pp. 176-223.

we all know, is always accompanied by a speeding up of movement, while a slowing down never fails to accompany a *diminuendo*.[73]

Such phrasing was commonly noted in the recordings of MSP violinists, especially Shumsky, Ricci, Perlman, Buswell, Mintz, Ehnes, Hahn, Fischer, Khachatryan, Tetzlaff (esp. in 2005) but also in the less radically HIP versions, for instance Beznosiuk and, to a lesser extent, Schröder.

The most noticeable differences with regards to dynamics and phrasing in the current dataset stem from decisions regarding the length or "identity" of a phrase. This finding is in line with the empirical research that asserts the existence of a combination of tempo curves in expressive performance, "with different weightings at different metrical levels, together with certain individual gestures corresponding to specific structural events."[74] As I have stated repeatedly, older and MSP violinists, especially those who play slow movements rather legato, tend to phrase in longer units while HIP and younger players have shorter arches progressing by single bar, half-bar, or pairs of bars. The difference in affect is profound. For contemporary sensibilities schooled on HIP, the phrase-arch approach sounds "romantic," especially when combined with vibrato tone, slower tempo, heavy bow pressure and legato articulation. By contrast, the more rapid, quasi chiaroscuro ebb and flow in performances that articulate shorter musical gestures sound "rhetorical," as if somebody is speaking or presenting an argument. The former may come across as sentimental, a pleading to and manipulation of emotions; or perhaps aggressive, forceful and demanding. The latter may strike as a genuine first-person story-telling, impassioned and authentic, or intimate and self-orientated. It does not force a reaction; it simply conveys a compelling account.[75]

---

[73] Igor Stravinsky, *Poetics of Music in the Form of Six Lessons* (1939), trans. by Arthur Knodel and Ingolf Dahl (New York: Knopf, 1960), p. 128.

[74] Cook, *Beyond the Score*, p. 156 referring to a study by Luke Windsor et al., 'A Structurally Guided Method for the Decomposition of Expression in Music Performance,' *Journal of the Acoustical Society of America*, 119 (2006), 1182-1193.

[75] The metric rubato one often hears in early recordings (when the tempo fluctuates in the melody only and at the bar level, with frequent *ritenutos* but few longer *accelerandos* and *rallentandos*) shares certain similarities with the "rhetorical" HIP approach. However a detailed comparative account is beyond the scope of the current study. For a discussion of metric rubato and its manifestation in recordings of artists born and trained well within the nineteenth century see Richard Hudson, *Stolen Time: The History of Tempo Rubato* (Oxford: Clarendon Press, 1994); Leech-Wilkinson, *The Changing Sound of Music* or; Neal Peres Da Costa, *Off the Record: Performing Practices in Romantic Piano Playing* (New York: Oxford University Press, 2012); and Dorottya Fabian, 'Commercial Sound Recordings and Trends in Expressive Music Performance: Why Should Experimental

Focusing on musico-technical elements contributing to these potential affective differences, recordings of the Largo from the C Major Sonata may serve us well to illustrate the point. The readings of Shumsky, Poulet, Mintz, Perlman and Hahn, among others, exemplify the legato approach where cadence points are subdued into ever continuing melodic lines. Tempo is relatively steady but the dynamics definitely have an arching profile, gradually building with each subsequent sub-phrase to climactic high notes and dropping only towards major structural moments, like b. 8 and b. 16 (Figure 4.12 bottom two panels). In contrast, Wallfisch, Zehetmair, Huggett and others articulate almost every harmonic figuration and make audible many temporary cadence points (Figure 4.12 top 3 panels; Audio example 4.18).

Violinists in the first group "bow-over" rests; e.g. bars 1-2, where the melody line is basically sustained in one continuous flow, in spite of the rests between its segments. In contrast, Wallfisch, Zehetmair and Huggett seem to relish the silences and create pauses even where there is none notated. In their reading, the four groups of semiquavers in bar 3 each has its own little dynamic and tempo arch and there is a little *rallentando* and pause on beat 3 of the next bar (cadence marked with trill in the manuscript). Typically they separate the sequential repetitions of bars 4-5 and create another mini cadence on the down-beat of bar 6. The next sequential repetition (bars 6-7) is again separately articulated and the second statement is not linked to the four semiquavers on the second beat of bar 7.

4.18. Articulated / "rhetorical" versus legato / "romantic" style in J. S. Bach, C Major Sonata BWV 1005, Largo, extract: bars 3-8. Five versions: Elizabeth Wallfisch © Hyperion, Monica Huggett © Virgin Veritas, Thomas Zehetmair © Teldec, Gerard Poulet © Arion, Oscar Shumsky © Musical Heritage Society. Duration: 4.14.

To listen to this extract online scan the QR code
or follow this link: http://dx.doi.org/10.11647/OBP.0064.24

Researchers Pay Attention?,' in *Expressiveness in Music Performance: Empirical Approaches across Styles and Cultures*, ed. by Dorottya Fabian, Renee Timmers, and Emery Schubert (Oxford: Oxford University Press), pp. 58-79.

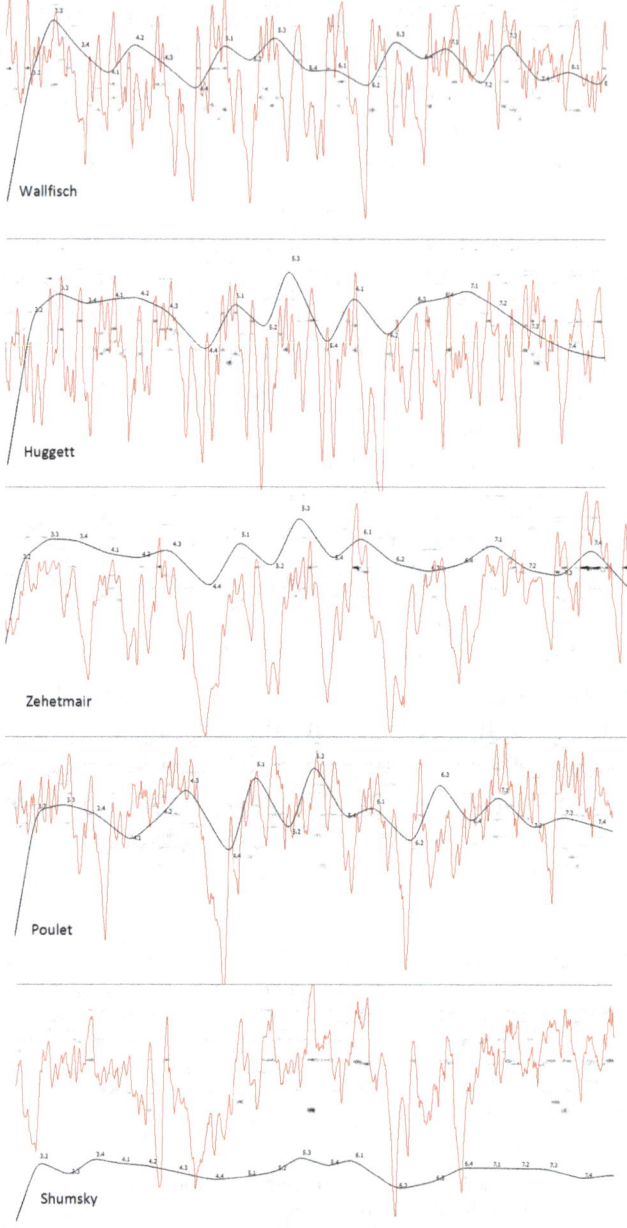

Figure 4.12. Comparison of tempo and power (dynamics) in bars 3-8 of the Largo from the C Major Sonata performed by (from top to bottom) Wallfisch, Huggett, Zehetmair, Poulet and Shumsky. Beat level tempo is indicated by the smoother line near bar and beat numbers. Power (dynamic) is indicated by the volatile slopes. Note the longer and clearer power arches in the bottom two panels as opposed to the near constant shifts in the more locally articulated versions above. Note also Shumsky's fairly even tempo line. I used *Sonic Visualiser* to prepare this analysis.

To various degrees, Wallfisch and the others also delineate the elision of the quavers cadence on beat 1 of bar 8 and the new start of the opening melody—the four semiquavers on the same beat. What is important to note, too, is that Wallfisch and others (e.g. Ibragimova) manage to keep the line going even though their articulation is very detailed and their phrasing locally nuanced. They manage to avoid the pitfall of creating a fragmented and over-accented reading that lacks flow.

Compared to this locally articulated phrasing, violinists listed in the first group (i.e. Shumsky et al.) tend to create one large phrase from the beginning to bar 8, even though some of them play the first two bars more separated than the others. Their over-legato approach geared towards a long-spun melody becomes most obvious from bar 4 onwards. One hears their performances as pushing ahead, using the momentum of the pairs of sequences. Continuously increasing intensity, vibrato and volume, they reach a climax on the high A of bar 7 where they slow down to emphasize the trilled cadence resolving on beat 1 of bar 8. They foster the perception of released tension by softening the dynamics.

4.6. Conclusions

In this chapter I continued to examine the similarities and differences between HIP and MSP versions taking a more detailed approach focusing on specific performance features. I wanted to see the degree of homogeneity present across these recordings and whether particular characteristics could be linked to time and place or violin school. Most importantly my aim was to gain a textured understanding of the complex nature, the "thousand layers" of music performance; the interactions of technical and musical, physical, acoustic and bodily features contributing to the process of emergent stylistic transformations. As this is the overarching aim of the entire book, I will draw only partial conclusions here. Additional information will come to light in the remaining chapters.

The analyses of performance features confirmed the more general points made in the previous chapter: MSP violinists, especially of the older generation and those associated with the Juilliard School tended to use similar bowing and more vibrato than HIP and HIP-inspired violinists. Beyond this very broad generalization however, it was difficult to categorize players and performances. The most important overlap between MSP and HIP was found in bowing. The overlap reflected generational differences:

older HIP players (especially Schröder) differed less from MSP violinists in their bowing while younger MSP players (except for Hahn) tended to emulate to a greater or lesser degree bowing typical of period practice. Investigation of tempo showed a greater alliance among HIP-inspired violinists with MSP customs in that they too tended to choose more extreme tempos than HIP violinists. On the other hand, ornamentation proved to be a strong indicator of HIP influence, with several MSP players considerably outperforming their period specialist colleagues in embellishing and ornamenting many movements of the Six Solos, especially since the mid-2000s.

Once the discussion moved into accounting for features such as rhythm, timing, articulation, dynamics and phrasing, the interaction of performance elements became palpable and made the previous attempts at categorizing styles rather futile. The masking effect of articulation and tempo on the perception of dotting was re-confirmed; the complex and interdependent impact of bow-strokes, articulation and dynamic nuance together with its contribution to diverse aesthetic affect was repeatedly noted. The detailed descriptions endeavoured to convey in words the myriads of audible differences across the selected recordings and explain what may constitute the complex of these differences; they endeavoured to identify "lines of flight" and "multiplicities" inhabiting the "rhizome" of solo violin Bach performance at the turn of the twentieth and twenty-first centuries.

In the face of the evidence one wonders why the notion of homogeneity in later twentieth-century performance is such a pervasive impression. Is it because there are so many more recordings available now that it is harder to pick out the salient ones compared to the "golden age" when only a handful of violinists made recordings and rarely of solo Bach?[76] Or could it be that solo performance, especially string and voice, tend to be more individualistic than piano, orchestral, or ensemble playing, and that these may have been the basis for drawing conclusions regarding homogeneity? Or is it simply the performance of baroque music, including Bach's that has changed so much providing opportunity for such diversity? These are

---

76 I am aware of only one or two recordings of the complete set made prior to 1950 (e.g. Yehudi Menuhin 1934-1936; George Enescu late 1940s or early 1950s), a few complete sonatas (e.g. Adolf Busch, Joseph Szigeti, Jascha Heifetz) and the D minor Partita (e.g. Borislav Huberman 1942, Adolf Busch 1929). However, most of the recordings from that period were of individual movements. James Creighton, *Discopaedia of the Violin, 1889-1971* (Toronto: University of Toronto Press, 1974) lists more than what I have but does not provide dates for the recordings.

realistic scenarios for potentially different conclusions, but research into string quartet practice also seems to point towards diversity[77] and important variations have been noted among pianists performing nineteenth-century music.[78] In my experience as intermittent listener to concertos (for instance Mozart's violin concertos), diversity seem harder to evidence in that repertoire whether one focuses on the soloists alone or the total experience. But in orchestral music I hear considerable differences between the interpretations of various conductors, like Simon Rattle, Claudio Abbado, Philippe Herreweghe or Nikolaus Harnoncourt, in repertoire as diverse as Berlioz, Mahler, Beethoven, Mendelssohn, and Brahms.[79] It could be that writers all too readily base their opinion on formative listening experiences during earlier times, perhaps ending by the 1980s. The lack of systematic attention to and analyses of current performances has allowed the casual impression to be reinforced by commercial propaganda or reviewers' choices that often favour the circulation of particular versions, and not always the most interesting ones. The striking differences between two almost concurrently released recent versions of the Bach Solos (Ibragimova and Faust, both recorded in 2009) should really make commentators rethink the validity of claiming uniformity in contemporary music performance. Whereas Ibragimova uses extreme tempos (very fast *allegros* and rather languid slow movements), adds no embellishments, plays with no vibrato and fairly softly almost all the time, Faust provides a varied, energetic reading full of bounce and a multitude of ornaments and embellishments. To me the first sounds stylish but "calculated"; the latter spontaneous and more "naturally" engaged and engaging. Expanding the variety, just a year later Khachatryan's set was issued, one that diverts only very lightly from the standard MSP approach, most typical of the 1970s and 1980s.

It is of course reasonable to posit that a notated musical composition defines the boundaries of its possible execution to a greater or lesser extent,

---

77 Richard Turner, 'Style and Tradition in String Quartet Performance: A Study of 32 Recordings of Beethoven's Op. 131 Quartet' (PhD Thesis Sheffield, University of Sheffield, 2004).

78 Bruno Repp, 'Diversity and Commonality in Music Performance: An Analysis of Timing Microstructure in Schumann's "Träumerei",' *Journal of the Acoustical Society of America*, 92/5 (1992), 2546-2568; Nicholas Cook, 'Methods for Analysing Recordings,' in *The Cambridge Companion to Recorded Music*, ed. by Nicholas Cook et al. (Cambridge: Cambridge University Press, 2009), pp. 221-245.

79 Performance (mostly tempo) trends in symphonic repertoire have been studied by Bowen, among others. José A. Bowen, 'Tempo, Duration, and Flexibility: Techniques in the Analysis of Performance,' *Journal of Musicological Research*, 16/2 (1996), 111–156.

contributing to potential homogeneity of performances. After all, we are in the habit of saying "performance *of* this or that piece" for some reason! The expression implies that a performance (or recording) is supposed to be a representation of the *work*. As discussed in chapter two, representational thought is restrictive because it requires the conceptualization of a piece of music to be a "faithful" copy of a supposed "original." Exposure to a hundred years of sound recordings has started to make us aware of how loose these boundaries might be and musicologists and theorists like Leech-Wilkinson[80] and Cook[81] have started unpacking the issue of representation and the nature of creativity in performance. Importantly, Deleuzian philosophy, to which I will refer increasingly in the final part of this book, encourages thinking of music as something without a stable entity; "music as process of becoming."

Nevertheless the perceived or very real boundaries conveyed by the score are upheld by our current training and associated value systems to a certain degree (quite a high degree in some cases as witnessed in the playing of Ehnes, Edinger, and Hahn, for instance). The question then is: how many *radically* different readings one can get of a piece? Or rather, to what extent readings must differ from each-other before one starts talking about homogeneity in performance? Only when we have many more detailed studies available of diverse repertoires, artists and periods shall we be in the position to answer these questions. For now, it seems cautionary to note the variety and beauty that the studied violinists bring to their interpretations, deepening and broadening our understanding of these seminal pieces composed by Bach.

The final point then is not to deny the existence of trends, but to emphasize their limited scope in helping to map twentieth-century developments of western music performance. To put it another way, analysis of individual interpretations seems more productive for an understanding of music as performance and creativity in performance, while establishing and examining trends maybe useful when thinking of music as culturally embedded communication.

---

80 Leech-Wilkinson, *The Changing Sound of Music*.
81 Nicholas Cook, 'Bridging the Unbridgeable? Empirical Musicology and Interdisciplinary Performance Studies,' in *Taking it to the Bridge: Music as Performance*, ed. by Nicholas Cook and Richard Pettengill (Ann Arbor: Michigan University Press, 2013), pp. 70-85.

5. Affect and Individual Difference: Towards a Holistic Account of Performance

Having focused on specific performance features in the previous chapter, I now turn to global matters in relation to specific moments of particular movements and increasingly enlist Deleuzian terms and thinking.[1] First I look for differences within the loose boundaries of MSP and HIP and then across multiple recordings of the same violinists. This is followed by a comparative exploration of musical character and affect in selected examples, concluding with a consideration of idiosyncratic versions and listeners' reactions.[2] Essentially, I argue that a more holistic approach to performance analyses brings to light the multitude of interactions at play that contribute to the overall effect of a performance. This might be best grasped subjectively paying attention to both measurable and felt features. I show that the seeming chaos of individual differences caused by the relative and diverse contributions and non-linear interactions of performance features can be illuminated, if not fully explained, by using a Deleuzian lens. Deleuze and Guattari offer a language to account for stabilizing (territorializing) and diversifying (de-territorializing) functions of technical and aesthetic traits and assist in pinpointing moments or

---

1 Gilles Deleuze and Felix Guattari, *A Thousand Plateaus: Capitalism and Schizophrenia* (London: Bloomsbury Academic, 2013).
2 As I state in the conclusions of this chapter, for me "affect" is a nameless sensation that precedes cognition and recognized emotion. It is a bodily reaction; a felt transition from one state to another.

performance solutions that push interpretations along the style vector from MSP to HIP; they help describe the "in between." Just like in the previous chapter, here too the detailed or more specific descriptions appear in boxed texts shaded grey for ease of navigation.

5.1. Differences within the MSP and within the HIP Styles

The Loure, the Gavotte en Rondeau, and the two Menuets of the E Major Partita have already received considerable attention especially in relation to ornamentation, rhythm and bowing. This provides a good foundation for further discussions of these movements. The focus now is on general interpretative differences within the two respective style categories rather than across them.

The Loure

According to Stowell, Schröder, and Ledbetter, several eighteenth-century French authors regard the loure to be a slow gigue, a dance in 6/4 metre with a heavy pace.[3] The German contemporaries of Bach—Mattheson and Walther—also concur regarding the slow tempo and the "arrogant and proud nature" of the dance.[4] Schröder further claims that the dotted rhythms underline the "fiery" jumps and complex steps of the dancer. However, the movement should never sound busy and should always retain a sense of "quiet nobility."[5] Somewhat contrastingly Ledbetter finds Wendy Hilton's description apt for Bach's loure: "a unique blend of gently expressed nobility, tenderness and tranquillity."[6]

Schröder recommends a moderate speed of crotchet = 96, "which allows the violinist to combine the *pesante* character with featherweight ornaments as well as distinguishing the light, arpeggiated upbeat chords from the

---

3 Jaap Schröder, *Bach's Solo Violin Works: A Performer's Guide* (London: Yale University Press, 2007), p. 171; Robin Stowell, *The Early Violin and Viola* (Cambridge: Cambridge University Press, 2001), p. 119; Ledbetter, *Unaccompanied Bach: Performing the Solo Works* (New Haven: Yale University Press, 2009), p. 170.
4 Stowell, *The Early Violin*, p. 119.
5 Schröder, *Bach's Solo Violin Works*, p. 171.
6 Ledbetter, *Unaccompanied Bach*, citing Wendy Hilton, *Dance and Music of Court and Theatre* (Stuyvesant, NY: Pendragon Press, 1997), pp. 407, 437.

strong ones on down-beats."[7] In contrast, the tempo Stowell suggests is crotchet = 80. He emphasizes the movement's "carefully balanced phrases [...] clear harmonies, and ornamented melody" contributing to a "languid" character.[8]

MSP Interpretations

As mentioned earlier, violinists tend to perform the E Major Loure as a slow, lyrical movement although quite a few of the more recently recorded versions show signs of a more dance-like approach. Still, the "fiery, proud and arrogant" character highlighted by Schröder is rare. Perhaps Zehetmair's version could be described as "fiery" due to its fast tempo and sharply defined rhythm. But the fast tempo seems to go against notions of "quiet nobility" and "languid character." Along the spectrum of the two basic approaches to interpreting this Loure—defined as lyrical and melodically orientated versus dance-like and rhythmically orientated—there is a great variety of grades and differences. Both approaches can be slower or faster, lighter or heavier overall, flowing or sturdy, more or less legato, detached or staccato, dotted to different degrees, ornamented or not, played on the string with quite intense bowing or with light, lifted bow strokes, and so on.[9]

Broadly speaking one might say that the MSP versions more commonly feature the melodically orientated approach and that these tend also to be fairly legato, with phrasing aided by arching dynamics

---

7   Schröder, *Bach's Solo Violin Works*, p. 172.
8   Stowell, *The Early Violin*, p. 119.
9   In an unpublished interview with Daniel Bangert, John Holloway explains why the Loure is a "very good example of needing to put information together in order to arrive at a credible interpretation." He states that violinists were "brought up with the idea that because the E Major Partita is how it is and that a piece with a lot of movements has to have a slow movement somewhere, [so] the Loure had to be the slow movement." This influenced bowing and rhythmic delivery fostering a legato and literalist rendering. In contrast, familiarity with French baroque dances and Muffat's teaching on bowing promotes a completely different approach. There are quotations from the interview and further discussion of Holloway's (and other's) view on bowing and interpretative approaches in Daniel Bangert, 'Doing without thinking: processes of musical decision-making in period instrument performance' (PhD Thesis, The University of New South Wales, 2012). For comments on the Loure see especially pp. 58-59. Holloway's performance of bars 1-8 of the Loure can be heard in Audio example 4.12.

(crescendo-decrescendo). The best examples are Hahn, Poulet, Shumsky, and Ehnes, but Tetzlaff's second recording may also be mentioned (the earlier is also fairly legato but lighter and less vibrato).

> Teasing out general differences among these MSP versions, it is worth noting that Hahn's and Tetzlaff's more recent interpretations focus on beauty of tone and melody. They both take lyricism to a level that may be perceived as emotive (cf. the intense vibrato on longer notes and extremely soft dynamics in Tetzlaff's), whereas the versions of Szenthelyi, Perlman, and Mintz project a gentle pulse that counteracts such an impression.[10] Szenthelyi plays with strong vibrato but less legato bowing which helps create some forward momentum. Ibragimova's version is rather different. She provides an articulated and more varied reading but she plays rather slow and soft and the performance becomes languid, making the music sound repetitive (cf. Audio example 4.12 and 5.1).
>
> Differences can be observed in the approach to repeats. Hahn, Mintz, Fischer, Shumsky, and Poulet do not differentiate between first play and repeat. Others often do. Tetzlaff varies ornamentations in 2005. Lev, Perlman and Tetzlaff in his earlier recording use softer and / or less fluctuating dynamics during repeats. Lev adds further variation by playing more legato.
>
> Further specific differences among MSP versions involve the use of dynamics and tempo fluctuation for the shaping of phrases. Many start the movement moderately loud and build towards a climax in b. 8. However, what happens in the next four measures tends to differ: For instance Perlman further intensifies through crescendo and vibrato whereas Zehetmair releases the tension and reduces dynamics. Barton Pine also relies on dynamics to aid phrasing while Kremer's recordings have considerable tempo fluctuations.
>
> Differences can also be noted in the large-scale phrasing of the second half of the Loure (bars 12-24). Several violinists tend to maintain the momentum to about bar 15 and then provide a brief relaxation of intensity

---

10   John H Planer discusses definitions of sentimentality in relation to musical performance in 'Sentimentality in the Performance of Absolute Music: Pablo Casals's Performance of Saraband from Johann Sebastian Bach's Suite No. 2 in D Minor for Unaccompanied Cello, S. 1008,' *The Musical Quarterly*, 73/2 (1989), 212-248. He mentions "emotional exaggeration" and refers to M. H. Abrams (among others) who defines sentimentality as "an excess of emotion, an overindulgence in the 'tender' emotions of pathos and sympathy." However, Planer notes Abrams' warning, that "excess or overindulgence is relative to the author and period" and therefore it is better to define it "by the use of clichés and commonplaces to express feeling." Planer, 'Sentimentality,' p. 214 referring to M. H. Abrams, 'Sentimentalism' in *A Glossary of Literary Terms*, 4th edn (New York: Holt, Rinehart and Winston, 1981), p. 175.

and dynamics. A building up of tension and crescendo then starts in b. 19 leading to a climax in b. 20. Zehetmair, in contrast, accelerates to b. 19 and starts this passage *f*, broadening the tempo in b. 20 with a concurrent diminuendo and strong *rall* to the dotted crotchet chord and then continuing *pp* from the up-beat to b. 21. A similar trajectory with less flexibility and contrast can be observed in Shumsky's performance as well. The last four bars (21-24) again vary regarding whether the tension is maintained to the end or tapered off to a soft conclusion. Those starting b. 21 *p* often create a little swell of dynamics in b. 22 before the final decrescendo and *rall* from beat 5 of b. 23 (Audio example 5.1).

5.1. Phrasing in J. S. Bach, E Major Partita BWV 1006, Loure, extract: bars 12-20. Three versions: Christian Tetzlaff 1994 © Virgin Veritas, Thomas Zehetmair © Teldec, James Ehnes © Analekta Fleurs de lys. Duration: 2.16.

To listen to this extract online scan the QR code
or follow this link: http://dx.doi.org/10.11647/OBP.0064.25

Some versions display a more localised, moment to moment variation. Tognetti, for instance, plays with dynamic nuance, achieved through stress and subtle-rapid changes in bow pressure and speed on the note or two-note level. Zehetmair changes dynamics to shape sub-phrase after sub-phrase (i.e. every two bars or so), while in his earlier recording Tetzlaff creates many little dynamic arches (*crescendo-decrescendo*) during the first play of each half of the movement. In the later version Tetzlaff's choice of agogic stresses and execution of trills often differ between first play and repeat (e.g. stress on downbeat B in b. 22 is only in first play; written out F on downbeat in b. 15 is played more like a longer appoggiatura in the first play but more as written during repeat; from b. 22 to the end of the movement is softer in repeat).

Another source of diversity is the manner in which chords are delivered. Among MSP players Lev, Tetzlaff, Tognetti, Barton Pine, and most of the younger violinists tend to play chords lightly, at times slightly arpeggiated. Older performers, especially Perlman, Kremer, and Shumsky, play with heavier strokes aiming to make the notes sound together. In spite of this broad generalization chords are generally played in diverse ways in most versions, depending on the musical context of the chord.

HIP Interpretations

Some of these characteristics typical of MSP recordings can be noticed in HIP versions as well, in particular Kuijken's and Schröder's but also van Dael's. Of these, Kuijken's is the most legato (with longer, fairly sustained bow strokes) and the least rhythmical, especially in 2001. Schröder and van Dael project the dance character in the first half of the movement but van Dael's tempo proves too slow to keep the momentum in the second half and Schröder slows down when the texture includes more double and triple stops. At times his bowing sounds weighty on the string and his strokes are longer in the second half with fewer metrical stresses. He adds an accented appoggiatura to almost every down-beat and half-bar beat during the first repeat and many in the second half. However, because of their regularity and uniformity they foster the impression of standardization rather than spontaneous embellishing (cf. Audio example 4.12).

The other HIP violinists tend to present a more rhythmically orientated reading. As I have shown in chapter four, some of them also add many ornaments (just like their younger MSP colleagues, such as Tetzlaff, Tognetti, and Gringolts, as well as Mullova and Faust). Nevertheless there are also many noticeable differences among these HIP versions as well.

> For instance, Wallfisch plays rather slower and very staccato, leaving gaps between notes. She leans on and holds the dotted notes while playing their short pairs as well as most third and sixth beats very short, with kerning. Her performance does not become mechanical because of subtle variations. The passage between bars 19 and 22, for instance, is played much less sharply articulated. In b. 20 the paired slurs are gently projected while the notes on beat three are shaped to form part of the cadence (chord) on beat four. Podger chooses a similar tempo but plays more legato and in a less overtly dotted, leaping manner. She does not add ornaments and plays the repeats as the first time round. Huggett's performance is similar to Podger's as it is more legato than Wallfisch's and she does not add ornaments either. On the other hand Huggett leans on the longer notes and suspensions like Wallfisch does. Luca's interpretation is more flowing and faster and in that it is similar to Huggett's. However, the added ornaments during repeat enhance the dotted character of the movement and he also plays some of the figures more staccato creating a very different overall effect (Audio example 5.2).

5.2. Comparison of HIP performances in J. S. Bach, E Major Partita BWV 1006, Loure, extracts: bars 19-22. Two versions: Elizabeth Wallfisch © Hyperion, Rachel Podger © Channel Classics; bars 17-22. Monica Huggett © Virgin Veritas; repeat of bars 12-24. Sergiu Luca © Nonesuch. Duration: 2.15.

To listen to this extract online scan the QR code
or follow this link: http://dx.doi.org/10.11647/OBP.0064.26

Importantly, Luca's ground-breaking playing finds its true descendants in the recordings of Mullova and Faust some 30 years later. These are not just straightforward next generation "improvements" on the past. They are new constellations; new "multiplicities." The lively energy, rich subtleties and luxuriantly varied and inventive ornamentations of Mullova's and Faust's performances are indicative of a liberated, non-literalistic performing style of baroque music becoming common as the new millennium enters its second decade. It is a testament to Sergiu Luca's visionary musicianship to have introduced-anticipated such "lines of flight" in the midst of the Urtext-orientated, "authentistic" 1970s.[11]

The Gavotte en Rondeau

The basic differences in performing the Gavotte relate to dynamics (whether fairly uniform or varied, and to what extent and how), bowing (whether lighter or heavier; shorter or longer), and to the shaping of the character of both the rondo theme and the various episodes (whether the contrasts in texture and thematic material are emphasized or downplayed and how each section is articulated and phrased). It is easy to see, then, that there could be a multitude of solutions and combinations of choices and this is indeed the case. A rough generalization is summarized in Table 5.1. For closer detail, and to enable insight into homogeneity or diversity

---

11   Term coined by Taruskin in 1988. See Taruskin, *Text and Act: Essays on Music and Performance* (New York: Oxford University Press, 1995), p. 99.

of performance practice within each overarching stylistic categories I offer comments on two HIP and two MSP versions recorded within a relatively short period of time: Wallfisch (1997) versus Huggett (1995) and Gringolts (2002) versus Lev (2002).

Table 5.1. A generalized summary of performance characteristics found in recordings of the E Major Gavotte en Rondeau movement. Date is provided if one version by the same artists differed from the other.

Dynamics		Bowing		Tempo		Episodes	
Uniform	Varied	Lighter (varied)	Heavier	Faster	Slower (slightly)	Contrasted (varied)	Uniform
Beznosiuk	Barton Pine	Barton Pine	Ehnes	Brooks	Beznosiuk	Barton Pine	Beznosiuk
Brooks	Buswell	Beznosiuk	Kremer'05	Faust	Buswell	Buswell	Brooks
Ehnes	Faust	Buswell	(episodes)	Gringolts	Fischer	Huggett	Ehnes
Fischer	Gringolts	Faust	Kuijken'01	Ibragimova	Hahn	Ibragimova	Fischer
Hahn	Huggett	Fischer	Perlman	Podger	Holloway	(a little)	Hahn
Holloway	Ibragimova	Hahn (episodes)	Shumsky (in	St John	Huggett	Khachatryan	Holloway
Kuijken	Mullova (esp.	Holloway	double stops	Wallfisch	Khachatryan	Faust	Kuijken
Luca	'08)	Huggett	of theme and	Zehetmair	Kuijken	(somewhat)	Luca
Matthews	Khachatryan	Ibragimova	episodes)		Luca	Kremer'80	Matthews
(terraced)	Lev	Khachatryan			Matthews	Lev	(mostly)
Mintz	Podger	Kremer'05			Mintz	Mullova	Mintz
Perlman	Shumsky	(theme)			Mullova	(more in '08)	Poulet
Poulet	St John	Kuijken'83			Perlman	Podger	Schröder
Schröder	Tetzlaff'05	Lev			Schröder	St John	Shumsky
Szenthelyi	Tognetti	Luca			Szenthelyi	Tognetti	Szenthelyi
Tetzlaff'94	van Dael	Mullova			van Dael	van Dael	Tetzlaff
	Wallfisch	Podger				Wallfisch	
	Zehetmair	Poulet				Zehetmair	
		Schröder					
		Shumsky (in					
		linear motion)					
		St John					
		Tetzlaff'05					
		Tognetti					
		van Dael					
		Zehetmair					

HIP: Wallfisch and Huggett

Elizabeth Wallfisch (1997) and Monica Huggett (1995) both play at a moderate tempo with mostly light, short bow strokes and subtle dynamic variations. Both articulate the score in great detail. Their performances are nevertheless very different.

Wallfisch mostly accentuates notes and figures by stressing the initial note (e.g. first quaver in bb. 53-57), by playing 'off-notes' very staccato and / or lightly (e.g. bb. 12-13 second group of four quavers or bb. 72-73 the second double stop in each quaver dyad), and by slight dynamic contrasts (bb. 24-26.1: *f*, b. 26.2-7: *p*, bb. 28-30.1: *f*, bb. 30.2-32: *mp*; bb. 82-83: *f*, bb. 84-85: *mp*, bb. 88-89: *pp*). She plays the rondo theme fairly flowingly, without any particular *caesura* after the minim in b. 2 or b. 6 (Audio example 5.3).

5.3. Articulation in J. S. Bach, E Major Partita BWV 1006, Gavotte en Rondeau, extract: bars 9-36. Elizabeth Wallfisch © Hyperion. Duration: 0.50

To listen to this extract online scan the QR code
or follow this link: http://dx.doi.org/10.11647/OBP.0064.27

In contrast, Huggett's version relies on tempo fluctuation and the timing of notes more than anything else. The theme itself is presented in a fairly straightforward manner but each episode includes subtle but constant shifts in tempo usually at the bar level, creating what amounts to rubato in the classical sense of the term: robbed time given back straight away.[12] In the first episode, for instance, there is a slight *accelerando* on the upward figures and a *ritenuto* on the other patterns. These fluctuations tend to go across the bar line as the upward figures occupy the second half of each bar, except in b. 11. Furthermore, both the *rits* and *accelerandos* may involve only two to three notes in an obvious or pronounced manner, so the effect is more to do with flow, shaping and articulation than tempo *per se* (see bb. 10-15, Audio example 5.4).[13]

---

12 Richard Hudson, *Stolen time: The History of Tempo Rubato* (Oxford: Clarendon Press, 1994).
13 Similar strategy is observed in the third episode but here the fluctuation of tempo is also reflected in subtly rising and falling dynamics, especially from b. 53 onwards. The first half of each bar is slightly slower while the second half is faster and crescendo, culminating in the emphasized (and held back) high notes of b. 59. In the other episodes the tempo fluctuation is less pattern-like but similarly enlisted to highlight the small motivic cells that make up sub-phrases and decorate harmonic progressions.

5.4. Timing and tempo fluctuations going across bars in J. S. Bach, E Major Partita BWV 1006, Gavotte en Rondeau, extract: bars 9-16. Monica Huggett © Virgin Veritas. Duration: 0.15

To listen to this extract online scan the QR code
or follow this link: http://dx.doi.org/10.11647/OBP.0064.28

Huggett's performance of the second episode is particularly noteworthy. She creates a little *rit.* in b. 28 as the figuration on beat one outlines the tonic. This is followed by a speeding up on beat two to lead into the next bar which is a repeat of the episode's opening gesture, this time in the dominant. However, by playing the second beat of this bar *ritenuto* Huggett allows the listener to momentarily relish the dominant for its own sake, for during the remainder of the episode Bach teases perception with the potential of making it the new tonic. Indeed, Huggett's performance engages with this teasing full on by alternatively accelerating (b. 31), slowing (b. 33) and holding back (b. 35) to draw out harmonic tensions and expectations. The final dominant preparing the tonic cadence at the end of the episode (bb. 38-39) is again played rapidly as if in a hurry to round it off at last and to end the game with a corresponding *rit.* (Audio example 5.5).

5.5. Articulation and timing in J. S. Bach, E Major Partita BWV 1006, Gavotte en Rondeau, extract: bars 24-40. Monica Huggett © Virgin Veritas. Duration: 0.30

To listen to this extract online scan the QR code
or follow this link: http://dx.doi.org/10.11647/OBP.0064.29

MSP: Lev and Girngolts

The two non-specialist violinists chosen for comparison are actually exhibiting HIP tendencies in their performances of the Gavotte en Rondeau.

So this discussion identifies further layers of diversity and complexity within HIP "territory" indicating "rhizomic" tendencies.

Lara Lev seems to play around more with tempo fluctuations whereas Ilya Gringolts more with dynamic shifts. He plays the theme through while Lev breaks it up with slight pauses at the minim double stops. Her detailed articulation of episode one creates an impression of slightly slower tempo and she uses similar speeding up and slowing down strategies to Huggett in episode 3, especially from b. 53 onward. In contrast Gringolts plays these bars in even tempo but with constantly fluctuating dynamics at the bar and half-bar level (Audio example 5.6).

5.6. Embellished rondo theme and comparison of MSP styles in J. S. Bach, E Major Partita BWV 1006, Gavotte en Rondeau, extracts: bars 40-72. Ilya Gringolts © Deutsche Grammophon; bars 48-64. Lara Lev © Finlandia Records. Duration: 1.09.

To listen to this extract online scan the QR code
or follow this link: http://dx.doi.org/10.11647/OBP.0064.30

In the final episode their dynamics are fairly similar although Gringolts has a greater contrast between loud and soft with *pp* in bars 74, 80, 84, and 88. Other differences include a *crescendo* by Gringolts as opposed to a *descrescendo* by Lev in bar 86; flexible (Gringolts) versus in-tempo (Lev) performance of bars 88-89; *crescendo / accelerando* followed by *decrescendo* in bars 90-1 in Lev's version and even dynamics with *rallentando* starting in the second half of bar 90 in Gringolts' performance. Lev plays the final rondo statement softly, Gringolts *forte*.

Menuet I-II

Before looking for diversity, it is worth pointing out overall conventions in performances of these paired dance movements, often but not always, delivered as Menuet I, Menuet II, and Menuet I *da capo*. These conventions are largely upheld by both HIP and MSP violinists.

The two menuets are generally contrasted so that the first one is livelier and louder while Menuet II is softer and lyrical, more legato. Whether HIP or MSP, the opening measures of Menuet I are usually played *forte* and with heavier (e.g. Gähler, Kremer, Szenthelyi, Shumsky) or lighter accents (e.g. Mintz, Zehetmair). Those opting for a heavier accenting and slower tempo tend to play it that way all the way to the repeat sign while others (e.g. Shumsky, Tognetti) might play the bars with quavers (bb. 4 and 6) lighter or more staccato and with greater flow. The standard interpretation of the second half is to contrast the multiple stopping of bb. 9-18 with the linear quaver motion of bb. 19-26; the latter being softer, lighter, and inflected; usually more staccato but following the slur marks of the score. Szenthelyi and Hahn are perhaps the only violinists who play these quavers almost legato. In Barton Pine 2007, Schröder, Podger, Kuijken (both), Wallfisch and van Dael's performances the quavers are lilted, creating a dotted effect, as I showed in chapter four under rhythmic alteration (cf. Audio example 4.5).

Clear four-bar phrases are the hallmark of most performances of Menuet II. Some articulate the slurred pairs of quavers more strongly than others (e.g. Perlman, Zehetmair, Shumsky) and in a few recordings (e.g. Huggett, van Dael) the figuration and slurring of bars 21-24 are emphatically articulated allowing for a shift of accents across the bar line (resulting in a sequence of quasi 5/4 + 4/4 bars). Phrasing is aided primarily either by gentle *crescendo-decrescendo* dynamic arches and tempo rubato (e.g. Luca, Tetzlaff, Barton Pine, Perlman, Huggett, Kuijken) or by agogic timing and rhythmic inflections (e.g. Gringolts, Tognetti, Lev, Shumsky). It is noteworthy that the names listed in brackets usually include both older and younger, MSP as well as HIP violinists.

The first half of Menuet II is often softer and more "reserved," especially in the first four bars. Greater dynamic fluctuations can be observed in the second half even though the whole movement might end in pp (e.g. Barton Pine). Mintz represents an exception by finishing Menuet II *forte*. The slurred pairs are highlighted in most versions through gentle accents or slight elongation of the first notes of each pair (except by Wallfisch who instead plays the second notes very short and lifted). The pairing of slurred notes—something HIP considers common practice—is the least obvious in the recordings of Hahn (MSP), Schröder (HIP) and Kuijken (HIP).

Within these general observations there is, of course, almost infinite variety. What might be instructive to discuss further are some striking individual features. Analysis of Kremer's two recordings and a comparison of Gringolts' and Huggett's version provide interesting insights into the complex interactions of performance elements as well as varied personal approaches; both contributing to subtle but significant interpretative differences.

> Kremer, in his 1980 recording, creates a stronger than usual contrast within Menuet I by playing bars 18-26 and 29-31 in a "featherweight" soft style while otherwise maintaining a detached, *marcato* bowing. Menuet II is also unique in that the repeat has a greater dynamic range than the first play: there are stronger accents in bb. 17-20 and a stronger crescendo to b. 29; the *f* is louder in bb. 29-30 followed by *p* both times.
>
> In the 2005 recording he plays both movements rather unevenly. Although bowing is fairly light, notes with triple stops as well as certain down-beats are forcefully accented. In Menuet I he creates a bar by bar change of *f-p-f* at the beginning of the second half which he did not do in 1980. He accents strongly other beats as well and there is a subito *pp* in b. 21 after which he plays faster, especially during the repeat.

Most of the interpretative strategies are already present in his earlier version, but in 2005 they are exaggerated. This is particularly true of the way he differentiates contrasting thematic materials in the first half of Menuet II through tempo fluctuations illustrated in Figure 5.1. With regards to interaction among performance features, it should be noted that the tempo fluctuation in Kremer's 1980 recording is less noticeable partly because the dynamics are softer and bowing lighter in the "drone" passage while in 2005 these bars are played louder and less legato, creating a broad sound underscoring the slower tempo and the musette-like, rustic quality of the music (Audio example 5.7).

5.7. Similarities between subsequent recordings of J. S. Bach, E Major Partita BWV 1006, Menuet II, extracts: bars 1-16. Gidon Kremer 1980 © Philips; bars 1-16 and repeat of bars 1-4. Gidon Kremer 2005 © ECM. Duration: 0.52.

To listen to this extract online scan the QR code
or follow this link: http://dx.doi.org/10.11647/OBP.0064.31

214 A Musicology of Performance

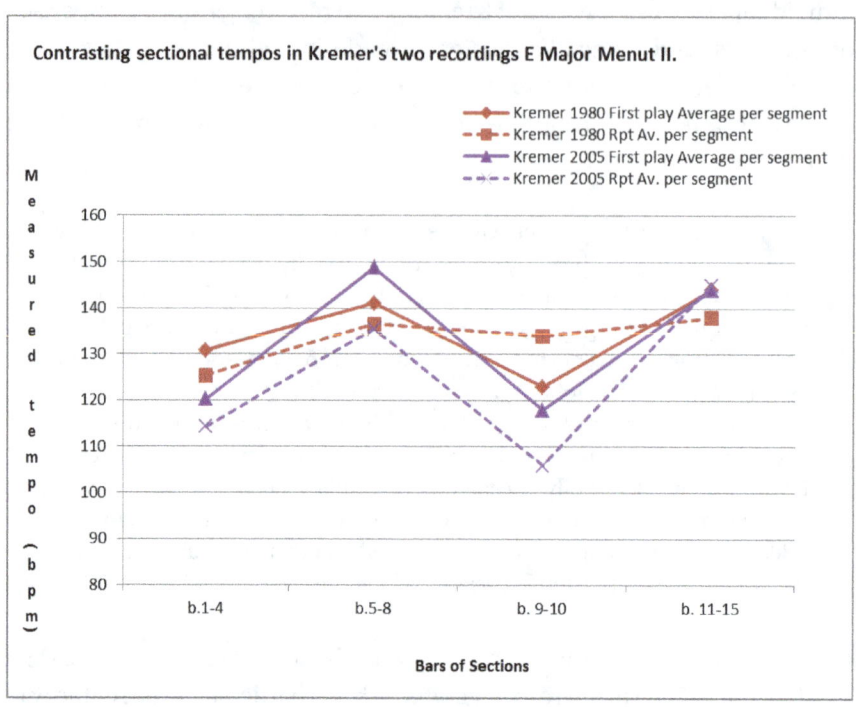

Figure 5.1. Summary of tempo fluctuation in Kremer's two performances of bars 1-16, Menuet II (E Major Partita) showing the averaged metronome value for each segment in the 1980 recording and the 2005 version.

Tempo fluctuation can also be observed in the other two versions selected for closer analysis. Both Huggett and Gringolts contrast to Kremer because the flexibility in these recordings is more to do with timing inflections (i.e. rhythmic rubato) than change of tempo between the contrasting groups of bars. Importantly, Huggett's and Gringolts' performances also differ from one-another. They show contrasting strategies regarding what aspect of the music to bring out.

> Gringolts highlights metric units; Huggett melodic-harmonic goals. Gringolts lays emphasis on downbeats (even in bars 21-22) by slightly delaying them and hurrying to the end of the measure. In contrast, Huggett follows melodic patterns across bar-lines creating shifted metric accents. Interestingly, Huggett's more fluctuating and "terraced" dynamics actually follow the metric units rather than the melodic ones that she shapes so emphatically through tempo. She also strongly accentuates particular downbeats, more than Gringolts (e.g. bb. 24 and 25). These differences are shown in Figures 5.2 and 5.3 (Audio examples 5.8, 5.9).

5. *Affect and Individual Difference* 215

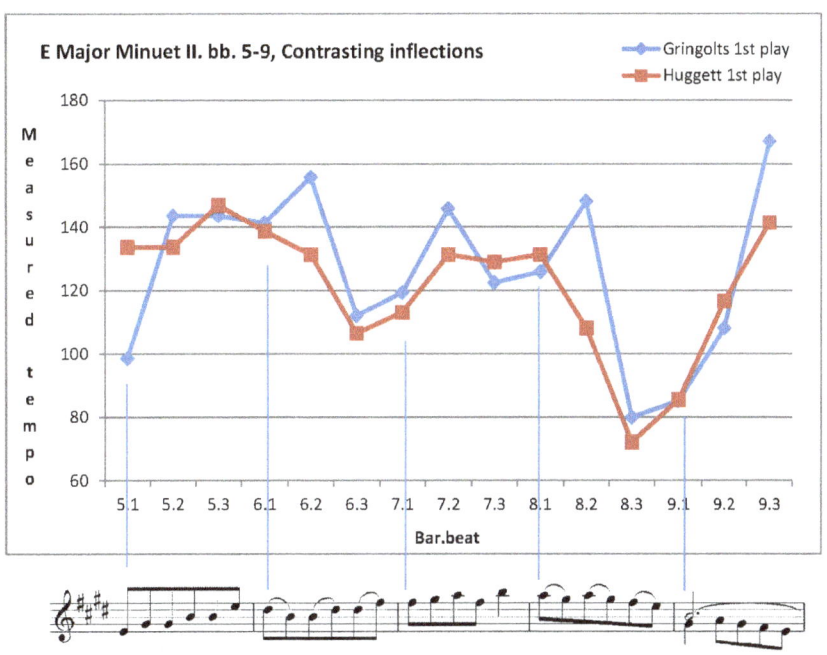

Figure 5.2. Comparison of beat-level timing data of bars 5-9 of Menuet II (E Major Partita) in Gringolts' and Huggett's recording (first play) showing different interpretative approaches. Huggett phrases in pairs of bars (accelerating in the first and slowing in the second); Gringolts articulates each bar (accelerating to the middle and then slowing).

5.8. Contrasting interpretative strategies in J. S. Bach, E Major Partita BWV 1006, Menuet II, extract: bars 5-9. Two versions: Ilya Gringolts © Deutsche Grammophon (highlights metric units); Monica Huggett © Virgin Veritas (highlights melodic-harmonic goals). Duration: 0.16.

To listen to this extract online scan the QR code
or follow this link: http://dx.doi.org/10.11647/OBP.0064.32

216   A Musicology of Performance

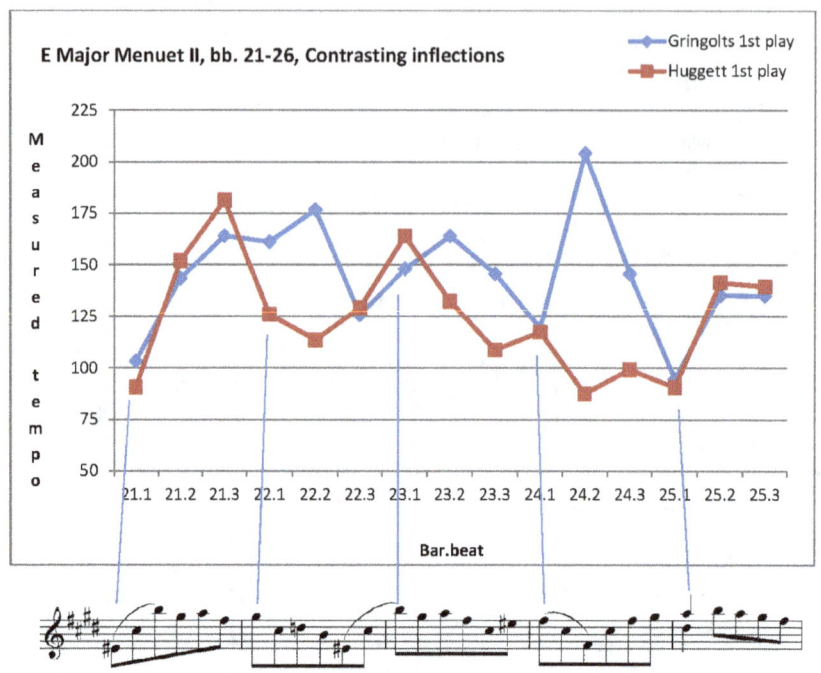

Figure 5.3. Comparison of beat-level timing data of bars 21-25 of Menuet II, E Major partita in Gringolts' and Huggett's recording (first play) showing different interpretative approach. Huggett tends to delay the second or third beat highlighting melodic contour or harmonic cadence. Gringolts tends to delay the downbeat and thus gives emphasis to the metric unit of the bar.

> 5.9. Contrasting interpretative strategies in J. S. Bach, E Major Partita BWV 1006, Menuet II, extract: bars 21-25. Two versions: Ilya Gringolts © Deutsche Grammophon (highlights metric units); Monica Huggett © Virgin Veritas (highlights melodic-harmonic goals). Duration: 0.14.
>
>
>
> To listen to this extract online scan the QR code
> or follow this link: http://dx.doi.org/10.11647/OBP.0064.33

The audible differences between Gringolts' and Huggett's performances are significant yet so fine-grained that explaining the nature of the difference in "assemblage" requires considerable analytical attention. Both of them play unevenly, flexing the timing of notes creating local nuance and tempo variation. Only close listening and software assisted analysis help reveal their different "molecular" lines that diversely "deterritorialize" the ostensibly common HIP "territory."[14]

In this section we have seen several examples of considerable diversity in "strata" formation ("thickening") as performance features ("assemblages") interacted within both the MSP and the HIP "territories" of the "milieus" of performance style. These differences underscore the complex, heterogeneous and dynamic inter-relationship of bowing, accenting, tempo, dynamics, timing, phrasing, articulation and ornamentation; at times leading away ("deterritorializing") from MSP, other times weakening ("deterritorializing") HIP, or moving towards a "nomad," idiosyncratic "multiplicity." To engage more with possible "rhyzomic" tendencies I now turn to the examination of multiple recordings of the same violinists.

5.2. Multiple Recordings of Violinists

There are five violinists who made more than one recording of the works (or certain sonatas or partitas) during the period under discussion (Table 5.2). Only one of them is a period specialist (Sigiswald Kuijken).

Table 5.2. Violinists who made more than 1 recording between 1977 and 2010.

Violinist	Recording 1	Recording 2	Recording 3
Kremer	Complete set 1980	Complete set 2005	
Kuijken	Complete set 1983	Complete set 2001	
Mullova	B minor Partita 1987	3 Partitas 1993-4	Complete set 2008
Tetzlaff	Complete set 1994	Complete set 2005	
Barton Pine	Complete set (concert) 1999	Gm and Dm 2004	Complete set (concert) 2007

It can be an interesting challenge to account for the differences among subsequent recordings of the same repertoire by the same artist. Such an exercise makes it rather explicit that we tend to find what we are looking for. The complex nature of performance allows for a multitude of observation points and some elements may be less prone to differ over time than others. If we focus on these we are likely to note similarities while features that might be more nuanced, hidden or harder to grasp may change more. The verdict also depends on where one draws the line: how big a difference counts as

---

14 These terms are introduced by Deleuze and Guattari (*A Thousand Plateaus*) and I have explained them in chapter two.

change? When does a "molar line" become a "molecular line" or even a "line of flight"? Are we looking for overarching characteristics, expressive-affective qualities or specific technical components and solutions? How many or what kinds of "molecular lines" and "lines of flight" do we need for transformation to occur; to arrive at a different "multiplicity," "assemblage," "territory"? Are we focusing on possible nuanced changes within one performer's interpretation of a piece in the context of this same performer's oeuvre or in comparison with the composition's performance history?

Musicians tend to lay emphasis on their changing sensibilities and insights when asked to give reasons for re-recording a composition. Yet systematic comparative analyses more often result in identifying similarities than radical differences. Exceptions that come to mind are Glenn Gould's 1955 and 1980 recordings of Bach's *Goldberg Variations*, Rubinstein's Chopin interpretation from the 1930s and from after the 1960s, or Leonhardt's 1953 recording of the *Goldberg Variations* compared to the later versions from 1965 and 1973. What transpires, generally, is that subsequent recordings take similar ideas further; the underlying interpretative choices become more obvious with the passing of time, perhaps because the musician is more comfortable or confident about their view of the pieces; the message they wish to convey. It is plausible that frequent performing of works ingrains certain solutions that are hard to change radically.[15] This seems to be the case here, too, especially in relation to the recordings of Kuijken, Barton Pine and Tetzlaff. However, some specific as well as conceptual differences can also be observed if one focuses less on the measurable and more on the affective aspects of these recorded performances.

Gidon Kremer

Among the violinists with multiple recordings of the works, Kremer seems to have changed his interpretation the most, if we discount for the moment

---

15 Dario Sarlo provides contrary examples when he argues that both Nathan Milstein and Joseph Szigeti have mellowed their virtuosic "moto perpetuo" approach to the E Major Preludio by playing it slower in later years. He also cites Szigeti confirming his changed aesthetic idea about the piece (*The Performance Style of Jascha Heifetz* (Farnham: Ashgate, forthcoming), chapter nine)). One might also think of Nikolaus Harnoncourt's two recordings of Bach's *Mass in B minor*; the 1967 version heralding the new HIP style while the 1986 version turning the clock back, or rather, taking HIP in a different direction.

the fundamental change between Mullova's early B minor Partita recording and the two later recordings (Table 5.2). Kremer's second version (2005) is much more strongly accented and articulated than his earlier playing (1980); he often chooses a slower tempo and his vibrato is narrower and less continuous. However, even he displays basic similarities in artistic approach.

We have already seen how the considerable tempo fluctuation observed in the 2005 version of the E Major Menuet II was, actually, just a stronger projection of the same idea regarding structural delineation of four-bar groups through contrasting tempo (Figure 5.1). Other examples include the A minor Grave and Fuga. Figure 5.4 clearly shows the strong similarities between the two recordings' dynamics profiles, indicating similar conceptualisation of large-scale form. In both versions of the Fuga movement Kremer plays the episodes of bars 111-124 and 206-220 softly. Both times he creates a crescendo from bars 45 to 61 (the return of fugal subject) and 232 to 271 (gradual "climb" of thematic material from lower to higher register with wider leaps and thicker texture). Similarly, having reached a climax in bar 166, he then starts a gradual decrescendo towards b. 206 in both recordings.

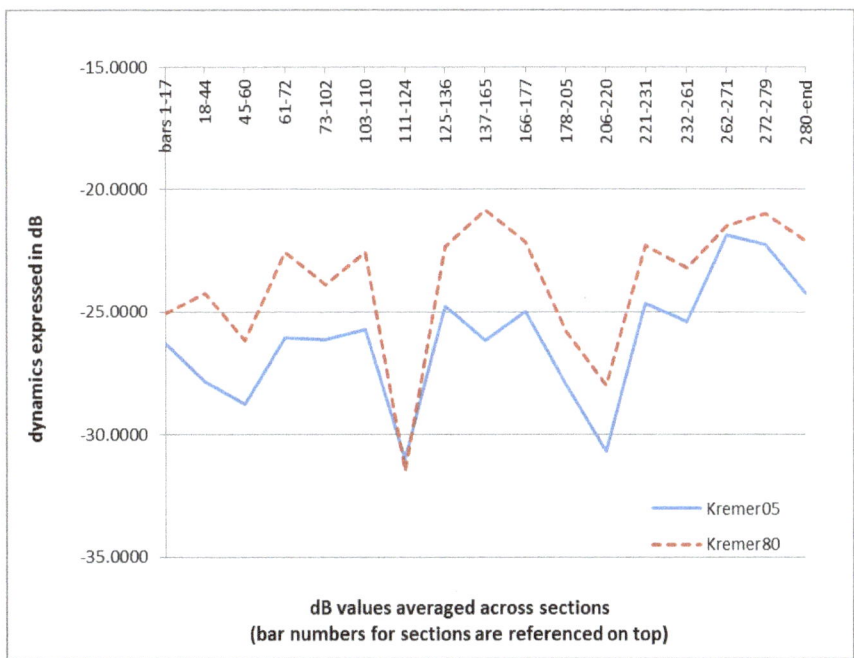

Figure 5.4. Dynamic profiles of Kremer's two recordings of the A minor Fuga.

Kremer plays the A minor Grave in a fairly intense, sustained (legato) style in both versions, with a clear distinction between louder multi-voiced moments of climax and softer-lighter linear and ornamental gestures. These dynamic contrasts are more extreme in the later recording but the interpretative principle remains essentially the same. In 2005 we can hear that the accent on the dotted F# in bar 8 is stronger but both times it is followed by a rapid decrease in dynamics in b. 9 before the new build-up of volume starts leading to a climax in b. 12, with the broadening and *ritenuto* being again more obvious in 2005. In the second half of b. 21 the low notes are played *forte* while the upward flourishes *piano* in both recordings but in the later version Kremer creates a stronger gesture by adding a breath (*'Luft-pause'*) followed by *subito piano* before the second *forte* G (Audio example 5.10).

5.10. Comparison of subsequent recordings by same violinist in J. S. Bach, A minor Sonata BWV 1003, Grave, extracts: bars 5-9. Two versions: Gidon Kremer 1980 © Philips, 2005 © ECM; bars 19-21. Two versions: Gidon Kremer 1980, 2005. Duration: 3.22.

To listen to this extract online scan the QR code
or follow this link: http://dx.doi.org/10.11647/OBP.0064.34

In a DVD documentary Kremer claimed that twenty years of life experience

> cannot simply vanish, they return in music. I expect that my own understanding of Bach and my own abilities have changed. But not so much that you could say an entirely different person is playing. I am still the same Gidon Kremer; with a different violin, in a different church but with the same music.[16]

At this point the film cuts excerpts from the two recordings of the Ciaccona next to each other and they sound rather similar. Much greater differences can be observed in other movements. Later in the same film he makes the important point:

> I also believe that we always remain in a composer's debt. This will never change. Generations of interpreters will come and go but the music of Bach, Mozart and Schubert will remain as will that of certain contemporaries such

---

16 Gidon Kremer, *Back to Bach*, A film by Daniel Finkernagel and Alexander Lück. EuroArts (2055638), 2006, 0.39:23-0.39:50.

as Shostakovich. And it will always be a mystery as to how it should be performed.[17]

Such statements are not fashionable nowadays in certain academic circles that question the existence of "works" and the composers' privileged position and authorship but illustrate well the attitude that contributes to Kremer's reputation as a musician with "great integrity."[18]

Rachel Barton Pine

Other violinists with multiple recordings show an even greater tendency to take their interpretation further in the same direction as before. The performances of Barton Pine are essentially similar. The general character of the movements tends to be the same across the versions even though surface differences can be noted. Overall, her 1999 broadcast recording sounds more "individual" or unique than her 2007 concert performance, but the latter is perhaps more polished and blends more with the performance tradition of the works. The metrically based gestures and more detailed articulation of the earlier version make that interpretation closer to HIP.

---

17 Kremer, *Back to Bach*, at 0.55:32.
18 An example of academia probing more deeply and practically (rather than theoretically) into the issues of interpretative styles and the contribution of performers is the Study Day organized by Daniel Leech-Wilkinson in May 2014 at Kings College London to explore "The Construction of Musical Performance Norms." The call for papers invited talks on "the ways in which norms of musical performance are tacitly agreed, taught, and maintained and on how they might be challenged." It suggested topics such as "teaching performance norms; ethics of performer obligation, the role of critics, agents, managers and producers in assuring performance norms; the examination and adjudication of performance style; performer anxiety in relation to perceived obligations and expectations; the implications of past recordings and beliefs about tradition; escaping, subverting or changing norms; the politics of performance; performance norms in relation to race, class and gender; the function of music as comfort or critique; music and utopia" and emphasized that "[c]ontributions need not be confined to western classical music." See Performance-studies-Network (perf-stud-net@jiscmail.ac.uk). Paraphrasing, reworking and "re-imagining" compositions are of course as old as our written records. These practices have again become popular especially among jazz musicians (e.g. Keith Jarrett, Jacques Loussier, Uri Caine, The Bad Plus) and some classical musicians (e.g. Red Priest, and Joe Chindamo, among many others). For a philosophical exposition and history of the "work" concept see Lydia Goehr, *The Imaginary Museum of Musical Works: An Essay in the Philosophy of Music*, rev. edn (New York: Oxford University Press, 2007). A few years ago I have also conducted a study to examine the possibility and implications of performing Schumann's *Träumerei* according to baroque performance conventions. See Dorottya Fabian, Emery Schubert, and Richard Pulley, 'A Baroque *Träumerei*: The performance and perception of a violin rendition,' *Musicology Australia*, 32/1 (2010), 25–42.

Her commercial disk from 2004 (that contains only two of the six works) also shows a nice balance of HIP and MSP characteristics.

> She plays the A minor Grave much more lightly and flowingly than Kremer, already in 1999. Some of her phrasing strategies and dynamics are similar to Kremer's but less extreme (e.g. *p* in bb. 4 and 12; slightly accented, louder high F#s in b. 8). By 2007 the relaxed flow is even more prominent because many dotted notes are simply stressed rather than dotted; played as if a starting note of an ornament (e.g. b. 9 beat 2) and the dynamics remain predominantly *mf* and *mp*. Noticeable expressive gestures are similar to the 1999 version. On both occasions she plays the F# in b. 8 louder, slightly stressed; the last two semiquavers of the first two beats in b. 19 staccato; and the low A and G in b. 21 (beats three and four) clearly separated. The phrase arches are also similar, highlighting the same moments of climax and repose (Audio example 5.11).

5.11. Comparison of subsequent recordings by same violinist in J. S. Bach, A minor Sonata BWV 1003, Grave, extracts: bars 5-12. Rachel Barton Pine 1999 © Chicago WFMT 98.7; bars 9-12. Rachel Barton Pine 2007 © The Artist; bars 19-23. Two versions: Rachel Barton Pine 1999, 2007. Duration: 3.25.

To listen to this extract online scan the QR code
or follow this link: http://dx.doi.org/10.11647/OBP.0064.35

She performs the A minor Allegro in virtuoso style on both occasions even though some details differ: Both are fast and have light detached bowing but in 1999 more notes are played staccato (e.g. in echo bars, in b. 33 during repeat, the un-slurred semiquavers in bb. 48-50). The flourish linking back to the repeat of the first half is more pronounced in 1999 (only a 3-note scale in 2007). She plays bars such as 17, 27, and 42 fast but with well-defined rhythm in 1999. There are also more stressed notes and slight "breathing pauses" (*luft pause*) that articulate the large-scale form and delineate sections, figurations, harmonic goals. The 2007 performance has a consistent level of dynamic while the echo effects are more pronounced than in 1999 (e.g. *p* in b. 56).

Other minor differences include the flourish at the end of the E Major Gigue. It is performed only in 1999. On the other hand, she plays Menuet I with slightly lilted *inégalité* only in 2007. Her playing seems to have more flow in 2007, probably because the shorter musical units are integrated into longer melodic lines (e.g. no echo effect in bars 22-3 of E Major Menuet II but rather played as part of one long phrase). But she adds more ornaments in 1999.

Barton Pine's tendency in the 2007 version towards a smoother, perhaps slightly more "mainstream" phrasing is already noticeable in her commercial disk from 2004 which includes the G minor Sonata and the D minor Partita only (compare, for instance, the D minor Allemanda or G minor Presto movements from 1999 and 2004). An exception is the D minor Sarabanda. Here articulation, phrasing, dynamics and bowing remain very much HIP-like (not to mention the vibrato-less tone) and it is the 2004 version that has added ornaments (bb. 6, 11-12, 18-19, cf. Audio example 4.6). She remains one of the few violinists (along with Tetzlaff and Mullova) who regularly perform the complete set in concert. A recent such occasion was on 23 August 2014 when she performed all six pieces along with other German baroque solo violin compositions in a marathon concert at the Ravinia Festival.[19] Her commercial recording of the complete set is scheduled for release in March 2016.

Christian Tetzlaff

The changes in Tetzlaff's two recordings show an overall increase in expressivity, at least in certain movements. Most noticeable is a larger range of dynamics in 2005, resulting in greater local detail and more obvious shaping of larger-scale units. These differences tend to be noted by commercial reviews as well. The earlier version is described as "intelligent, carefully considered [...] musically imaginative without any effusions of Romantic sentiment"[20] while the second recording as having "a remarkable air of spontaneity, the result of a pervasive *rubato* [...]."[21]

According to an interview in *Strad*, at the time of the first recording Tetzlaff found it "most important not to make [the Sonatas] sound like contrapuntal exercises." He relished their "speaking, dramatic quality."[22]

---

19 At 2pm she played the first two sonatas and first partita interspersed with a piece each by Baltzar and Pisendel. This was followed with Part 2 of the concert at 8pm when she delivered the remaining Bach Solos together with compositions by Westhoff and Biber. *eNewsletter* received from v-adventures@aweber.com on 21 August 2014. See also *Voices, Chicago Sun-Times* blog 20 August, 2014, available at http://voices.suntimes.com/arts-entertainment/the-daily-sizzle/rachel-barton-pine-undertakes-marathon-concert-program-at-ravinia-festival/ [last accessed October 2015].

20 Robin Stowell, 'Reviews: CDs—Bach Sonatas and Partitas for Solo Violin, Christian Tetzlaff (violin) Virgin VCD 45089 2,' *Strad*, 106/1261 (May 1995), 541-542.

21 Duncan Druce, 'Reviews: Bach 3 Sonatas and 3 Partitas BWV1001-BWV1006, Christian Tetzlaff *vn*, Hänssler Classic CD98 250 (130 minutes DDD),' *Gramophone*, 85/1021 (August 2007), 71.

22 Herbert Glass, 'A Reasoning Romantic—Profile: Christian Tetzlaff,' *Strad*, 106/1259 (March 1995), 260-265.

He considered the Partitas to be "quite different—a secular counterpart, with lots of dances." Tellingly, he added "But for a long time no one would really dance in this music," hinting at his allegiance to HIP.[23]

Tetzlaff's current views on the Bach pieces are explored in a 2012 interview for the *New Yorker* which seems to confirm that nowadays he aims for a more personally involved and intimate reading of the pieces.[24] In the article Tetzlaff is attributed seeing "the cycle as Bach's 'personal prayer book,'" and the interviewer claims that "Tetzlaff's mystical side comes out most strongly when he speaks of Bach." He reports a concert of the Solos in Dresden during which the "slower movements were almost uncomfortably introverted," Tetzlaff exposing "layer after layer of vulnerability, creating an atmosphere of naked confession." And in conversation Tetzlaff confides:

> Bach's music confronts the player and the audience in a very personal situation, in a very alone way.[25] And I try at that moment to put away pretensions—in levels of violin playing, pretensions of being a strong man,

---

23 Idid.
24 Jeremy Eichler, 'String Theorist: Christian Tetzlaff Rethinks How a Violin Should Sound' [Profiles], *The New Yorker* (27 August 2012), 34-39. All citations from p. 39. Tetzlaff also discusses his views of the Bach Solos in an interview with Edith Eisler, 'Christian Tetzlaff from Bach to Bartók,' *Strings* (February-March 1999), 50-56 (Here and elsewhere italics in original unless otherwise stated).
25 Apparently Tetzlaff believes the incorrect Italian grammar on the title page of Bach's autograph score from 1720 (*Sei Solo* instead of *Sei Soli*, i.e. *Six Solos*) is actually a "spiritual double-entendre, since Sei Solo can also be rendered as 'You are alone.'" (Eichler, 'String Theorist,' p. 39). This interpretation is also mentioned by Elizabeth Wallfisch in 'Masterclass: Bach's Solo Violin Sonata in G Minor,' *Strad* (July 2007), 64-67. She highlights that Bach's first wife died the same year this beautiful autograph was penned. The suggestion that Sei Solo might mean "you are alone" may have been inspired by Helga Thoene's papers retold in the liner notes to Christoph Poppen and The Hilliard Ensemble's *Morimur* compact disk as these emphasize the tragedy Bach experienced when, upon returning from Karlsbad to Cöthen in 1720 he found his wife of thirteen years, Maria Barbara dead and buried. Thoene shows that the manuscript paper used by Bach for the fair autograph copy of the Six Solos originates from near Karlsbad. She speculates that therefore it is likely Bach prepared the copy in the wake of his wife's death. Helga Thoene, 'Geheime Sprache—Verborgener Gesang in J. S. Bch's "Sei Solo a Violino,"' in *Morimur* CD ECM New Series 1765, 461895-2 (München: ECM Records, 2001), pp. 19-28 (p. 20). Thoene's theory gained considerable following among violinists (while hardly any among Bach scholars), probably because of Poppen's disk or because she herself is a violin professor at the University of Düsseldorf. I have heard Simone Standage speak (in an early music performance masterclass held in Sopron, Hungary around 2002) of Thoene's suggestion that the D minor Ciaccona is a "tombeau for Maria Barbara" as if it was a historical fact. See also Helga Thoene, 'Johann Sebastian Bach Ciaccona: Tanz oder Tombeau—Verborgene Sprache eines berühmten Werkes,' *Köthener Bach-Hefte*, 6 (Köthen: Historisches Museum Köthen/Anhalt, 1994), 15-81; and Helga Thoene, '"Ehre sey dir Gott gesungen"— Johann Sebastian Bach Die Violin-Sonata G-Moll BWV 1001, Der Verschlüsselte Lobgesang,' *Köthener Bach-Hefte*, 7 (Köthen: Bach-Gedenkstätte und Historisches Museum Köthen/Anhalt, 1998), 1-113.

of being invulnerable—and instead say, 'This is where all of us have common ground.' Most of the time, we try to tell ourselves 'I am confident' or 'I am doing well.' But then, in a moment alone at home, you feel how close you are to some kind of abyss. [...] Music, even at terrible moments, can make you accept so much more—accept your dark sides, or the things that happen to you. Maybe it's just because you see that this is a common trait for all of us. You see that *we are not alone*. [...] And that's what the concert situation is about for me, when I am sitting in the hall and also when I am playing myself. It's about communication—I almost want to say 'communion.' As a player, you really don't interpret anymore. You listen, together, with the audience.

I read this article long after I had completed my analyses of the recordings and cited it at length because it is a very personal confirmation of the observations I was struggling to put into scholarly language. A reviewer of this second recording has actually found that while his "interpretations have deepened" some listeners "may find them fussy."[26]

> The fugues of the A minor and G minor sonatas are good examples of the changes towards greater expression and detail in Tetzlaff's second recording. Both movements are played rather softly in 1994 with an easy flow and forward momentum, but there are only few and very discretely shaped cadence points that might aid the listener in hearing or identifying the different structural sections and phrases. Furthermore, Tetzlaff shapes and groups melodic-harmonic-rhythmic gestures much more obviously in 2005 and throughout these fugal movements, not just at the beginning. He creates many more "mini goals" towards which the music is moving and then arrives, mostly achieved through surges in dynamics and increased stresses on crucial harmonic or melodic notes. At times he also uses slight ritardandos to highlight moments of arrival. The cadence points in bars 18, 45, 73 of the A minor Fuga are much more audible in the 2005 recording than in the earlier version. Comparing the ending of the two performances one can notice that Tetzlaff starts a crescendo in measure 240 on both occasions but in 1994 it seems aborted, it does not develop. In 2005, on the other hand, it leads to bars 250-251 and restarts in 252 with a climax in b. 257 and cadence in 262 followed by a decrescendo in 268-269. He creates a new rise and fall between bars 269-280 with a final crescendo leading to the climax of the fioritura in 286-287 and the final two bars. Furthermore, the slurred pairs of quavers and various groups of semiquavers are much more strongly articulated in 2005. He shapes them by leaning on the first note in each group and playing the rest faster and lighter (Audio example 5.12).

---

26 Joseph Magil, 'Bach: Solo Violin Sonatas and Partitas [Christian Tetzlaff],' *American Record Guide*, 70/4 (July/August 2007), 69-70 (p. 70).

5.12. Comparison of subsequent recordings by same violinist in J. S. Bach, A minor Sonata BWV 1003, Fuga, extract: bars 240-289. Two versions: Christian Tetzlaff 1994 © Virgin Veritas, 2005 © Virgin Classics. Duration: 2.46.

To listen to this extract online scan the QR code
or follow this link: http://dx.doi.org/10.11647/OBP.0064.36

The greater expressiveness can also be observed in the G minor Adagio. Both readings have an air of improvisation but the flexibilities in the 2005 version are more linked to harmony and melody and less to the bar and metre. This makes the later performance sound freer, more gestural. However, as I have shown in earlier discussions (chapter four), at times this surge in musical expression leads to quite romantic sounds, especially when vibrato is used more prominently, when both tone and dynamics exploit extreme ranges of *ppp* and when bowing is more sustained serving a longer-spun melody, such as in the A minor Andante or the E Major Loure. It is perhaps this change in the underlying artistic approach from ostensibly HIP to more subjectively grounded that Tetzlaff has referred to when stating in an interview, "I have new ideas about them [i.e. the Bach Solos] and I would love to record them again."[27]

The greater expressivity notwithstanding, Tetzlaff's two recordings also show many crucial similarities, especially in surface detail. Importantly, when these surface details differ, the gesture or shaping tends to become stronger (i.e. more noticeable) rather than going in the opposite direction. But doesn't this contradict what I have just claimed, namely a change in the underlying artistic conception? The complexity of music performance becomes quite obvious when one wishes to tease out these differences and similarities. What is the underlying conception and what is surface / technical detail? When does an effect become a cause? Which elements ("lines of flight") create a sense of different aesthetics (new "multiplicity") and which seem to make the same point simply more audible (thickening "molar lines"; territorializing the "assemblage")? When do we cross an

---

27 Anthony Tommasini, 'A Violin Virtuoso and Total Bach,' *New York Times*, 28 April 2000, p. E4, available at http://www.nytimes.com/2000/04/28/movies/a-violin-virtuoso-and-total-bach.html

aesthetic threshold by making a gesture stronger? Harnoncourt said many years ago that "when we emphasize one specific aspect, another specific aspect is weakened until it disappears. We do not just have more and more expression."[28]

Contemplating these issues illuminates what Deleuzian language might formulate as "expression is not simply an effect of material relations, but in turn acts on those relations."[29] If a performance is considered to be an "assemblage," a "multiplicity of heterogeneous elements" unified by the co-functioning of the role the components play and whether these contribute to stability ("territorialisation") or to loss of identity ("deterritorialisation"),[30] then pondering thresholds of interpretative solutions, technical details, affect, aesthetics and style is an exercise where Deleuzian thinking may be harvested usefully.[31] It is an interrogation of the processes of interactions, of transformation, the process of performing; the moment that we listeners perceive holistically, in its totality. The analyst, on the other hand, while trying to describe the moment and account for the perceptual experience, is stuck in the domain of words. By the time the interactive elements are dissected and the phenomenon described, the whole is somewhat lost and we seem to be left with scattered debris, interesting bits and pieces that once belonged to the object of our wonder and to our sensed experience. More importantly, perhaps, by the time the analysts has accounted for the elements contributing to the experience, the perceived moment has long passed and the multiplicity of heterogeneous elements has already configured (transformed into) a different assemblage. Therefore it is important to emphasize that the analytical observations refer to more global impressions, they are not trying to pin down moments, to explain moment to moment causes and effects. My aim is to explore the overall nature of each interpretation; I consider the totality of a movement or piece as the "assemblage" and "territory" even when highlighting specific moments (bars, beats, notes) in the recorded performances. When I look for

---

28 'Podiumdiskussion: Zur Situation der Aufführungspraxis Bachscher Werke 1978,' in *Bachforschung und Bachinterpretation heute: Wissenschaftler und Praktiker im Dialog*, ed. by Reinhold Brinkmann (Kassel: Bärenreiter, 1981), pp. 185-204 (p. 196).

29 Jason Read, 'Review Essay—The Full Body: Micro-Politics and Macro Entities,' *Deleuze Studies*, 2/2 (2008), 220-228 (p. 227). I thank Ellen Hooper for this reference.

30 Read: 'Review Essay,' p. 221. Here I used Read's spelling of territorialization and deterritorialization.

31 I am grateful to Ellen Hooper for our thought-provoking discussions of such approaches to performance analysis.

similarities and differences I am thinking of "molar" and "molecular" lines that thicken or thin the "territory" as represented by the whole.

In that sense, when investigating similarities between Tetzlaff's two versions I am able to note only one major difference between his two interpretations of the B minor Allemanda, for instance: the considerably greater dynamic differentiation of the first repeat in 2005. The repeats of both halves are played softer in the later recording, but only the first half is performed louder than *mf* the first time, so the contrast is most striking in that section. Otherwise the light, quasi legato dotting, the "flowing-continuous" style is the same in both recordings, and similar notes or note groups are stressed on both occasions and in both first plays and repeats. This single difference in dynamics does not have transformative or "fracturing" power. The two recordings of this movement portray an essentially identical "territory," but perhaps with slight variation in "assemblage." At the same time, interpretative gestures become somewhat stronger in the later version: The elongation of each first triplet note in b. 15 is more pronounced and cadence points are highlighted by greater *Rits* (e.g. bb. 8-9 and, especially, 18-19) in 2005. For me these represent "molecular lines" as they "deterritorialize"; they contribute to the process of transforming the later recording into a more expressive reading or "territory" (Audio example 5.13).

5.13. Comparison of subsequent recordings by same violinist in J. S. Bach, B minor Partita BWV 1002, Allemanda, extract: bars 15-19. Two versions: Christian Tetzlaff 1994 © Virgin Veritas, 2005 © Virgin Classics. Duration: 0.51.

To listen to this extract online scan the QR code
or follow this link: http://dx.doi.org/10.11647/OBP.0064.37

Greater dynamic contrast between first play and repeat is the most striking difference between Tetzlaff's two versions of the A minor Andante as well. Both recordings provide a gentle, lyrical reading with the first play utilizing "reverse swells" (leaning on main notes followed by release (*decrescendo*)) to highlight appoggiaturas while in the repeat these are played more like accented notes. Both "assemblages" have similar phrasing and fluctuating dynamics, with the later version using greater contrasts and a more forward-moving and flexible tempo. *Crescendos* and *diminuendos* are stronger and broader, creating a more passionate and dynamically varied performance.

Bars 16-17 are played louder, with more intensity, while bb.21-23 are softer, Tetzlaff keeping the dynamic nuances within the *pp-mp* region. The accents on the G-D-F triple stop in b. 13 and the first and third semiquavers of the final beat of b. 23, the *Rit* in bb. 8-9 as well as the *Rall* in b. 25 are much stronger in the later version but do not represent new interpretative decisions. They are simply thicker "molar lines" contributing to stability; to a clearer delivery of interpretative intent. In neither version are the paired slurs in b. 15 emphasized; on both occasions Tetzlaff plays them in a straightforward legato manner (Audio example 5.14).

5.14. Comparison of subsequent recordings by same violinist in J. S. Bach, A minor Sonata BWV 1003, Andante, extract: bars 15-19. Two versions: Christian Tetzlaff 1994 © Virgin Veritas, 2005 © Virgin Classics. Duration: 0.43.

To listen to this extract online scan the QR code
or follow this link: http://dx.doi.org/10.11647/OBP.0064.38

Sigiswald Kuijken

Throughout chapters three and four I repeatedly claimed that Kuijken's two versions are surprisingly less HIP in many respects than one would expect and what critical reception tends to assert. This is an impression I have developed through long hours of comparative listening and it is only true to a certain extent; or relatively speaking. When I first heard it in the 1980s (and before I heard Luca's), it sounded very different to those I grew up with (e.g. Grumiaux, Milstein, Szeryng). However, close listening to Kuijken's first version in comparison with other period violinists' recordings (especially that of Luca and later Podger, Huggett and many others) made me more aware of the range of possibilities and the scope of historically informed playing in this music. I was eager to hear his second version when it came out in 2001. I thought Kuijken would make his interpretation more radical, given the extra twenty years of experience and stylistic developments as well as the evidence of his recordings with *La Petite Bande*, for instance. However, overall there is not much difference between the two, at least not in terms of basic conception and approach (cf. Table 3.3 for rating of performance features in both but also Tables 4.4 [vibrato] , 4.7 [dotting], 4.8 [Gm Fuga]). In the next section of this chapter

I will discuss some interesting and telling differences that close listening and analysis can reveal (cf. Audio examples 5.17 and 5.21). These tend to show a return to less detailed, more even or literal playing, in other words, towards more "authentistic" style, just like we saw when comparing performances of Rachel Barton Pine. But here I rather briefly summarize the main similarities.

Tempo, phrasing, bowing and movement characters are fairly similar throughout the two recordings but particularly noticeable in the C Major Largo and Allegro assai, the D minor Allemanda and Sarabanda and the G minor Siciliana and Presto. The later recording has a different ambience — much more reverberant acoustics — that often calls forth a different initial impression, one that feels "heavier," more laboured, especially in the fast finale movements. This feeling is supported by the somewhat slower tempos. At times bowing is also broader (more sustained) and the articulation and phrasing more legato. But these are just slight differences in degree, not in kind. The consistent dynamics, the similarity of accents, added ornaments (e.g. b. 12 in D minor Sarabanda), and phrasing across the two recordings impress the casual listener more than these slight differences that one notices when listening more attentively.

Viktoria Mullova

If Barton Pine, Tetzlaff and Kuijken seem to have toned down the HIP elements of their playing in their later recordings, the trajectory of Mullova's performances illustrates the opposite path. I have already shown ample evidence of her playing becoming increasingly similar to how period violinists perform baroque music. Not just similar, but in many respects at the cutting edge, leading the way.[32] This is revealed in her phrasing, bowing and ornamentation, in particular. The deliberate and radical change in her approach emerged in the early 1990s and in that she is similar to Leonhardt,

---

32 Joseph Magil does not agree. In his review he claims that "Viktoria Mullova conveys a bland studiousness. As usual, she plays like a student who has just learned a work and isn't yet sure what to make of it. Her attitude toward period performance practice is that it is a set of rules to be followed rather than a key to unlocking any of the music's mysteries." One wonders what CD he listened to, but the publication clearly lists the Onyx album! See 'Guide to Records—Bach: Violin Sonatas & Partitas; Pauset: "Kontrapartita,"' *American Record Guide*, 72/5 (September 2009), 61.

for instance, whose 1953 *Goldberg Variations* recording is nothing like his 1965 or 1973 versions.

Mullova once said she was pleased that Philips agreed not to release her recording of the Bach Solos from the 1990s because she really disliked them.[33] She must have been thinking of the three Sonatas only because the three Partitas have been issued and already show the HIP-Mullova in the making. Interestingly, although the *Gramophone* reviewer finds her playing on this disk "a breath of fresh air" and notes that "Her dance movements are light on their feet (helped by her quickness of bowing through chords) and her nuancing of tone and volume is full of subtlety—warm and expressive but with no trace of romanticism," he nevertheless compares her disk with Kagan's and Shumsky's MSP versions.[34] As if the HIP qualities were not recognized as such, given Mullova's reputation at the time as a virtuoso soloist of romantic concertos! Such slippage helps maintain false views of trends and under-informs readers. Still, the reviewer "tentatively add[s] the disk to [his] 'treasure island' collection" and decides to wait "hopefully for the sonatas to join it." Although he had to wait for more than ten years, John Duarte would probably agree that it was worth it. What Mullova achieves on the complete set recorded in 2007-2008 for the Onyx label is not so much the radical change from her interpretation of the B minor Partita in 1987—this is already witnessed on the 1993-1994 disk of the three Partitas—but *mastery* of period technique and complete freedom of play that comes with full command and "ownership" of style.

The 1992-1993 recordings can still sound a little mechanistic due to consistency of pulse and accents. Several movements of the B minor Partita are played at a considerably slower tempo than in 1987 and with more staccato bowing; both contributing to a somewhat laboured and artificial effect; a self-conscious attempt at HIP. By 2008 the bowing is shorter and bouncier; accents more varied, delineating shorter or longer segments; tempo a little faster (similar to 1987) assisting greater flow; phrasing is freer; ornamentation more abundant. Movements like the D minor Giga have no time to become mechanistic because there is a constant ebb and flow of dynamics—partly due to varied bowing—and accentual detail.

---

33 Andrew Palmer, 'Viktoria Mullova: The Individualist,' in *Violin Virtuosos*, ed. by Mary VanClay and Stacey Lynn (San Anselmo: String Letter Publishing, 2000), pp. 47-57.

34 John Duarte, 'Bach Partitas—No. 1 in B Minor, BWV 1002; No. 2 in D minor, BWV 1004; No. 3 in E, BWV 1006, Viktoria Mullova *vn*, Philips 434 075-2 PH (77 minutes DDD),' *Gramophone*, 72/853 (June 1994), 80.

The three recordings of the Tempo di Borea movement from the B minor Partita illustrate these observations well. The 1987 version has a moderate speed (minim = ca. 77 beat per minute) and a detached style of bowing. Accents fall on each crotchet creating a 4/4 rather than cut C (₵) pulse. The quavers are played evenly. Typically for performances of this movement, the second half includes contrasting dynamics where the more linear measures are played softer and with shorter bow strokes. The 1992 version is considerably slower (ca. 67 bpm) and much more staccato. This combination eventually makes the movement sound rather choppy. However, the 4/4 pulse is weaker, at times the accents hinting at ₵. The approach to dynamics is similar to the earlier recording. The 2007-2008 recording is the fastest (ca. 82 bpm), has fewer accents and the notes and bars are much more strongly grouped bringing forth the cut C pulse. Dynamics fluctuate primarily as a result of bowing, although the linear bars of the second half are played softer on this occasion as well. In this version the performance has not simply regained some of the flow and richer tone of the 1987 version but took the interpretation to a different level. The flow is of a different kind. It is a "line of flight" that projects and follows the ₵ metre. Because the accenting often seems to be simply a side-effect of differences between up- and down-bow strokes, the pulse does not become mechanistic or repetitive-predictable; it does not "territorialize" but rather "moves between." Bow pressure and speed contribute to a chiaroscuro effect enriching the dynamic palette. In hindsight, the staccato bowing in the 1992 version seems like an artificial and abortive attempt (a rhizomic molecular line getting lost) at what the 2007-2008 recording achieved through mastery of baroque bowing (Audio example 5.15).

5.15. Comparison of subsequent recordings by same violinist in J. S. Bach, B minor Partita BWV 1002, Tempo di Borea, extract: repeat of bars 39-50. Three versions: Viktoria Mullova 1987 © Philips, 1992 © Philips, 2008 © Onyx. Duration: 0.57.

To listen to this extract online scan the QR code
or follow this link: http://dx.doi.org/10.11647/OBP.0064.39

In sum, the program notes to a concert of Beethoven's sonatas by Mullova and Kristian Bezuidenhout justifiably claimed that "Her recent recording of Bach's Solo Sonatas and Partitas represents a significant milestone in

Viktoria's personal journey into this music."[35] Tim Ashley enthused already in 2000 after a concert showcasing the E Major, G minor and D minor works that "In Viktoria Mullova—whose technical perfection combines with matchless, uncompromising interpretative subtlety—they [the Bach Solos] find perhaps their ideal interpreter. [...] To hear Mullova play Bach is, simply, one of the greatest things you can experience [...]."[36]

5.3. The Holistic Analysis of Interpretations

The previous section has already engaged with issues that underscore the complexity of analysing music performance. Here I focus on these matters by teasing out further the subtle differences ("territorializations" and "deterritorializations") between multiple versions recorded by the same violinists. Bringing the various elements together and weighing up their relative contribution to the "multiplicity" each performance assembles lead to addressing the interpretations in terms of affect and / or musical character. In my consideration of the complex interactions of both compositional and performance features prompting the potential affective response, I often resort to metaphor and formulate arguably subjective judgements. In some instances "objective" measurements of any one of these elements would simply give undue emphasis to something that does not act alone but in tandem with several other (non-measurable) elements, creating in-the-moment effects and transformations of meaning. In these cases aural analysis, or what might be called "musicological" or "close / focused listening,"[37] better equips the researcher to ponder what one perceives than quantified data. It also enables ecologically valid propositions. In other

---

35 Concert presented on 12 March 2011 as part of the 2010/2011 Camerata Musica International Artists series in Cambridge (UK), available at http://www.cameratamusica.org.uk/past-concerts/

36 *The Guardian*, Monday 10 April 2000, available at http://www.theguardian.com/culture/2000/apr/10/artsfeatures4

37 "Musicological listening" is a term used in Nicholas Cook, *Music, Imagination and Culture* (Oxford: Clarendon Press, 1992), p. 152. However, "close" or "focused listening" is more commonly used; e.g. Nicholas Cook, *Beyond the Score: Music as Performance* (New York: Oxford University Press, 2014); Daniel Leech-Wilkinson, *The Changing Sound of Music: Approaches to Studying Recorded Musical Performance* (London: CHARM, 2009), chapter eight, paragraphs 20-21, http://www.charm.rhul.ac.uk/studies/chapters/chap8.html.

instances software assisted analysis is important to clarify perception. It can "guard against mistakes such as when an accent is attributed to dynamics [but] was in fact the result of an agogic (temporal) emphasis."[38] I continue comparing primarily the multiple recordings of Kuijken, Tetzlaff, Kremer, Barton Pine and Mullova because these can serve as good test cases for both approaches. The differences are usually rather subtle and often quite hard to put into words: The analyst is forced to face the challenge of interrogating the *interaction* of performance features—the "relations of causality" to use Deleuzian language—and to grasp each reading holistically as well as in the complexity of their detail. This way the truism that each performance is different may open up to scholarly explanation.

"Subjective" Aural Analysis: The D minor Giga

Take the various versions of the D minor Giga, for example. Focused listening would observe the projection of pulse, the presence of accents, tempo, bowing, articulation, and delivery of the marked terraced dynamics. The overall effect may be virtuosic or dance-like or perhaps a bit of both. These could then be regarded as either tending towards MSP (virtuosic) or towards HIP (dance-like). In this regard the general observation is that the more recent versions of Barton Pine, Kuijken, and Tetzlaff tend to be less detailed and more virtuosic.

> Barton Pine plays a little faster in 2007 and with fewer accents and agogic stresses than earlier. The pulse is still very perceivable and there are obvious phrases but because of the faster tempo, more evenly flowing, "uninterrupted" stream of semiquavers it sounds more virtuosic, overall. Alternatively, I could say that the 1999 version has more ebb and flow in terms of dynamics as well as tempo and the agogic stresses are part of that ebb and flow, making the performance sound more phrased and detailed while being virtuosic. Her 2004 version is closer to the earlier than the later reading and I would be hard pressed to pinpoint any perceivable difference apart from variation in the ambiance of the recording (the 2004 version seems to have a thinner tone, a more "distant" sound, perhaps due to microphone placement). In her three recordings then it is tempo that is perhaps the "thickest molar line" "territorializing" the virtuosic effect. The molecular lines of ebb and flow, dynamics, and agogic stresses "deterritorialize" but do not transform the virtuosic character to something else, such as dancing (Audio example 5.16).

---

38   Cook, *Beyond the Score*, p. 143.

5.16. Comparison of subsequent recordings by same violinist in J. S. Bach, D minor Partita BWV 1004, Giga, extracts: bars 1-5. Two versions: Rachel Barton Pine 1999 © Chicago WFMT 98.7, 2004 © Cedille; bars 1-11. Rachel Barton Pine 2007 © The Artist. Duration: 1.03.

To listen to this extract online scan the QR code
or follow this link: http://dx.doi.org/10.11647/OBP.0064.40

Kuijken's two versions of the D minor Giga are not about virtuosity overall. The 1981 recording projects a strong pulse and groups shorter units and phrases. Bowing is light, terraced dynamics are observed. It sounds like a standard HIP reading; bouncy and dance-like, with easy flow and clear architecture based on the piece's harmonic structure. The 2001 version has a more relaxed tempo (ca. 74 bpm in contrast to ca. 85 in 1981) but also much less detail. It quickly starts sounding mechanistic. It is not that there are fewer accents but that the accents are uniformly executed without the ebb and flow of dynamic shades and subtlety of bowing. Perhaps a slightly faster tempo would push the performance towards the virtuosic type, but the rather routine delivery of semiquavers and regular accents would probably counter-act anyway. Together with the slower tempo, these instead create a performance that evokes the old-fashioned, "sewing-machine" or clockwork-like MSP style of the 1950s and 1960s (Audio example 5.17).

5.17. Comparison of subsequent recordings by same violinist in J. S. Bach, D minor Partita BWV 1004, Giga, extract: bars 1-10. Two versions: Sigiswald Kuijken 1983 © Deutsche Harmonia Mundi, 2001 © Deutsche Harmonia Mundi. Duration: 1.02.

To listen to this extract online scan the QR code
or follow this link: http://dx.doi.org/10.11647/OBP.0064.41

Tetzlaff's two versions further support some of my claims about Kuijken's 2001 recording in the above two sentences. Tetzlaff's playing is virtuosic on both occasions. In 1994 he uses relatively short bow strokes, plays with light pulse, and light tone. From about bar 9 onwards he starts to phrase in shorter units and introduces clearer accents. The performance does not sound mechanistic because of the near constant ebb and flow of dynamics and shadings of tone through bowing. In contrast, the 2005 recording takes virtuosity a step further by increasing tempo (from ca. 83 to ca. 89 bpm). The section between bars 3 and 9 is quite smoothly virtuosic with even, rapid flow. Although obvious downbeat accents and clearer phrasing are introduced from bar 10, the overall impression becomes mechanistic because, perhaps due to the fast tempo, the accents are uniform and routine; there seems to be no time to shape the tone, the phrase, the harmonic or melodic unit (Audio example 5.18).

5.18. Comparison of subsequent recordings by same violinist in J. S. Bach, D minor Partita BWV 1004, Giga, extract: bars 1-12. Two versions: Christian Tetzlaff 1994 © Virgin Veritas, 2005 © Virgin Classics. Duration: 1.05.

To listen to this extract online scan the QR code
or follow this link: http://dx.doi.org/10.11647/OBP.0064.42

In the four versions played by Kuijken and Tetzlaff, tempo, accenting, bowing, dynamics and shades of tone interact in ways that create diverse "multiplicities." The interaction of tempo and regular accenting form "molar lines" causing thickening in the "strata." Slower tempo combined with regular accents creates "assemblages" belonging to the "territory" frequently described as "sewing-machine-style" or modernist-authentistic HIP (Kuijken 2001).[39] Assemblages where the combination of regular accents and faster tempo are the key stabilizing features "territorialize" virtuosic readings (Tetzlaff 2005). The impact of these "molar lines" is weakened, the territories of virtuoso and authentistic HIP are deterritorialized when bow-strokes and pulse are varied and become "multiplicities" in themselves. They make room for the "in between molecular lines" of ebb and flow, rapidly shifting dynamics and the "betweeness" of tonal shades (Tetzlaff 1994).

The two other violinists who made more than one recording of the piece during the period are Kremer and Mullova. Contrary to those discussed above, in their case it is the later, more recent recording that is more detailed (and less categorizable, i.e. more "deterritorialized").

---

39 Taruskin introduced the term "authentistic" as a descriptor of what, in my view, Dreyfus called "sewing-machine" style. See Taruskin, *Text and Act* (esp. pp. 99-143) and Lawrence Dreyfus, 'Early Music Defended against its Devotees: A Theory of Historical Performance in the Twentieth Century,' *The Musical Quarterly*, 69/3 (1983), 297-322.

Kremer's two recordings have similar tempos (the earlier being faster at ca. 85 compared to ca. 81 bpm in 2005) and overall approach. However, in the later recording Kremer uses stronger and more frequent accents, often quite harsh and sharp. These tend to sound ugly (e.g. tied E in bb. 14-15; G natural in b. 19) because they lack purpose; they are not properly integrated into the flow of the music. These accents interrupt an otherwise even and virtuosic rattling off of uniformly controlled passage work (Audio example 5.19). These "lines of flight" break away from the normative but the transformation is not for the better; just leading to randomness.

5.19. Comparison of subsequent recordings by same violinist in J. S. Bach, D minor Partita BWV 1004, Giga, extract: bars 12-20. Two versions: Gidon Kremer 1980 © Philips, 2005 © ECM. Duration: 0.52.

To listen to this extract online scan the QR code
or follow this link: http://dx.doi.org/10.11647/OBP.0064.43

The crucial role of tempo when interacting with accenting, phrasing and dynamics is highlighted again when comparing Mullova's two versions. Her 1993 recording of the D minor Giga has a relaxed tempo (ca. 74 bpm). The pulse is perceptible and the phrases are pointed out. She observes the terraced dynamics. However, the regularity of accents tends to make the music sound mechanistic, especially in bars 7-15 and 25-30. This is all the more obvious when one compares it to her 2008 recording. Here she plays faster (ca. 85 bpm), with similarly short bowing but stronger and more frequent accents and stresses. In fact she articulates shorter units of various lengths. This helps counteract any sense of uniformity because the faster tempo and constantly shifting tone, dynamics and accentual detail combine to draw attention to melodic-harmonic directions, pulse, ebb and flow (Audio example 5.20).

5.20. Comparison of subsequent recordings by same violinist in J. S. Bach, D minor Partita BWV 1004, Giga, extract: bars 6-16. Two versions: Viktoria Mullova 1993 © Philips, 2008 © Onyx. Duration: 1.10.

To listen to this extract online scan the QR code
or follow this link: http://dx.doi.org/10.11647/OBP.0064.44

While Tetzlaff's faster tempo seemed to limit the opportunity for phrasing and shaping and contributed to a more mechanistic impression, Mullova's faster tempo seems to serve flow and aids the moulding of musical units. The "multiplicity" of each performance feature (not just their interaction with other elements) is shown here. At times they territorialize, other times they deterritorialize to a greater or lesser extent; at times a feature may be the thickest molar line, while other times it works in tandem with other elements. In Mullova's 2008 recording the performance features seem to be completely rhizomic and non-categorical. To describe their full nature, function and interactions is beyond words, they are "in between," constantly shifting and breaking away; they have to be heard.

"Objective" Measures:
The A minor Grave and G minor Adagio

Software assisted analysis is also helpful in clarifying what is going on in a performance. Listening to Kuijken's two versions of the A minor Grave I noted that the earlier recording sounded freer, more improvisatory while the more recent interpretation more measured but still flexible. I guessed that perhaps there was less tempo fluctuation in the second recording and the tone also sounded more even, indicating less tonal inflections with the bow. Bowing felt more legato, with fewer swells and gaps between groups of notes or at phrase ends. Nevertheless changes in dynamics were quite clearly audible but perhaps serving a conception of the music on a larger-scale; conveying greater order and progressing in bigger chunks.

Trying to mark up the sound files for detailed observations in *Sonic Visualiser* immediately clarified how much more measured the 2001 recording was, indeed.[40] Marking beats were reasonably straightforward as most flexibility unmistakably fitted with metric units. In contrast, working with the earlier sound file was quite hard. The kind of flexibility Kuijken adopted in 1981 followed gestural content and had little to do with pulse or metre. When I was marking perceived phrase boundaries I rarely found

---

40 *Sonic Visualiser* is an open access computer program developed at Queen Mary University for viewing and analysing the contents of music audio files available at http://www.sonicvisualiser.org/ or Chris Cannam, Christian Landone, and Mark Sandler, 'Sonic Visualiser: An Open Source Application for Viewing, Analysing, and Annotating Music Audio Files,' in *Proceedings of the ACM Multimedia 2010 International Conference* (Florence: October 2010), 1467-1468.

myself noting downbeats, or beginning of beats, but much more often the second or third beat of a bar or the off-note of the downbeat or another beat. It is this lack of pulse that lands the 1981 performance a "preluding" character, an improvisation that sounds as if freely following the fancy of the player—a fantasia (Audio example 5.21).

5.21. Comparison of subsequent recordings by same violinist in J. S. Bach, A minor Sonata BWV 1003, Grave, extract: bars 1-8. Two versions: Sigiswald Kuijken 1983 © Deutsche Harmonia Mundi, 2001 © Deutsche Harmonia Mundi. Duration: 2.27.

To listen to this extract online scan the QR code
or follow this link: http://dx.doi.org/10.11647/OBP.0064.45

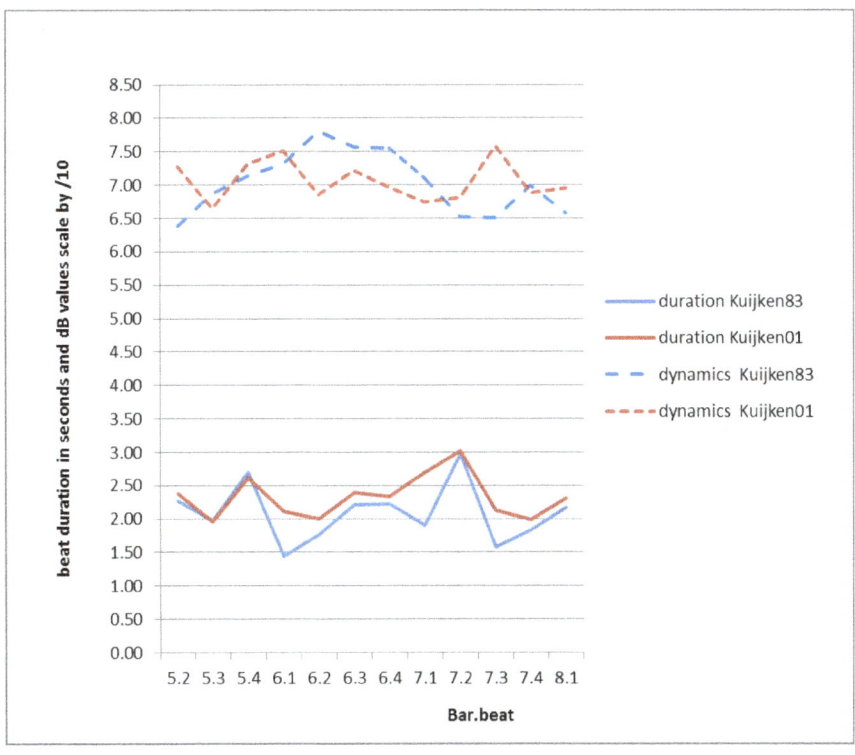

Figure 5.5. Beat-durations and dynamics in Kuijken's two recordings of the A minor Grave bb. 5-8

In Figure 5.5 the tempo lines for bars 5 to 8 of each recording show how much more volatile the 1981 version is. The power curves confirm that the use of dynamics is also different. The bigger and more frequent slopes in the 2001 version indicate a greater role of standard crescendos— decrescendos in aid of grouping the notes of metrical units. The relatively more arch-like dynamic line of the 1981 version hides its many rapid oscillations within a more gradually changing range. Perhaps the frequency of data capture or the algorithm that *Sonic Visualiser* uses to measure power would need to be changed to register the dynamic nuance that results from varied bow speed and pressure as Kuijken's fingers and bow glide through the rapid notes, crossing strings to remain in the lower positions and creating a series of typical baroque chiaroscuro effects.

In the earlier version the intricate rhythms of the notated score are played with fluidity and an exclusive focus on harmonic and melodic goals (rather than metre / pulse). Although I can illustrate and evidence my observations by providing graphs of tempo and dynamic fluctuations, these quantified measurements certainly do not tell the entire story. Rather, they simply signal aspects of the performance that subsume all the other key contributing elements: tone, shades, bowing, as well as the fundamental decision that governs the interpretation, namely whether metre rules or freedom of melody and harmony.

Another potential limitation of measurements can be illustrated by presenting the graphs of phrase durations in Kuijken's two recordings of the A minor Grave (Figure 5.6). In this case the data show up the similarities between the recordings, namely that both are flexible and "improvisatory." However, given the discussed perceptual experience of close listening that could be demonstrated by graphing beat durations (Figure 5.5) such a graph is somewhat misleading and certainly hides important information regarding the fundamental differences between the two versions: the alternative approach each utilizes to create flexibility and the diverse effects these changes achieve. If only the graph at Fig 5.6 is offered, homogeneity in performance might be evidenced, completely missing and thus denying the existence of crucial musical and affective variances and transformations.

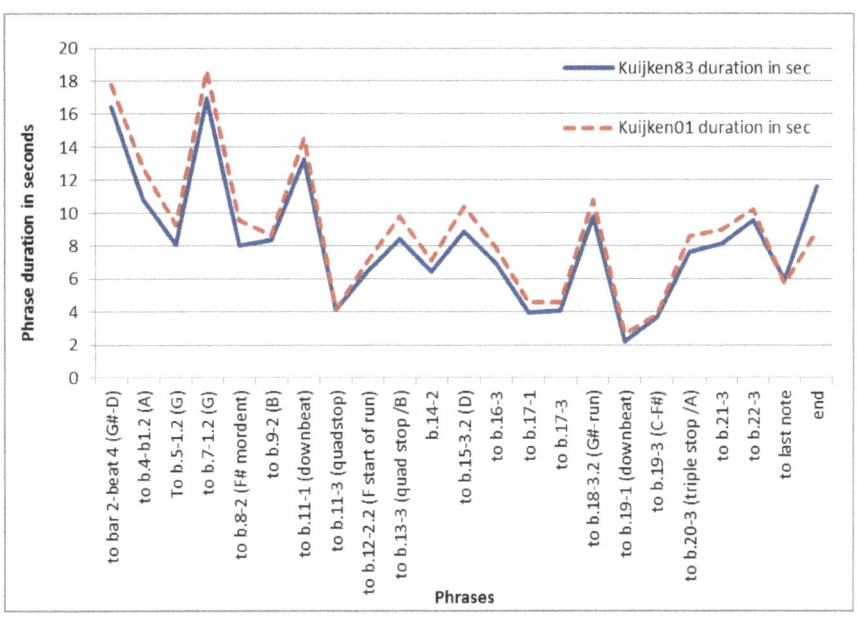

Figure 5.6. Comparison of phrase durations in Kuijken's two recordings of the A minor Grave misleadingly showing similarities in tempo flexibilities

Analysis of Kuijken's two recordings of the G minor Adagio provides similar results. The later recording sounds improvisatory and reasonably flexible with some dynamic nuances and swells on notes but closer inspection shows a much more measured delivery of ornamental groups (e.g. bb. 6-7) that is anchored in the underlying metre / pulse. The earlier recording is much more improvisatory because of metrical freedom, greater flexibility of tempo rubato, and constant shifts in tone and bowing. The ornamental groups are often hurried or rushed-over capriciously as they lead to melodic high- or low notes, meditative-exploratory gestures—for instance melodic re-starts, repetitions, wayward, indecisive turns, momentary harmonic goals that continue on unexpectedly—and cadence points.

Perception of Affect

In a recent study, Spitzer and Coutinho referred to my 2005 paper on the performance history of Bach's solo violin works and lamented the fact that it "has not touched on the affective dimension."[41] They found this regrettable

---

41 Michael Spitzer and Eduardo Coutinho, 'The Effects of Expert Musical Training on the Perception of Emotions in Bach's Sonata for Unaccompanied Violin No. 1 in G Minor (BWV 1001),' *Psychomusicology: Music, Mind, and Brain*, 24/1 (2014), 35-57 (p. 36).

especially because of "an entrenched school of thought," promoted among others by Daniel Leech-Wilkinson,[42] "that holds that emotional expression in music is mostly influenced by performance style, rather than the music's acoustic features or formal structure." They embarked on an initial investigation to "ascertain whether the acoustic features of musical emotion [...] converge with analytical findings [...]" and used Kremer's 2005 recording of the G minor Sonata to test their case.[43]

The listeners in Spitzer and Coutinho's study found Kremer's 2005 recording of the Adagio movement to express "sadness, sorrow, melancholy, tenderness" but also "tension" and "being moved."[44] Spitzer and Coutinho did not analyze Kremer's performance in detail. Instead their reasoning for affective response was largely based on score analysis linked to contemporary psychological investigations of emotional expression in music.[45] They claimed that the G minor Adagio's "structural features suggest sadness":

> a slow tempo, minor-mode key, narrow intervals, legato articulation, variability of texture, preponderance of descending melodic contours, and high level of dissonance, especially involving semitone appoggiaturas (an ornament which "leans on" the main note a step above). In musical semiotics, such appoggiaturas are historically associated with *pianti*, or crying, figures (Monelle, 2000), as if the musical contour were iconically representing the sound of a sobbing voice.[46]

---

42 Daniel Leech-Wilkinson, 'The Emotional Power of Musical Performance,' in *The Emotional Power of Music: Multidisciplinary Perspectives on Musical Arousal, Expression, and Social Control*, ed. by Tom Cochrane, Bernardino Fantini, and Klaus R. Scherer (Oxford: Oxford University Press, 2013), pp. 41-54.

43 I have shown the impact of performance features on affective and aesthetic response in relation to recordings of the D minor Sarabanda; Dorottya Fabian and Emery Schubert, 'Baroque Expressiveness and Stylishness in Three Recordings of the D minor Sarabanda for Solo Violin (BWV 1004) by J. S. Bach,' *Music Performance Research*, 3 (2009), 36-55. See also fn. 51 below.

44 Spitzer and Coutinho, 'The Effects of Expert Musical Training,' p. 48, Figure 10.

45 In relation to the Adagio movement of the G minor Sonata Spitzer and Coutinho refer to David Huron, 'A Comparison of Average Pitch Height and Interval Size in Major— and Minor-Key Themes: Evidence Consistent with Affect-Related Pitch Prosody,' *Empirical Musicology Review*, 3 (2008), 59-63; Alf Gabrielsson and Erik Lindström, 'The Role of Structure in the Musical Expression of Emotions,' in *Handbook of Music and Emotions: Theory, Research, Applications*, ed. by Patrik Juslin and John Sloboda (Oxford: Oxford University Press, 2010), pp. 367-400; Patrik Juslin, 'Emotional Communication in Music Performance: A Functionalist Perspective and Some Data,' *Music Perception*, 14/4 (1997), 383-418; and Sarha Moore, 'Interval Size and Affect: An Ethnomusicological Perspective,' *Empirical Musicology Review*, 7/3-4 (2012), 138-143.

46 Spitzer and Coutinho, 'The Effects of Expert Musical Training,' p. 37. The internal citation refers to Raymond Monelle, *The Sense of Music: Semiotic Essays* (Princeton: Princeton University Press, 2000).

They also noted that

> David Huron has made the connection between sadness in music and the "detailed-oriented thinking" of "depressive realism" (Huron, 2011, p. 48). Our analysis of the Adagio reveals it to be highly fragmentary in its texture and tonal structure, and this 'atomistic' quality could be related to the detail-oriented quality of its sad affect.[47]

"In the Adagio," Spitzer and Coutinho assert on p. 42, "the ideas evolve fluidly from measure to measure." And on p. 43 they claim that "The atomization of the schema in the *Adagio* suggests the lack of goal—lethargy—connected with sadness or depression." All these points can be useful as one considers differences among recorded performances.

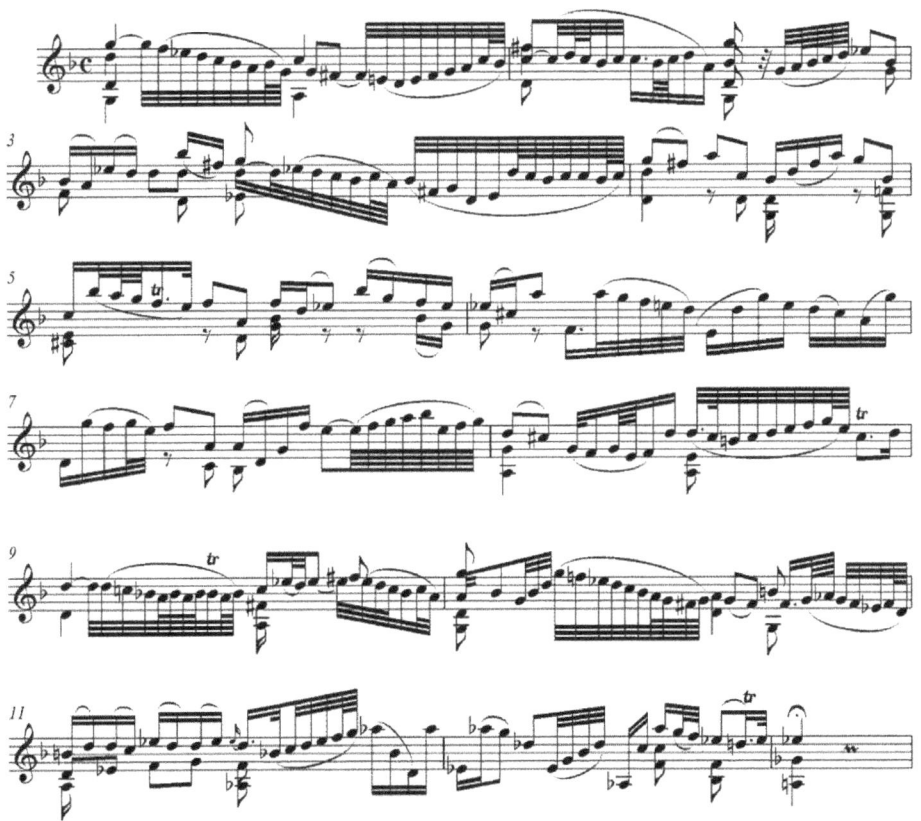

Figure 5.7. Score of G minor Adagio, bars 1-12

---

47   Spitzer and Coutinho, 'The Effects of Expert Musical Training,' 40. The internal citation refers to David Huron, 'Why is Sad Music Pleasurable? A Possible Role for Prolactin,' *Musicae Scientiae*, 15 (2011), 146-158.

When I listen to Kremer's 2005 version I can hear a flexibility that is nevertheless somewhat jolted, not at all fluid and certainly contributing to a fragmented, atomistic quality. The bars with demi-semiquaver and smaller note values have considerably more fluency than bars with only semiquavers (e.g. b. 6). These are played in a rhythmically literal way, without a sense of pulse, direction or shape. Whether this results in lethargy is arguable. Some of the notes—for instance the triple stops in bars 3 and 4 (especially the first and last) but also the double stops in bar 7 and, quite surprisingly, the E tied quaver in the middle of the same bar—are harshly accented, in a way that does not make any musical sense to me even in the context of Kremer building a climax to the cadence point at the end of bar 8. Together with the increased bow-pressure, considerably swelling volume and broadening of tempo, in my view these accents create an "angry" or "tense" effect rather than lethargic depression. But when Kremer follows these attacks with soft and mellow, almost caressing sounds, as in bars 9-10, I can hear why the overall rating of emotional expression might be "melancholy," "sadness" and "sorrow." For me, however, an inescapable impression is the fragmented nature of this reading. It just does not flow enough to take me to a sublime, affective state, but keeps jarring and thus falling into self-aware / self-conscious bits, making the technical components all too obvious (Audio example 5.22).

5.22. Phrasing in J. S. Bach, G minor Sonata BWV 1001, Adagio, extract: bars 1-8. Gidon Kremer 2005 © ECM. Duration: 1.27

To listen to this extract online scan the QR code or follow this link: http://dx.doi.org/10.11647/OBP.0064.46

In contrast, the relatively more even style of Perlman's interpretation (apparently also rated in a follow-up study by Spitzer[48]), for instance, conveys a strong sense of unity (Audio example 5.23).

---

48   Michael Spitzer, 'Affektive Shapes and Shapings of Affect in Bach's Sonata for Unaccompanied Violin No. 1 in G Minor (BWV 1001),' in *Music and Shape*, ed. by Daniel Leech-Wilkinson and Helen Prior (New York: Oxford University Press, forthcoming). I had no opportunity to access this paper while completing this manuscript.

5.23. Phrasing in J. S. Bach, G minor Sonata BWV 1001, Adagio, extract: bars 1-8. Itzhak Perlman. © EMI Classics. Duration: 1.37

To listen to this extract online scan the QR code
or follow this link: http://dx.doi.org/10.11647/OBP.0064.47

I propose that the main contributing elements are his sustained style of bowing and fairly uniform dynamics. In Perlman's playing the difference between flexible gestures and more measured moments is mild and well integrated. Unity and stability are achieved through continuity of phrasing and tone. The overall effect, however, is less personal. It speaks to me more as if somebody was making an appeal for some common cause; it sounds "public"; an objectified performance of "the music" rather than a personally invested communication.[49] The additional affective element that I believe contributes importantly to such a perception is best grasped by stating what the performance is lacking. In psychological terms it is lacking what Huron might link to the "detailed-oriented thinking" of "depressive realism." In terms of emotional expression it is lacking everything that characterizes the flip-side of the sustained style: it does not "breathe," let alone "sob," "yearn," "plead" or "implore." In Perlman's rendering there is no sense of vulnerability, of conveying upheavals of the soul.

In light of Spitzer and Coutinho's propositions, we can now briefly revisit Kuijken's two versions of the opening movements from the G minor and A minor Sonatas. Perhaps the more measured and thus less flowing and more "atomized" later versions are closer to conveying "dogged"

---

49 Jonas Kaufmann and Helmut Deutsch have recently discussed the issue of concentration and conscious control while performing highly emotional music. In this interview Kaufmann evokes "Karajan's famous remark about 'controlled ecstasy.' Everyone, myself included, should have the impression that I am abandoning myself completely to the emotion that I'm depicting, but a final controlling authority ensures that I don't damage my voice or become overexcited." (See, 'You can't simply carry on as usual afterwards—Jonas Kaufmann and Helmut Deutsch in conversation with Thomas Voigt,' *Schubert: Winterreise,* Jonas Kaufmann [tenor], Helmut Deutsch [piano]. Sony Classical 88883795652 (USA: Sony Classical Records, 2014), CD Booklet, pp. 7-12 (pp.11-12)). Perhaps in Perlman's performance this "final controlling authority" is given too much room and nobody, perhaps not even the violinist, has the impression that he is abandoning himself to the expressive power of the music.

depression that feels hopeless and circular. The more freely flowing, improvisatory, melodic-harmonic goal orientated earlier versions, on the other hand, express heartfelt sadness that nevertheless has hope to heal. The way the performer conveys a sense of free musical fancy that seemingly obeys only the passions of his soul carries within the seeds of consolation and redemption—just like an uncontrolled, cathartic grieving-crying, saying out loud, has the potential of letting go, of accepting, of moving on.

Is all (or any) of this in the music, in the performance? Or do we, listeners project our emotions or personal predispositions onto what we hear? Surely all three, as countless empirical studies and philosophical arguments have shown.[50] My point here is more to note: firstly, that compositions carry a range of affective potential; secondly, therefore subtle differences in performance can shift ("de-" and "re-territorialize") the affective meaning communicated; and thirdly, that listeners may prefer performances that convey moods that more closely match their own psychological predispositions. When I find Kuijken's later recording more "mechanistic," perhaps I react against possible affective qualities that may evoke "depressive realism." Whether the explanation of these subjective reactions sounds plausible is open to debate. But it is undeniable that aspects of these differences among the performances can be quantified. They certainly exist, how we interpret them is another matter.[51]

As noted above, how people identify the performance as well as compositional elements that contribute to overall aesthetic or emotional effect is something music psychologists have been investigating for several decades by now. I hope my discussion makes it apparent that I am not so much interested in the question whether basic emotions are conveyed or experienced when listening to music performance. Rather, I am trying to find a language to describe the *affect*—the pre-conscious, felt meaning—and to pinpoint the potential performative and bodily reasons for it. I have also

---

50 *Handbook of Music and Emotions: Theory, Research, Applications*, ed. by Patrik Juslin and John Sloboda (Oxford: Oxford University Press, 2010). Peter Kivy, *Sound Sentiment: An Essay on the Musical Emotions* (Philadelphia: Temple University Press, 1989).

51 I have investigated "emotion" or what I prefer to call "musical character" empirically in relation to thirty-three recordings of Variation 7 from Bach's *Goldberg Variations*. This investigation revealed five different clusters of "affect" but the ninety-eight participants chose a variety of specific (synonymous) words available within the emergent five categories to describe the performances. This demonstrated considerable subjective differences within broad agreements. See Dorottya Fabian and Emery Schubert, 'Musical Character and the Performance and Perception of Dotting, Articulation and Tempo in Recordings of Variation 7 of J.S. Bach's *Goldberg Variations* (BWV 988),' *Musicae Scientiae*, 12/2 (2008), 177-203.

collected listeners' aesthetic response to selected movements performed by a range of violinists and in the next section I will draw on these as I comment on some of the most idiosyncratic versions available on record: those made by Huggett and Zehetmair.

5.4. Idiosyncratic Versions and Listeners' Reactions

So far we have explored recent performance trends along the categories of MSP and HIP. We have also observed individual signatures and personal interpretative trajectories. At all times the discussion ended with the manifestation of problems regarding classifications, the establishing of boundaries for "territories." The differences in degree (de-territorializing "molecular lines") turned out to be as important as differences in kind (break away "lines of flight" causing transformation and moving towards re-territorialization). In this final section I explore how we might discuss essentially "rhizomic" interpretations that are so idiosyncratic that they seem to fit what Deleuze and Guattari may call the "nomad" because they are "open-ended."[52] The two performances that I believe fit this "category" are the recordings of Zehetmair (1983) and Huggett (1996).

Thomas Zehetmair

Zehetmair's idiosyncratic style is hinted at by his tempo choices which often show more than 2 Standard Deviation (SD) from the average of over sixty studied recordings, especially in faster movements (D minor Corrente and Giga, B minor Corrente, E Major Gavotte en Rondeau).[53] Other times they are more than 1 SD from the norm (first 3 movements of the G minor Sonata;

---

52   Deleuze and Guattari contrast "representational thought" which is analogical and structured with "nomadic thought" that "moves freely in an element of exteriority. It does not repose on identity; it rides difference" (Brian Massumi, 'Translator's Foreword: Pleasures of Philosophy,' in Deleuze and Guattari, *A Thousand Plateaus*, pp. x-xi). It is the open-endedness and freedom from categories (representation) that make me label Zehetmair and Huggett's recordings of the Bach Solos "rhizomic" and "nomad." Gringolts' version might also fit such a description but as it has already received much attention I am not discussing it here any further.

53   As explained at fn. 5 in chapter four, Standard Deviation (SD) is defined as the average amount by which scores in a distribution differ from the mean. It shows how much variation there is from the mean. Generally three standard deviations account for 99.7% of the studied data. One SD accounts for about 68% of the data set while two SD about 95%. When SD is close to 0 this indicates that the data points are very close to the mean. In the current study negative values indicate a deviation slower than the mean score while positive values are faster than average.

first and last movements of the A minor Sonata, first and third movement of the C Major Sonata, B minor Tempo di Borea, D minor Sarabanda, E Major Loure, Menuet I and Bourée). His tempo is 4.16 SD from average in the A minor Andante! If one compares his tempos to only MSP violinists the results can be even more extreme than when the calculations are made within the pool of HIP and HIP-inspired violinists Table 5.3).

Table 5.3. Comparison of Zehetmair's tempo SD scores in the E Major Partita when compared to the combined group of 34 MSP and 12 HIP-inspired violinists (columns A) as opposed to the group of 12 HIP and 12 HIP-inspired players (columns B).

	Preludio		Loure		Gavotte		Menuet I		Menuet II		Bourée		Gigue	
	A	B	A	B	A	B	A	B	A	B	A	B	A	B
Zehetmair SD scores	.43	.19	1.64	.99	2.94	2.08	1.4	1.31	1.1	1.13	.91	.56	.6	.43

His use of vibrato is also highly unusual. As noted in chapter four (Table 4.4), Zehetmair's vibrato is often slow and wide. He obviously uses it to give emphasis to certain melodically or harmonically charged notes because few notes are vibrated but when they are it is very noticeable. However, his idiosyncratic style is primarily a result of the interaction of volatile phrasing, unpredictable bowing and accents, sudden changes in dynamics and extreme fluctuations of tempo. His delivery of notated ornamental groups is often extremely rapid and light with a gliding bow stroke. The effect is not particularly "decorative," and at times reminds one of Gringolts' recording (which is also highly idiosyncratic but has already received much attention to be interrogated here).

Given the earlier discussion of the G minor Adagio, I exemplify my claim regarding Zehetmair's distinctively personal style by commenting on his performance of this movement. Overall he projects a tri-partite structure of the movement with bars 9-14 representing the contrasting middle section of a quasi ABA form.[54] Such an outline of large-scale structure is quite unique among the recorded performances studied here. Most sound more like a through-composed movement.

---

54 This is so even though there are "in-between" cadential gestures in Zehetmair's performance (e.g. bars 3-4, 13-14, and 20-21). Like Kuijken in 1981, his shaping of phrases follow harmonic and melodic goals with several overlaps or elisions of ending-beginnings that fall on metrically stronger points.

Zehetmair starts off in the "melancholy" improvisatory style with gentle dynamics, legato bowing and a relaxed tempo. He takes the upward slide to the Eflat in bar 2 rather fast and light and not so much accents the Eflat but lets it ring out creating a slight gap (silence) before moving on with the last G-Bflat double stop quaver of the bar. This indeed lends the gesture a feel of "new beginning"; much more so than Kremer's in 2005, lending support to Spitzer and Coutinho's score analysis.[55] The ornamental figure in bar 3 is shaped through tempo flexibility and bowing so that the first note of the fourth beat (Bflat semiquaver) gains an agogic stress by being held a little longer (score at Figure 5.7). From bar four onwards there are strong dynamic contrasts linked to dissonances and their resolution as well as particular melodic groups. There is a constant and sharp fluctuation of dynamics that is created through a combination of accents, swells, and reverse swells, faster and slower bow-strokes. The effect is further fostered by rapid acceleration and deceleration that was already noticeable in bar 3. At the end of bar 5 all this suddenly comes to a halt; tempo slows, rhythm becomes measured, and dynamics drop to subito *ppp* (Audio example 5.24).

5.24. Phrasing in J. S. Bach, G minor Sonata BWV 1001, Adagio, extract: bars 1-8. Thomas Zehetmair © Teldec. Duration: 1.10

To listen to this extract online scan the QR code
or follow this link: http://dx.doi.org/10.11647/OBP.0064.48

The non-vibrato precisely controlled tone has an otherworldly, "from a distance" effect. This only lasts till the second beat of bar 6, however, at which point the more volatile style returns. He repeats this vibrato-less *ppp* effect at the turn of bars 18-19, where the musical content is similar to bb. 5-6. But first we get a passionate, impetuous outburst between bars 10 and 12 during which Zehetmair plays with urgency, pressing ahead with tempo, tone and dynamics. There is nothing melancholic about these bars, even sadness is forgotten. One particularly individual solution is the staccato, almost thrown bowing of the three demisemiquavers (G-Bflat-D) leading to the second beat of bar 10. This creates enormous energy and changes the affective landscape instantaneously (Audio example 5.25).

---

55   Spitzer and Coutinho, 'The Effects of Expert Musical Training,' p. 40.

> 5.25. Phrasing in J. S. Bach, G minor Sonata BWV 1001, Adagio, extract: bars 9-14.
> Thomas Zehetmair © Teldec. Duration: 0.39
>
>
>
> To listen to this extract online scan the QR code
> or follow this link: http://dx.doi.org/10.11647/OBP.0064.49

But what might be the emotion communicated? What kinds of hermeneutical metaphors come to mind as I listen to it holistically? I began my description in the previous paragraph by noting that the performance starts off similarly to many other versions. So melancholy and sadness seem obvious and reasonable associations. But the sense of immanent volatility conveyed through constant shifting of tone, tempo and intensity together with a sense of brewing impulsiveness that eventually bursts to the fore in bar 10 undermine such a simplistic association. Is it then a soliloquy going through a variety of emotions? Or is it perhaps a dialogue between a desperate, passionate, sad but angry soul and a calming consoler? Imagining two voices in "ardent dialogue" makes sense to me as it explains the rapid shifts in intensity, dynamics and tempo—it feels more plausible, more in line with how the performance unfolds than hearing it, for instance, as the hysterics of a grieved protagonist.

Zehetmair's approach to Bach's Six Solos for Violin is certainly not MSP. His bow strokes, articulation, rhythmic projection may be inspired by HIP but he takes these HIP characteristics out of their "territory" and infuses them with subjectivity. In other words, he interprets HIP "rules" liberally. The shorter, more lifted bow strokes, the locally nuanced and "airy" articulation mix freely with longer legato lines, sustained and heavier bowing. Vibrato-less tone alternates with strongly vibrated, emotive timbres; rapidly delivered fast and homogeneous passages and movements alternate with closely articulated, highly differentiated ones that dance and bounce. The ostensibly "molar lines" that create the HIP or MSP sound mix together in such fine grain of multiplicities that something entirely differently is born, especially if one takes into account the set as a whole.

Whether this "nomad" recording is considered appealing or mannered depends on the listener's preferences; I certainly was positively stunned by the power of its individuality when I first heard it around the turn of the millennium, more than fifteen years after it was recorded. However, when I collected subjective responses from participants with varied musical background to various renditions of selected movements of the Bach Solos,[56] Zehetmair's received the most conflicting comments ranging from "Lovely performance, beautiful phrases and line of the melody" to "Terrible performance. Wrong phrasing, not musical; the performer doesn't understand the music at all." Some considered it to be by a "self-indulgent, ill-informed performer" playing in a "very performer-centred" way. Comments also tapped into the idiosyncratic nature of Zehetmair's reading: "[The] exaggerated phrasing, that is very extreme crescendos and decrescendos in very short spaces of time, made it come across as a less emotionally genuine performance." And: "Quite flexible and spontaneous. It makes it interesting. A bit too fast though and rough at times."

The unique blend of MSP and HIP in Zehetmair's performance was also remarked upon: "Even though this performance wasn't on a period instrument, I felt that the performer showed quite a good understanding of Baroque style and phrasing." Another participant considered it to "almost capture [her own] concept of how this piece should sound. The only things lacking are the right kind of instrument, i.e. a baroque setup violin, and less vibrato and better ornaments. Affectually, it is pleasing. Intonation could be a little nicer too." However, others felt that "While [it is] somewhat historically informed, it is not expressive i.e. does not try to exaggerate the affect of the piece, and this exaggeration is an integral part of baroque musical oration. Such plain performance is a hallmark of the modern style which emphasises faithfulness to the score, and to the mastery of the composer at the expense of the performer's vital interpretative authority."

Monica Huggett

Apart from Gringolts, the other violinist who tends to provide the most highly idiosyncratic readings of the works is Huggett. In many respects she is the opposite of Zehetmair. Not only is she a period specialist using historical apparatus but she also tends to play slowly while Zehetmair's playing is usually fast, as discussed above (Table 5.3). When compared to the approximately sixty recordings in my collection issued since 1903, the slow tempos of Huggett's readings are particularly noteworthy in the nominally faster movements, such as the finales for the Sonatas and the E Major Preludio, but also the fugues. She tends to play slower in the dance movements of the Partitas as well, but less markedly (Tables 5.4 and 5.5). It

---

56 These included the D minor Sarabanda, the A minor Andante and the E Major Loure. However, due to randomization not all participants heard all versions of all movements. Most of the cited comments refer to Zehetmair's performance of the D minor Sarabanda.

should also be noted that her tempos are even slower relative to the pool of HIP and HIP-inspired violinists. For instance in such a comparison her SD score for the E Major Preludio is -1.37, for the E Major Gavotte en Rondeau it is -2.15 and for the E Major Tempo di Borea it is -1.61.

Table 5.4. Standard Deviations of Monica Huggett's tempo choices in Sonata movements compared to the average of approximately 60 recordings made since 1903. High negative SD values indicate considerably slower tempos.

	Gm Fugue	Gm Presto	Am Fugue	Am Allegro	CM Fugue	CM Allegro assai
SD, Huggett	-2.32	-1.58	-1.55	-2.42	-1.77	-.187

Table 5.5. Standard Deviations of Monica Huggett's tempo choices in Partita movements compared to the average of approximately 60 recordings made since 1903. Negative SD values indicate slower than average.

	Bm Allemanda	Bm Borea	Bm Borea DL	Dm Allemanda	Dm Giga	EM Preludio	EM Gavotte	EM Tempo di Borea
SD, Huggett	1.14	-1.2	-1.29	-1.05	-1.33	- 0.87	-1.63	-1.58

I should come clean and admit that my "relationship" with the recording is ambivalent. I like it, essentially, but then I also find it frustrating. It is full of beautiful and original detail; relished dissonances, broken chords, highlighted harmonic or melodic moments, ornaments (written out or added), clear polyphony, gorgeous violin timbre recorded well for sonorous effect, and even vitality in certain sections. Yet there is also a sense of laboriousness, lack of flow, angular and erratic phrasing; as if all this magnificent detail and precision were a huge struggle (which I am sure is not)! Both these characteristics of her version are remarked upon by reviewers and also the participants in the above mentioned experiment.

Reviewers find that "her fussiness with phrasing often disrupts the flow of the music";[57] that her "constant stop-go approach undermines the rhythmic integrity of (many) movements";[58] and that "Her rhythmic

---

[57] Joseph Magil, 'Bach: Solo Violin Sonatas and Partitas' [Monica Huggett], *American Record Guide*, 61/4 (July 1998), 88-89.

[58] Bernard Jacobson, 'CD Review: Bach: Sonatas and Partitas for Solo Violin—Monica Huggett (vn) (period instrument), VIRGIN 7243 5 45205 2 5(152:33),' *Fanfare*, 22/1 (September 1998), 116-117 (p. 116).

flexibility (very marked in the Chaconne) may upset some traditionalists, but it gives her readings a thoughtfully spontaneous air."[59] In contrast, Stowell notes "her remarkable intonation, technical precision and tone quality" and considers "rhythmic flexibility" her "greatest interpretative asset." In his view Huggett's "shaping and articulation of phrases generally allow the music to unfold naturally and with a sense of spontaneity." However, even he mentions that "some may [...] dislike her occasional 'stop-start' approach."[60] In the accompanying booklet Huggett notes that "the bass must always be given extra attention so that the balance between harmony and melody is not tipped too far in melody's favour."[61] According to Jacobson, this "explains her meticulous way of dwelling on the lower notes" in many passages but can lead to an entire movement being "repeatedly thrown off course by the apparent establishment of a whole new tempo unrelated to what went before." He also finds it "odd" that she embellishes only in a few repeats. Jacobson's overall opinion is the same as mine: it is "hard to arrive at a balanced critical conclusion."[62]

Participants in the listening experiment liked the "serenity" of Huggett's playing but also noted the fragmentation and sense of effort: "[the] piece seemed to be performed in chunks punctuated by the performer breathing! but a sense of time could still be established." Or: "although [it is] regular, the performer allows breathing and small variations within the beat. It makes it expressive without being overly expressive"; and "[the] tempo felt more painful, as if it was more work to play the notes, and the harmonies." One participant specifically noted the uniqueness of Huggett's style: "The performer plays this piece with their own style," while another conveyed her approval by stating, "flexible within phrases to allow more expression. I like that. Also, time for breaths between phrases."

Given my earlier discussion of various performances of the G minor Adagio, it would make sense to choose this movement for a detailed discussion of Huggett's unique style. Indeed, her playing of it is very different to all I have analysed so far. Yet describing it may not necessarily be worth an attempt. It is a hybrid between the detailed, articulated,

---

59 Lionel Salter, 'Reviews: Bach 3 Sonatas and 3 Partitas, BWV10010-06, Monica Huggett *vn*, Virgin Classics CD 545205-2 (152 minutes),' *Gramophone*, 75 (January 1998), 78.
60 Robin Stowell, 'Reviews: CDs—J.S. Bach: Sonatas and Partitas for Solo Violin BWV 1001-6. Monica Huggett (violin) VIRGIN VERITAS 7243 5 45205 2 5,' *Strad*, 109/1297 (May 1998), 539.
61 Monica Huggett, 'A Performer's View of Bach's Sonatas and Partitas for Solo Violin,' *J. S. Bach: Sonatas and Partitas BWV 1001*-1006. Virgin Veritas 7243 5-45205-2 5 (Holland: Virgin Classics, 1997), CD booklet, pp. 12-13 (p. 13).
62 Jacobson, 'CD Review,' 116-117.

improvisatory style and the more measured and fragmented versions (Audio example 5.26).

5.26. Phrasing in J. S. Bach, G minor Sonata BWV 1001, Adagio, extract: bars 4-8, 13-15. Monica Huggett © Virgin Veritas. Duration: 1.24

To listen to this extract online scan the QR code
or follow this link: http://dx.doi.org/10.11647/OBP.0064.50

In contrast, picking a fast movement for study should provide pertinent insights. In these her attention to articulation and the underlying harmony makes her readings especially characteristic and unique (just like in the E Major Gavotte en Rondeau, as discussed earlier; see Audio examples 5.4 and 5.5). So for an interrogation of her performing style I turn to the E Major Partita, yet again. I discuss Huggett's performance of its opening Preludio movement in relation to many other versions because this helps to illuminate how idiosyncratic her playing is.

The E Major Preludio

This movement has an improvisatory character based on broken chords. The even semiquaver figuration has traditionally been interpreted in a sleek virtuoso style. Such clockwork-like perpetual motion (*moto perpetuo*) reading is also typical among the recordings studied here, most obviously those by Kremer, Ehnes, Hahn, St John, Brooks, Ibragimova, Kuijken, Lev, and Tetzlaff.

5.27. Virtuosic style in J. S. Bach, E Major Partita BWV 1006, Preludio, extract: bars 1-33. Lara St John © Ancalagon. Duration: 0.38

To listen to this extract online scan the QR code
or follow this link: http://dx.doi.org/10.11647/OBP.0064.51

5. Affect and Individual Difference   255

In his forthcoming exhaustive monograph on Jascha Heifetz's performance style, Dario Sarlo provides an interesting discussion of recorded interpretations of the E Major Preludio.[63] He examines the threshold of what may count as the "Italian virtuoso *moto perpetuo*" style (where rapid figuration is persistently maintained)[64] compared to the "French improvised preluding style" which Sarlo labels "expressive." To arbitrate performance style he examines tempo and tempo fluctuation, as can be stipulated from differences in calculated metronome estimates based on durations of larger sections. Through score analysis and a review of analytical literature, Sarlo identifies eight sections summarized in a table, reproduced here from his pre-publication manuscript as Table 5.6. He then compares the duration of each section in eleven recorded performances. By calculating the percent deviation from the overall average metronome value he is able to conclude whether the performance is closer to the virtuoso *moto perpetuo* style (i.e. less fluctuation) or the expressive improvisatory style (higher percentage deviation).

Table 5.6. Eight structural subdivisions of the E Major Preludio according to Sarlo (forthcoming)[65]

Part	Bars	Description	% of piece
1	1–32	Theme, bariolage	23.2
2	33–58	Transition	18.8
3	59–82	Theme, bariolage	17.4
4	83–89	Build-up to harmonic climax	5.1
5	90–108	Build-up to and from harmonic climax	13.8
6	109–122	Dominant progression	10.1
7	123–129	Final dominant	5.1
8	130–138	Resolution	6.5

The eleven recorded performances investigated by Sarlo on this occasion include three of those studied here: Kremer 2005, Wallfisch and Huggett. Out of all eleven, he found the highest fluctuation in Huggett's performance

---
63   Sarlo, *Heifetz* (forthcoming), chapters six-ten.
64   Sarlo uses the definition provided by Michael Tilmouth, 'Moto perpetuo,' in *Grove Music Online*. *Oxford Music Online* (Oxford—New York: Oxford University Press, 2007-2015), available at http://www.oxfordmusiconline.com/subscriber/article/grove/music/19224
65   Sarlo, *Heifetz*, Table 10.2 (as presented in the original MS Word manuscript in 2014, before typesetting and publishing).

(9%). He listed Wallfisch's fluctuation as 6.2% while Kremer's as only 4.2%, one of the lowest and similar to the classic, stereo-typical *moto perpetuo* style exhibited by Sarasate in a recording from 1904.

Sarlo's data provide neat empirical evidence for differences between a smooth, "clockwork-like" performance and one that has more agogic details and tempo fluctuations. He asserts that the former falls into the *moto perpetuo* style because of the fast delivery.[66] But does *moto perpetuo* have to be fast? Can a performer "persistently maintain rapid figuration" while playing at a moderate tempo? Or how slow can it be before it transforms into something else? Put another way, how fast can be an "expressive" version before the tempo prohibits playing around with agogic accents and timing? Would a more holistic or comprehensive examination of performance characteristics substantially enrich the process of labelling? Would it refine our understanding of differences between performances or the range along the two ends of the spectrum from *moto perpetuo* (alias virtuosic) to "expressive"? To answer some of these questions I re-examine these three recordings and a few others that are good cases in point. But first a brief overview of my data set seems useful.

All versions since Luca's recording in 1977 tend to project the underlying harmonic progressions to a greater or lesser degree, outlining large-scale structural units.[67] Smaller units and more localised events are highlighted by agogic stresses, accents and inflections. These are introduced to various degrees by most players with Gringolts, Huggett, Schröder, and van Dael providing the least clockwork-like and most detailed readings. Huggett, Gringolts and Matthews employ considerable tempo modifications as well, for instance starting the *bariolage* section at bar 64 slowly and then speeding up, or playing the echo measures faster than the more independently articulated notes of the louder complementary bars. Huggett's, van Dael's, and especially Schröder's version may sound somewhat laboured due

---

66 To be fair, in discussing his results Sarlo refines the point when he states: "There is clearly a link between playing the piece more slowly and playing it less persistently. Based upon the evidence, it is not only the total durations of these recordings that differs with the virtuosic early 1900s recordings, but also the approach to persistent figuration. [...] Unlike many of the other slower-paced period instrument performances, Wallfisch takes a different approach to the Prelude, since hers is the fifth fastest of all 136 recordings. It is therefore not simply in duration that Wallfisch diverges from the other period performances—the more persistent nature of the Wallfisch figuration, identified with a lower fluctuation percentage, suggests a closer link to the virtuosic and *moto perpetuo* approach of Sarasate [...] than to the period performances of [...] Huggett." Sarlo, *Heifetz* (forthcoming), chapter ten.

67 Sarlo identifies eight sections: bb. 1-32, 33-58, 59-82, 83-89, 90-108, 109-122, 123-129, and 130-138 (cf. Table 5.6). As I will show performers do not necessarily highlight these boundaries but often chose other moments.

to the slower tempo and uneven delivery that often outlines bar by bar grouping of notes. Gringolts' faster tempo gives his interpretation a more flowing quality. Among the more virtuosic versions Podger and Matthews mark arrival points and new figurations by accenting or slightly stressing notes (e.g. every downbeat between bb. 79-98) whereas Wallfisch tends to accent most downbeats except in the *bariolage* sections (bb. 17-29; 67-79) and when the music seems to be moving in pairs of bars. Wallfisch performs the Preludio very fast resulting in a rather rough sound (Audio examples 5.28; see also Audio examples 5.29 and 5.30 discussed at Figures 5.8 and 5.9).

5.28. Expressive versus virtuosic "moto perpetuo" style in J. S. Bach, E Major Partita BWV 1006, Preludio, extracts: bars 1-17. Jaap Schröder © NAXOS; bars 29-63. Rachel Podger © Channel Classics; bars 101-138. Lucy van Dael © NAXOS. Duration: 2.44.

To listen to this extract online scan the QR code
or follow this link: http://dx.doi.org/10.11647/OBP.0064.52

The marked dynamics (echo effects) are observed by all players but some make the contrast stronger (e.g. Kremer 1980 and Shumsky less obviously) while others tend to remain within a relative dynamic range of *mf-f* (e.g. Wallfisch, Barton Pine, Mintz, Poulet, etc.). The most homogenous dynamics are observed in Brooks,' Kuijken's, and Ehnes' recordings. Podger seems to achieve *piano* by using shorter bow strokes. She marks slurred notes and louder sections by longer strokes.

> It is important to further explore the violinists' varied approach to dynamics. This contributes significantly to the impression of diverse clusters among these recordings. Kuijken, Huggett, Zehetmair, Kremer, Holloway, Podger, Faust, and St John use a smaller range of dynamics. St John's performance is softer and lighter than the others while Kremer's and Podger's are relatively louder overall. In all these versions there are also longer periods with fairly consistent dynamics. Although terraced dynamics are also found, the contrast in these recordings is not necessarily strong. Wallfisch's version differs because of her sharply accented f and p dynamics. In spite of the narrow range, these violinists all use crescendos and diminuendos as well, primarily to shape longer segments.
>
> Kremer and Barton Pine create a strong decrescendo during the bariolage sections (to bars 29 and 79, respectively) while Zehetmair and Kuijken play these at consistent dynamics. Schmid creates a crescendo from b. 63 to 73 and then a decrescendo to b. 79. Zehetmair's tempo in these sections is unsteady

with slight acceleration. His tempo settles after the accented new figuration in bars 29 and 79. In contrast to the relatively uniform dynamics of Kuijken, Zehetmair, Kremer, Holloway, Podger, St John and Faust, Barton Pine utilizes fluctuating dynamics on a larger dynamic scale and more frequently. For instance she creates many crescendos and diminuendos between bars 79 and 109 (starting with a diminuendo to b. 79, then crescendo to 89, a renewed crescendo to 93 then diminuendo to 97 and a crescendo with rallentando to 109). Otherwise her tone and bowing is very similar to Kremer's in both of her concert recordings and her tempo only slightly slower in 1999 than Kremer's (the duration of the performances are 3:20 for Barton Pine versus 3:12 for Kremer).

The overview of general characteristics indicates that distinguishing between *moto perpetuo* and "expressive" styles cannot be limited to a study of tempo fluctuations. Close listening draws attention to three important components of the differing approaches: Firstly, whether the structural points identified by Sarlo are signified in some way, for instance by temporal accents or dynamics; secondly, whether the performer highlights other moments more obviously; and thirdly, how dynamics are used throughout. A further issue is the degree of tempo fluctuation but from a perceptual point of view. How perceptible is it? Are the reported percentages of deviation clearly audible? Does one hear Kremer's tempos less fluctuating than Wallfisch's, for instance? Is the difference statistically or perceptually significant?

As Table 5.7 shows, the performers selected for closer study (Wallfisch, Kremer 2005, Huggett, Zehetmair, Schmid, Holloway, St John, Mathews, Podger, Faust, both Kuijken, and both Barton Pine) rarely highlight in an obviously audible manner the eight structural points identified by Sarlo on the basis of score analytical literature.[68] The most commonly highlighted ones are the beginning of sections two (b. 33), six (b.109), and eight (b. 130). These violinists much more typically accent new figurations, whether through dynamics or temporal elongation (e.g. bb. 7, 9, 29, 42, etc.). At times one feels that the agogic (temporal) accents also serve technical control, providing just a touch of extra time to adjust-alter bowing, position or secure pitch. In other words, the physicality of performance is very much in the fore during most versions of this movement.

---

68 This discrepancy between analyses and performance illustrates how "irrelevant" music analysis literature can be for performance analysis (and for performers) once the attention is to describe rather than to prescribe what performers are (*not* should be) doing, even if the analysts might behave as if they had the "upper hand." This of course has implications for the tertiary training of performers and also for practice-led research discussed in chapters two and six.

5. Affect and Individual Difference   259

Table 5.7. Summary of aural analysis of selected recordings of the E Major Preludio according to the 8 sections identified by Sarlo.

Violinist, duration, comment	b. 1-32	b. 33-58	b. 59-82	b. 83-89	b. 90-108	b. 109-22	b. 123-29	b. 130-38
Huggett 4:07	Very angular; stops & starts with every figuration Dynamics fairly consistent Decrescendo from bb.17 to 28 New start in b.29	Big Rit. to b.43; Bowing is varied (shorter/longer) Certain bars accelerate	Bariolage uneven dynamically as well b.79: accelerates to b.82 (with crescendo-decres.)	bb.83-89 accelerates (with crescendo-decres.)	b.90: new start; Tenuto on second beats in bb. 102-3	Agogic and p Scale up in b.117 accelerates, then tenuto and rallentando	Last beat in b.129 has Rit..	Trills in bb.134, 135 b.136: in tempo b.138: slight Rit..
Wallfisch 2:58 Dynamic accents to mark new figurations or downbeats	Dynamics as score; New start in b.29	b.33 marked; Stresses also in bb. 34, 35, 42, etc.	Some fast accents (e.g. b.63); terraced dynamics; bariolage starts f; b.79: p	b.83 marked; slight pause before moving to b. 90	Every downbeat marked (bb.90, 91, 92); Slight pause for b.107	Slightly slower from b.109; Most flexible tempo in this section	Not marked	Slight tenuto on high E (b.130); Fast pick-up of tempo)
Kremer 2005 3:13	Considerable decrescendo during bariolage Crescendo bb.29-32	Crescendo bb. 33-39; Accents on second beats of bb. 39-40; Score dynamics	Decrescendo during bariolage (to b.79)	Accented notes (each beat) Crescendo: bb.79-94	Crescendo: bb.79-94; Decrescendo: bb.94-7	Accented b.108, b.119	Slows down to b.129	Broadens a little to end
Barton Pine 1999 3:20 Similar to Kremer (tone, bowing) and her own 2007.	Decrescendo to b.29; crescendo to b.33	New figurations articulated	Decrescendo to b.79 followed by crescendo	Crescendo to b.93	Decrescendo to b.97; Crescendo to 101 Slows to end of b.108	Restart in b.109 and again in b.119	Slight Rit. to bb.129-130	Trill in bb.134, 135
Barton Pine 2007 3:37 Similar to 1999, more relaxed	Decrescendo to b.29; Crescendo to b. 42;	Crescendo to b.42; agogic stress in b.43 Fluctuating tempo	Score dynamics + constant cresc-decresc. Decrescendo to b.79	Crescendo to b.89	Crescendo to 93; decrescendo to b.97; Crescendo to 109	Slowing to (with crescendo) 109	Crescendo from b.122 to b.129; Ritenuto over bb.129-30	Ritenuto over bb.129-30 Trill in b.135

Table 5.7, cont. Summary of aural analysis of selected recordings of the E Major Preludio according to the 8 sections identified by Sarlo.

Kuijken '83 3:28	Articulated; fluctuating timing/tempo; score dynamics; Smoother from b.16; Shorter bow for p bars; b.29 marked	Consistent to b.43; Score dynamics; b.55: f	Score dynamics to b.67 then consistent; Crescendo starts in b.79		Accent b.90; Slows to b.94; consistent dynamics; Light accents in b.103-4	Consistent playing		Slight Rit. to b.134 from b.131. Trill in bb. 134 & 135
Kuijken 2001 3:48 Homogenous, consistent dynamics, few accents, even bowing	bb.1-4: short bows score dynamics (narrow range); bariolage even w. consistent dynamics	Very few accents (e.g. bb.39-40), little contrast between f and p	Score dynamics (bb.61-66); Bariolage consistent; New start in b.79	Perhaps the most moto perpetuo – "persistently maintained," even though it is NOT fast, but rather undifferentiated.				Slight Rit. to b.134 Trill in bb.134 & 135
Schmid 3:13 Relaxed, fairly consistent	Staccato eighths; score dynamics; slight accelerando at b.17; slight diminuendo to b.30	Softer, short bow; b.43 terraced dynamics; strong accents in bb.51-2	Not marked. cresc. to b.63; decresc. bb.73-8; cresc. from b.79	Smooth dynamics; few accents	Few accents	p start; Terraced dynamics Descending lines p; ascending lines f	Slight tenuto in b.129;	Rit. to b.134
Holloway 3:30 relaxed	p bits slightly faster; Bariolage accelerates at beginning b. 29: new start	Agogics in bb.39-40	Fluctuates a lot but smoothly; Decrescendo bb. 67-78	Fairly consistent dynamics	Accelerates slightly at 90; Tenuto agogic in b. 102	Agogic accent in b.109		Slight tenuto for 130; Rit. in bb.133 to 134 Trill in b.135
Zehetmair 3:35 Score dynamics	Accelerando at b.17; Steady tempo, consistent dynamics from b.29	Accent in b.39; score dynamics from b.45	Accelerando from 67 (uneven bariolage) Accented b.79 then crescendo	Crescendo to b.93	Crescendo to b.93; decresc. to b.101 then cresc. b.102 (ff)	Decrescendo to b.109 More legato bowing; fluctuating tempo; many short crescendos	Broader b.123; b.129 not really marked	Trill in b.135

5. Affect and Individual Difference   261

Matthews 4:05	Agogics in bb.3, 5 Bariolage has slight decrescendo Accelerando from b.29	Accelerando from b.33 Agogic in b.48 each f and p also in bb.55, 57	Very gradual decrescendo in bariolage (67-78) Accelerando bb.79-82	Accelerando bb.83-7 Agogic in bb.90, 91, 92	Slight agogic in bb.102, 103 (on second beats)			Agogic in b.130. Improvised Cadenza in bb.134-5
Podger 3:29	f and p are not accented, dynamic change almost gradual; bariolage has slight crescendo no marking of b.29	Smoothly linked b.33; light stress on low notes (bb.45, 46, etc.). Terraced dynamics are not accented; Stressing 4 notes of down-beats (bb.55, 56)	Bariolage is smooth, fairly consistent dynamics	Slightly stressed b.83; slightly stressed 2nd sixteenth note in bb.87-8	Slight agogic in bb.90, 94 Bottom notes staccato Slight accent on repeated slurred notes (bb.102-3 second beat)	Not marked Tenuto high G (b.118) then p Accented low notes (bb.119-21)	Very slight stress on first 2 semiquavers (b.123) Slight Rit. at end of b.129	Slight tenuto on E in b.130 Trill in b.135
St John 2:55	Rapid blur of sixteenth notes beyond first note in bar; Bariolage rushes ahead and has crescendo-diminuendo to b.29	Most 1st notes in bb. 43-55 stressed f in b.55 stressed	second beat of b.59 accented; Terraced then consistent dynamics; diminuendo bb.74-9	Soft until b.91	Crescendo bb.92-4; Broadening bb.94-6 Softer from b.97; Slows from third beat b. 107 (accent on third beats bb.107-8)	Rit. to b.109; tempo little slower thereafter; Fluctuating dynamics bb.113-4, then p; Tempo fluctuates most from here on	Broadens a little to downbeat (4note groups) bb.123-4	Tenuto in b.130 Rit. to b.134 Trill in b.135 Diminuendo in b.138 pp end
Faust 3:34	Small dynamics contrast between f and p Slight tenuto on E (b.9) Tempo little unsteady during bariolage, consistent dynamics p from b.29	Smooth, few accents (e.g. second beat bb.39-41; low notes in bb.43-51 esp. in f measures; Smooth contrast of terraced dynamics	Small range terraced dynamics; bb.67-78: consistent dynamics Slight Rit. to b.79	Very slightly stressed down beats throughout	Very slightly stressed down beats throughout; Slight Rit. to b.109	Slightly stressed b.109; bb.119-22: Bass notes stressed	Light Rall. into and Rit. on E in b.130	Consistent dynamics Trill in b.135

Among violinists using dynamic accents, Wallfisch stands out because of the frequency and strength of her accenting. She uses bowing and dynamics to strongly accent most new figurations and many downbeats, for instance in bb. 33-35 and 90-92. At the speed of her playing these seem to enhance virtuosity and do not impact negatively on the "persistent maintaining of rapid figuration." Kremer accents fewer new figurations and less sharply. However, he, and to a lesser extent Holloway and also Kuijken, among many others, accents the second beats in bars 39-41, creating a momentary shift in the metrical pattern. The other performer who uses primarily dynamic accents is St John. Although Kuijken's 1981 recording is fairly detailed with clearly articulated groups, agogic stresses, and terraced dynamics, he hardly plays any accents in his second version from 2001. This version has more consistent dynamics and is also twenty seconds slower than the earlier one! Strong temporal (agogic) accents are more common in the recordings of Holloway and Matthews as well as Huggett (Audio examples 5.29 and 5.30 discussed at Figure 5.8 and Figure 5.9).

Another noteworthy difference in relation to the use of accents, whether dynamic or temporal, lies in their effect or function. Wallfisch accents single notes, rapidly and sharply. They are "stabbed." Podger and Faust, on the other hand briefly lean on *groups* of notes, not just emphasizing them but shaping and integrating them into the flow of the music. This adds ebb and flow and thus perhaps makes the performance less strictly *moto perpetuo* but still squarely in the virtuoso style. This shaping-grouping of two to four notes at the beginning of certain bars has a different effect to both the short and sharp dynamic accent and the longer temporal stress on a single note. The former rarely impacts on perceived tempo because it is simply a fast stab. The latter arrests the flow of the music much more than when the temporal elongation involves the entire metric unit (here this means four semiquavers) because of the distribution of extra time. When two to four notes are elongated and thus grouped (as opposed to a single "bass note"), this functions as a shaping mechanism; and shape assists flow as it creates a sense of direction.

Although I would categorize both Kremer and Barton Pine's performances as in *moto perpetuo* style, Barton Pine's might impress more like "virtuosic" because of the dynamic variety. Kremer's is more etude-like because of its homogeneity. St John's performance is also unquestionably virtuosic, and not just because of the very fast tempo. Her light bowing, rapid accents and fluctuating dynamics within a narrow (and fairly soft) range all contribute to this impression. Her tempo tends to rush ahead somewhat in the bariolage sections but otherwise it sounds steady. It noticeably fluctuates only from bars 109 onwards, in preparation for the climax. The rapidly delivered, diminuendo final bars confirm the virtuoso approach.

As for the other versions, practically all of them are shaped as *moto perpetuo*, except Huggett's and perhaps Schröder's, Matthews' and Holloway's. Why? Because they all tend to play in a smooth style using dynamics and dynamic accents to highlight moments rather than temporal (agogic) accents and locally nuanced tempo fluctuations as Huggett does. Even Holloway's tempo fluctuations are more smoothly executed and over longer periods of time. Schröder's and Matthews's versions are closer to being deemed "expressive" rather than *moto perpetuo*. He plays rather slowly with fairly frequent accenting and detailed articulation (cf. first item in Audio example 5.28). She also creates stresses frequently (e.g. bars 3, 5, 7), and always with temporal elongation. However, otherwise the tempo in Matthews' recording is fairly fast and steady except for two sections: She accelerates from bar 29-32 and then from 33-36 and also at the analogous bars of 79-82 and 83-87. Even so, there are extended periods, notably the two bariolage sections, where the music moves smoothly and evenly, with consistent dynamics, tempo, and bowing (cf. first item in Audio examples 5.29 and 5.30, respectively).

Huggett, on the other hand, constantly stops and restarts the flow, articulating figurations bar by bar or as seem to fit her reading of harmonic and melodic motions. There are no sections longer than two to four bars that might have any fluency and consistency. Apart from tempo fluctuation and agogic timing she also varies her bowing much more than others. So even when the tempo remains reasonably steady her change to more staccato bowing, for instance, interferes with and counters the "persistent maintaining of rapid figuration." In sum, the degree and extent of her tempo fluctuation and the frequency of stopping and accelerating make her performance individual and unusual to the extreme (cf. second item in Audio examples 5.29 and 5.30).

These aural impressions are not easily shown through measurements. When bars and beats are marked up the results indicate greater fluctuation than what my perceptual "threshold" would notice. This is particularly true when beat-level tempo is visualized (see Wallfisch or Kuijken in Figures 5.8b and 5.9b). However, the listening mind automatically adjusts minor differences and fluctuations—it receives the performance as a Gestalt with no regards for such micro variations. In Figures 5.8 and 5.9 two excerpts are illustrated in four of the versions studied: the opening bars of the movement (Figure 5.8) and a longer section between bars 29 and 63 that includes several agogic accents as well as dynamic contrasts (Figure 5.9). The smoother tempo curves of Kuijken and Wallfisch are quite obvious when bar-level tempo fluctuation is graphed. Wallfisch's strong accents are seen at beat level but her tempo graph is reasonably smooth when bar-level fluctuations are presented. Although the beat-level mapping shows constant fluctuation for Kuijken and Wallfisch, even here their versions are smoother than Matthews' or Huggett's, confirming the *moto perpetuo* style (Figures 5.8b and 5.9b). The differences between Matthews' and Huggett's "expressive" style also show up with Huggett's graph demonstrating more frequent and deeper fluctuations both at bar and beat levels.

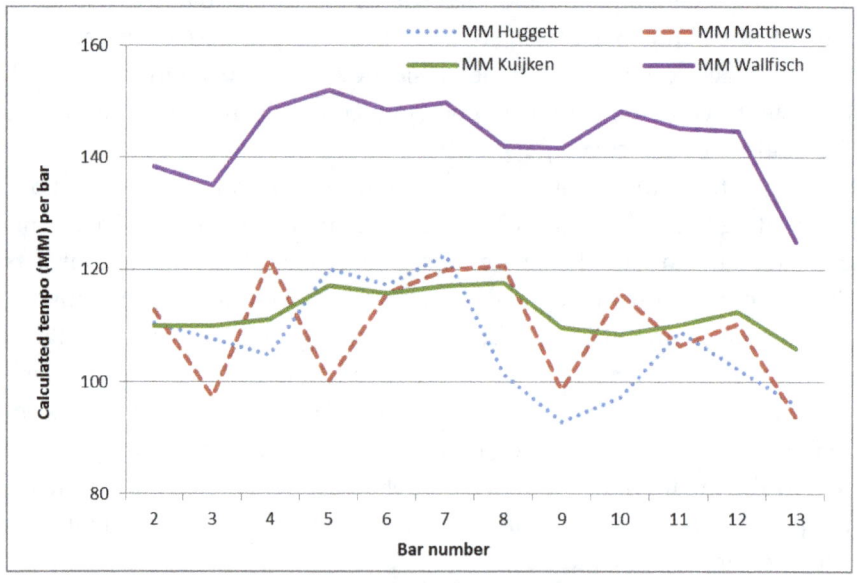

Figure 5.8a. E Major Preludio, bars 1-12. Bar level tempo fluctuation in four recordings (Matthews, Huggett, Kuijken 2001 and Wallfisch).

5. Affect and Individual Difference   265

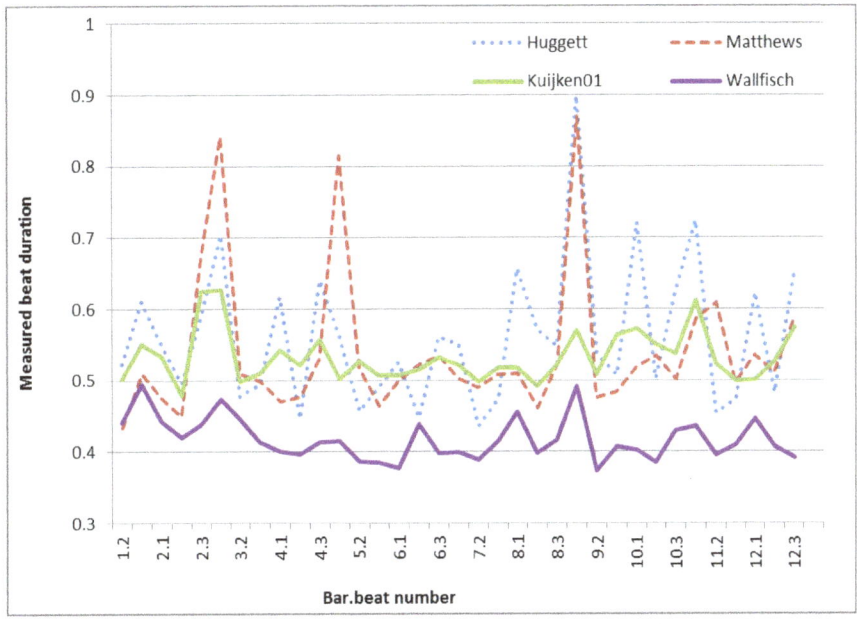

Figure 5.8b. E Major Preludio, bars 1-12. Beat durations in 4 recordings (Matthews, Huggett, Kuijken 2001 and Wallfisch).

5.29. Expressive versus virtuosic "moto perpetuo" style in J. S. Bach, E Major Partita BWV 1006, Preludio, extract: bars 1-12. Four versions: Ingrid Matthews © Centaur, Monica Huggett © Virgin Veritas, Sigiswald Kuijken 2001 © Deutsche Harmonia Mundi, Elizabeth Wallfisch © Hyperion. Duration: 1.20.

To listen to this extract online scan the QR code
or follow this link: http://dx.doi.org/10.11647/OBP.0064.53

266   A Musicology of Performance

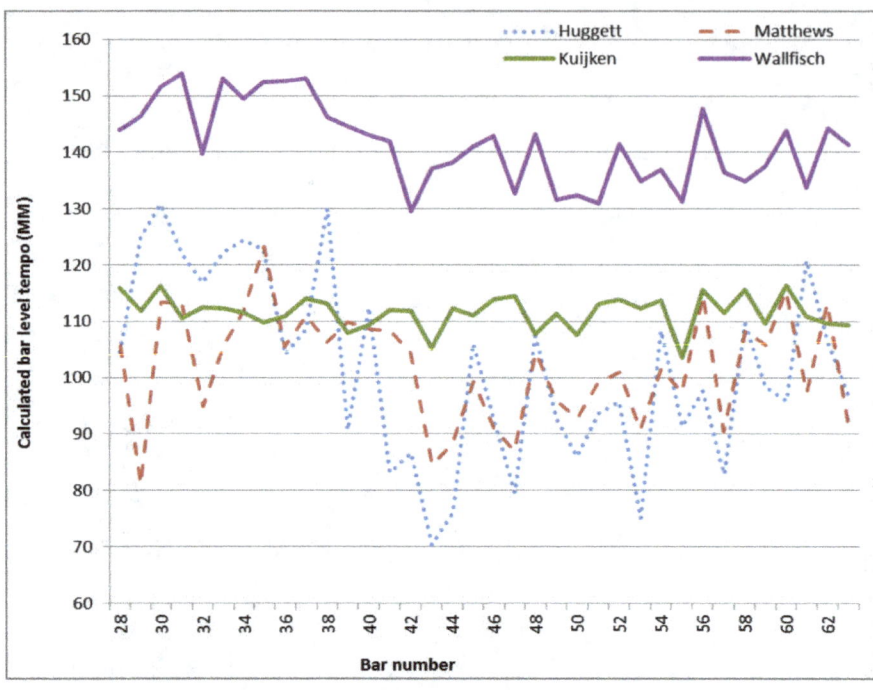

Figure 5.9a. E Major Preludio, bars 29-63. Bar level tempo fluctuation in 4 recordings (Huggett, Matthews, Kuijken 2001 and Wallfisch).

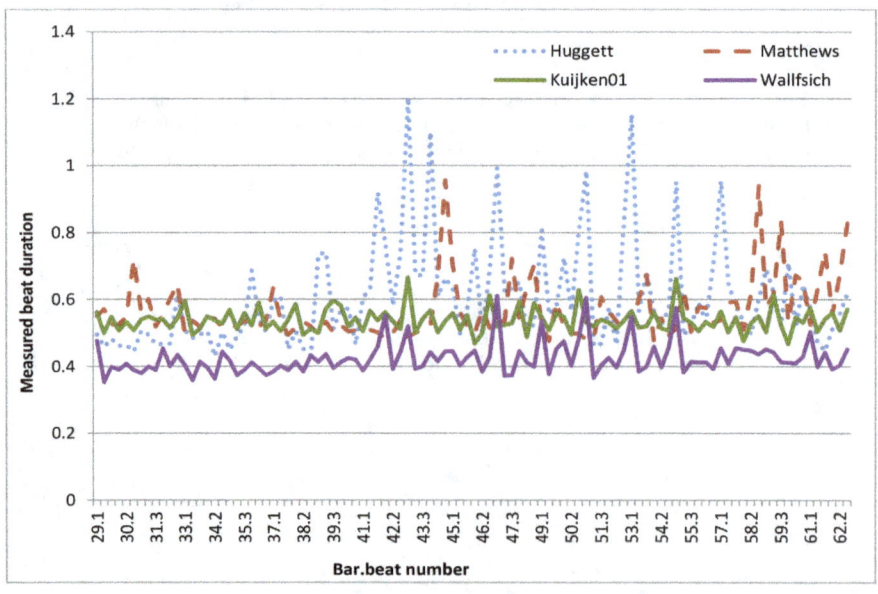

Figure 5.9b. E Major Preludio, bars 29-63. Beat durations in 4 recordings (Huggett, Matthews, Kuijken 2001 and Wallfisch).

5.30. Expressive versus virtuosic "moto perpetuo" style in J. S. Bach, E Major Partita BWV 1006, Preludio, extract: bars 29-62. Four versions: Ingrid Matthews © Centaur, Monica Huggett © Virgin Veritas, Sigiswald Kuijken 2001 © Deutsche Harmonia Mundi, Elizabeth Wallfisch © Hyperion. Duration: 3.53.

To listen to this extract online scan the QR code
or follow this link: http://dx.doi.org/10.11647/OBP.0064.54

Clearly, Sarlo is right when he asserts "a link between playing the piece more slowly and playing it less persistently." The two least persistent versions in the above sample are also the slowest (Huggett 101 beat per minute; Matthews 102 bpm).[69] However, quite a few of other slower versions deliver the figuration just as "persistently" and regularly as the fastest versions (St John 142 bpm; Wallfisch 140 bpm), perhaps even more so. Figures 5.8 and 5.9 show that Kuijken's slowish 2001 version (109 bpm) has a fairly even tempo, generally steadier than Wallfisch's.[70] The fast speed of St John's interpretation impresses with its whirl-like virtuosity, partly because of its hushed, light tone quality that makes it sound even faster. The stabbed accents and rough tone in Wallfisch's version create a performance that sounds like being on edge, "just made it." In contrast, the relaxed, hardly differentiated second version of Kuijken, the more even tone and consistent dynamics of Kremer or Schmid (both players' tempo is around 129 bpm) make these versions more than comply with the idea of "persistent delivery." Kuijken's 2001 recording is so homogenous and steady that it easily takes the palm for being "clockwork-like" *moto perpetuo*, even if not that virtuosic.

Although I set out to show how idiosyncratic Huggett's interpretation is, I ended up discussing other versions more. Individuality is often more obvious against the relief of the common. By commenting on similarities and differences within that common backdrop Huggett's radically different way of playing emerges. Not only that, but we can also see the range of

---

69 In my entire collection Schröder (99 bpm) and Beznosiuk (98 bmp) are the only two that are slower than Huggett and Matthews. The next slowest is Ehnes (104 bmp) and then Szeryng (105 bpm).

70 Because I calculated beat per minute tempos from duration it might be useful to provide the base durations I used when working with these Preludio recordings. Huggett: 4:04, Matthews: 4:04, St John: 2:55, Wallfisch: 2:58, and Kuijken 3:47.

diversity within even such straightforward musical character as the *moto perpetuo*. And, if that would not be fascinating enough, the complexity of music performance also manifests, yet again. The empirical evidence measurement of tempo fluctuation provided for the distinguishing of performance styles in the E Major Preludio (between *moto perpetuo* and "expressive") turned out to be but the tip of the iceberg. To tease out the constituent performance elements contributing to a perception of "rapid figuration [being] persistently maintained" we had to examine delivery of accents (dynamic or temporal), use of dynamics and bowing, as well as tempo choice and relate them to each-other. This helped to see how perception of tempo stability and overall effect of persistency are formed.

5.5. Conclusions

In this chapter I recaptured differences between the broad and increasingly loosened MSP and HIP categories primarily through close analysis of four movements from the E Major Partita, multiple recordings of the same violinists, and an examination of affect and musical "meaning" in the D minor Giga, A minor Grave and G minor Adagio. The final section focused on two sets of idiosyncratic versions, one each of nominally MSP or HIP-inspired (Zehetmair) and HIP (Huggett) . Here I drew upon the opinions of general and musically trained listeners as well to support my view of these recordings being highly individual. Throughout the chapter my aim was to engage with the performances at a "holistic" level and to show the multitude of interactions at play. At times this enabled me to point out the usefulness of Deleuzian thinking and terminology when attempting to explain differences in kind and degree or to distinguish between kind and degree.

One of the main conclusions of this chapter stems from the comparisons of subsequent recordings made by the same violinists. The findings refine Daniel Leech-Wilkinson's[71] and Eitan Ornoy's[72] observations that artists tend to develop their approach to compositions early in their career; subsequent recordings by the same musician take the pieces further in the

---

71 Daniel Leech-Wilkinson, 'Recordings and Histories of Performance Style' in *The Cambridge Companion to Recorded Music*, ed. by Nicholas Cook et al. (Cambridge: Cambridge University Press, 2009), pp. 246-262.
72 Eitan Ornoy, 'Recording Analysis of J. S. Bach's G minor Adagio for Solo Violin (excerpt): A Case Study,' *JMM: Journal of Music and Meaning*, 6 (Spring 2008), section 2, available at http://www.musicandmeaning.net/issues/showArticle.php?artID=6.2

same direction. Although by and large this was found to be true in the current data set as well, complicating factors have also come to light. Slight differences were noted between the earlier and later recordings of Tetzlaff who increased his vibrato both in terms of frequency and prominence and created more extreme dynamic contrasts in places where the earlier recording displayed only modest contrast. However, some of these differences, although ostensibly representing the same idea (e.g. contrast), actually led the overall character of the playing towards different aesthetics and affect. The difficulty of unpacking cause and effect or the hierarchy of similarity and difference became transparent, questioning the feasibility of the task.

More significant differences were noted in Kremer's two versions. The 2005 release was found to be rather wayward and uneven in tempo and more forcefully articulated, perhaps as a somewhat individualized understanding of HIP principles developed through collaborations with Harnoncourt and others in performances of post-baroque repertoire. Kremer radically decreased the use of vibrato, chose more extreme tempos and dynamics and delivered more powerful accents. Nevertheless basic interpretative choices remained intact even in his two recordings, as exemplified in discussion of the A minor Grave and Fuga, as well as the E Major Menuet II, for instance.[73] To recall Kremer himself again, as cited earlier, "I am still the same Gidon Kremer; with a different violin, in a different church but with the same music."

The only violinist who has radically changed her approach to performing Bach's *Six Sonatas and Partitas for Solo Violin* is Viktoria Mullova. In her case we witness a total transformation from MSP to "beyond" HIP, or what I would currently regard the ideal (HIP) Bach performance—now, at the beginning of the second decade of the new millennium.

Although it could be argued that the music sets the boundaries of possible expressive gestures and phrasing as well as affective communication, the findings of this chapter provided further confirmation of the results of previous chapters: the interpretative differences among players show a broader range than what one finds within the two versions of any one violinist (except for Mullova in the current data set). Importantly, this chapter demonstrated that differences within MSP and within HIP versions can be considerable. This is particularly noteworthy in

---

[73] In earlier sections of the book my comments on Kremer's performances of other movements also noted many similarities between his two recordings.

relation to MSP which has been much criticised for lacking individuality. Close examination underscored my position that generalizations are not particularly useful. They hide more than what they reveal. Furthermore, what might be typical in one movement of a given recording might not be true for another. Therefore I compared specific instances (e.g. D minor Giga, E Major Preludio, Loure, Gavotte and Menuet) and examined the level of uniformity in these particular cases. Although I offered some cautiously formulated general conclusions about particular violinists' performance styles, more often than not the results prompted questions and highlighted the problem of dealing with complex dynamical systems.

Performance is non-linear and complex, rather than complicated. Its analysis does not deal with simple steps but the simultaneous irruption of many variables. I aimed to show that idiosyncratic performances are extreme examples of complexity because they are "unpredictable" and full of deterritorializing "lines of flight." As Latour notes, "The more disorderly the message, the higher its information content [...] [and] the less able the receiver is to predict" what will happen next. "A message high in information is one low in predictable structure, and therefore high in 'entropy.'"[74] However, there is tension between predictability and information content: unpredictability may eventually become randomness. When it does, the listener may feel disengaged; the music, the performance does not make sense anymore, it may seem mannered, tasteless, out of style, may be lacking flow, coherence. Some of the comments from the listening study imply that the unique styles of Zehetmair and Huggett are verging on this thin line of tension between "meaning" and idiosyncrasy.

The structure of any system must have some meaning; it "must somehow 'represent' the information important to its existence." In other words a performance has to make musical sense whether in terms of a particular convention such as HIP or MSP or in terms of compositional style, or musical character. And because the "notion of 'distributed representation' [means that] the elements of the system have no representational meaning by themselves, but only in terms of patterns of relationships with many other elements"[75] (i.e. patterns of relationships involving bowing, articulation, tone, tempo, timing, dynamics and so on), these unique versions often fall outside easy categorizations. In Huggett's and Zehetmair's recordings the

---

74 Bruno Latour, *Pandora's Hope: Essays on the Reality of Science Studies* (Cambridge, MA: Harvard University Press, 1999), p. 7.
75 Latour, *Pandora's Hope*, p. 11.

"patterns of relationships" among the performance elements are porous, malleable, unpredictable, and at times seemingly incongruent. Their rich information content makes them particularly interesting to study and extremely challenging to "evaluate."

This chapter's more holistic explorations of recorded performances increasingly called upon subjective reflections and the contemplation of affective response. Affect is a nameless sensation that precedes cognition and recognized emotion. It is a bodily reaction; a felt transition from one state to another. It can be argued that aesthetics may be thought of as this capacity of sensing affectively. Since music performance unfolds in sound and penetrates the body in its entirety at once through the auditory system, we experience it holistically and affectively. In contrast to language and the written world music is first "comprehended" through the body, empathetically. Cognition, analytical dissecting and meaning-making occur only afterwards. Explaining the parts, however, rarely leads to a full understanding of the whole, underscoring the importance of allowing for the use of metaphoric language in an attempt to convey the felt experience. Musical complexity remains resistant to meaningful theoretical formulations or models. This is good because theories incline towards closure and thus stifle creativity; they are "the gravestones of musical invention."[76] If we want music performance to thrive, to be relevant and meaningful for ever new generations of listeners and musicians alike, we should not strait-jacket performers into theoretical constructs of normative performance rules and conventions. Nor should we deny or be silent about the listeners' (including analysts') holistic-affective experience, even if it is hard to find scholarly language for it.

---

76 Richard Toop, 'Against a Theory of Music (New) Complexity,' in *Contemporary Music: Theoretical and Philosophical Perspectives*, ed. by Max Paddison and Irène Deliège (Aldershot: Ashgate, 2010), pp. 89-98 (p. 97).

6. Conclusions and an Epilogue: The Complexity Model of Music Performance, Deleuze and Brain Laterality

As I was completing this manuscript Nicholas Cook's most recent monograph *Beyond the Score: Music as Performance* was published. It is a magisterial overview of the field, detailed yet summative, covering more than one could think of—and in a page-turner style of writing! It makes my project fade into insignificance, at least in terms of the broader issues regarding the study of performance. There is no point to the discussion of the different approaches to investigating music performance, nor to their respective limitations. Instead I put forth my proposition for a theoretical framework that a musicology of performance could adopt and formulate what I believe might enrich our thinking about how to overcome the problems encountered in current research.

My analytical discussions conveyed my credo that is in agreement with what Cook writes in the final chapter of *Beyond the Score*:

> It is not obvious that there is a limit on the number, or nature, or viable performance options, whether these are informed by historical precedent, structural interpretation, rhetorical effect, or personal taste. In every instance there will be some reasons for doing it one way, and some for doing it another. Each will have its own consequences, which can be explored and evaluated. There are lots of ways of making sense of music as performance, and lots of sense there for the making. It really is as simple, and as complicated, as that.[1]

---

1 Nicholas Cook, *Beyond the Score: Music as Performance* (New York: Oxford University Press, 2014), p. 402.

The many ways of making sense of music as performance, and of the *activity* of performing, are all valid and contribute to our understanding of the phenomenon and our engagement with it. Arguing about the best method is therefore not my goal. But arguing for an increased attempt to find ways of dealing with it in its complexity; to synthesize approaches and analytical detail, is. There are two issues I raised early on in this book to which I need to return now: the importance of aural communication that takes place where music is performed (see Epilogue) and the claim that music performance is a complex dynamical system.

Based on Cilliers,[2] in chapter two I listed eight characteristics of complex dynamics systems that are easy to relate to musical performance and promised to discuss them further here. The first point stated that complex systems require not only a large number of elements but that these interact in a dynamic way and therefore change over time. Performing classical music has many technical as well as musical and emotional-psychological-cognitive elements. It also has a history and a cultural-social dimension. Different approaches to studying music performance tend to focus on any one of these: Empirical analyses of performance focus on features such as tempo, dynamics or vibrato; ethnographic and psychological studies on musicians' practice behaviour, ensemble coordination, decision-making processes, memory, body movements, emotional communication, social interaction; historical-cultural investigations on musicians' biographies, performing tradition lineages, concertizing, receptions, diaries, and memoires; music analytical and historical performance practice research on technical and historical requirements and the fulfilment of stipulated intentions and historical requirements; and so on.

As we have seen these "large number of elements" are indeed present and play a role not just in how a performance is acted out but also how it is heard and received. The physical interactions between instrument and player, between acoustic and affective elements and between violinist and listener are also supplemented by interactions between musicians, between historical and contemporary violinists, teachers and students, and a variety of written sources evidencing "transference of information." The detailed analysis of performance features discussed many specific interactions (for instance between tempo, articulation and dotting). Biographical information, citations from interviews, reviews, and compact disk liner

---

2 Paul Cilliers, *Complexity and Postmodernism: Understanding Complex Systems* (London: Routledge, 1998), pp. 3-7.

notes confirmed interactions among musicians, history, culture and audiences. Comparison of recordings hinted at formations of practice—an often unspoken "interaction" among players as they form communities with each-other, their forbearers and the music they perform. The tracing of mutual influence of MSP and HIP and the often futile attempt to deliberate between the two styles showed what a melting pot music performance can be. The various complex interactions of these diverse elements from the cultural-historical through the technical-musical and ultimately to the personal were all noted. Their role and the nature and network of interactions differed in various ways according to the individual instances.

Still, it is quite remarkable how much performances change over time. Here I focused only on the last 30 years, hardly more than two generations (if you consider a generation to be 10-15 years) yet change was in evidence everywhere. Diversity of approaches could be observed in relation to most movements of Bach's works for solo violin and the change was not necessarily one-directional; some MSP features resurfaced in slightly different form (e.g. longer phrases but lighter bowing) while HIP features were taken to more extreme levels (e.g. metrical grouping of notes and ornamentation). The variety found among the most recent recordings was perhaps the most interesting and reassuring discovery: Bach performance is in a healthy state at the beginning of the new millennium. The plurality of styles available on record is as good as—if indeed not *much better* than—during the proverbial golden age at the dawn of sound recording a hundred years ago. It is also obvious that performers (and listeners) vote with their playing and heart: by now it is certainly not only "the composer's voice [that] is worth listening to when devising performance approaches."[3] I have shown many examples of interpretations of the Solos that could be severely critiqued by people with "Urtext mentality," yet provide thoroughly enjoyable readings that exude vitality and (personal) authenticity.

The second point on my list based on Cilliers was the requirement that the interaction be rich; any element in the system influences, and is influenced by, quite a few other ones. This was observed primarily as I discussed the various specific performance features and when I described selected recordings in a holistic manner.

---

3   Kenneth Hamilton, *After the Golden Age: Romantic Pianism and Modern Performance* (New York: Oxford University Press, 2008), p. 281. To be sure, Hamilton is asking the question "is the composer's voice the only one worth listening to when devising performance approaches?" and arguing for "a more liberal attitude."

Remember, for instance, how often tempo, a seemingly straightforward matter, interacted with various other features impacting on perceived speed, flow and overall aesthetic effect. The perception of tempo could be influenced by articulation as well as bowing, either together or singularly. Heavier bow pressure and / or more sustained articulation tended to make the performance sound slower. Tempo, on the other hand, could influence the perception of rhythm and so did articulation which in turn interacted with bowing. As bowing is the instrument of articulation in violin playing, it is perhaps more accurate to say that bowing *acted out* or delivered articulation. And of course bowing also depends on the bow, very much so. Players often say it is harder to find the right bow than one's life partner! Quite a few violinists use particular bows for particular repertoire; and the differences between a modern and an early eighteenth-century bow are considerable. Its contribution to particular musical effects has been frequently pointed out.

Nevertheless it is *phrasing* that is without doubt *the* feature that occupies the ultimate seat of interactions; it emerges from the composite of most other features and is affected by personal disposition, cultural heritage, education, age, experience and so on. Most of my attempts at holistic-descriptive analysis of interpretations engaged with verbalising the constituent parts of what we call the performer's shaping or phrasing of music. Being the most complex "element" of performance—well, this is an oxymoron, surely, as something is either an element or a complex, so it might be better to think of phrasing as a higher-level feature; a construct of interactive elements such as articulation, timing, dynamics and tempo— it certainly influences other elements, not just being influenced by them. The overall aesthetic perception and affective response largely depends on our (the listener's) interaction with phrasing. I mentioned how trills and grace notes, even added embellishments did not matter much unless they were shaped in a particular way; usually through bowing that enhanced a sense of pulse or highlighted harmonic motion. I also discussed how phrasing could limit or boost the impression of improvisatory freedom. A comparison of Kuijken's two recordings of the A minor Grave and G minor Adagio, among others, showed phrasing to interact with either metric organization (leading to more regularity) or harmony and melody (leading to more improvisatory freedom). Added to the mix are bowing (pressure, speed, length and distribution affecting tone and shaping and significance of notes), dynamics, tempo and timing of notes. Eventually

I even ventured to mention possible affective states that the complex of phrasing may engender in a listener like me.

The third point listed in chapter two referred to the characteristics of interactions; that they are non-linear, that small causes can have large results and vice versa. This is considered a precondition of complexity. With regards to music performance it is arguable what a "small cause" and "large results" might be. Perhaps a more locally nuanced articulation is a reasonably small cause in the context of detached articulation yet it has a very significant impact (large result). The difference between metrically shaping groups and rattling them off in a motoric-mechanistic manner has become the hallmarks of HIP *vis a vie* the "modernist" (or "authentistic") style.[4] Another instance of a potentially small cause having a large result is Gringolts' delivery of embellishments in the B minor Sarabande. As discussed in chapter four, the figures he adds and the places where he ornaments are similar to Mullova's in 2007-2008. Yet her version sounds completely different because of the more metrical delivery and period bowing style: a potentially small technical detail having a large result.

A more complicated situation came to light in my discussion of the E Major Preludio in chapter five. I understood Sarlo to claim that small differences in tempo fluctuation could create large differences in interpretative style.[5] I argued the opposite; that seemingly large differences can have rather small results. Or to be more precise, I argued that details matter. For me neither the relatively large overall tempo differences nor the small tempo fluctuations necessarily caused a large change; they did not *per se* shift a performance from the Italian *moto perpetuo* style into the French "expressive" interpretative option (compare Kuijken 2001 with Wallfisch or Kremer 2005). Rather, these differences simply weakened ("deterritorialized"[6]) the virtuosic element that I could still hear even in the "expressive" versions (e.g. Matthews, Holloway). Similarly, the considerable difference in the strength of accents or dynamic range or the way dynamics were used had little impact on the overall aesthetics: Wallfisch's accented playing or Barton Pine's dynamically shaped versions still sounded virtuosic and *moto perpetuo*, exemplifying situations when

---

[4] The term "authentistic" was coined by Richard Taruskin. See his *Text and Act: Essays on Music and Performance* (New York: Oxford University Press, 1995), esp. pp. 99ff.

[5] Dario Sarlo, *The Performance Style of Jascha Heifetz* (Farnham: Ashgate, forthcoming).

[6] A term borrowed from Gilles Deleuze and Felix Guattari, *A Thousand Plateaus* (London: Bloomsbury, 2013) and explained in chapter two.

easily noticeable (large) causes in a complex system have relatively small results.

The fourth point referred to "loops in the interactions"; when the effect of any activity can feed back onto itself, sometimes directly, sometimes after a number of intervening stages. This can be best observed when the recordings and violinists are placed in their historical-cultural context. The spiral model of performance trends that I proposed in 2003 aims to explain exactly this looping:[7] Performance features that have gone out of fashion may reappear again after a while but although they are similar they are never the same. The rhythmic flexibility and expressive freedom witnessed in some contemporary violinists' playing is different to that observed in the recordings of Joachim and his contemporaries.

In the current study we could witness such differences and "spiralling" primarily through the examination of multiple recordings by the same violinists. This showed two contrasting tendencies: Firstly, that musicians take their conceptions witnessed on the earlier version further in the same direction, and secondly, that they may return to previous, in the interim abandoned, aesthetic ideals and playing technique. However, just as it is impossible to step in to the same river twice, so it is with music performance. For instance, if a player re-introduces vibrato after he or she had been convinced of its historical inauthenticity, she will use it differently: perhaps less frequently, probably not as part of tone production but as an expressive device. The performer interacts with her past, his changing aesthetic sensibilities. However much they change, a part of them will still be there—as we saw Kremer explain on the DVD *Back to Bach* cited in chapter five. For some musicians the similarities are stronger, the looping is tighter and the radius of the loops shorter. For others more radical interactions may occur.

The effect of playing baroque music in decidedly HIP manner may even have a global influence, impacting on the musician's playing of Beethoven or Brahms or Bartók ("activity feeding back onto itself"). This can be observed in the not-at-all nineteenth-century manner of performing Brahms, Verdi or Chopin by musicians nominally associated with HIP.[8] Mullova, Barton Pine, Ibragimova, Faust have all worked with period ensembles and

---

[7] Dorottya Fabian, *Bach Performance Practice, 1945-1975: A Comprehensive Review of Sound Recordings and Literature* (Aldershot: Ashgate, 2003), pp. 246-248.

[8] I have discussed examples in Dorottya Fabian, 'Is Diversity in Performance Truly in Decline? The Evidence of Sound Recordings,' *Context*, 31 (2006), 165-180. See also Clive Brown, 'Performing Nineteenth-Century Chamber Music: The Yawning Chasm between Contemporary Practice and Historical Evidence,' *Early Music*, 38 (2010), 476-480.

6. *Conclusions and an Epilogue* 279

specialists whose influence they acknowledge. In Mullova's case we have recorded evidence of how these activities influenced her playing of the Bach Solos "after a number of intervening stages" (exemplified by the 1992-1993 recordings of the Partitas). In hindsight, Gringolts' 2001 disk studied here is a record of an early stage in his growing interest in baroque violin playing. Nowadays he is often seen playing with a baroque bow and both his technical and musical approaches to baroque repertoire have gained depth and seem to have lost some of their idiosyncratic qualities.[9] He referred to this "looping back" already in 2003 when he noted in an interview:

> I'd say playing good music is like reading a great book—each time you read it you gain more understanding by reading between the lines. Each word can have a double or triple meaning and you will never reach the bottom. That's how it is with good music—it is completely boundless and that's why, in the case of Bach's solo violin works, it is still being played more than 300 years after its creation.[10]

It remains to be seen how he will play Bach in ten or twenty years' time.

Schröder's case may also be best understood in terms of this "loops in the interactions." His early commitment to historical investigation, to the re-discovery of seventeenth-century violin repertoire, his role as chamber musician (especially of classical string quartets), his pedagogical activities and publications, his participation in Holland's vibrant and experimental early music scene all formed various loops of interactions, some resulting in more ground-breaking contributions than others. Judging his role or the importance of his contribution based exclusively on his solo Bach recording would be a fatal mistake.

The fifth point asserted that complex systems are usually open systems, they interact with their environment. This aspect of music performance is shown in many ethnographic studies. Quite pertinently it is evidenced in the large survey Ornoy conducted among HIP musicians at the end of the 1990s. He clearly pinpoints the complexity of this interaction with the environment when he notes:

---

9 See the Medici TV youtube broadcast of a concert excerpt (held during the Verbier Festival in July 2011) where he and Masaaki Suzuki perform the Largo from Bach's Sonata in C minor BWV 1017, available at https://www.youtube.com/watch?v=fY-rbsei_rY

10 From a post by Greg Cahill on the *All Things Strings* website available at http://www.allthingsstrings.com/layout/set/print/News/Interviews-Profiles/For-violinist-Ilya-Gringolts-It-s-Bach-and-Beyond [last accessed October 2015].. See also the interview cited in chapter three, talking about the "experimental" stage he was in at the time of recording the disk studied here.

> The conspicuous discrepancy between the wide, multicolored ideological spectrum found in various writings and the somewhat uniform values of the performers' actual practice might also indicate the lack of interaction between the two domains: many early music performers have been found to be "behind the times" with current ideologies, since they perform according to attitudes formed many generations ago. [...] practical considerations took priority over ideological aspirations, and contradiction between the two domains might easily evolve.[11]

On the one hand musicians interact with their environment through "practical considerations," while on the other hand they remain aloof of larger cultural-ideological movements and continue doing what they are used to, showing "conservative" / "behind times" traits. Such contradictions can be traced among the most prominent performer—writers of the early music movement; the verbal pronouncements frequently not matching musical outcomes.[12]

This duality is also seen in contemporary discussions of western classical music and its performance. These often criticise the "industry" for being inward looking and stratified. This attitude is considered to contribute to the perceived decline in audiences or mass demand for classical music. However, this is not necessarily the case at all, especially not in relation to the performance of baroque music and HIP.[13] There are also obvious signs of constant renewal and interaction with the environment. I noted, for instance, that even The Juilliard School of Music has now introduced postgraduate studies in historical performance practice; that even James Ehnes (if not Hilary Hahn) has changed his Bach performance by the time he recorded the accompanied sonatas (chapter three). In *Beyond the Score* Cook lists many initiatives coming from Conservatoires, soloists, ensembles, orchestras, and opera houses. The pluralistic society we currently live in inspires musicians to experiment with new ways of performing, of mixing styles, of improvising, of enjoying and incorporating into their

---

11   Eitan Ornoy, 'In Search of Ideologies and Ruling Conventions among Early Music Performers,' *Min-Ad: Israel Studies in Musicology Online*, 6 (Special Issue 2007-2008), 1-19 (p. 18).
12   I have mentioned a few examples in earlier chapters and pointed out many more in Fabian, *Bach Performance Practice*.
13   The reporting about audiences is often inaccurate and misleading as Lyndon Terracini of Opera Australia explains in *Australian Book Review* (02 September 2014), for instance, available at https://www.australianbookreview.com.au/arts-update/arts-commentary/101-arts-update/2151-opera-australia-s-lyndon-terracini-replies-to-peter-tregear

own practice good music of any kind and tradition. All this has an impact on their approach to the Bach Solos as well, as seen in the increased level of ornamentation and embellishing of several movements. They do not "interpret" the music as much as they *play* with it. They "proclaim a loyalty to the playful and emotive elements which are music's greatest joy."¹⁴

This demonstrates that "the value of studying the stylistic features of what Hamilton calls the 'golden age' of pianism does not lie so much in rehabilitating specific stylistic practices. It lies in recapturing the pluralism that was so prominent a feature of nineteenth-century musical culture."¹⁵ Although in a study like this I had no opportunity to discuss the wide spectrum of evidence for this pluralism, the growing experimentation and freedom from the letter of the score was clearly in evidence as we progressed through the last 30 years.¹⁶ The added embellishments and cadenzas (cf. E Major Gavotte and Rondeau, Loure, Menuet I and the two Sarabandes); the sheer physicality of some of the fast movements; the abundant expressive gestures everywhere, all signified younger performers' responses to their environment—and I did not even include Stefano Montenari's richly embellished recording issued in 2013. The more literal, evenly balanced "perfect violin performances" of earlier MSP versions similarly reflected an interaction between the expectations of society (especially the profession) and the musicians. Back in the 1970s and 1980s and earlier "modernist" times, even tone, powerful and seamless bowing, and perfect control were the aesthetic ideals. There was only one way of "honouring the composer's

---

14 Lawrence Dreyfus, 'Beyond the Interpretation of Music,' *Dutch Journal of Music Theory*, 12/3 (2007), 253-272 (p. 272).
15 Cook, *Beyond the Score*, p. 401.
16 Think of projects and ensembles like *Officium* (Jan Garbarek with the Hilliard Ensemble), The Red Priest (*Johann I am only dancing*), O'Stravaganza, All'Improviso, Yo Yo Ma's *Inspired by Bach*, Uri Cane's Goldberg Variations (among others), Joe Chindamo's *Reimaginings*, or Matthew Barley's various projects. His website sums up this new generation's attitude: "[Matthew Barley's] musical world is focused on projects that connect people in different ways, blurring the boundaries that never really existed between genres and people." See http://www.matthewbarley.com/wordpress/?page_id=2. Consider also the new courses in classical improvisation convened by pianist David Dolan at the Guildhall School of Music and Drama and reported in, for instance, David Dolan et al., 'The improvisatory approach to classical music performance: An empirical investigation into its characteristics and impact,' *Music Performance Research*, 6 (2013), 1-38. In May 2015 they advertised a masterclass / lecture recital with Robert Levin entitled "Creative Repetition." The abstract informed that the lecture recital is "focusing on how to approach repeats creatively. His performance will include two piano sonatas by Mozart (K. 330 in C major and K. 576 in D major) with improvised repeats as well as improvised interlude between them […]."

score," so everybody at a certain level of professionalism tended to sound much the same.

How performers dedicated to the early music movement have interacted with their environment in the UK during the past few decades is traced, to a certain extent, by Nick Wilson in his 2014 book, *The Art of Re-enchantment*.[17] I eagerly await a cultural historian's or ethnographer's more detailed account and explanation (perhaps in collaboration with a music performance analyst) of the *stylistic* changes in performance that reflect such interactions. Richard Taruskin drew important parallels between modernism and the mainstream style of classical music performance during the middle of the twentieth century.[18] John Butt expanded on this work and showed parallels with postmodernism and other, perhaps more particular and personal matters.[19] I have also discussed these largely theoretical propositions in chapters two and three. My main position, however, is to reiterate the importance of *detail*. The interaction of performance features, the differences between artists, and the complexity of music performance should not be dealt with a cavalier cherry-picking method for the sake of a plausible argument. Nuanced, systematic and comprehensive coverage is needed before broad conclusions can be drawn. And this of course means that my results speak only of performing Bach's solo violin works. We may find different tendencies even in recordings of his Cello Suites, let alone the music of other composers and periods.

The interaction between trends in music performance and the cultural-social environment is complex and non-linear. The pluralism and diversity displayed by the studied recordings, and especially the trend toward greater freedom and individuality, clearly parallel other cultural turns. Nevertheless the link is not necessarily straightforward or veridical. In one of his essays, Fredric Jameson interpreted the "end of art" notion as originally being a left-wing idea as opposed to the "markedly right-wing spirit of the current 'end of history.'"[20] This would imply that the new "loosened

---

17 Nick Wilson, *The Art of Re-enchantment: Making Early Music in the Modern Age* (New York: Oxford University Press, 2013).
18 Taruskin, *Text and Act*, pp. 90-154, 164-172.
19 John Butt, *Playing with History: The Historical Approach to Musical Performance* (Cambridge: Cambridge University Press, 2002). See also John Butt, 'Bach Recordings since 1980: A Mirror of Historical Performance,' in *Bach Perspectives 4*, ed. by David Schulenberg (Lincoln and London: University of Nebraska Press), pp. 181-198, where he discusses the potential of the "anxiety of influence" one generation of musicians might feel vis-à-vis their forebears and teachers.
20 Fredric Jameson, '"End of Art" or "End of History"?,' in *The Cultural Turn: Selected Writings on the Postmodern, 1983-1998* (London: Verso, 2009), 73-92 (p. 76).

HIP" has something to do with this less radical, more conformist-populist attitude. Perhaps it is so in certain cases. But for me it seems more likely that instead of trivialization the HIP performance approach has gained depth through liberation from the tyranny of the "purists" who tried to make it an alternative establishment and money-making machine. It is not at all true that "anything goes," that the tendency is towards facile readings. Pluralism notwithstanding, these recorded performances of Bach's solo violin works still fall within palpable boundaries (Deleuzian "territories" and "multiplicities"). Important criteria include the vitality of performance and the technical command of the violinist. Without one or the other the playing may perfectly parallel cultural trends, might even be a "perfect performance of a musical work" but not at all a "perfect performance."[21]

This leads me to the sixth point about complex systems. Namely that they operate under conditions far from equilibrium. There has to be a constant flow of energy to ensure survival. This energy is supplied primarily by the ever new generations reaching maturity and starting a professional career. Their responses to their teachers and musical "parentage," to refer to Hilary Hahn's formulation cited in chapter three, are complex in themselves. Some feel more comfortable with continuing their tradition, others prefer rebelling against them. The lack of stability is also manifest in the anxiety over how to carve a career; how to find the balance between pleasing competition and audition judges' expectations, yet be innovative and original, arresting and attention-grabbing with your performances. The anxiety of influence also lends energy and instability to the complex of music performance. We have seen how Mullova suffered while trying to play Bach the way she was expected to in the Moscow Conservatory (chapter three). In her 2011 book *From Russia to Love* she talks about living in fear and playing the violin "to get out of the USSR." Once in the West she came to enjoy performing, came to *love* making music, playing Bach's Solos.[22] Volatility, instability, flow of energy from teacher to student, from performer to audience and back are part and parcel of a musician's life and

---

21 Lydia Goehr, 'The Perfect Performance of Music and the Perfect Musical Performance,' *New Formations*, 27 (1996), 1-22.
22 Viktoria Mullova and Eva Maria Chapman, *From Russia to Love: The Life and Times of Viktoria Mullova* (London: Robson Press, 2012). See also interviews with Eric Jeal 'Viktoria Mullova: From Russia in a Blond Wig,' *The Guardian*, Wednesday 17 August 2011, available at http://www.theguardian.com/music/2011/aug/16/viktoria-mullova-russia-interview,' or with Jamie Crick on Classic FM 'Classic FM speaks to Viktoria Mullova,' available at https://www.youtube.com/watch?v=Kf83eztSVtg

evidenced by far too many interviews, reflections and other publications to recount any more here. But given the generally held view—especially from within western classical music's walls—that audiences are aging and the style has lost its contemporary relevance, it is worth noting the number of extremely young faces in the Berlin Philharmonic, for instance, and the mushrooming number of smaller and larger ensembles or the oversubscription by students at prestigious conservatoires.

The energy of renewal and the palpable physical vitality emanating from a symphony orchestra performing Mahler or Beethoven or Stravinsky, or anything else for that matter, speak for themselves. This physical energy becomes particularly perceivable when watching DVDs and digital broadcasts (for instance from the Berlin Philharmonic's Digital Concert Hall). The close-ups of intensely focused faces, moving bodies, eye contacts, breathing, and the physical effort and concentration involved when sounding loud, fast, or deeply expressive passages all add to the impact of performance. Although it is unlikely that anything would go wrong, it is possible to sit on edge and feel one's adrenaline and heart-rate rise as the musicians negotiate being in a state "far from equilibrium."

The seventh point claimed that complex systems have history. Not only do they evolve through time, but their past is co-responsible for their present behaviour. In music performance this manifests quite clearly in debates around historical performance practice and the current state of affairs. Changes in performance style are often brought about by a reaction to the past. The matter-of-fact, literalist style of the 1950s to the 1980s certainly had such an element. I remember our discussions of performers and performances when I was a student at the Franz Liszt Academy of Music in Budapest (Hungary); what and whom we liked and why. Precision, relentless tempi and anti-romantic expression were highly prized—but as a result certain music, especially baroque music, sounded boring or trivial. All this had changed when musicians started playing it with inflections and dancing movement. Alternatively, the success of the historically informed performance movement must be "co-responsible" for the increasing number of recordings demonstrating HIP influence. Among the studied recordings that were made in the new millennium hardly any could be categorized as entirely MSP. Even Julia Fischer's and Sergey Khachatryan's versions displayed aspects of the HIP style.

Tracing the co-responsibility of the past might lead us back to the issue of aging audiences and the die-hard view that performances have become all too uniform. The focus on technical perfection and big sound during the 1960s to 1980s may be held responsible for this prevalent view. The history of the recording industry, its promotion of a star cult that continues to be the norm with established "legacy" concert organizers relying on snobbish audiences may also be responsible for the much more limited opportunities and exposure of many excellent musicians without good agents. The present behaviour of pluralisation, of self-recording, of direct marketing and accessing potential audiences is a reaction to that historical development and a sign of the dynamic energy with which performers embrace new technologies and technologically mediated opportunities. These show the evolving history of music performance. Although making a middle-class living as a young, up-and-coming classical musician is admittedly rather hard under current circumstances,[23] it is not a viable expectation "that classical music should occupy the role it did a hundred years ago, in a far more monolithic culture."[24] Such an attitude is not commensurate with characteristics of complex systems. The history of a complex system evolves and renews; it contributes to and is co-responsible for the present functioning of the system. It is never static. Therefore what we see developing now is yet another sign of performance being a complex, dynamic system. What we see is a transformation and pluralisation that fulfils the "more reasonable expectation" identified by Cook as the expectation "that classical music should be a *successful* niche culture, or set of niche cultures."

The final, eighth point referred to potential clusters in dynamic complex systems; interactions that take the form of clusters of elements which co-operate with each other and also compete with other clusters. An element in the system may belong to more than one clustering. Clusters should not be interpreted in a special sense, or seen as fixed, hermetically sealed entities. They can grow or shrink, be subdivided or absorbed, flourish or decay. We have seen many instantiations of this characteristic. The cluster of bowing and articulation both co-operated and competed

---

23 See, for instance, interview with Monica Huggett by Laurence Vittes, 'From Rock to Bach,' *Strings*, 21/6 (January 2007), 53-57: "Unfortunately, while musicians like Huggett continue to refine and deepen their understanding of Baroque performing practices, the outlook for the commercial side of their musical lives is not so positive. 'In London,' Huggett says, 'It is *shrink* of the Baroque. I don't envy my young colleagues. There are a lot of players still playing concerts who want to live a middle-class life, but it's a real struggle. [Baroque] musicians may be highly intelligent and highly trained, but when it comes to financial reward, they are very little respected.'" (p. 56).

24 Cook, *Beyond the Score*, p. 403.

with the cluster of tempo and dynamics, for instance, while bowing belonged to other clusters as well, forming one with phrasing and tone and another with ornamentation. Actually these clusters (or "multiplicities" and "assemblages" to use Deleuzian language) tended to have more than the named interacting elements, blurring the distinction between clusters. In other words, it was impossible to consider them as "fixed, hermetically sealed entities." They did indeed fluctuate in size and significance at times allowing one specific element to "rule," other times interacting so tightly that it proved impossible to tease them apart.

6.1. Summary

Throughout this book I have developed and evidenced a novel theory of music performance using the analogy of complex dynamical systems. This theory overcomes the problem of contrasting and contradictory explanations that arise from reliance on limited and generalized information. The new theory accommodates (1) the distinction between various overarching trends and individual performing styles; (2) differences in degree not just in kind; and (3) the interactions among various technical and musical elements of performing. It also clarifies the distinctive roles of aurality versus literacy in musical practice and allows for a more comprehensive and subtle explanation of the relationship between performing styles and broader social-cultural-historical trends. The model fosters interdisciplinary approaches and the combination of qualitative and quantitative methods. Moreover, the theory of complexity highlights the fact that each individual may display contrasting traits in diverse repertoires and thus cautions against generalisation. The theory accounts for and unifies all the parts in the puzzle, offering solutions for long standing debates and mutually contradictory stand points. It is complex but complex systems cannot be adequately described by means of a simple theory. The models themselves have to be at least as complex as the systems they model.

Such a conceptualization of music performance is an important contribution to this field of research. Complex dynamical systems are always more than the sum of their parts; they are constituted also by the intricate relationships between their components. By placing emphasis on the interaction of the various expressive and technical elements, the theory draws attention to the limitations of researching particular aspects of performances and maps a new path for empirical and experimental research, and research into creative practice. Such a new path has also been argued for by cognitive scientist Patrik Juslin in his recently proposed theory of musical emotions.[25]

Significantly, the theory enables a valid argument for aesthetic criteria in judging performances. This is especially useful in an age of pluralism and relativism when sceptics critique the assumed "anything goes" and revert to authoritarian, absolutist and normative ideologies. Just as the unpredictability of complex systems may turn into randomness, ad hoc execution in performance may result in mannerisms, stylistic incoherence and a lack of musical flow. The holistic approach fostered by the adoption of the complexity theory helps explain and evaluate the artistic-aesthetic qualities of performances.

6.2. Where to from here? — Epilogue

If music performance is complex, should we just put it in the "too hard" basket and give up studying it? Or should we accept that we can only study aspects of it and perhaps never be able to complete the jigsaw puzzle? Throughout my analysis I referred to contemporary philosophies that offer methods of approaching complex dynamical systems. In particular, I used the analytical concepts developed by Gilles Deleuze and Felix Guattari and Bruno Latour's questioning of science. These concepts and ways of thinking proved plausible for studying and understanding processes that are complex and dynamic.[26]

Deleuze and Guattari's book *A Thousand Plateaus* provides a performed model of what they call the "rhizome," where immediate connections between any of its points are allowed. In essence, as I understand it, they use the insights of dynamical systems theory and extend the notion of self-organizing material systems to other realms. I showed how the resultant de-centred network ("rhizome") may be used as a metaphor for music performance or, rather, as a model for analysing music performance. My cross-referencing to their terms indicated how their description of processes they call territorialization (ordering "hierarchical bodies" in "assemblages"), deterritorialization (breaking of habits), and reterritorialization (formation of habits) can be applied in investigations

---

25 Patrik N. Juslin, 'From Everyday Emotions to Aesthetic Emotions: Towards a Unified Theory of Musical Emotions,' *Physics of Life Review*, 10 (2013), 235-266.
26 Manuel De Landa is one writer who attempted to show in his book, *Intensive Science and Virtual Philosophy* (London: Continuum, 2003) how Deleuze's philosophy may be linked to contemporary "chaos" or "dynamical system's" theory.

of changes in performing styles. They call an "assemblage" an emergent unity that joins together heterogeneous bodies in a "consistency." We can replace the term "heterogeneous bodies" with "performance elements" or "performance features" while "assemblage" could be the emergent style that joins ("territorializes") these elements or features creating overall aesthetic effect ("consistency") and perhaps even affect.

Non-linear thinking in the humanities and social sciences has taken root during the past decade or so, especially through the work of Manuel De Landa[27] and Bruno Latour, on whose ideas I relied upon more. Such approaches have become fashionable in certain musicological circles as well.[28] However, most remain fairly theoretical and abstract. I have not seen these ideas applied consistently in analytical studies of performance. Nick Nesbitt presents a specific argument for the case of using Deleuzian thinking (or rather, Latour's Actor Network Theory that is an analytical tool kit developed from Deleuze and Guattari's concept of the *agencement*) to unpack the processes of jazz improvisation. Still, his paper also lacks a demonstration or modelling of how such an analysis might unfold.[29] Reading such literature can make one feel that plain language would be just as good and would aid comprehension. But of course the fault could be with the reader. In any case, even though I did show the obvious parallels and applicability, I am more inclined to turn to science and empirical evidence to find viable routes and explanations. I found what I was looking for in Iain McGilchrist's volume, *The Master and his Emissary* (Yale University Press, 2009).

The Brain and its Two Worlds

I am no neuroscientist and am familiar with only the smallest fraction of that literature, more out of curiosity than research.[30] McGilchrist's argument is

---

27 Manuel De Landa, *A Thousand Years of Non-linear History* (New York: Swerve Editions, 2000). I thank Ellen Hooper for this reference. See also dozens of articles in *Deleuze Studies*, http://www.euppublishing.com/journal/dls.
28 See for instance *Sounding the Virtual: Gilles Deleuze and the Theory and Philosophy of Music*, ed. by Brian Hulse and Nick Nesbitt (Farnham: Ashgate, 2010). I am grateful to Ellen Hooper for alerting me to some of this literature.
29 Nick Nisbett, 'Critique and Clinique: From Sounding Bodies to the Musical Event,' in *Sounding the Virtual: Gilles Deleuze and the Theory and Philosophy of Music*, pp. 159-180.
30 So I am more familiar with books for "general" audiences than scientific papers. My thinking is informed by, for instance, David Huron, *Sweet Anticipation: Music and the Psychology of Expectation* (Cambridge, Mass: MIT Press, 2007); Daniel Levitin, *This is Your Brain on Music: Understanding a Human Obsession* (London: Atlantic Books, 2006); Antonio Damasio, *The Self Comes to Mind: Constructing the Conscious Brain* (New York:

compelling to me because of the wide range of research and scholarship he refers to from neurology and psychology to anthropology, art history, literature, history, music, and philosophy, as well as their sub disciplines and much else (the notes in the paperback edition run to over 50 pages and at the start of the "Select Bibliography" (p. 518) the reader is referred to a more complete list to be found at http://www.iainmcgilchrist.com/ TMAHE/biblio). Still, I am aware that his near 500 pages (in small print) long volume was first published in 2009. Six years is a long period in the rapidly developing field of brain science. So I perhaps trust my intuition and prejudices here, but I am comforted by the many overtly enthusiastic reviews the book received from all corners (including neurology, neuroscience, neurobiology, behavioural neurology and neuropsychiatry) when it appeared.[31] Ultimately I simply find the distinctions he draws useful for explaining the difficulties and short-comings of performance research and to emphasize the importance of aurality and bodily understanding. For me the distinctions also provide biological support for philosophies that promote a non-linear and experiential way of being, thinking and knowing.

The Master and his Emissary is a book about laterality; about the processes and functions of the left and right brain hemispheres. However, McGilchrist is at pains to stress, if not on every page then almost as frequently as that: "we now know that every type of function— including reason, emotion, language and imagery—is subserved not by one hemisphere alone, but by both."[32] Essentially the book argues that what matters most is a consideration of *how* the hemispheres use the "skills" they possess; how each contributes to the various functions the brain fulfils. Overall the book explores the characteristics and consequences of an over-reliance on analytical, abstract thinking. I see this over-reliance to be particularly detrimental, misleading, and limiting when applied to music performance studies.

To put simply, the left hemisphere tends to be logical, inward-looking, self-referential, working with what it already knows, good at focused attention, categorizing and abstraction; "analysis by parts, rather than as

---

Vintage, 2012); Oliver Sacks, *Musicophilia: Tales of Music and the Brain* (New York: Alfred Knopf, 2007); *The Psychology of Music*, ed. by Diana Deutsch, 2nd edn (San Diego: Academia Press, 1999), among others.

31 The positive responses are available at http://www.iainmcgilchrist.com/comments. asp#content. A critical view that is explored and replicated here is available at http://www.iainmcgilchrist.com/exchange_of_views.asp#content

32 Cited from the book's abstract on McGilchrist's website: available at http://www.iainmcgilchrist.com/brief_description.asp#content

a whole."³³ In contrast, the right hemisphere tends to be holistic, is good at detecting anomalies, has an "open" attention, looks outside of itself, feels to "be a part of something much bigger," is concerned with "everything that goes on in [its] purview."³⁴ This, McGilchrist points out, "requires less of a wilfully directed, narrowly focused attention, and more of an open, receptive, widely diffused alertness to whatever exists, with allegiances outside of the self."³⁵

Melodic contours and unexpected harmonic events are processed primarily in the right hemisphere, which is also the dominant hemisphere for emotions.³⁶ Empathy, our ability to relate to others, to see their perspective and be attuned to their feelings depends primarily on the function of the right hemisphere. Music encourages empathy, even entrainment. Some argue that "mental representation of music may occur simultaneously in different areas" and it is true that "musical training shifts some music processing from the right hemisphere to the left."³⁷ But the separation is not clearly delineated and perhaps it is *not* in our best interest to encourage a take-over by the left-hemisphere. Rather, the evidence of my analytical discussions and the parallels drawn with oral cultures compel to approach musical training and performance more holistically; to engage the right hemisphere for a more complex and complete understanding as well as creative renewal.³⁸

McGilchrist draws upon study after study to illustrate and evidence the differences between left and right hemisphere processes. He covers an impressively wide spectrum of sources—both in terms of time and disciplines—that lend overall weight and *philosophical* credibility to the argument. Together these provide an explanation why it is so difficult to

---

33 McGilchrist, *The Master and his Emissary*, p. 24.
34 Ibid., p. 25.
35 Ibid.
36 Anne Dhu McLucas, *The Musical Ear: Oral Tradition in the USA* [SEMPRE Studies in The Psychology of Music] (Farnham: Ashgate, 2011), p. 120.
37 Ibid.
38 Perhaps it is no coincidence that the less analytical, more existentially orientated Continental philosophers' work seems to have greater potential to assist explaining the phenomenological experience of musical performance. I mostly adopted Deleuze's ideas, but see also Husserl and Merleau-Ponty, among others I drew upon in chapter one: Edmund Husserl, *The Idea of Phenomenology* (The Hague: Martinus Hijhoff, 1964); Maurice Merleau-Ponty, *Phenomenology of Perception* (London: Routledge and Kegan Paul, 1962). In his wonderful study *Reason and Resonance: A History of Modern Aurality* (New York: Zone Books, 2010), Veit Erlmann also shows a long tradition of Continental writers and thinkers who have considered hearing as important as seeing, if not more so.

study creativity and artistic practices; why it is easy to feel disappointed upon reading scientific examinations that impress as simplistic and beside the point regardless of their increasingly sophisticated experimental apparatus and measuring techniques. By dissecting and analysing the parts (something the left hemisphere is good at and what empiricism and sciences set out to do since the Enlightenment) we lose the whole—which is what we would like to understand and for which we would need to rely more on our right hemisphere's capacity. As I pointed out in chapter five, "complexity does not accumulate, it proliferates."[39] The elements of complex systems "have no representative meaning by themselves but only in terms of patterns of relationships with other elements."[40] Self-referential, categorizing cognition is not well positioned to help us understand such dynamisms; meaning is created globally and needs to be understood that way.

Early on in the book McGilchrist refers to a study by Goldberg and Costa from 1981 to start explaining the main differences between *how* the hemispheres work.[41] He notes that we use the word "know" in at least two different ways which languages other than English often express with different words. One sense in which we use the word "know" is for what the German calls "kennen," that refers to experiential knowledge, an encounter, an understanding of what is known.[42] The other sense in which the word "know" is used refers to factual knowledge or "wissen" in German. This kind of knowledge is constructed by "putting things together from bits." He writes (p. 95):

> [Factual knowledge] is not usually well applied to knowing people. [...] 'born on 16 September 1964,' 'lives in New York,' '5ft 4 in tall,' 'red hair,' 'freckles,' and so on. Immediately you get the sense of somebody—who you *don't* actually know. [...] What's more, it sounds as though you're describing an inanimate object—'chest of drawers, two single over three double, bun feet, circa 1870, 30 x 22 x 28in'—or a corpse.

---

39 Richard Toop, 'Against a Theory of Music (New) Complexity,' in *Contemporary Music: Theoretical and Philosophical Perspectives*, ed. by Max Paddison and Irène Deliège (Aldershot: Ashgate, 2010), pp. 89-98 (p. 91).
40 Bruno Latour, *Pandora's Hope: Essays on the Reality of Science Studies* (Cambridge, Mass.: Harvard University Press, 1999), p. 11.
41 Elkhonon Goldberg and Louis D. Costa, 'Hemispheric Differences in the Acquisition and use of Descriptive Systems,' *Brain and Language*, 14/1 (1981), 144-173.
42 McGilchrist, *The Master and his Emissary*, pp. 94-97.

This type of knowledge is valued by science because its findings are repeatable, disengaged from the subjective, general, impersonal, fixed. It is the kind of knowledge that the left hemisphere is good at generating. However, such knowledge "doesn't give a good idea of the whole, just of partial reconstruction of aspects of the whole." For a holistic, experiential knowledge we rely on the right hemisphere.

So far so good, but why is this relevant for studying music performance? Because, as McGilchrist points out, music apparently "requires us to know it in the sense of *kennen* rather than *wissen*." I will cite him at length here to make the argument clear:

> To approach music is like entering into relation with another living individual, and research suggests that understanding music is perceived as similar to knowing a person; we freely attribute human qualities to music, including age, sex, personality characteristic and feelings. The empathic nature of the experience means that it has more in common with encountering a person than a concept or an idea that could be expressed in words. It is important to recognise that music does not *symbolise* emotional meaning, which would require that it be interpreted; it *metaphorises* it—'carries it over' direct to our unconscious minds. Equally it does not symbolise human qualities: it conveys them direct, so that it acts on us, and we respond to it, as in a human encounter. In other words, knowing a piece of music, like knowing other works of art, is a matter of *kennenlernen*. Coming to us through the right hemisphere, such living creations are seen as being essentially human in nature. In an earlier book I argued that works of art—music, poems, painting, great buildings—can be understood only if we appreciate that they are more like people than texts, concepts or things. But the perception is ancient: Aristotle, for example, compared tragedy to an organic being (p. 96).

Whether these different ways of knowing relate to the hemispheres of the brain or some other neuro-biological mechanisms, is not for me to say. Music is processed in the brain in multiple and parallel ways. Nevertheless I certainly agree with the conclusions, and especially with regards to complex dynamic systems, that "To know (in the sense of *kennen*) something is never fully to know it (in the sense of *wissen*) at all, since it will remain for ever changing, evolving, revealing further aspects of itself." On the other hand, "To know (in the sense of *wissen*) is to pin down so that it is repeatable and repeated, so that it becomes familiar in the other sense: routine, inauthentic, lacking the spark of life." (Ibid.).

It seems a crucial loss when, due to analytical pinning down, due to writing rather than listening and observing or participating, "[k]nowledge of the whole is all too soon followed by knowledge of the parts" only.⁴³ Scholarship of creativity, of improvisation or of artistic processes dissects the whole. While it might get closer to knowing the elements at work, it gets further away from understanding the phenomenon. If we insist that musicians and artists become researchers rather than deepen their experiential "kennen"; if we insist that musicians develop "left-brain capacities" such as abstraction, rational thinking, linearity, and logic, we will miss out on the capacity of music and the aural domain to "activate other parts of the brain (mostly in the right hemisphere [...]) [and to] bring into play new kinds of ideas."⁴⁴ By encouraging musicians to become researchers, by limiting discussions of performance to empirically-experimentally measurable or verifiable "facts," we distance ourselves further both from the object of study as well as the creative practice itself. It is crucial to integrate the two ways of knowing and to celebrate both instead of prioritizing analytical-abstract knowledge in written up peer-reviewed publications. As Veit Erlmann has argued,

> The error of modern epistemology is that, eager to declare [...] a distanced stance as the sine qua non of reason, it excluded [...] formations of complementarity as too complex to be known and named. And because complex formations exist only as capacity, "as a black memory, a middle between presence and absence, forgetting and memory," they are ill suited for founding the subject in modernity's either-or logic.⁴⁵

To be sure, I am not advocating for sloppiness or personal "confessionals"; not at all. I believe in the rational project and am curious and keen to understand what I think I know, but I want it all, "and / as well as", *not* "either / or". If we keep it constantly in mind that music performance is like a complex dynamic system we will have a lesser chance of falling back on just dissecting; of losing sight of the whole or of becoming prescriptive and normative in our conclusions. Just like musicians who "never leave a piece of music alone" but "are always tangling with it, wrestling with it, [are] seduced by it," the analyst of music performance must also always toy with and be completely "entangled" by her object of study.⁴⁶

---

43   Ibid., p. 97
44   McLucas, *The Musical Ear*, p. 158.
45   Erlmann, *Reason and Resonance*, p. 314. The internal quote is from Michel Serres, *The Troubadour of Knowledge* (Ann Arbor: University of Michigan Press, 1997), pp. 20-21.
46   Laurence Dreyfus, 'Beyond the Interpretation of Music,' *Dutch Journal of Music Theory*, 12/3 (2007), 253-272 (p. 272).

In chapter two (at notes 110 and 113) I cited Bruno Latour to underline the "limiting and inhibiting effect of becoming too explicitly aware of the process"[47] and the sense of wonder one feels when achieving something semi-consciously. I also suggested we need to gain a better understanding of how knowledge is gained, understood, and transmitted in oral cultures, as the locus of music performance is in the aural realm (also shown above when discussing the fourth and fifth points of complex dynamics systems). The "written word tends inevitably towards [...] [a] specialised and compartmentalised world,"[48] and before long the holistic perception of listening could also be endangered: "the more the eye and ear are capable of thought, the more they reach that boundary line where they become asensual. *Joy is transferred to the brain; the sense organs themselves become dull and weak.* More and more, the symbolic replaces that which exists."[49]

This of course resonates with Deleuze's philosophy. Another such instance is when McGilchrist notes that "Language enables the left hemisphere to represent the world 'off line,' a conceptual version, distinct from the world of experience." Language individuates. Music reinforces empathy and helps maintain a commune, being attuned to the whole, the domain of the right hemisphere. Importantly McGilchrist also notes:

> Isolating things artificially from their context brings the advantage of enabling us to focus intently on a particular aspect of reality and how it can be modelled, so that it can be grasped and controlled.
>
> But its losses are in the picture as a whole. Whatever lies in the realm of the implicit, or depends on flexibility, whatever can't be brought into focus and fixed, ceases to exist as far as the speaking hemisphere is concerned.[50]

---

47 McGilchrist, *The Master and his Emissary*, p. 107.
48 Ibid., p. 105.
49 *The Complete Works of Friedrich Nietzsche 3: Human All too Human I* [1878]. Translated with Afterword by Gary Handwerk (Stanford: Stanford University Press, 1995), §217, p. 145 (emphasis added). Another translation reads: "The more capable of thought eye and ear become, the closer they approach the point at which they become asensual: pleasure is transferred to the brain, the sense-organs themselves grow blunt and feeble, the symbolical increasingly replaces the simple being." *Cambridge Texts in the History of Philosophy: Nietzsche*. Trans. by R. J. Hollingday (Cambridge: Cambridge University Press, 1996), p. 100. A third translation gives p. 115: "The more capable of thought that eye and ear become, the more they approach the limit where they become senseless, the seat of pleasure is moved into the brain, the organs of the senses themselves become dulled and weak, the symbolical takes more and more the place of the actual." *Dover Philosophical Classics*, ed. and trans. by Oscar Levy (New York: Dover Publications, 2006 [London and Edinburgh: T. N. Foulis, 1909-1913]).
50 McGilchrist, *The Master and his Emissary*, p. 115.

McGilchrist then asserts the importance of metaphor, which he claims to be "a function of the right hemisphere, and [to be] rooted in the body." It is important because "Metaphoric thinking [...] is the *only* way in which understanding can reach outside the system of sign to life itself. It is what links language to life."[51] Metaphoric language bridges us to the experiential world because "words are used so as to activate a broad net of connotations, which though present to us, remains implicit, so that the meanings are appreciated as a whole, at once, to the whole of our being [...] rather than being subject to the isolating effects of sequential, narrow-beam attention."[52]

Inevitably, there is much discussion of music in McGilchrist book. Although many of the points he makes are familiar to students of music, he tends to shed new light on them or draws novel conclusions that seem useful when considering an emergent musicology of performance. For instance, on p. 121 he states that "skills are embodied, and therefore largely intuitive: they resist the process of explicit rule following. [...] a skill cannot be formulated in words or rules, but can be learnt only by watching and following with one's eyes, one's hands and ultimately one's whole being: the expert himself is unaware of how he achieves what he does." This explains why music, especially the playing of an instrument has to be taught through the "apprenticeship model" and why Conservatoires need to remain practical institutions with plenty of time for experimentation and experiential learning that is best fostered by one-on-one tuition and lots of doing and modelling. It also explains why practitioners may not be the best auto-ethnographers writing practice-led or practice-based / practice-informed research (recall Latour cited in chapter two, fn. 110). Once we move out of the zone of demonstration and talking in metaphors (as is most often the case during lessons and rehearsals), and adopt a scientific language, we have lost the whole and have only (some of) the (not necessarily most important) constituent parts.

Being immersed in the experiential world is second nature to musicians and all the difficulties about studying this world, the difficulties I have been trying to highlight here, had long been summed up in the saying that "writing about music is like dancing about architecture." So I might ask again, should we just put it in the "too hard" basket, go home and continue experiencing it through playing, composing, improvising, listening? I

---

51   Ibid.
52   Ibid., p. 116.

certainly would not advocate for that! What I do advocate for is a more balanced, humble, and open-ended approach, or indeed a more "right hemisphere" approach: the right to do things (research, that is) differently, to partly remain in "oral culture mode," to use metaphor, to "proclaim a loyalty to the playful and emotive elements,"[53] to engage with aesthetics not as attitude but as capacity of sensing, to not shy away from describing subjective experiences, to present performances *as performance*, as *play*.

---

53 Dreyfus, 'Beyond the Interpretation of Music,' 272.

List of Audio Examples

4.1 Literal versus ornamental delivery of small rhythmic values in J. S. Bach, G minor Sonata BWV 1001, Adagio, extract: bars 1-2. Six versions: Monica Huggett © Virgin Veritas, Oscar Shumsky © Musical Heritage Society, Shlomo Mintz © Deutsche Grammophone, Julia Fischer © PentaTone Classics, Sergey Khachatryan © Naïve, Alina Ibragimova © Hyperion. Duration: 2.08.   151

4.2 Ornamentation in J. S. Bach, A minor Sonata BWV 1003, Andante, extract: repeat of bars 1-11. Two versions: Sergiu Luca © Nonesuch, Ilya Gringolts © Deutsche Grammophon. Duration: 1.07.   155

4.3 Ornamentation in J. S. Bach, E Major Partita BWV 1006, Loure, extract: repeat of bars 5-20. Ilya Gringolts © Deutsche Grammophon [edited sound file, first time play of bars 12-20 eliminated to show only the repeats]. Duration: 0.58.   157

4.4 Ornamentation in J. S. Bach, B minor Partita BWV1002, Sarabande, extract: repeat of bars 9-16. Five versions: Viktoria Mullova 1987 © Philips, 1992 © Philips, 2008 © Onyx, Ilya Gringolts © Deutsche Grammophon, Sergiu Luca © Nonesuch. Duration: 2.31.   158

4.5 Ornamentation and lilted rhythm in J. S. Bach, E Major Partita BWV1006, Menuet I, four extracts: bars 1-8. Jaap Schröder © NAXOS; bars 1-8 with repeat. Rachel Podger © Channel Classics; bars 1-8. Lara St John © Ancalagon; embellished repeats from Menuet I and its Da Capo. Isabelle Faust © Harmonia Mundi [edited sound file to show repeats only]. Duration: 2.31.   162

4.6 Ornamentation in J. S. Bach, D minor Partita BWV 1004, Sarabanda, six extracts: repeat of bars 1-8. Two versions: Pavlo Beznosiuk © Linn Records, Isabelle Faust © Harmonia Mundi; repeat of bars 16-21. Two versions: Isabelle Faust, Pavlo Beznosiuk; repeat of bars 4-21. Rachel Barton Pine 2004 © Cedille [edited to show only repeats]; repeat of bars 1-8 and 25-29. Monica Huggett © Virgin Veritas. Duration: 5.05.   163

4.7 Ornamentation in J. S. Bach, E Major Partita BWV 1006, Loure, 165
extract: repeat of bars 1-3. Seven versions: Ilya Gringolts © Deutsche
Grammophon, Isabelle Faust © Harmonia Mundi, Viktoria Mullova
2008 © Onyx, Lucy van Dael © NAXOS, Elizabeth Wallfisch ©
Hyperion, Sergiu Luca © Nonesuch, and Richard Tognetti © ABC
Classics. Duration: 1.53.

4.8 Interpretations of the notation at the end of J. S. Bach, A minor 168
Sonata BWV 1003, Grave, extract: bars 22-23. Eight versions: James
Ehnes (© Analekta Fleurs de lys) trilling both notes in both dyads;
James Buswell (© Centaur) trilling the top notes of the dyads; Miklós
Szenthelyi (© Hungarton) strongly vibrating the first dyad and then
trilling the top note; Lara St John (© Ancalagon) trilling the top note
and then both notes; Pavlo Beznosiuk (© Linn Records) producing a
trillo (bow-vibrato) on the first dyad followed by a trill on the second;
Brian Brooks (© Arts Music) performing a less obvious bow vibrato;
Benjamin Schmid (© Arte Nova) playing a crescendo with increasing
vibrato leading to trill on second dyad followed by decrescendo; Alina
Ibragimova (© Hyperion) playing without vibrato, creating a small
mezza-di-voce on the first dyad then a trill with diminuendo on the
second. Duration: 2.43.

4.9 Dotting and accenting in J. S. Bach, D minor Partita BWV 1004, 176
Corrente, extract: bars 1-6. Three versions. Sergiu Luca © Nonesuch,
Ingrid Matthews © Centaur, Julia Fischer © PentaTone Classics.
Duration: 0.30.

4.10 Articulation and perceived dotting in J. S. Bach, B minor Partita BWV 178
1002, Allemanda, extract: bars 1-3. Two versions. Gidon Kremer 1980
© Philips, 2005 © ECM. Duration: 0.26.

4.11 Articulation and perceived dotting in J. S. Bach, B minor Partita BWV 179
1002, Allemanda, extract: bars 1-3. Three versions. Viktoria Mullova
1987 © Philips, 1992 © Philips, 2008 © Onyx. Duration: 0.42.

4.12 Tempo, articulation and musical character in J. S. Bach, E Major Partita 180
BWV 1006, Loure, extract: bars 1-8. Four versions: Hillary Hahn ©
Sony, Miklós Szenthelyi © Hungaroton, John Holloway © ECM, Alina
Ibragimova © Hyperion; repeats of bars 1-8: Jaap Schröder © Naxos.
Duration: 3.13.

4.13 Sturdy style of evenly emphasized beats in J. S. Bach, E Major Partita 182
BWV 1006, Menuet I, extract: bars 1-8. Rudolf Gähler (curved "Bach-
bow") © Arte Nova Classics. Duration: 0.13.

4.14 Different bowings within HIP style in J. S. Bach, G minor Sonata BWV 185
1001, Fuga, extract: bars 1-6. Six versions: Sigiswald Kuijken 1983 ©
Deutsche Harmonia Mundi, Rachel Podger © Channel Classics, Elizabeth
Wallfisch © Hyperion, John Holloway © ECM, Pavlo Beznosiuk © Linn
Records, Monica Huggett © Virgin Veritas. Duration: 2.11.

4.15 Different interpretations in J. S. Bach, G minor Sonata BWV 1001, Fuga 188
extract: bars 35-42. Seven versions: Ingrid Matthews © Centaur, Rachel
Podger © Channel Classics, Jaap Schröder © NAXOS, Sergiu Luca ©
Nonesuch, Elizabeth Wallfisch © Hyperion, Sigiswald Kuijken 1983 ©
Deutsche Harmonia Mundi, John Holloway © ECM. Duration: 3.09.

4.16 Performance of multiple stops in J. S. Bach, G minor Sonata BWV 1001, 191
Adagio, extract: bar 1, chord 1. Four versions: James Ehnes © Analekta
Fleurs de lys, Ruggiero Ricci © One-Eleven, Ingrid Matthews ©
Centaur, John Holloway © ECM. Duration: 0.18.

4.17 Increasingly lighter bowing, less legato articulation and stronger 192
pulse in J. S. Bach, B minor Partita BWV 1002, Sarabande, extract: bars
9-17. Eleven versions: Ruggiero Ricci © One-Eleven, James Ehnes ©
Analekta Fleurs de lys, Sergey Khachatryan © Naïve, Gerard Poulet
© Arion, Julia Fischer © PentaTone Classics, Benjamin Schmid © Arte
Nova, Richard Tognetti ©ABC Classics, John Holloway © ECM, Lara
St John © Ancalagon, Ingrid Matthews © Centaur, Elizabeth Wallfisch
© Hyperion. Duration: 5.46.

4.18 Articulated / "rhetorical" versus legato / "romantic" style in J. S. Bach, 195
C Major Sonata BWV 1005, Largo, extract: bars 3-8. Five versions:
Elizabeth Wallfisch © Hyperion, Monica Huggett © Virgin Veritas,
Thomas Zehetmair © Teldec, Gerard Poulet © Arion, Oscar Shumsky
© Musical Heritage Society. Duration: 4.14.

5.1 Phrasing in J. S. Bach, E Major Partita BWV 1006, Loure, extract: bars 205
12-20. Three versions: Christian Tetzlaff 1994 © Virgin Veritas, Thomas
Zehetmair © Teldec, James Ehnes © Analekta Fleurs de lys. Duration:
2.16.

5.2 Comparison of HIP performances in J. S. Bach, E Major Partita BWV 207
1006, Loure, extracts: bars 19-22. Two versions: Elizabeth Wallfisch
© Hyperion, Rachel Podger © Channel Classics; bars 17-22. Monica
Huggett © Virgin Veritas; repeat of bars 12-24. Sergiu Luca ©
Nonesuch. Duration: 2.15.

5.3 Articulation in J. S. Bach, E Major Partita BWV 1006, Gavotte en 209
Rondeau, extract: bars 9-36. Elizabeth Wallfisch © Hyperion. Duration:
0.50.

5.4 Timing and tempo fluctuations going across bars in J. S. Bach, E Major   210
     Partita BWV 1006, Gavotte en Rondeau, extract: bars 9-16. Monica
     Huggett © Virgin Veritas. Duration: 0.15

5.5 Articulation and timing in J. S. Bach, E Major Partita BWV 1006,   210
     Gavotte en Rondeau, extract: bars 24-40. Monica Huggett © Virgin
     Veritas. Duration: 0.30.

5.6 Embellished rondo theme and comparison of MSP styles in J. S. Bach,   211
     E Major Partita BWV 1006, Gavotte en Rondeau, extracts: bars 40-
     72. Ilya Gringolts © Deutsche Grammophon; bars 48-64. Lara Lev ©
     Finlandia Records. Duration: 1.09.

5.7 Similarities between subsequent recordings of J. S. Bach, E Major   213
     Partita BWV 1006, Menuet II, extracts: bars 1-16. Gidon Kremer 1980 ©
     Philips; bars 1-16 and repeat of bars 1-4. Gidon Kremer 2005 © ECM.
     Duration: 0.52.

5.8 Contrasting interpretative strategies in J. S. Bach, E Major Partita   215
     BWV 1006, Menuet II, extract: bars 5-9. Two versions: Ilya Gringolts
     © Deutsche Grammophon (highlights metric units); Monica Huggett
     © Virgin Veritas (highlights melodic-harmonic goals). Duration: 0.16.

5.9 Contrasting interpretative strategies in J. S. Bach, E Major Partita BWV   216
     1006, Menuet II, extract: bars 21-25. Two versions: Ilya Gringolts ©
     Deutsche Grammophon (highlights metric units); Monica Huggett ©
     Virgin Veritas (highlights melodic-harmonic goals). Duration: 0.14.

5.10 Comparison of subsequent recordings by same violinist in J. S. Bach,   220
     A minor Sonata BWV 1003, Grave, extracts: bars 5-9. Two versions:
     Gidon Kremer 1980 © Philips, 2005 © ECM; bars 19-21. Two versions:
     Gidon Kremer 1980, 2005. Duration: 3.22.

5.11 Comparison of subsequent recordings by same violinist in J. S. Bach,   222
     A minor Sonata BWV 1003, Grave, extracts: bars 5-12. Rachel Barton
     Pine 1999 © Chicago WFMT 98.7; bars 9-12. Rachel Barton Pine 2007
     © The Artist; bars 19-23. Two versions: Rachel Barton Pine 1999, 2007.
     Duration: 3.25.

5.12 Comparison of subsequent recordings by same violinist in J. S. Bach,   226
     A minor Sonata BWV 1003, Fuga, extract: bars 240-289. Two versions:
     Christian Tetzlaff 1994 © Virgin Veritas, 2005 © Virgin Classics.
     Duration: 2.46.

5.13 Comparison of subsequent recordings by same violinist in J. S. Bach, B   228
     minor Partita BWV 1002, Allemanda, extract: bars 15-19. Two versions:
     Christian Tetzlaff 1994 © Virgin Veritas, 2005 © Virgin Classics.
     Duration: 0.51.

List of Audio Examples 301

5.14 Comparison of subsequent recordings by same violinist in J. S. Bach, A minor Sonata BWV 1003, Andante, extract: bars 15-19. Two versions: Christian Tetzlaff 1994 © Virgin Veritas, 2005 © Virgin Classics. Duration: 0.43. — 229

5.15 Comparison of subsequent recordings by same violinist in J. S. Bach, B minor Partita BWV 1002, Tempo di Borea, extract: repeat of bars 39-50. Three versions: Viktoria Mullova 1987 © Philips, 1992 © Philips, 2008 © Onyx. Duration: 0.57. — 232

5.16 Comparison of subsequent recordings by same violinist in J. S. Bach, D minor Partita BWV 1004, Giga, extracts: bars 1-5. Two versions: Rachel Barton Pine 1999 © Chicago WFMT 98.7, 2004 © Cedille; bars 1-11. Rachel Barton Pine 2007 © The Artist. Duration: 1.03. — 235

5.17 Comparison of subsequent recordings by same violinist in J. S. Bach, D minor Partita BWV 1004, Giga, extract: bars 1-10. Two versions: Sigiswald Kuijken 1983 © Deutsche Harmonia Mundi, 2001 © Deutsche Harmonia Mundi. Duration: 1.02. — 235

5.18 Comparison of subsequent recordings by same violinist in J. S. Bach, D minor Partita BWV 1004, Giga, extract: bars 1-12. Two versions: Christian Tetzlaff 1994 © Virgin Veritas, 2005 © Virgin Classics. Duration: 1.05. — 236

5.19 Comparison of subsequent recordings by same violinist in J. S. Bach, D minor Partita BWV 1004, Giga, extract: bars 12-20. Two versions: Gidon Kremer 1980 © Philips, 2005 © ECM. Duration: 0.52. — 237

5.20 Comparison of subsequent recordings by same violinist in J. S. Bach, D minor Partita BWV 1004, Giga, extract: bars 6-16. Two versions: Viktoria Mullova 1993 © Philips, 2008 © Onyx. Duration: 1.10. — 237

5.21 Comparison of subsequent recordings by same violinist in J. S. Bach, A minor Sonata BWV 1003, Grave, extract: bars 1-8. Two versions: Sigiswald Kuijken 1983 © Deutsche Harmonia Mundi, 2001 © Deutsche Harmonia Mundi. Duration: 2.27. — 239

5.22 Phrasing in J. S. Bach, G minor Sonata BWV 1001, Adagio, extract: bars 1-8. Gidon Kremer 2005 © ECM. Duration: 1.27 — 244

5.23 Phrasing in J. S. Bach, G minor Sonata BWV 1001, Adagio, extract: bars 1-8. Itzhak Perlman. © EMI Classics. Duration: 1.37 — 245

5.24 Phrasing in J. S. Bach, G minor Sonata BWV 1001, Adagio, extract: bars 1-8. Thomas Zehetmair © Teldec. Duration: 1.10 — 249

5.25 Phrasing in J. S. Bach, G minor Sonata BWV 1001, Adagio, extract: bars 9-14. Thomas Zehetmair © Teldec. Duration: 0.39 — 250

5.26 Phrasing in J. S. Bach, G minor Sonata BWV 1001, Adagio, extract: bars   254
      4-8, 13-15. Monica Huggett © Virgin Veritas. Duration: 1.24

5.27 Virtuosic style in J. S. Bach, E Major Partita BWV 1006, Preludio,   254
      extract: bars 1-33. Lara St John © Ancalagon. Duration: 0.38

5.28 Expressive versus virtuosic "moto perpetuo" style in J. S. Bach, E   257
      Major Partita BWV 1006, Preludio, extracts: bars 1-17. Jaap Schröder ©
      NAXOS; bars 29-63. Rachel Podger © Channel Classics; bars 101-138.
      Lucy van Dael © NAXOS. Duration: 2.44.

5.29 Expressive versus virtuosic "moto perpetuo" style in J. S. Bach, E Major   265
      Partita BWV 1006, Preludio, extract: bars 1-12. Four versions: Ingrid
      Matthews © Centaur, Monica Huggett © Virgin Veritas, Sigiswald
      Kuijken 2001 © Deutsche Harmonia Mundi, Elizabeth Wallfisch ©
      Hyperion. Duration: 1.20.

5.30 Expressive versus virtuosic "moto perpetuo" style in J. S. Bach, E Major   267
      Partita BWV 1006, Preludio, extract: bars 29-62. Four versions: Ingrid
      Matthews © Centaur, Monica Huggett © Virgin Veritas, Sigiswald
      Kuijken 2001 © Deutsche Harmonia Mundi, Elizabeth Wallfisch ©
      Hyperion. Duration: 3.53.

List of Tables

1.1	Studied Recordings Listed by Chronology of Violinists' Year of Birth.	19
3.1	Definition of Stylistic Features as Listed in Column Headings in Table 3.3.	110
3.2	Movement by Movement Tendency of Selected Violinists' Interpretative Styles.	112
3.3	Average scores of subjectively rated HIP and MSP performance features in forty selected recordings.	114
4.1	Summary of Tempo Trends 1977-2010.	132
4.2	Average MSP and HIP Tempos across All Studied Recordings Made since 1903 (Joachim).	132
4.3	Average Tempos in Recordings Made Pre and Post 1978 (before or after Luca).	134
4.4	Vibrato Rate, Width (depth) and Frequency of Use.	141
4.5	Most Embellished Movements Listed in Order of Amount of Ornamentation.	154
4.6	Summary of Solutions in the Penultimate Bars of the A minor Grave.	168
4.7	Average Dotting Ratios in the D minor Corrente, C Major Adagio, and B minor Allemanda.	174
4.8	Summary of *Basic* Difference in Executing Bars 35-41 of the G minor Fuga.	187
4.9	Summary of Modifications in the B minor Sarabande.	191
5.1	E Major Gavotte en Rondeau, A Generalized Summary of Performance Characteristics.	208
5.2	Violinists who made more than one recording of the Solos between 1977 and 2010.	217

5.3 Standard Deviations of Zehetmair's tempo choices in the E Major Partita.   248

5.4 Standard Deviations of Monica Huggett's tempo choices in Sonata movements.   252

5.5 Standard Deviations of Monica Huggett's tempo choices in Partita movements.   252

5.6 Structural Subdivisions of the E Major Preludio according to Dario Sarlo.   255

5.7 E Major Preludio—Summary of Aural Analysis of selected recordings according to the 8 sections identified by Sarlo.   260

List of Figures

2.1	Hellaby's *Interpretative tower*	45
3.1	Collated subjective scores of albums showing overall MSP and HIP points expressed as percentages	113
4.1	Spectrograms of bars 5-6 of the D minor Sarabanda	139
4.2	G minor Adagio, Bars 1-2 [Score]	150
4.3	A minor Andante, Bars 12-24. Transcription of melodic embellishments in Gringolts' performance during repeat	156
4.4a	B minor Sarabande. Transcription of embellishments in Gringolts' performance of the repeats	159
4.4b	B minor Sarabande. Transcription of embellishments in Mullova's 2008 performance of the repeats	160
4.4c	B minor Sarabande. Transcription of embellishments in Luca's performance of the repeats	161
4.5	E Major Gavotte en Rondeau. Theme and its major variants in five recordings	164
4.6	E Major Loure. Transcription of seven different ornamentations during the repeat of bars 1-3	165
4.7	A minor Grave. Facsimile of final bars	166
4.8	B minor Allemanda bars 1-3. Spectrograms of Gidon Kremer's two recorded performances	178
4.9	B minor Allemanda bars 1-3. Spectrograms of Viktoria Mullova's three recorded performances	179
4.10	E Major Loure bars 4-7 [Score]	181
4.11	G minor Fuga bars 35-41. Bach's original scoring and performed interpretations	188

4.12 C Major Largo bars 3-8. Comparison of tempo and power (dynamics) in five performances — 196

5.1 E Major Menuet II bars 1-15. Summary of tempo contrast in Kremer's two performances — 214

5.2 E Major Menuet II bars 5-9. Comparison of beat-level timing data in Gringolts' and Huggett's recording — 215

5.3 E Major Menuet II bars 21-25. Comparison of beat-level timing data in Gringolts' and Huggett's recording — 216

5.4 Dynamic profiles of Kremer's two recordings of the A minor Fuga — 219

5.5 Beat-durations and dynamics in Kuijken's two recordings of the A minor Grave, bars 5-8 — 239

5.6 Comparison of phrase durations in Kuijken's two recordings of the A minor Grave — 241

5.7 G minor Adagio, bars 1-12 [Score] — 243

5.8a E Major Preludio bars 1-12. Bar-level tempo fluctuation in four recordings — 264

5.8b E Major Preludio bars 1-12. Beat durations in 4 recordings — 265

5.9a E Major Preludio bars 28-63. Bar-level tempo fluctuation in 4 recordings — 266

5.9b E Major Preludio bars 29-63. Beat durations in 4 recordings — 266

Discography of Recordings Studied[1]

Bach, Johann Sebastian: Sonatas and Partitas for Unaccompanied Violin

Barton Pine, Rachel (1999). Complete set. Concert – WFMT 98.7 FM Broadcast, Chicago [recording sourced from the artist].

Barton Pine, Rachel (2004). Baroque bow. G minor Sonata, D minor Partita. Cedille 90000 078.

Barton Pine, Rachel (2007). Baroque bow. Complete set. Concert, Montreal Chamber Music Festival: 'The majesty of Bach: The complete six Sonatas and Partitas', May 12, 2007 [private recording sourced from the artist].

Beznosiuk, Pavlo (2011 (Rec. 2007)). Baroque violin. Complete set. Linn Records CKD 366.

Brooks, Brian (2001). Baroque violin. Complete set. Arts Music 47581-2.

Buswell, James (1995 (Rec. 1989). Centaur CRC 2147/48.

Edinger, Christiane (1991). 'Sonatas and Partitas Volume 2', D minor partita, C Major sonata, E Major Partita. NAXOS 8.55057.

Ehnes, James (1999). Complete set. Analekta Fleurs de lys FL 23147-8.

Faust, Isabelle (2010). 'Sonatas and Partitas BWV 1004-1006 Volume 1', D minor, C Major, E Major. Harmonia Mundi HMC 902059 [vol. 2 issued in 2012: HMC 902124].

Fischer, Julia (2005). Complete set. PentaTone Classics 5186072.

Gähler, Rudolf (1999). Curved 'Bach-bow'. Complete set. Arte Nova Classics 74321 67501-2.

---

1   Date refers to release.

Gringolts, Ilya (2001). 'Bach', B minor Partita, A minor Sonata, E Major Partita. Deutsche Grammophone DG 474 235-2.

Hahn, Hilary (1999). D minor Partita, C Major Sonata, E Major Partita. SONY SK 62793.

Holloway, John (2006 (Rec. 2004)). Baroque violin. Complete set. ECM New Series 1909/10 B0007621-02.

Huggett, Monica (1995). Baroque violin. Complete set. Virgin Veritas 5452052.

Ibragimova, Alina (2009). Complete set. Hyperion CDA67691/2.

Khachatryan, Sergey (2010). Complete set. Naïve V5181.

Kremer, Gidon (1980). Complete set. Philips 416651-2.

Kremer, Gidon (2005). Complete set. ECM New Series 1926/27.

Kuijken, Sigiswald (1983 (Rec. 1981)). Baroque violin. Complete set. Deutsche Harmonia Mundi DHM 77043.

Kuijken, Sigiswald (2001). Baroque violin. Complete set. Deutsche Harmonia Mundi DHM 5472775272.

Lev, Lara (2001). 'Bach: Sonatas and Partitas Volume 2', D minor partita, C Major Sonata, E Major Partita. Finlandia Records, Warner Classics APEX 092-4808-2.

Luca, Sergiu (1977). Baroque violin. Complete set. Nonesuch 7559-73030-2.

Matthews, Ingrid (2001 (Rec. 1997)). Baroque violin. Complete set. Centaur CRC 2472/2473.

Mintz, Shlomo (1984). Complete set. Deutsche Grammophone DG 413810-2.

Mullova, Viktoria (1990 (Rec. 1987)). B minor Partita. Philips 420948.

Mullova, Viktoria (1992-3). Three Partitas. Philips 4757451.

Mullova, Viktoria (2009 (Rec. 2007-2008)). Baroque bow. Complete set. Onyx 4040.

Perlman, Itzhak (1986). Complete set. EMI Classics 7 49483 2.

Podger, Rachel (1999). Baroque violin. Complete set. Channel Classics CCS 12198.

Poppen, Christoph (2000). Baroque violin. D minor Partita. 'Morimur.' ECM 1765.

Poulet, Gerard (1996). Complete set. Arion 268296.

Ricci, Ruggiero (1988). Concert: A minor Sonata, D minor Partita. 'Ricci: Celebrating Six Decades on Stage'. One-Eleven URS 92033.

Ricci, Ruggiero (1991). Concert: B minor Partita. 'Ricci: Celebrating Six Decades on Stage'. One-Eleven URS 92033.

Schmid, Benjamin (1999). Complete set. Arte Nova 74321 72113 2.

Schröder, Jaap (2005 (Rec. 1985)). Baroque violin. Complete set. NAXOS 8.557563-64.

Shumsky, Oskar (1983). Complete set. Musical Heritage Society Recording ASV ALHB 306. [According to a NIMBUS 2010 release (NI2557), the original recording was made in 1979 by Amreco Inc.]

St John, Lara (2007 (Rec. 2006-7)). Complete set. Ancalagon AR 132.

Szenthelyi, Miklós (2002). Complete set. Hungaroton HCD 32071-72.

Tetzlaff, Christian (1996). Complete set. Virgin Veritas 545089-2.

Tetzlaff, Christian (2005). Complete set. Virgin Classics 545668-2.

Tognetti, Richard (2005). Complete set. ABC Classics 476 8051.

van Dael, Lucy (1996). Baroque violin. Complete set. NAXOS 8.554423.

Wallfisch, Elizabeth (1997). Baroque violin. Complete set. Hyperion Dyad CDD 22009.

Zehetmair, Thomas (1984). Complete set. Teldec 903176138-2.

Other Recordings Mentioned

Bach, Johann Sebastian: Sonatas and Partitas for Solo Violin (BWV1001-1006)

Enescu, George (1999 (Rec. ca. 1949)). Instituto Discografico Italiano IDIS 328/29.

Menuhin, Yehudi (1989 (Rec. 1934-6)). EMI Reference (mono) CHS 763035 2.

Montanari, Stefano (2012 (Rec. 2011)). Amadeus Elite Paragon DDD AMS 108/109-2 SIAE.

Bach, Johann Sebastian: Selected Sonatas and Partitas

Busch, Adolf (1994 (Rec. 1929)). Partita in D minor. EMI Japan TOCE 6781-97.

Busch, Adolf (1983 (Rec. 1934)). G minor Sonata. Danacord DACO 136.

Huberman, Borislav (1997 (Rec. 1942)). Partita in D minor. Arbiter 105.

Heifetz, Jascha (1992 (Rec. 1935)). Sonata in G minor, Sonata in C Major, Partita in D minor. EMI References CDH 7 64494 2.

Szigeti, Joseph (1999 (Rec. 1927-1933)). Sonata in G minor, Sonata in A minor. Biddulph LAB 153.

Bach, Johann Sebastian: Goldberg Variations BWV 988

Gould, Glenn (1992 (Rec. 1955)). Sony SMK 52685.

Gould, Glenn (1981). CBS DBL 37779.

Leonhardt, Gustav (1992 (Rec. 1953)). Vanguard OVC 2004.

Leonhardt, Gustav (1995 (Rec. 1965)). Teldec DAW 4509-97994-2.

Leonhardt, Gustav (1990 (Rec. 1978)). Deutsche Harmonia Mundi GD 77149.

Bach, Johann Sebastian: Various Other Works

Accompanied Violin Sonatas (BWV 1014-1023). James Ehnes violin, Luc Beauséjour harpsichord, with Benoit Loiselle cello (2008 (Rec. 2004-2005)). Analekta AN 2 2016-7.

Accompanied Violin Sonatas (BWV 1014-1023). Viktoria Mullova violin, Ottavio Dantone harpsichord and organ, with Vittorio Ghielmi viola da gamba and Luca Pianca lute (2007). Onyx 4020.

Brandenburg Concertos Nos. 1-6 (BWV 1046-1051), soloistic recording with Sigiswald Kuijken violin, Frans Brüggen recorder, Anner Bijlsma cello, and Gustav Leonhardt harpsichord, among others (1999 (Rec. 1976-1977)). Sony Essential Classics SBK 61814-5.

Mass in B minor (BWV 232), Harnoncourt, Nikolaus conductor, Concentus Music Wien, Wiener Sängerknaben, Chorus Viennensis (1994 (Rec. 1968)). Teldec DAW 4509-95517-2.

Mass in B minor (BWV 232), Harnoncourt, Nikolaus conductor, Concentus Musicus Wien, Arnold Schoenberg Chor (1995 (Rec. 1986)). Teldec 2292-42676-2.

St Matthew Passion (BWV 244), Harnoncourt, Nikolaus conductor, Concentus Musicus Wien et al. (1994 (Rec. 1971)). Teldec DAW 2292-42509-2.

Six Suites for Solo Cello (BWV 1007-1012), Wispelwey, Pieter (2012). Compact Disk Recording with DVD documentary. Evil Penguin Records Classics EPRC 0012.

Six Suites for Solo Cello (BWV 1007-1012), Angela East (2009 (Rec. 2001-2004)). Red Priest Recording RP006 2009.

Six Suites for Solo Cello (BWV 1007-1012), David Watkin (2015 (Rec. 2013)). Resonus Limited RES10147.

Bach—Violin and Voice (2010). Hilary Hahn violin, Mattias Goerne and Christine Schäfer voice, Munich Chamber Orchestra, Alexander Liebreich conductor. Deutsche Grammophon 477 8092.

Beethoven, Ludwig van: Violin Sonatas

Complete set. Rachel Barton Pine violin and Matthew Hagle piano (2005). Concert broadcast by WFMT Radio. Chicago [sourced from the artist].

Complete set. Isabelle Faust violin and Alexander Melnikov piano (2009). Harmonia Mundi 902025-27.

Complete set. Viktoria Mullova violin and Kristian Bezuidenhout piano (2010). Onyx 4050.

Complete set. Sophie Mutter violin and Lambert Orkis piano (1998). Deutsche Grammophon DG 457 623-2.

Sonatas Op. 23 and Op. 30 No. 2. Daniel Sepec violin and Andreas Staier piano (2006). Harmonia Mundi 901919.

Mozart, Wolfgang Amadeus

Sonatas for Fortepiano and Violin (3 vols). Malcolm Bilson fortepiano, Sergiu Luca classical violin (1985). Nonesuch Digital 9 79112.

Violin Concerto No. 5 in A Major (K219), Andrew Manze violin, The English Concert (2006). Harmonia Mundi HMU 807385.

Violin Concerto No. 5 in A Major (K219), Hilary Hahn violin, Deutsche Kammerphilharmonie Bremen, Paavo Järvi conductor (2015). Deutsche Grammophon 0289 479 3956 6 CD DDD GH.

Other

All'Improviso, L'Arpeggiata, Christina Pluhar (2004). Alpha Productions Alpha 512.

American Virtuosa: Tribute to Maud Powell (Miscellaneous works), Rachel Barton Pine violin, Matthew Hagle piano (2007). Cedille 9000 097.

Inspired by Bach: The Cello Suites, Yo Yo Ma in collaborations with other non-musician artists (2000). 3 Vols. DVD. Sony Pictures.

Officium, Jan Garbarek with The Hilliard Ensemble (1994). ECM New Series ECM 1523 NS.

O'Stravaganza – Vivaldi in Ireland, Hughes de Courson (2001). Virgin Classics VC 545494-2.

Red Priest: Johann I am only Dancing – Masterworks by J.S. Bach (2009). Red Priest Recordings RP007.

Reimaginings, Joe Chindamo piano and Zoe Black violin (2012). Which Way Music WWM013.

Powell Maud: Complete Recordings 1904-1917. Volumes 1-3, NAXOS Historical 8.110961-8.110963.

Schubert: Winterreise, Jonas Kaufmann tenor, Helmut Deutsch piano (2014). Sony Classical 88883795652.

Vivaldi [Five Violin Concertos], Viktoria Mullova, Il Giardino Harmonico, Giovanni Antonini conductor. (2004). Onyx 4001.

References

Abrams, M[eyer] H[oward], *A Glossary of Literary Terms*, 4th edn (New York: Holt, Rinehart and Winston, 1981).

Adorno, Theodor Wesendunk, 'Bach Defended against its Devotees', in *Prisms*, Engl. trans. by Shierry and Samuel Weber (Cambridge, MA: MIT Press, 1981 [1967]), pp. 133-146 (Original German publication in 1951 as *Bach gegen seine Liebhaber verteidigt*).

Aldrich, Putnam, *Ornamentation in Bach's Organ Works* (New York: Coleman-Ross, 1950).

[Anders] Stern, Günther, 'Philosophische Untersuchungen zu musikalischen Situationen', typescript, Österreichisches Literaturarchiv der Österreichischen Nationalbibliothek, Vienna. Nachlass Günther Anders. ÖLA 237/04.

Anonymous, 'Viktoria Mullova and Kristian Bezuidenhout', Concert Program Notes for concert presented on 12 March 2011 as part of the 2010-2011 *Camerata Musica International Artists Series* in Cambridge (UK), http://www.cameratamusica.org.uk/past-concerts/

Anonymous, 'One to Watch: Sergey Khachatryan, Violinist' [For the Record], *Gramophone*, 80/962 (January 2003), 11.

Applebaum, Samuel, ed., *The Way They Play: Illustrated Discussions with Famous Artists and Teachers*, Books 1, 4 (Neptune City, NJ: Paganini Publications, 1975-1983).

Ashley, Tim, 'Viktoria Mullova – Concert Review', *The Guardian*, Monday 10 April 2000, http://www.theguardian.com/culture/2000/apr/10/artsfeatures4

Auer, Leopold, *Violin Master Works and Their Interpretation* (New York: Carl Fischer, 2012).

Auslander, Philip, 'Musical Personae', *The Drama Review*, 50/1 (2006), 100-119, http://dx.doi.org/10.1162/dram.2006.50.1.100

Babbitt, Milton, 'The Composer as Specialist', reprinted in *The Collected Essays of Milton Babbitt*, ed. by Stephen Peles, Stephen Dembski, Andrew Mead, and Joseph Straus (Princeton: Princeton University Press, 2003), pp. 48-54 [originally published in *High Fidelity* (February 1958) as 'Who Cares if you Listen'].

Babbitt, Milton, 'A Life of Learning', *Charles Homer Haskins Lecture for 1991*. ACLS Occasional Paper, 17 (New York: American Council of Learned Societies, 1991).

Badel, James, 'On Record: Christopher Hogwood', *Fanfare*, 9/2 (November-December 2005), 90.

Bangert, Daniel, 'Doing without Thinking: Processes of Musical Decision-Making in Period Instrument Performance' (PhD Thesis, The University of New South Wales, 2012).

Bangert, Daniel, Dorottya Fabian, Emery Schubert, and Daniel Yeadon, 'Performing Solo Bach: A Case Study of Musical Decision Making', *Musicae Scientiae*, 18/1 (2014), 35-52, http://dx.doi.org/10.1177/1029864913509812

Barton Pine, Rachel, *On-line Biography*, http://industry.rachelbartonpine.com/bio_medium.php

Barton Pine, Rachel, *The Rachel Barton Pine Collection: Original Compositions, Arrangements, Cadenzas and Editions for Violin* (New York: Carl Fischer, 2009).

Baudelaire, Charles, 'The Painter of Modern Life', in *The Painter of Modern Life and Other Essays*, ed. and trans. by Jonathan Mayne (London: Phaidon Press, 2012 [1995]), pp. 1-41.

Bazzana, Kevin, *Glenn Gould: The Performer in the Work* (New York: Oxford University Press, 1997).

Bazzana, Kevin, *Wondrous Strange: The Life and Art of Glenn Gould* (Toronto: McClelland and Stewart, 2003).

Ben-Amos, Dan, *Do We Need Ideal Types (in Folklore)? An Address to Lauri Hinko* (Turku, Finland: Nordic Institute of Folklore, 1992).

Berkowitz, Aaron L., *The Improvising Mind: Cognition and Creativity in the Musical Moment* (New York: Oxford University Press, 2010), http://dx.doi.org/10.1093/acprof:oso/9780199590957.001.0001

Berry, Wallace, *Musical Structure and Performance* (New Haven: Yale University Press, 1989).

Bharucha, Jamshed J., 'Neural Nets, Temporal Composites, and Tonality', in *The Psychology of Music* (2nd edn), ed. by Diana Deutsch (San Diego: Academia Press, 1999), pp. 413-440, http://dx.doi.org/10.1016/b978-012213564-4/50012-3

Bononcini, Giovanni, *Sonate da chiesa a due violini* (Venice: [n.p.], 1672).

Bowen, José A., 'Tempo, Duration, and Flexibility: Techniques in the Analysis of Performance', *Journal of Musicological Research*, 16/2 (1996), 111-156, http://dx.doi.org/10.1080/01411899608574728

Bowen, José A., 'Performance Practice versus Performance Analysis: Why Should Performers Study Performance?', *Performance Practice Review*, 9/1 (1996), 16-35, http://dx.doi.org/10.5642/perfpr.199609.01.03

Bowen, José A. 'Finding the Music in Musicology: Performance History and Musical Works', in *Rethinking Music*, ed. by Nicholas Cook and Mark Everist (Oxford and New York: Oxford University Press, 1999), pp. 424-451.

Brown, Clive, 'Performing Nineteenth-Century Chamber Music: The Yawning Chasm between Contemporary Practice and Historical Evidence', *Early Music*, 38 (2010), 476-480, http://dx.doi.org/10.1093/em/caq060

Burney, Charles, *The Present State of Music in France and Italy* (London, T. Becket & Co., 1771).

Burney, Charles, *A General History of Music* (New York: Dover Books, 1957 [1776]).

Butt, John, *Bach Interpretation: Articulation Marks in Primary Sources* (Cambridge: Cambridge University Press, 1990).

Butt, John, *Bach: B minor Mass* (Cambridge: Cambridge University Press, 1991), http://dx.doi.org/10.1017/cbo9781139166379

Butt, John, 'Bach Recordings since 1980: A Mirror of Historical Performance', in *Bach Perspectives 4*, ed. by David Schulenberg (Lincoln and London: University of Nebraska Press, 1999), pp. 181-198.

Butt, John, *Playing with History: The Historical Approach to Musical Performance* (Cambridge: Cambridge University Press, 2002), http://dx.doi.org/10.1017/cbo9780511613555

Cannam, Chris, Christian Landone, and Mark Sandler, 'Sonic Visualiser: An Open Source Application for Viewing, Analysing, and Annotating Music Audio Files', in *Proceedings of the ACM Multimedia 2010 International Conference* (Florence, October 2010), 1467-1468, http://dx.doi.org/10.1145/1873951.1874248

Carman, Taylor, 'The Body in Husserl and Merleau-Ponty', *Philosophical Topics*, 27/2 (1999), 205-226, http://dx.doi.org/10.5840/philtopics199927210

Chaffin, Roger, Gabriela Imreh, and Mary E. Crawford, *Practicing Perfection: Memory and Piano Performance* (Mahwah, NJ: Lawrence Erlbaum, 2002), http://dx.doi.org/10.4324/9781410612373

Cilliers, Paul, *Complexity and Postmodernism: Understanding Complex Systems* (London: Routledge, 1998).

Clarke, Eric, 'Structure and Expression', in *Musical Structure and Cognition*, ed. by Peter Howell, Ian Cross, and Robert West (London: Academic Press, 1985), pp. 209-236.

Clarke, Eric, 'Expression in Performance: Generativity, Perception and Semiosis', in *The Practice of Performance*, ed. by John Rink (Cambridge: Cambridge University Press, 1995), pp. 21-54, http://dx.doi.org/10.1017/cbo9780511552366.003

Clarke, Eric, 'Empirical Methods in the Study of Performance', in *Empirical Musicology: Aims, Methods, Prospects*, ed. by Eric Clarke and Nicholas Cook (Oxford and New York: Oxford University Press, 2004), pp. 77-102, http://dx.doi.org/10.1093/acprof:oso/9780195167498.003.0005

Coulter, Todd J., 'Editorial: Music as Performance—The State of the Field', *Contemporary Theatre Review*, 21/3 (2011), 259-260, http://dx.doi.org/10.1080/10486801.2011.585983

Cook, Nicholas, *Music, Imagination and Culture* (Oxford: Clarendon Press, 1992).

Cook, Nicholas, 'The Domestic *Gesamtkunstwerk*, or Record Sleeves and Reception', in *Composition, Performance, Reception: Studies in the Creative Process in Music*, ed. by Wyndham Thomas (Aldershot: Ashgate, 1998), pp. 105-117.

Cook, Nicholas, 'Between Process and Product: Music and/as Performance', *Music Theory Online*, 7/2 (April 2001), http://www.mtosmt.org/issues/mto.01.7.2/mto.01.7.2.cook.html

Cook, Nicholas, 'Methods for Analysing Recordings', in *The Cambridge Companion to Recorded Music*, ed. by Nicholas Cook, Eric F. Clarke, Daniel Leech-Wilkinson, and John Rink (Cambridge: Cambridge University Press, 2009), pp. 221-245, http://dx.doi.org/10.1017/ccol9780521865821.027

Cook, Nicholas, Eric Clarke, Daniel Leech-Wilkinson, and John Rink, eds., *The Cambridge Companion to Recorded Music* (Cambridge: Cambridge University Press, 2009), http://dx.doi.org/10.1017/ccol9780521865821

Cook, Nicholas, 'Introduction: Refocusing Theory', *Music Theory Online*, 18 (2012), http://mtosmt.org/issues/mto.12.18.1/mto.12.18.1.cook.pdf

Cook, Nicholas, 'Bridging the Unbridgeable? Empirical Musicology and Interdisciplinary Performance Studies', in *Taking it to the Bridge: Music as Performance*, ed. by Nicholas Cook and Richard Pettengill (Ann Arbor: University of Michigan Press, 2013), pp. 70-85.

Cook, Nicholas, *Beyond the Score: Music as Performance* (New York: Oxford University Press, 2014), http://dx.doi.org/10.1093/acprof:oso/9780199357406.001.0001

Couperin, François, Preface to *Pièces de clavecin*, Book 3 (Paris, 1722).

Cowan, Rob, 'Bach: Violin Sonatas and Partitas, BWV 1001-1006, Julia Fischer *vn*, Pentatone PTC 5186072 (150 minutes DDD)', *Gramophone*, 89/993 (June 2005), 72.

Creighton, James, *Discopaedia of the Violin, 1889-1971* (Toronto: University of Toronto Press, 1974).

Crick, Jamie, 'Classic FM speaks to Viktoria Mullova', https://www.youtube.com/watch?v=Kf83eztSVtg.

Cross, Ian, and Iain Morley, 'The Evolution of Music: Theories, Definitions and the Nature of the Evidence', *Communicative Musicality: Exploring the Basis of Human Companionship*, ed. by Stephen Malloch and Colwyn Trevarthen (Oxford: Oxford University Press, 2009), pp. 61-81.

Cullingford, Martin, 'The Experts' Expert—Violinists', *Gramophone*, 82/986 (November 2004), 46.

Damasio, Antonio, *The Self Comes to Mind: Constructing the Conscious Brain* (New York: Vintage, 2012).

Danton, David, 'Bach Partitas no. 1 in B minor BWV 1002 & no. 3 in E Major BWV 1006, Sonata No. 2 in A minor BWV 1003. Ilya Gringolts (violin). Deutsche Grammophon 474 235-2', *The Strad*, 114/1363 (Nov 2003), 1269.

Davies, Stephen, *Musical Works and Performances: A Philosophical Exploration* (New York: Oxford University Press, 2001), http://dx.doi.org/10.1093/0199241589.001.0001

Davidson, Jane W., 'What Type of Information is Conveyed in the Body Movements of Solo Musician Performers?', *Journal of Human Movement Studies*, 6 (1994), 279-301.

Day, Timothy, *A Century of Recorded Music: Listening to Musical History* (New Heaven and London: Yale University Press, 2000).

De Landa, Manuel, *A Thousand Years of Non-linear History* (New York: Swerve Editions, 2000).

Deleuze, Gilles, *Difference and Repetition*, Engl. trans. by Paul Patton (New York: Columbia University Press, 1994).

Deleuze, Gilles, and Felix Guattari, *A Thousand Plateaus*, Engl. trans. by Brian Massumi (London: Bloomsbury Academic, 2013).

Deutsch, Diana, ed., *The Psychology of Music*, 2nd edn (San Diego: Academia Press, 1999).

Dirst, Matthew, 'Bach's French Overtures and the Politics of Overdotting', *Early Music*, 25/1 (1997), 35-44, http://dx.doi.org/10.1093/em/25.1.35

Distler, Jed, 'Review: Bach 3 Sonatas and 3 Partitas, BWV1001-1006, Gidon Kremer *vn*, ECM New Series 4767291 (131 minutes: DDD)', *Gramophone*, 83/1001 (January 2006), 63.

Doğantan-Dack, Mine, 'Philosophical Reflections on Expressive Music Performance', in *Expressiveness in Music Performance: Empirical Investigations across Styles and Cultures*, ed. by Dorottya Fabian, Renee Timmers, and Emery Schubert (Oxford: Oxford University Press, 2014), pp. 3-21, http://dx.doi.org/10.1093/acprof:oso/9780199659647.003.0001

Dolan, David, John A. Sloboda, Henrik Jeldtoft Jensen, Björn Crüts, and Eugene Feygelson, 'The Improvisatory Approach to Classical Music Performance: An Empirical Investigation into its Characteristics and Impact', *Music Performance Research*, 6 (2013), 1-38, http://mpr-online.net/Issues/Volume%206%20%5B2013%5D/MPR0073.pdf

Dolmetsch, Arnold, *The Interpretation of the Music of the Seventeenth and Eighteenth Centuries* (London: Novello, 1949/1915 [R1969]).

Donington, Robert, *The Interpretation of Early Music* (London: Faber, 1963 [2nd edn: 1965; rev. 1974, reprinted with corrections 1975, 1977, rev. 1989, R1990]).

Dreyfus, Laurence, 'Early Music Defended against its Devotees: A Theory of Historical Performance in the Twentieth Century', *The Musical Quarterly*, 69/3 (1983), 297-322, http://dx.doi.org/10.1093/mq/lxix.3.297

Dreyfus, Laurence, 'Beyond the Interpretation of Music', *Dutch Journal of Music Theory*, 12/3 (2007), 253-272.

Druce, Duncan, 'Reviews: Bach 3 Sonatas and 3 Partitas BWV1001-1006, Christian Tetzlaff *vn*, Hänssler Classic CD98 250 (130 minutes DDD)', *Gramophone*, 85/1021 (August 2007), 71.

Druce, Duncan, 'Reviews: Bach 3 Sonatas and 3 Partitas, BWV1001-1006, Sigiswald Kuijken *vn*, Deutsche Harmonia Mundi 05472 775 27-2 (135 minutes DDD)', *Gramophone*, 79/947 (2001), 93.

Druce, Duncan, 'Reviews: Bach 3 Sonatas and 3 Partitas BWV1001-1006, Richard Tognetti *vn*, ABC Classics CD ABC 4768051 (145 minutes: DDD)', *Gramophone*, 84/1010 (October 2006), 80.

Druce, Duncan, 'Sergey Khachatryan – An Engaging and Persuasively Virtuosic Debut from a Young Violinist to Note', EMI Debut 575684-2 (71 minutes DDD), *Gramophone*, 80/962 (January 2003), 56.

Duarte, John, 'Reviews: Bach Partitas – No. 1 in B Minor, BWV 1002; No. 2 in D minor, BWV 1004; No. 3 in E, BWV 1006, Viktoria Mullova *vn*, Philips 434 075-2 PH (77 minutes DDD)', *Gramophone*, 72/853 (June 1994), 80.

Dulak, Michelle, 'The Quiet Metamorphosis of "Early Music"', *Repercussions*, 2/ 2 (1993), 31-61.

Eales, Adrian, 'The Fundamentals of Violin Playing and Teaching', in *The Cambridge Companion to the Violin*, ed. by Robin Stowell (Cambridge: Cambridge University Press, 1992), pp. 92-121, http://dx.doi.org/10.1017/ccol9780521390330.007

Efrati, Richard, *Treatise on the Execution and Interpretation of the Sonatas and Partitas for Solo Violin and the Suites for Cello by Johann Sebastian Bach* (Zürich: Atlantis Verlag, 1979).

Eichler, Jeremy, 'String Theorist: Christian Tetzlaff Rethinks How a Violin Should Sound', *The New Yorker* (27 August 2012), 34-39.

Eisler, Edith, 'Christian Tetzlaff from Bach to Bartók', *Strings* (February-March 1999), 50-56.

Elste, Martin, *Meilensteine der Bach-Interpretation 1750-2000: Eine Werkgeschichte im Wandel* (Stuttgart and Weimar: Metzler; Kassel: Bärenreiter, 2000).

Erlmann, Veit, *Reason and Resonance: A History of Modern Aurality* (New York: Zone Books, 2010).

Fabian, Dorottya, *Bach Performance Practice, 1945-1975: A Comprehensive Review of Sound Recordings and Literature* (Aldershot: Ashgate, 2003).

Fabian, Dorottya, 'Towards a Performance History of Bach's Sonatas and Partitas for Solo Violin: Preliminary Investigations', in *Essays in Honor of László Somfai*, ed. by László Vikárius and Vera Lampert (Lanham, MD: Scarecrow Press, 2005), pp. 87-108.

Fabian, Dorottya, 'The Recordings of Joachim, Ysaÿe and Sarasate in Light of their Reception by Nineteenth-Century British Critics', *International Review of the Aesthetics and Sociology of Music*, 37/2 (2006), 189-211.

Fabian, Dorottya, 'Is Diversity in Performance Truly in Decline? The Evidence of Sound Recordings', *Context*, 31 (2006), 165-180.

Fabian, Dorottya 'Classical Sound Recordings and Live Performances: Artistic and Analytical Perspectives', in *Recorded Music: Philosophical and Critical Reflections*, ed. by Mine Doğantan-Dack (London: Middlesex University Press, 2008), pp. 232-260.

Fabian, Dorottya, 'Ornamentation in Recent Recordings of J. S. Bach's Solo Sonatas and Partitas for Violin', *Min-Ad: Israel Studies in Musicology Online*, 11/2 (2013), 1-21, http://www.biu.ac.il/hu/mu/min-ad/

Fabian, Dorottya, 'Commercial Sound Recordings and Trends in Expressive Music Performance: Why Should Experimental Researchers Pay Attention?', in *Expressiveness in Music Performance: Empirical Approaches across Styles and Cultures*, ed. by Dorottya Fabian, Renee Timmers, and Emery Schubert (Oxford: Oxford University Press, 2014), pp. 58-79, http://dx.doi.org/10.1093/acprof:oso/9780199659647.003.0004

Fabian, Dorottya, and Eitan Ornoy, 'Identity in Violin Playing on Records: Interpretation Profiles in Recordings of Solo Bach by Early Twentieth-Century Violinists', *Performance Practice Review*, 14 (2009), 1-40, http://dx.doi.org/10.5642/perfpr.200914.01.03

Fabian, Dorottya, and Emery Schubert, 'Musical Character and the Performance and Perception of Dotting, Articulation and Tempo in Recordings of Variation 7 of J.S. Bach's *Goldberg Variations* (BWV 988)', *Musicae Scientiae*, 12/2 (2008), 177-203, http://dx.doi.org/10.1177/102986490801200201

Fabian, Dorottya, and Emery Schubert, 'Baroque Expressiveness and Stylishness in Three Recordings of the D minor Sarabanda for Solo Violin (BWV 1004) by J. S. Bach', *Music Performance Research*, 3 (2009), 36-55, http://mpr-online.net

Fabian, Dorottya, and Emery Schubert, 'A New Perspective on the Performance of Dotted Rhythms', *Early Music*, 38/4 (2010, November), 585-588, http://dx.doi.org/10.1093/em/caq079

Fabian, Dorottya, Emery Schubert, and Richard Pulley, 'A Baroque Träumerei: The Performance and Perception of a Violin Rendition', *Musicology Australia*, 32/1 (2010), 25-42, http://dx.doi.org/10.1080/08145851003793986

Farach-Colton, Andrew, 'Perlman', *The Strad*, 116/1387 (November 2005), 44-51.

Flesch, Carl, *The Art of Violin Playing: I. Technique in General*, English text by Frederick H. Martens (New York: Carl Fischer, 2000).

Flesch, Carl, *The Memoirs of Carl Flesch*, Eng. trans. by Hans Keller (Bois de Boulogne: Centenary Edition, 1973).

Flynn, James, 'Why our IQ Levels are Higher than our Grandparents?', https://www.ted.com/talks/james_flynn_why_our_iq_levels_are_higher_than_our_grandparents?language=en

Friberg, Anders, and Andreas Sundström, 'Swing Ratios and Ensemble Timing in Jazz Performance: Evidence for a Common Rhythmic Pattern', *Music Perception*, 19/3 (2002), 333-349, http://dx.doi.org/10.1525/mp.2002.19.3.333

Friberg, Anders, and Erica Bisesi, 'Using Computational Models of Music Performance to Model Stylistic Variations', in *Expressiveness in Music Performance: Empirical Approaches across Styles and Cultures* ed. by Dorottya Fabian, Renee Timmers, and Emery Schubert (Oxford: Oxford University Press, 2014), pp. 240-259, http://dx.doi.org/10.1093/acprof:oso/9780199659647.003.0014

Gabrielsson, Alf, 'The Performance of Music', in *The Psychology of Music* (2nd edn), ed. by Diana Deutsch (San Diego: Academic Press, 1999), pp. 501-602, http://dx.doi.org/10.1016/b978-012213564-4/50015-9

Gabrielsson, Alf, 'Music Performance Research at the Millennium', *Psychology of Music*, 31 (2003), 221-272, http://dx.doi.org/10.1177/03057356030313002

Gabrielsson, Alf, and Erik Lindström, 'The Role of Structure in the Musical Expression of Emotions', in *Handbook of Music and Emotions: Theory, Research, Applications*, ed. by Patrik Juslin and John Sloboda (Oxford: Oxford University Press, 2010), pp. 367-400, http://dx.doi.org/10.1093/acprof:oso/9780199230143.003.0014

Galamian, Ivan, *Principles of Violin Playing and Teaching*, 3rd edn with postscript by Elizabeth A. H. Green (Englewood-Cliff: Prentice Hall, 1985 [1962]).

Gelfand, Stanley, *Hearing: An Introduction to Psychological and Physiological Acoustics*, 2nd edn (New York & Basel: Marcel Dekker, 1990).

Gibson, James, *The Senses Considered as Perceptual Systems* (London: Unwin Bros, 1966).

Gibson, James, *The Ecological Approach to Visual Perception* (New Jersey: Lawrence Erlbaum, 1979).

Gilman, Benjamin Ives, 'Report on an Experimental Test of Musical Expressiveness', *The American Journal of Psychology*, 4/4 (1892), 558-576, http://dx.doi.org/10.2307/1410803

Glass, Herbert, 'A reasoning Romantic—Profile: Christian Tetzlaff', *The Strad*, 106/1259 (March 1995), 260-265.

Godlovitch, Stan, *Musical Performance: A Philosophical Study* (London: Routledge, 1998).

Godøy, Rolf Inge, 'Gestural Affordances of Musical Sound', in *Musical Gestures: Sound, Movement, and Meaning*, ed. by Rolf Inge Godøy and Marc Lehman (New York and London: Routledge, 2010), pp. 103-125.

Godøy, Rolf Inge, and Marc Lehman, eds., *Musical Gestures: Sound, Movement, and Meaning* (New York and London: Routledge, 2010).

Goehr, Lydia, 'The Perfect Performance of Music and the Perfect Musical Performance', *New Formations*, 27 (1996), 1-22.

Goehr, Lydia, *The Imaginary Museum of Musical Works: An Essay in the Philosophy of Music*, rev. ed. (New York: Oxford University Press, 2007 [1994]).

Goldberg, Elkhonon, and Louis D. Costa, 'Hemispheric Differences in the Acquisition and Use of Descriptive Systems', *Brain and Language*, 14/1 (1981), 144-173, http://dx.doi.org/10.1016/0093-934x(81)90072-9

Greenfield, Edward, 'Itzhak Perlman Talks to Edward Greenfield', *Gramophone*, 66/787 (1988), 967.

Gritten, Anthony, and Elaine King, eds., *Music and Gesture* (Farnham: Ashgate, 2006).

Gritten, Anthony, and Elaine King, eds., *New Perspectives on Music and Gesture* (Farnham: Ashgate, 2011).

Gritten, Anthony, 'The Subject (of) Listening', *Journal of the British Society for Phenomenology*, 45/3 (2015), 203-219, http://dx.doi.org/10.1080/00071773.2014.966461

Hamilton, Kenneth, *After the Golden Age: Romantic Pianism and Modern Performance* (New York: Oxford University Press, 2008), http://dx.doi.org/10.1093/acprof:oso/9780195178265.001.0001

Hanslick, Eduard, *On the Musically Beautiful*, Engl. trans. by Geoffrey Payzant (Indianapolis: Hackett Publishing, 1986) [German original: *Vom Musikalisch-Schönen* (Leipzig: R. Weigel, 1854 [8th edn 1891])].

Harmen, Kjell-Ake, 'French master' [Profile: Jaap Schröder], *The Strad*, 113/1349 (September 2002), 954-957.

Harnoncourt, Nikolaus, *Baroque Music Today: Music as Speech* (Portland, Oregon: Amadeus Press, 1988). Engl. trans. by Mary O'Neill of German original: *Musik als Klangrede* (Salzburg: Residenz, 1982).

Haskell, Harry, *The Early Music Revival: A History* (London: Hudson, 1988).

Hasty, Christopher, 'The Image of Thought and Ideas of Music', in *Sounding the Virtual: Gilles Deleuze and the Theory and Philosophy of Music* (Farnham: Ashgate, 2010), pp. 1-22.

Haynes, Bruce, *The End of Early Music: A Period Performer's History of Music for the Twenty-First Century* (New York: Oxford University Press, 2007), http://dx.doi.org/10.1093/acprof:oso/9780195189872.001.0001

Hefling, Stephen, *Rhythmic Alteration in Seventeenth- and Eighteenth-Century Music* (New York: Schirmer, 1993).

Hellaby, Julian, *Reading Musical Interpretation – Case Studies in Solo Piano Performance* (Farnham: Ashgate, 2009).

Hilton, Wendy, *Dance and Music of Court and Theatre* (Stuyvesant, NY: Pendragon Press, 1997).

Houle, George, *Meter in Music, 1600-1800: Performance, Perception and Notation* (Bloomington: Indiana University Press, 1987).

Hudson, Richard, *Stolen Time: The History of Tempo Rubato* (Oxford: Clarendon Press, 1994).

Huggett, Monica, 'A Performer's View of Bach's Sonatas and Partitas for Solo Violin', in *J. S. Bach: Sonatas and Partitas BWV 1001-1006* Virgin Veritas 7243 5-45205-2 5 (Holland: Virgin Classics, 1997), CD booklet, pp. 12-13.

Hulse, Brian, and Nick Nesbitt, eds., *Sounding the Virtual: Gilles Deleuze and the Theory and Philosophy of Music* (Farnham: Ashgate, 2010).

Huron, David, *Sweet Anticipation: Music and the Psychology of Expectation* (Cambridge, MA: MIT Press, 2007).

Huron, David, 'A Comparison of Average Pitch Height and Interval Size in Major- and Minor-Key Themes: Evidence Consistent with Affect-Related Pitch Prosody', *Empirical Musicology Review*, 3 (2008), 59-63, http://hdl.handle.net/1811/31940

Huron, David, 'Why is Sad Music Pleasurable? A Possible Role for Prolactin', *Musicae Scientiae*, 15 (2011), 146-58, http://dx.doi.org/10.1177/1029864911401171

Husserl, Edmund, *The Idea of Phenomenology*, Engl. trans. by W. Alston and G. Nakhnikian (The Hague: Martinus Hijhoff, 1964).

Jacobson, Bernard, 'CD Review: Bach: Sonatas and Partitas for Solo Violin – Monica Huggett (vn) (period instrument), VIRGIN 7243 5 45205 2 5(152:33)', *Fanfare*, 22/1 (September 1998), 116-117.

Jameson, Fredric, 'Postmodernism and Consumer Society', in *The Cultural Turn: Selected Writings on the Postmodern, 1983-1998* (London: Verso, 2009 [1998]), pp. 1-20.

Jameson, Fredric, '"End of Art" or "End of History"?', in *The Cultural Turn: Selected Writings on the Postmodern, 1983-1998* (London: Verso, 2009 [1998]), pp. 73-92.

Jameson, Fredric, *A Singular Modernity* (London and New York: Verso, 2012 [2002])

Jeal, Eric, 'Viktoria Mullova: From Russia in a Blond Wig', interview, *The Guardian*, 17 August 2011, http://www.theguardian.com/music/2011/aug/16/viktoria-mullova-russia-interview

Johnson, Lawrence A., 'An Interview with Rachel Barton', *Fanfare*, 21/1 (September/October 1997), 81-84.

Josipovici, Gabriel, *What Ever Happened to Modernism?* (New Haven: Yale University Press, 2010).

Juslin, Patrik N., 'Emotional Communication in Music Performance: A Functionalist Perspective and Some Data', *Music Perception*, 14/4 (1997), 383-418, http://dx.doi.org/10.2307/40285731

Juslin, Patrik N., 'From Everyday Emotions to Aesthetic Emotions: Towards a Unified Theory of Musical Emotions', *Physics of Life Reviews*, 10 (2013), 235-266. http://dx.doi.org/10.1016/j.plrev.2013.05.008

Juslin, Patrik N., and John Sloboda, eds., *Handbook of Music and Emotions: Theory, Research, Applications* (Oxford: Oxford University Press, 2010).

Kane, Brian, 'Excavating Lewin's "Phenomenology"', *Music Theory Spectrum*, 33 (2011), 27-36, http://dx.doi.org/10.1525/mts.2011.33.1.27

Katz, Mark, 'Beethoven in the Age of Mechanical Reproduction: The Violin Concerto on Record', *Beethoven Forum*, 10 (2003), 38-54.

Katz, Mark, *Capturing Sound: How Technology has Changed Music* (Berkeley and Los Angeles: University of California Press, 2004).

Katz, Mark, 'Portamento and the Phonograph Effect', *Journal of Musicological Research*, 25 (2006), 211-232, http://dx.doi.org/10.1080/01411890600860733

Keller, Peter, 'Ensemble Performance: Interpersonal Alignment of Musical Expression', in *Expressiveness in Music Performance: Empirical Investigations across Styles and Cultures*, ed. by Dorottya Fabian, Renee Timmers, and Emery Schubert (Oxford: Oxford University Press, 2014), pp. 260-282, http://dx.doi.org/10.1093/acprof:oso/9780199659647.003.0015

Kemp, Lindsay, 'Going Solo — Monica Huggett on Playing Solo Bach', *Gramophone*, 75/897 (January 1998), 16.

Kenyon, Nicholas, ed., *Authenticity and Early Music* (Oxford: Oxford University Press, 1988).

Kerman, Joseph, *Musicology* (London: Fontana Press, 1985).

Kirnberger, Johann, *Die Kunst des reinen Satzes in der Musik* [*The Art of Strict Composition in Music*] (Berlin and Königsberg: G. J. Decker and G. L. Hartung, 1774).

Kivy, Peter, *Sound Sentiment: An Essay on the Musical Emotions, Including the Complete Text of The Corded Shell* (Philadelphia: Temple University Press, 1989).

Kjemptrup, Inge, 'Ilya Gringolts: The Man, the Myth, the Musician on the Move', WEB interview posted February 2011, https://www.allthingsstrings.com/layout/set/print/News/Interviews-Profiles/Ilya-Gringolts-The-Man-the-Myth-the-Musician-on-the-Move

Kleinerman, Shulamit, 'A Mix of Images: Women in Baroque Music', *Early Music America*, 10/4 (Winter 2004), 28-34.

Kolneder, Walter, *Amadeus Book of the Violin*, Engl. trans. by Reinhard G. Pauly (Pompton Plains, N.J.: Amadeus Press, 1998).

Kopiez, Reinhard, Andreas C. Lehmann, and Janina Klassen, 'Clara Schumann's Collection of Playbills: A Historiometric Analysis of Life-Span Development, Mobility, and Repertoire Canonization', *Poetics*, 37 (2009), 50-73, http://dx.doi.org/10.1016/j.poetic.2008.09.001

Kozinn, Allan, 'Jascha Brodsky, 90, Violinist at Curtis Institute' [Obituary], *The New York Times* [Arts], 6 March 1997, http://www.nytimes.com/1997/03/06/arts/jascha-brodsky-90-violinist-at-curtis-institute.html

Kremer, Gidon, *Back to Bach*, a film by Daniel Finkernagel and Alexander Lück, DVD. EuroArts (2055638), 2006.

Kurzbauer, Heather, 'Reviews CDS: Bach Sonatas and Partitas for Solo Violin BWV1001-1006, Sigiswald Kuijken (violin) Deutsche Harmonia Mundi 05472 775 272', *The Strad*, 113/1341 (January 2002), 81.

Latour, Bruno, *Pandora's Hope: Essays on the Reality of Science Studies* (Cambridge, MA: Harvard University Press, 1999).

Lawson, Colin, and Robin Stowell, *Historical Performance: An Introduction* (Cambridge: Cambridge University Press, 1999), http://dx.doi.org/10.1017/cbo9780511481710

Ledbetter, David, *Unaccompanied Bach: Performing the Solo Works* (New Haven: Yale University Press, 2009).

Lee, Heejung, 'Violin Portamento: An Analysis of its Use by Master Violinists in Selected Nineteenth-Century Concerti' (Doctor of Education Thesis, Columbia University, 2006).

Leech-Wilkinson, Daniel, 'What We Are Doing with Early Music Is Genuinely Authentic to such Small Degree that the Word Loses most of its Intended Meaning', *Early Music*, 22/1 (1984), 13-25, http://dx.doi.org/10.1093/earlyj/12.1.13

Leech-Wilkinson, Daniel, *The Changing Sound of Music: Approaches to Studying Recorded Musical Performance* (London: CHARM, 2009), http://www.charm.rhul.ac.uk/studies/chapters/intro.html

Leech-Wilkinson, Daniel, 'Recordings and Histories of Performance Style', in *The Cambridge Companion to Recorded Music*, ed. by Nicholas Cook, Eric F. Clarke, Daniel Leech-Wilkinson, and John Rink (Cambridge: Cambridge University Press, 2009), pp. 246-262, http://dx.doi.org/10.1017/ccol9780521865821.028

Leech-Wilkinson, Daniel, 'Compositions, Scores, Performances, Meanings', *Music Theory Online*, 18/1 (2012), 1-17, http://www.mtosmt.org/issues/mto.12.18.1/mto.12.18.1.leech-wilkinson.php

Leech-Wilkinson, Daniel, 'The Emotional Power of Musical Performance', in *The Emotional Power of Music: Multidisciplinary Perspectives on Musical Arousal, Expression, and Social Control*, ed. by Tom Cochrane, Bernardino Fantini, and Klaus R. Scherer (Oxford: Oxford University Press, 2013), pp. 41-54, http://dx.doi.org/10.1093/acprof:oso/9780199654888.003.0004

Leech-Wilkinson, Daniel, and Helen Prior, 'Heuristics of Expressive Performance', in *Expressiveness in Music Performance: Empirical Investigations across Styles and Cultures*, ed. by Dorottya Fabian, Renee Timmers, and Emery Schubert (Oxford: Oxford University Press, 2014), pp. 34-57, http://dx.doi.org/10.1093/acprof:oso/9780199659647.003.0003

Le Huray, Peter, and James Day, eds., *Music and Aesthetics in the Eighteenth and Early Nineteenth Centuries* (Cambridge: Cambridge University Press, 1981).

Leonhardt, Gustav, 'Dirigieren ist der leichteste Beruf', Interview, *Concerto*, 2/1 (1984), 61-64.

Leonhardt, Gustav, '"One Should not Make a Rule": Gustav Leonhardt on Baroque Keyboard Playing', in *Inside Early Music: Conversations with Performers*, ed. by Bernard D. Sherman (New York: Oxford University Press, 1997), pp. 193-206, http://dx.doi.org/10.1093/acprof:oso/9780195169454.003.0011

Lester, Joel, *Bach's Works for Solo Violin: Style, Structure, Performance* (Oxford-New York: Oxford University Press, 1999), http://dx.doi.org/10.1093/acprof:oso/9780195120974.001.0001

Levitin, Daniel, *This is Your Brain on Music: Understanding a Human Obsession* (London: Atlantic Books, 2006).

Lewin, David, 'Music Theory, Phenomenology, and Modes of Perception', *Music Perception*, 3/4 (Summer 1986), 327-392, http://dx.doi.org/10.2307/40285344

Lincoln, Stoddard, 'Bach in Authentic Performance: The Technically Impossible Becomes Merely Difficult (recording)', *Stereo Review*, 40/4 (April 1978), 86-87.

Lindström, Erik, Patrik Juslin, Roberto Bresin, and Aaron Williamon, '"Expressivity Comes from within Your Soul": A Questionnaire Study of Music Students' Perspectives on Expressivity', *Research Studies in Music Education*, 20/1 (2003), 23-47, http://dx.doi.org/10.1177/1321103x030200010201

Lord, Albert B., *The Singer of Tales*, 2nd edn (Cambridge, MA: Harvard University Press, 2000 [1960]).

Luca, Sergiu, 'Going for Baroque', *Music Journal*, 32/8 (1974), 16-34.

Lussy, Matisse, *Musical Expression: Accents, Nuances, and Tempo in Vocal and Instrumental Music*, Engl. trans. by M. E. von Glehn (London: Novello, 1874).

Lyotard, Jean-François, *The Postmodern Condition*, Engl. trans by Geoff Bennington and Brian Massumi (Minneapolis: University of Minnesota Press, 1984).

Magil, Joseph, 'Bach: Solo Violin Sonatas and Partitas' [Monica Huggett], *American Record Guide*, 61/4 (July 1998), 88-89.

Magil, Joseph, 'Bach: Solo Violin Sonatas and Partitas' [Ingrid Matthews], *American Record Guide*, 63/4 (July/August 2000), 83-84.

Magil, Joseph, 'Bach Solo Violin Partitas 1+3, Sonata 2. Ilya Gringolts DG 315', *American Record Guide*, 66/6 (November 2003), 75-76.

Magil, Joseph 'Bach: Solo Violin Sonatas and Partitas' [Christian Tetzlaff], *American Record Guide*, 70/4 (July/August 2007), 69-70.

Magil, Joseph, 'Guide to Records—Bach: Violin Sonatas & Partitas; Pauset: 'Kontrapartita' [Viktoria Mullova]', *American Record Guide*, 72/5 (September 2009), 61.

March, Ivan, Edward Greenfield, and Robert Layton, *The Penguin Guide to Compact Discs* (London: Penguin, 1990).

Maxham, Robert, 'Bach Violin Partitas: No. 1 in B; No. 3 in E. Solo Violin Sonata No. 2 in A Ilya Gringolts (vn) Deutsche Grammophon B0000315-02 (58:56)', *Fanfare*, 27/ 2 (November 2003), 111-112.

Macarthur, Sally, *Towards a Twenty-first Century of Feminist Politics of Music* (Farnham: Ashgate, 2010).

McCaleb, J. Murphy, *Embodied Knowledge in Ensemble Performance*, SEMPRE Studies in the Psychology of Music (Farnham: Ashgate, 2014).

McGilchrist, Iain, *The Master and his Emissary: The Divided Brain and the Making of the Western World* (New Haven: Yale University Press, 2009).

McLucas, Anne Dhu, *The Musical Ear: Oral Tradition in the USA*, SEMPRE Studies in The Psychology of Music (Farnham: Ashgate, 2011).

Melrose, Susan, *A Semiotics of the Dramatic Text* (London: Macmillan, 1994).

Mendel, Arthur, ed., *Bach: St John Passion – Vocal Score* (New York: Schirmer, 1951).

Merleau-Ponty, Maurice, *Phenomenology of Perception*, Engl. trans. by Colin Smith (London: Routledge and Kegan Paul, 1962 [1945]).

Mertl, Monika, *Vom Denken des Herzes. Alice und Nikolaus Harnoncourt – Eine Biographie* (Salzburg and Vienna: Residenz Verlag, 1999).

Miller, Richard, *The Structure of Singing* (New York and London: Schirmer Books, 1986).

Milsom, David, *Theory and Practice in Late Nineteenth-Century Violin Performance: An Examination of Style in Performance, 1850-1900* (Aldershot: Ashgate, 2003).

Milstein, Nathan, and Solomon Volkov, *From Russia to the West: The Musical Memoirs and Reminiscences of Nathan Milstein* (New York: Limelight Editions, 1990).

Moens-Haenen, Greta, 'Vibrato', *Grove Music Online. Oxford Music Online*, available at http://www.oxfordmusiconline.com

Monelle, Raymond, *The Sense of Music: Semiotic Essays* (Princeton: Princeton University Press, 2000).

Monsaingeon, Bruno, *The Art of Violin*, DVD Warner Music Vision NVC Arts (8573-85801-2), 2001.

Moore, Sarha, 'Interval Size and Affect: An Ethnomusicological Perspective', *Empirical Musicology Review*, 7/3-4 (2012), 138-143.

Mozart, Leopold, *Gründliche Violinschule*. Fascimile-Nachdruck der 3. Auflage, Augsburg, 1789 (Leipzig: VEB Deutscher Verlag für Music, 1968).

Mullova, Viktoria, and Eva Maria Chapman, *From Russia to Love: The Life and Times of Viktoria Mullova as Told to Eva Maria Chapman* (London: Robson Press, 2012).

Nancy, Jean-Luc, *Listening*, Engl. trans. by Charlotte Mandell (New York: Fordham University Press, 2007).

Neumann, Frederick, *Ornamentation in Baroque and Post-Baroque Music* (Princeton: Princeton University Press, 1978).

Neumann, Frederick, *Performance Practices of the Seventeenth and Eighteenth Centuries* (New York: Schirmer, 1993).

Neumann, Frederick, 'Some Performance Problems in Bach's Unaccompanied Violin and Cello Works', in *Eighteenth-Century Music in Theory and Practice: Essays in Honour of Alfred Mann*, ed. by Mary Parker (Stuyvesant, NY: Pendragon Press, 1994), pp. 19-48.

Newman, Anthony, *Bach and the Baroque: A Performing Guide to Baroque Music with Special Emphasis on the Music of J.S. Bach* (New York: Pendragon Press, 1985).

Nietzsche, Friedrich, *The Complete Works 3: Human All too Human I*, Engl. trans. with Afterword by Gary Handwerk (Stanford: Stanford University Press, 1995 [1878]).

Nietzsche, Friedrich, *Human, All too Human: A Book of Free Spirits*, Engl. trans. R. J. Hollingdale (Cambridge: Cambridge University Press, 1996 [1878]).

Nisbett, Nick, 'Critique and Clinique: From Sounding Bodies to the Musical Event', in Brian Hulse and Nick Nesbitt (eds.), *Sounding the Virtual: Gilles Deleuze and the Theory and Philosophy of Music* (Farnham: Ashgate, 2010), pp. 159-180.

Oesch, Hans, *Die Musikacademie der Stadt Basel* (Basel: Schwabe, 1967).

Ong, Walter J., *Orality and Literacy: The Technologizing of the Word* (London: Routledge, 1988).

Onwuegbuzie, Anthony J., and Nancy L. Leech, 'On Becoming a Pragmatic Researcher: The Importance of Combining Quantitative and Qualitative Research Methodologies', *International Journal of Social Research Methodology*, 8/5 (2005), 375-387, http://dx.doi.org/10.1080/13645570500402447

Ornoy, Eitan, 'Between Theory and Practice: Comparative Study of Early Music Performances', *Early Music*, 34/2 (2006), 233-247, http://dx.doi.org/10.1093/em/cah008

Ornoy, Eitan, 'In Search of Ideologies and Ruling Conventions among Early Music Performers', *Min-Ad: Israel Studies in Musicology Online*, 6 (2007-2008), 1-19, http://www.biu.ac.il/hu/mu/min-ad/

Ornoy, Eitan, 'Recording Analysis of J. S. Bach's G minor Adagio for Solo Violin (Excerpt): A Case Study', *JMM: Journal of Music and Meaning*, 6 (Spring 2008), http://www.musicandmeaning.net/issues/showArticle.php?artID=6.2

Ortega y Gasset, José, *The Dehumanization of Art and Other Essays on Art, Culture and Literature*, Engl. trans. by Helene Weyl (Princeton: Princeton University Press, 1968).

Paddison, Max, *Adorno's Aesthetics of Music* (Cambridge: Cambridge University Press, 1993).

Palmer, Andrew, 'Victoria Mullova: The Individualist', in *Violin Virtuosos*, ed. by Mary VanClay and Stacey Lynn (San Anselmo: String Letter Publishing, 2000), pp. 47-57.

Palmer, Caroline, 'Mapping Musical Thought to Musical Performance', *Journal of Experimental Psychology*, 15 (1989), 331-346, http://dx.doi.org/10.1037//0096-1523.15.2.331

Parncutt, Richard, 'Introduction: "Interdisciplinary musicology"', *Musicae Scientiae*, 10/1 (Special Issue 2005-2006), 7-11, http://dx.doi.org/10.1177/1029864906010001011

Parrott, Andrew, *The Essential Bach Choir* (Woodbridge: The Boydell Press, 2000).

Pearson, Ingrid E., 'Practice and Theory; Orality and Literacy: Performance in the Twenty-first Century', paper presented at the *Performa '11 Conference*, Aveiro (Portugal), 19-21 May 2011.

Peres Da Costa, Neal, *Off the Record: Performing Practices in Romantic Piano Playing* (New York: Oxford University Press, 2012), http://dx.doi.org/10.1093/acprof:oso/9780195386912.001.0001

[Perlman, Itzak], 'Itzhak on Bow Grip', http://www.youtube.com/watch?v=6r0WW-KN6VM

Persché, Gerhard, 'Authentizität ist nicht Akademismus – ein Gespräch mit Chrtistopher Hogwood', *Opernwelt*, 25/2 (1984), 58-61.

Philip, Robert, *Performing Music in the Age of Recording* (New Haven: Yale University Press, 2003).

Philip, Robert, 'Studying Recordings: The Evolution of a Discipline', keynote paper at the CHARM/RMA Conference *Musicology and Recordings* (Egham, Surrey), September 2007, http://www.charm.rhul.ac.uk/content/events/r.philip_keynote.pdf

Planer, John H., 'Sentimentality in the Performance of Absolute Music: Pablo Casals's Performance of Saraband from Johann Sebastian Bach's Suite No. 2 in D Minor for Unaccompanied Cello, S. 1008', *The Musical Quarterly*, 73/2 (1989), 212-248, http://dx.doi.org/10.1093/mq/73.2.212

'Podiumdiskussion: Zur Situation der Aufführungspraxis Bachscher Werke 1978', in *Bachforschung und Bachinterpretation heute: Wissenschaftler und Praktiker im Dialog*, Bericht über das Bachfest-Symposium 1978 der Philipps-Universität Marburg, ed. by Reinhold Brinkmann (Kassel: Bärenreiter, 1981), pp. 185-204.

Quantz, Johann Joachim, *Versuch einer Anweisung die Flöte traversiere zu spielen* (1752), Engl. trans. by Edward Reilly, *On Playing the Flute*, 2nd edn (Boston: Northeastern University Press, 1985 [1975]).

Quinn, Michael, 'Bach to the future [Hilary Hahn Interview]', *Gramophone*, 81/973 (Awards/Special Issue 2003), 30-31.

Read, Jason, 'Review Essay – The Full Body: Micro-Politics and Macro Entities', *Deleuze Studies*, 2/2 (2008), 220-228, http://dx.doi.org/10.3366/e1750224108000299

Repp, Bruno, 'Patterns of Expressive Timing in Performances of a Beethoven Minuet by Nineteen Famous Pianists', *Journal of the Acoustical Society of America*, 88 (1990), 622-641, http://dx.doi.org/10.1121/1.399766

Repp, Bruno, 'Diversity and Commonality in Music Performance: An Analysis of Timing Microstructure in Schumann's "Träumerei"', *Journal of the Acoustical Society of America*, 92/5 (1992), 2546-2568, http://dx.doi.org/10.1121/1.404425

Repp, Bruno, 'A Constraint on the Expressive Timing of a Melodic Gesture: Evidence from Performance and Aesthetic Judgment', *Music Perception*, 10/2 (1992), 221-241, http://dx.doi.org/10.2307/40285608

Rink, John, 'In Respect of Performance: The View from Musicology', *Psychology of Music*, 31/3 (2003), 303-323, http://dx.doi.org/10.1177/03057356030313004

Rink, John, 'The State of Play in Performance Studies', in *The Music Practitioner*, ed. by Jane Davidson (Aldershot: Ashgate, 2004), pp. 37-51.

Rolland, Paul, *Basic Principles of Violin Playing* (American String Teacher's Association, 1959).

[Rosand, Aron], 'Aaron Rosand on How to Produce a Beautiful Tone', http://www.thestrad.com/latest/blogs/aaron-rosand-on-how-to-produce-a-beautiful-tone

Sacks, Oliver, *Musicophilia: Tales of Music and the Brain* (New York: Alfred Knopf, 2007).

Sadler, Naomi, 'Unpredictable Passions – Monica Huggett [Profile]', *The Strad*, 110/1310 (June 1999), 595.

de Saint Lambert, Michel, *Principes de Clavecin* (Amsterdam: Estienne Roger, 1702).

Salter, Lionel, 'Reviews: Bach 3 Sonatas and 3 Partitas, BWV10010-06, Monica Huggett *vn*, Virgin Classics CD 545205-2 (152 minutes)', *Gramophone*, 75 (January 1998), 78.

Sand, Barbara Lourie, *Teaching Genius: Dorothy DeLay and the Making of a Musician* (New Jersey: Amadeus, 2000).

Sarlo, Dario, 'Investigating Performer Uniqueness: The Case of Jascha Heifetz' (PhD Thesis Goldsmith College, University of London, 2010).

Sarlo, Dario, *The Performance Style of Jascha Heifetz* (Farnham: Ashgate, forthcoming).

Schachter, Carl, 'The *Gavotte en Rondeaux* from J.S. Bach's Partita in E Major for Unaccompanied Violin', *Min-Ad: Israel Studies in Musicology*, 4 (1987), 7-26.

Schenker, Heinrich, *The Art of Performance*, ed. by Heribert Esser, Engl. trans. by Irene Schreier Scott (New York: Oxford University Press, 2000), http://dx.doi.org/10.1093/acprof:oso/9780195151510.001.0001

Schröder, Jaap, 'Jaap Schröder Discusses Bach's Works for Unaccompanied Violin', *Journal of the Violin Society of America*, 3/3 (Summer 1977), 7-32.

Schröder, Jaap, *Bach's Solo Violin Works: A Performer's Guide* (London: Yale University Press, 2007).

Schubert, Emery, and Dorottya Fabian, 'Perception and Preference of Dotting in 6/8 Patterns', *Journal of Music Perception and Cognition*, 7/2 (2001), 113-132.

Schwarz, Boris, *Great Masters of the Violin: From Corelli and Vivaldi to Stern, Zukerman and Perlman* (New York: A Touchstone Book, 1983).

Schwarz, Vera, 'Aufführungspraxis als Forschungsgegenstand', *Österreichische Musikzeitschrift*, 27/6 (1972), 314-322.

Seashore, Carl, 'Approaches to the Science of Music and Speech', *University of Iowa Studies: Series of Aims & Progress of Research*, 41 (1933), 15.

Serres, Michel, *The Troubadour of Knowledge* (Ann Arbor: University of Michigan Press, 1997).

Sherman, Bernard D., ed., *Inside Early Music: Conversations with Performers* (New York: Oxford University Press, 1997).

Sherman, Bernard, 'The Bach Violin Glut of the 2000s and its Strange Gender Gaps', http://bsherman.net/BachViolinGlutofthe2000s.htm

Smith, Harriet, 'Interview: Julia Fischer', *Gramophone*, 83/993 (June 2005), 19.

Sweeting, Adam, 'Hilary Hahn [Cover Story]', *Gramophone*, 78/927 (May 2000), 8-13.

Shave, Nick, 'Star of the North [Zehetmair]', *The Strad*, 116/1377 (January 2005), 18-22.

Silvia, Paul J., *Exploring the Psychology of Interest* (New York: Oxford University Press, 2006), http://dx.doi.org/10.1093/acprof:oso/9780195158557.001.0001

Spitzer, Michael, and Eduardo Coutinho, 'The Effect of Expert Musical Training on the Perception of Emotions in Bach's Sonata for Unaccompanied Violin No. 1 in G minor (BWV 1001)', *Psychomusicology: Music, Mind and Brain*, 24/1 (2014), 35-57, http://dx.doi.org/10.1037/pmu0000036

Spitzer, Michael, 'Affektive Shapes and Shapings of Affect in Bach's Sonata for Unaccompanied Violin No. 1 in G Minor (BWV 1001)', in *Music and Shape*, ed. by Daniel Leech-Wilkinson, and Helen Prior (New York: Oxford University Press, forthcoming).

Stevens, Denis, ed., *The Art of Ornamentation and Embellishment in the Renaissance and Baroque* (New York: Vanguard Records BGS 70697/8, 1967).

Stowell, Robin, 'Technique and Performing Practice', in *The Cambridge Companion to the Violin*, ed. by Robin Stowell (Cambridge: Cambridge University Press, 1992), pp. 122-142, http://dx.doi.org/10.1017/ccol9780521390330.008

Stowell, Robin, 'Reviews: CDs – Bach Sonatas and Partitas for Solo Violin, Christian Tetzlaff (violin) VIRGIN VCD 45089 2', *The Strad*, 106/1261 (May 1995), 541-542.

Stowell, Robin, 'Reviews: CDs – J.S. Bach: Sonatas and Partitas for Solo Violin BWV 1001-6. Monica Huggett (violin) Virgin Veritas 7243 5 45205 2 5', *The Strad*, 109/1297 (May 1998), 539.

Stowell, Robin, *The Early Violin and Viola: A Practical Guide* (Cambridge: Cambridge University Press, 2001), http://dx.doi.org/10.1017/cbo9780511481833

Stravinsky, Igor, *Poetics of Music in the Form of Six Lessons* (1939), Engl. trans. Arthur Knodel and Ingolf Dahl (New York: Knopf, 1960).

Sung, Alistair, and Dorottya Fabian, 'Variety in Performance: A Comparative Analysis of Recorded Performances of Bach's Sixth Suite for Solo Cello from 1961 to 1998', *Empirical Musicology Review*, 6/1 (2011), 20-42, http://hdl.handle.net/1811/49760

Sweeting, Adam, 'Hilary Hahn', *Gramophone*, 78/927 (May 2000), 10-15.

Szigeti, Joseph, *Szigeti on the Violin* (New York: Dover Books, 1979).

Taruskin, Richard, 'On letting the Music Speak for Itself: Some Reflection on Musicology and Performance', *Journal of Musicology*, 1/3 (July 1982), 101-117, http://dx.doi.org/10.2307/763881

Taruskin, Richard, *Text and Act: Essays on Music and Performance* (New York: Oxford University Press, 1995).

Taruskin, Richard, 'How Things Stand Now?', keynote address delivered at the *Performa '11* Conference, Aveiro Portugal, 19 May 2011.

Telemann, Georg Friedrich, *Sonate metodiche for Violin or Flute* (Hamburg: [n.p.], 1728).

Terracini, Lyndon, 'Opera Australia's Lyndon Terracini responds to Peter Tregear', *Australian Book Review* (2 September 2014), https://www.australianbookreview.com.au/arts-update/arts-commentary/101-arts-update/2151-opera-australia-s-lyndon-terracini-replies-to-peter-tregear

Thoene, Helga, 'Johann Sebastian Bach Ciaccona: Tanz oder Tombeau – Verborgene Sprache eines berühmten Werkes', *Köthener Bach-Hefte*, 6 (Köthen: Historisches Museum Köthen/Anhalt, 1994), 15-81.

Thoene, Helga, '"Ehre sey dir Gott gesungen" — Johann Sebastian Bach Die Violin-Sonata G-Moll BWV 1001, Der Verschlüsselte Lobgesang', *Köthener Bach-Hefte*, 7 (Köthen: Bach-Gedenkstätte und Historisches Museum Köthen/Anhalt, 1998), 1-113.

Thoene, Helga, 'Geheime Sprache – Verborgener Gesang in J. S. Bach's "Sei Solo a Violino"', in *Morimur*, CD ECM New Series 1765, 461895-2 (München: ECM Records, 2001), pp. 19-28.

Tilmouth, Michael, 'Moto perpetuo', *Grove Music Online. Oxford Music Online*, http://www.oxfordmusiconline.com

Timmers, Renee, 'On the Contextual Appropriateness of Expression', *Music Perception*, 20/3 (Spring 2003), 225-240.

Todd, Neil, 'A Model of Expressive Timing in Tonal Music', *Music Perception*, 3 (1985), 33-57, http://dx.doi.org/10.2307/40285321

Todd, Neil, 'Towards a Cognitive Theory of Expression: The Performance and Perception of Rubato', *Contemporary Music Review*, 4 (1989), 405-416, http://dx.doi.org/10.1080/07494468900640451

Todd, Neil, 'The Dynamics of Dynamics: A Model of Musical Expression', *Journal of the Acoustical Society of America*, 91/6 (1992), 3540-3550, http://dx.doi.org/10.1121/1.402843

Tommasini, Anthony, 'A Violin Virtuoso and Total Bach', *New York Times* (28 April 2000), p. E4, http://www.nytimes.com/2000/04/28/movies/a-violin-virtuoso-and-total-bach.html

Tomes, Susan, *Beyond the Notes: Journey with Chamber Music* (Woodbridge: The Boydell Press, 2004).

Toop, Richard 'Against a Theory of Music (New) Complexity', in *Contemporary Music: Theoretical and Philosophical Perspectives*, ed. by Max Paddison and Irène Deliège (Aldershot: Ashgate, 2010), pp. 89-98.

Tosi, Pier Francesco, *Opinioni de cantori antichi sopra il canto figurato* (1723), http://www.haendel.it/interpreti/old/tosi_opinioni.htm

Treitler, Leo, and Wye Jamison Allanbrook, eds., *Strunk's Source Readings in Music History: The Late Eighteenth Century* (New York: Norton, [revised edn] 1998).

Turner, Richard, 'Style and Tradition in String Quartet Performance: A Study of 32 Recordings of Beethoven's Op. 131 Quartet' (PhD Thesis, University of Sheffield, 2004).

Urdan, Timothy C., *Statistics in Plain English* (New Jersey: Lawrence Erlbaum Associates Inc., 2005).

Vittes, Laurence, 'From Rock to Bach – Monica Huggett', *Strings*, 21/6 (January 2007), 53-57.

Vittes, Laurence, 'Profile: Violinist Isabelle Faust', *Strings* (April 2009), http://www.stringsmagazine.com/article/default.aspx?articleid=23900

Voices, Chicago Sun-Times blog, 20 August 2014, http://voices.suntimes.com/arts-entertainment/the-daily-sizzle/rachel-barton-pine-undertakes-marathon-concert-program-at-ravinia-festival/

Voigt, Thomas, 'You Can't Simply Carry on as Usual Afterwards – Jonas Kaufmann and Helmut Deutsch in Conversation with Thomas Voigt', *Schubert: Winterreise*, Jonas Kaufmann [tenor], Helmut Deutsch [piano]. Sony Classical 88883795652 (Sony Classical Records, 2014), CD Booklet, pp. 7-12.

Volioti, Georgia, 'Playing with Tradition: Weighing up Similarity and the Buoyancy of the Game', *Musicae Scientiae*, 14/2 (2010). Special issue (CHARM II), 85-111, http://dx.doi.org/10.1177/102986491001400204

Wen, Eric, 'The Twentieth Century', in *The Cambridge Companion to the Violin*, ed. by Robin Stowell (Cambridge: Cambridge University Press, 1992), pp. 79-91, http://dx.doi.org/10.1017/ccol9780521390330.006

Widmer, Gerhard, 'Machine Discoveries: A Few Simple, Robust Local Expression Principles', *Journal of New Music Research*, 31/1 (2002), 37-50, http://dx.doi.org/10.1076/jnmr.31.1.37.8103

Wilson, Nick, *The Art of Re-enchantment: Making Early Music in the Modern Age* (New York: Oxford University Press, 2013), http://dx.doi.org/10.1093/acprof:oso/9780199939930.001.0001

Windsor, Luke W., 'Gesture in Music-making: Action, Information and Perception', in *New Perspectives on Music and Gesture*, ed. by Anthony Gritten and Elaine King (Farnham: Ashgate, 2011), pp. 45-66.

Windsor, Luke W., and Eric Clarke, 'Expressive Timing and Dynamics in Real and Artificial Music Performance: Using an Algorithm as an Analytical Tool', *Music Perception*, 15/4 (1997), 127-152, http://dx.doi.org/10.2307/40285746

Windsor, Luke W., Peter Desain, Amandine Penel, and Michiel Borkent, 'A Structurally Guided Method for the Decomposition of Expression in Music Performance', *Journal of the Acoustical Society of America*, 119 (2006), 1182-1193, http://dx.doi.org/10.1121/1.2146091

Wiora, Walter, ed., *Alte Musik in unserer Zeit – Referate und Diskussionen der Kasseler Tagung 1967* (Kassel: Bärenreiter, 1968).

Wispelwey, Pieter, *Bach: Six Suites for Solo Cello*, Compact Disk Recording with DVD Documentary (Evil Penguin Records Classics, 2012), EPRC 0012.

Wolff, Christoph, ed., *The New Bach Reader – A Life of Johann Sebastian Bach in Letters and Documents* (New York and London: Norton, 1998).

Zbikowski, Lawrence M., 'Musical Gesture and Musical Grammar: A Cognitive Approach', in *New Perspectives on Music and Gesture*, ed. by Anthony Gritten and Elaine King (Farnham: Ashgate, 2011), pp. 83-98.

Yeo, Adrian, 'A Study of Performance Practices in Recordings of Bach's Violin Sonata BWV 1003 from 1930-2000' (BMus (Honours) Thesis, Edith Cowan University, 2010).

Index

Adorno, Theodor W. 39, 46
aesthetics 7, 10-12, 21-24, 28-45, 48-50, 55, 58, 86, 90, 92-93, 95-96, 99, 104, 121, 127-129, 136, 146-149, 153, 155, 163, 170-172, 185, 198, 201, 226, 246, 269-271, 276-278, 281, 287-288, 296
affect 4, 9, 23, 41, 44, 51, 58, 60, 121, 137, 151-155, 194-195, 198, 201-272, 276-277, 288
A minor Sonata 76, 84, 245, 248
  Allegro 222
    terraced dynamics of 193
  Andante 15, 20, 119, 129, 144
    comparison of recordings 157-158, 228
    embellishment of 84
    legato in 108
    melody of 226
    tempo of 248
  Fuga 190, 225-226, 269
    tempo of 135, 219
  Grave 85, 219-220, 222, 268
    comparison of recordings 119, 238-241, 276
    legato in 220
    rhythm of 109
    tempo of 219, 238
    variety of interpretation of 167-168
Anders, Günther Stern 3, 72
arpeggio (arpeggiating chords) 57, 104, 118, 119, 186-193, 202, 205
articulation 12, 15, 23, 28, 43, 56, 60, 66, 70, 95-96, 120, 128, 129, 136, 163, 167, 171, 172, 184-198, 204, 206-212, 217, 219, 221-223, 234, 237, 253-254, 256, 262-263, 270, 274-277. *See also* figuration and phrasing
  altering of 153, 160
  and dotted rhythm 176-181, 198
  comparison of HIP and MSP styles 99-118, 223, 250
  relationship to bowing 93, 95, 101, 107, 276, 285
  style
    detached 192, 277
    detailed 101, 197, 211, 221, 263
    forceful 225, 269
    legato 180, 194-197, 230, 242, 250
    nuanced 21, 198, 277
    refined 88
    sustained 276
    varied 41, 186
  subjective nature of 107-109
Auer, Leopold 76, 87-91
aurality 4-5, 65-73, 286, 289, 293-294
  aural analysis 22, 233, 233-238
  aural communication 6, 65-73, 274
  aural experience 6, 13, 25, 73, 156
  aural perception 5, 30, 58, 65, 157, 163
authentistic style 38, 43, 101, 104, 207, 230, 236, 277

Bach, Johann Sebastian 7, 21, 27, 31, 33, 35, 38, 39, 61, 81, 88, 89, 96, 97-100, 106, 119, 124, 127, 136, 153, 158, 172, 181, 200, 202, 220, 224

Brandenburg Concertos 29, 33, 167, 173
Goldberg Variations 218, 231
Mass in B minor 29, 37, 218
notation practices 148-153, 166, 169, 171, 181, 186, 189
Passions 29, 32, 37, 173
Six Sonatas and Partitas for Solo Violin 2, 10, 11, 13, 15, 18-21, 22, 31, 38, 72, 73-74, 93, 95, 100, 103, 105, 122-126, 127-200, 201-272, 273-282. *See* G minor Sonata; B minor Partita; A minor Sonata; D minor Partita; C Major Sonata; E Major Sonata
baroque bow. *See* bowing
Bartók, Béla 84, 278
Barton Pine, Rachel 18-20, 46, 57, 79, 83, 85, 95, 104-105, 108, 121, 123, 143, 144, 145, 151, 162, 186, 190, 192, 204-205, 212, 218, 221-223, 230, 234, 257-263, 277, 279
Baudelaire, Charles 32
Beethoven, Ludwig van 7, 26, 35, 49, 53, 72, 145, 199, 232, 278, 284
Berlioz, Hector 199
Beznosiuk, Pavlo 104, 116, 117, 135, 137, 154, 155, 162, 185-186, 194
Birnbaum, Johann Abraham 148-149
B minor Partita 83, 84, 219, 231-232
    Allemanda 228
        dotted rhythm of 118, 173-180
    Corrente 247
    Sarabande 191
        Double 118, 135
            embellishment of 15, 84, 156-161, 170, 277
            rhythm of 181-183
    Tempo di Borea 118, 248
        comparison of recordings 232
bodily experience 1, 3-7, 25, 58, 64-69, 137, 153, 246, 271, 274, 284, 296. *See also* aurality; cognition; and kinaesthesia
bowing 10-11, 12, 20-21, 23, 56, 57, 88-90, 92, 93, 95, 99-104, 107-120, 128, 140, 144-146, 155, 163-167, 171, 173, 180, 184-198, 202, 203-208, 213-217, 222-223, 230-232, 234-241, 244, 248-250, 257-268, 270, 276-277, 285

"Bach-bow" 21, 144
Baroque bow 18, 21, 56, 83, 84, 85, 95, 104, 105, 110, 117, 124, 184, 185, 190, 232, 279. *See also* period instruments
"bow vibrato" 163-167
grip 88-90
style
    inflected 105, 117, 238
    legato 10, 105, 108, 118, 176, 180, 192-193, 194-197, 203-206, 212, 213, 220, 229, 238, 249
    lifted 77, 104, 119, 140, 184, 192, 203, 235, 248, 250, 262, 275
    nuanced 235, 250
    seamless 21, 56, 145, 184
    sustained 108, 119, 178, 206, 226, 230, 245, 281
    varied 41, 57, 84, 88, 101, 107, 117, 145, 186, 205, 231, 236, 240, 241, 249, 263
    weighted 58, 101, 119, 194, 206, 250, 276
Brahms, Johannes 72, 145, 199, 278
brain function 22, 24, 65, 69, 153, 288-296. *See also* cognition and music psychology
Brendel, Alfred 74
Brodsky, Adolph 87
Brodsky, Jascha 86, 90, 97
Burney, Charles 41
Buswell, James 79, 83, 85, 91, 100, 108, 116, 117, 140, 151, 184, 190, 194
Butt, John 12, 30, 32, 38, 95, 107, 148, 282

Capet, Lucien 90, 91
Casals, Pablo 8
Chopin, Frédéric 218, 278
Cilliers, Paul 52, 57, 60-61, 274, 275
C Major Sonata 84, 118-119, 248
    Adagio 118-119
        dotted rhythm of 118, 173-181
    Allegro 135, 230
    Largo 108, 119
        legato in 108, 195
cognition 3, 5-6, 25, 42, 66, 69, 271, 274. *See also* brain function and music psychology

complex systems 2, 14, 17, 22, 25, 52, 56-61, 74, 270, 279-280, 273-287, 291-294
Cook, Nicholas 2, 7, 42, 50-52, 177, 193, 200, 273, 280, 285
Costello, Elvis 1
Czerny, Carl 26, 53, 65

DeLay, Dorothy 77, 82, 90-93, 97, 105
Deleuze, Gilles 22, 25, 52-56, 61, 123, 201, 247, 268, 283, 286-288, 294
Descartes, René 31
D minor Partita 76, 84, 85, 233
  Allemanda 118, 131, 223, 230
  Ciaccona
    notation of 189
  Corrente 118, 247
    dotted rhythm of 173-180, 183
  Giga 118, 131, 193, 231, 247, 268, 270
    aural analysis of 234-238
    HIP characteristics of 106
  Sarabanda 144, 162, 223, 230, 248
    embellishment of 81, 154, 230
Doğantan-Dack, Mine 66, 68
Dolmetsch, Carl 27, 104
Donington, Robert 37
dynamics 5, 41, 66, 100-101, 108-109, 116-120, 129, 137-140, 167, 171, 191-198, 217, 219-225, 248-250, 257-268, 270, 274, 276-278
  comparison of recordings 233-240
  complex dynamical systems. *See* complex systems
  fluctuation of 204, 211, 228, 248-249, 258, 262
  in Gavotte en Rondeau 207-211
  shifting of 140, 153, 172, 183, 189, 205
  style
    arched 203
    consistent 230, 245, 257, 263, 267
    emotionalized 101, 108
    exaggerated 116
    expressive 117
    extreme 123, 226, 269
    HIP-style 117, 193-197
    long-range 105, 119

  MSP-style 117, 119, 204
  multiple stops 191-193
  terraced dynamics 21, 193, 214, 234-238, 258, 262

early music movement 12, 27, 36, 77, 80, 93-95, 102, 170, 279-282
Ehnes, James 18, 79, 86, 96-97, 100, 105, 108, 144, 151, 184, 190, 192, 193, 194, 200, 204, 254, 257, 280
Elman, Mischa 87-90
E Major Partita 84, 118-119, 129, 153-155, 179-183, 202-216, 217, 233, 254-268
  Bourée 248
  Gavotte en Rondeau 118, 247, 254, 270
    comparison of HIP and MSP versions 207-211
    embellishment of 15, 81, 281
    HIP characteristics of 106
    tempo of 252
  Gigue 118, 222
    HIP characteristics of 106
  Loure 119, 144, 226, 248, 270
    comparison of HIP and MSP versions 202-207
    dotted rhythm of 179
    embellishment of 154, 156, 281
  Menuets 119, 123, 161, 183, 219, 222, 248, 269, 270
    comparison of HIP and MSP versions 211-217
    dotted rhythm of 181
    embellishment of 281
  Preludio 108, 118, 270, 277
    comparison of recordings 254-268
    MPS characteristics of 106
    tempo of 131, 136, 251, 254-268, 277
    terraced dynamics of 193
  reworking for lute 152
embellishment 15, 41, 81, 84, 95, 103, 104, 117-118, 121, 124, 146-163, 169-172, 198, 199, 206, 253, 276, 277, 281. *See also* ornamentation

emotion 32, 44, 63, 127, 136-140, 152, 194, 241-247, 250-251, 271, 274, 287, 292, 289-293
  emotional expression 101, 108, 137, 241-247, 274
  emotional memory 65
Erlmann, Veit 68, 290, 293

Faust, Isabelle 18, 79, 83-84, 95, 104-106, 121, 123, 124, 145, 154-155, 161-162, 169, 171, 183, 190, 193, 199, 206-207, 257-258, 279
figuration 70, 152, 153, 195, 210, 212, 254-268. *See also* articulation
Fischer, Julia 18, 77, 78, 85, 96-98, 100, 105, 108, 116, 118, 140, 151, 180, 184, 190, 194, 204, 284

Gähler, Rudolf 18, 21, 100, 135, 144, 186, 190, 212
Galamian, Ivan 80, 82, 83, 89-93, 97, 103, 105
Gibson, James 6
Gigli, Beniamino 8
G minor Sonata 84, 85, 100, 223, 225-227, 233, 245, 247
  Adagio 85, 109, 119, 129, 238-247, 248, 253, 268, 276
    embellishment of 150-151, 153
    expressiveness of 226, 242
    notation of 150-151
    opening chord 190
  Fuga 129, 193
    comparison of recordings 185-189
    nuance in 123
  Presto 150-151, 223, 230
  Siciliana 230
Godøy, Rolf 5
Gringolts, Ilya 18, 77-78, 95, 100, 104, 121, 123-126, 135, 144, 154-160, 163, 171-172, 190, 206, 208, 211-217, 248, 251, 257, 277, 279
Gritten, Anthony 68
Guattari, Felix 55-57, 123, 201, 247, 287-288

Hahn, Hilary 18, 79, 86, 90, 96, 97-98, 100, 105, 108, 145, 184, 195, 198, 200, 204, 212, 254, 280, 283
Hanslick, Eduard 40
harmony 21, 23, 44, 67-68, 95, 99, 106-108, 118, 123, 140, 144, 149, 155-158, 171, 173, 181-184, 189, 192, 195, 203, 210, 214, 216, 222, 225-226, 235-237, 246, 248, 252-254, 256, 263, 276, 290
  harmonic goals 123, 240
  harmonic-metric groups 108, 183, 184
Harnoncourt, Nikolaus 20, 27, 29, 82, 94, 105, 199, 227, 269
Haskell, Harry 12
Haynes, Bruce 12, 30
Heifetz, Jascha 8, 46, 87, 88, 97, 175, 255
Hellaby, Julian 44-48
historically informed performance (HIP) 43-44, 52, 53, 55, 57, 77-87, 130-137, 154, 161-162, 166
  and modernism 27-31, 43
  blended with MSP 75, 83, 250
  compared to MSP 15, 18, 20-22, 52, 61, 95-126, 127-200, 268-270, 275
    bowing 184-190
    dotting 173-181
    multiple stops 190-193
    phrasing and dynamics 193-197
    tempo choice 130-137
    vibrato 137-146
  differences within 201-247
  evolution of 33-41, 57, 72, 73, 277-284
  influence on MPS 94-126
  origins of 12-13
Hogwood, Christopher 33, 94, 169
holistic experience 22-24, 59, 68, 92, 140, 153, 176, 201-272, 275-277, 287, 289-296
Holloway, John 104, 108, 160, 181, 182, 186-188, 190, 192, 257-263, 277
Huggett, Monica 15, 79, 80-82, 104, 121, 123, 135, 140, 151, 154, 162, 166, 186, 190, 192, 195, 206-216, 229, 247, 251-269, 270

Husserl, Edmund 3, 5, 290

Ibragimova, Alina 18, 21, 77, 79, 95, 104, 131, 151, 166, 190-192, 197, 199, 204, 254, 279

imagination 1, 7, 16, 44, 49, 54, 66, 85, 107, 169, 223

improvisation 35, 46, 97, 121, 146-152, 170, 239, 246, 255, 280, 288, 293, 295
  improvisatory freedom 119, 121, 171, 240-241, 246, 276
  improvisatory style 85, 117-119, 152, 163, 169-170, 173, 226, 241, 249, 253-254

Jameson, Fredric 33-41, 282
Juslin, Patrik 63, 287

Karajan, Herbert von 74, 82
Katz, Mark 10
Khachatryan, Sergey 18, 77-79, 96-99, 100, 108, 116, 118, 151, 180, 184, 192, 194, 199, 284
kinaesthesia 3, 64, 65, 137. *See also* aurality; bodily experience and cognition
Koopman, Ton 80
Kreisler, Fritz 8, 46, 76, 97
Kremer, Gidon 20, 79, 82, 96, 100, 108, 117, 135, 143, 177, 186-189, 190, 193, 204, 212, 214, 218-222, 234, 237, 244, 249, 254, 255, 262-263, 267, 269, 277, 278
Kreutzer, Rudolphe 65
Kuijken, Sigiswald 18, 20, 79, 80, 81, 101-104, 108, 116, 143, 155, 190, 206, 212, 217-218, 229-230, 234, 246, 254-257, 264-267, 276, 277
Kuijken, Wieland 81

Landowska, Wanda 27, 104
Latour, Bruno 62-65, 73, 270, 287, 288, 294, 295
Leech-Wilkinson, Daniel 200, 242, 268
legato. *See* articulation and bowing
Lennon, John 4
Leonhardt, Gustav 27, 29, 43, 49, 77, 80, 81, 93, 104, 218, 230

Lev, Lara 79, 82, 104, 116-117, 144, 184, 204, 205, 208, 210-212, 254
Lewin, David 3
Luca, Sergiu 18, 73, 80, 103-104, 121, 154-158, 171, 175, 181, 182, 186-187, 189, 193, 206, 212, 229, 256
Lyotard, Jean-François 34

Mahler, Gustav 35, 199, 284
mainstream performance (MSP) 13, 53, 55, 56, 73, 86, 201-247
  compared to HIP. *See* historically informed performance (HIP)
  origins 25-26
Matthews, Ingrid 83, 86-87, 104, 181, 183, 187-189, 190, 192, 256, 263-267, 277
McGilchrist, Ian 24, 71, 288-296
McLaughlin, John 81
melody 11, 14, 21, 32, 44, 100, 106, 121, 140, 144, 147-151, 154-158, 169, 171, 179-182, 185, 190, 192-193, 195-197, 203-204, 214, 225-226, 240-242, 251-253, 263, 276
  melodic embellishment 149, 153, 163, 170-171
memory 1, 3, 7, 16, 65-67, 69, 72, 274, 293
Mendelssohn, Felix 199
Merleau-Ponty, Maurice 3, 5, 290
Milstein, Nathan 46, 77, 83, 87-88, 97, 156, 229
modernism 14, 31-42, 52, 59, 62
Mozart, Leopold 107
Mozart, Wolfgang Amadeus 12, 49, 80, 83, 89, 199, 220
MSP. *See* mainstream performance
Mullova, Viktoria 20, 79, 83, 95, 99-100, 103-104, 108, 116, 117, 121, 123, 124, 140-141, 145, 151, 154-158, 163, 169, 171, 178, 181-182, 184, 186, 190-193, 207, 219, 223, 230-233, 236-238, 269, 277, 279, 283
music psychology 4-6, 25-26, 42, 47-49, 64-66, 96, 128, 242-247, 274, 289. *See also* brain function and cognition

Neumann, Frederick 37, 148, 152, 166, 173, 189
notes inégales. *See* rhythm

Ong, Walter J. 67-70
oral cultures 24, 61, 65-73, 290, 294
ornamentation 12, 15, 23, 30, 35, 43, 50, 56, 70, 85, 95, 100, 104, 107, 116-118, 122-125, 128, 143, 146-172, 173, 182-183, 189, 193, 198, 199, 202-207, 217, 220-221, 222, 230-231, 241, 248, 251, 252, 275, 277, 281, 286. *See also* embellishment
   and improvisation 169-170
   importance of 120-121
Ornoy, Eitan 20, 75, 124, 268, 279

Paderewsky, Ignacy Jan 8, 14
period instruments 12, 21, 27, 37, 39, 43, 56, 73, 79, 80, 82, 84-85, 93-95, 98-99, 101-106, 110, 117-118, 120, 124, 154, 184, 229, 230, 251
period orchestras 80, 82, 94, 117
Perlman, Itzhak 32, 39, 77, 79, 82, 96, 100, 105, 108, 143, 184, 189, 190-192, 194, 204-205, 212, 244-246
phrasing 9, 23, 50, 60, 66, 79, 97-101, 106, 108-109, 116-118, 119-120, 140, 180, 183, 184, 193, 198, 203-205, 207, 217, 222-223, 225, 228, 230-231, 251-253, 253, 276-277, 286. *See also* articulation
   crucial impact of 276-277
   style
      arched 193-194, 203, 222
      "emotionalized" 108
      expressive 269
      flexible 23, 95, 253
      HIP-style 116-117, 193-197, 222-223
      legato 108, 230
      long 10, 21, 95, 99, 101, 103, 106, 108, 118, 119, 194, 222, 275
      melodic 95, 106, 180, 185
      MSP-style 117, 203-205, 212
   subjective nature of 109-110, 128

playfulness 41, 161-163, 171, 183, 281, 296
Podger, Rachel 15, 79, 83, 86, 101, 104, 108, 121, 123, 154, 161, 171, 181, 186-189, 206, 212, 229, 257-262
Poppen, Christoph 84, 95, 224
postmodernism 28-42, 52, 59, 62, 95, 282
Poulet, Gérard 18, 77, 96, 100, 108, 144, 184, 195, 204, 257
psychology. *See* music psychology

rhythm 10, 15, 21, 41, 44, 54, 61, 66, 79, 95, 100, 101, 106-109, 116-120, 150, 153-158, 163, 171-184, 192, 198, 202-203, 206, 212, 222, 225, 240, 244, 249, 252, 276
   dotted rhythm 23, 37, 43, 107, 118, 128, 129, 158, 173-180, 192, 202
   notes inégales 173, 181, 183
   rhythmic flexibility 23, 30, 35, 81, 103, 107, 109, 116, 128, 173, 182-183, 253-254, 278
   rhythmic projection 118, 120, 184, 250
Ricci, Ruggiero 18, 76, 100, 194
Richter, Karl 32
Richter, Sviatoslav 74
Rostal, Max 80, 83
rubato. *See* tempo

Scheibe, Johann Adolf 148-149
Schenker, Heinrich 1
Schmid, Benjamin 83, 95, 100-101, 104, 117, 184, 192, 257, 258, 267
Schröder, Jaap 10, 18, 76, 77, 88, 100, 101-104, 116, 136, 151, 156, 161, 185, 194, 198, 206, 212, 256, 263, 279
Shumsky, Oscar 18, 32, 76, 96, 100, 108, 144, 151, 184, 190-197, 204-205, 212, 231, 257
St John, Lara 18, 79, 83, 85, 104, 108, 140, 161-162, 183, 184, 190, 193, 254, 257-268
Stravinsky, Igor 28, 33, 35, 193, 284
Sublime, the 39-42

Taruskin, Richard 9, 12, 13, 27-40, 43, 71, 97, 124, 282

tempo 9, 15, 28, 44, 56, 57, 60, 66, 81, 84, 100, 108, 116-118, 120, 128-137, 173, 176-180, 189, 192, 194-198, 202-217, 219, 230, 231, 234-241, 244, 247-250, 252-253, 255-268, 269, 270, 276-277, 286
  choice of 23, 106, 128-137, 247
  flexibility of 35, 104, 128, 228, 241, 249
  fluctuation of 204, 209-211, 213-217, 219, 238, 240, 248, 255-268, 277
  perception of 15, 61, 131, 262, 276
  rubato 30, 107, 116, 117-118, 118, 120, 209, 212, 214, 223, 241
  steadiness of 9, 10, 101, 195, 263, 267
terraced dynamics. *See* dynamics
Tetzlaff, Christian 20, 21, 79, 83-84, 95, 104-105, 108, 116, 117, 121, 123, 135, 143, 155, 160, 184, 186-189, 194, 204-206, 212, 218, 223-229, 230, 234-238, 254, 269
timbre 11, 23, 60, 66, 82, 119-120, 172, 184-190, 192, 250, 252
timing 15, 23, 95, 107, 109, 128-129, 140, 163, 171, 172, 183, 198, 209, 212, 214-217, 256, 263, 270, 276

Tognetti, Richard 15, 21, 79, 83, 84-85, 95, 104-105, 108, 121, 123, 124, 135, 155, 160, 169, 171, 181, 182, 186, 190, 205, 212
Toscanini, Arturo 28, 74

Ughi, Ugo 18, 100
Urtext 35, 44, 53, 207
  "Urtex mentality" 46, 53, 96, 172, 275

vibrato 10-11, 21, 23, 35, 85, 91, 95, 99, 100, 101, 104, 106, 108, 116-118, 119, 129, 137-146, 153, 166-167, 194, 197, 199, 204, 219, 223, 226, 229, 248-251, 269, 274, 278
Vivaldi, Antonio 35

Wallfisch, Elizabeth 79, 81, 104, 108, 151, 154, 161-163, 190, 197, 206-210, 212, 255, 257-267, 277
Wen, Eric 10
Windsor, Luke 6

Ysaÿe, Eugène 84, 87, 90

Zbikowski, Lawrence 6
Zehetmair, Thomas 21, 79, 83, 95, 104-105, 116-117, 135, 143, 184, 190-195, 195, 203-205, 205, 212, 247-251, 257-258, 268, 270
Zimbalist, Efrem 76, 87, 90

This book need not end here...

At Open Book Publishers, we are changing the nature of the traditional academic book. The title you have just read will not be left on a library shelf, but will be accessed online by hundreds of readers each month across the globe. OBP publishes only the best academic work: each title passes through a rigorous peer-review process. We make all our books free to read online so that students, researchers and members of the public who can't afford a printed edition will have access to the same ideas. This book and additional content is available at:

https://www.openbookpublishers.com/isbn/9781783741526

Customise

Personalise your copy of this book or design new books using OBP and third-party material. Take chapters or whole books from our published list and make a special edition, a new anthology or an illuminating coursepack. Each customised edition will be produced as a paperback and a downloadable PDF. Find out more at:

https://www.openbookpublishers.com/section/59/1

Donate

If you enjoyed this book, and feel that research like this should be available to all readers, regardless of their income, please think about donating to us. We do not operate for profit and all donations, as with all other revenue we generate, will be used to finance new Open Access publications:

https://www.openbookpublishers.com/section/13/1/support-us

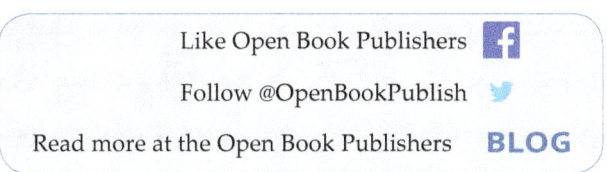

You may also be interested in:

Verdi in Victorian London
Massimo Zicari

https://www.openbookpublishers.com/product/437

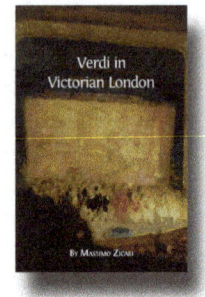

Denis Diderot 'Rameau's Nephew' – 'Le Neveu de Rameau': A Multi-Media Bilingual Edition
Edited by M. Hobson. Translated by K.E. Tunstall and C. Warman. Music researched and played by the Conservatoire National Supérieur de Musique de Paris under the direction of P. Duc

https://www.openbookpublishers.com/product/498

Tellings and Texts: Music, Literature and Performance in North India
Edited by Francesca Orsini and Katherine Butler Schofield

https://www.openbookpublishers.com/product/311

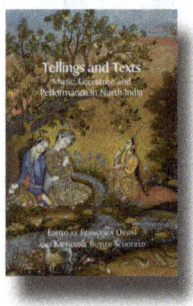